OUMA'S COOKERY BOOK

COMPILED BY

MRS. ROY HENDRIE

NATAL

JUTA & CO. LTD.
CAPE TOWN/WETTON/JOHANNESBURG

First Edition   Pretoria, March 1940
Reprinted 1992
Reprinted 1995

© **JUTA AND CO, LTD**
P.O. Box 14373, Kenwyn 7790

O Thou Who kindly dost provide
For every creature's want,
We bless Thee, God of nature wide
For all Thy goodness lent;
And if it please Thee, Heavenly Guide,
May never worse be sent,
But whether granted or denied,
Lord bless us with content.

BURNS

This book is copyright under the Berne Convention. In terms of the Copyright Act, No 98 of 1978, no part of this book may be reproduced or transmitted in any form or by any means, electronic or mechanical, including photocopying, recording or by any information storage and retrieval system, without permission in writing from the Publisher.

ISBN 0 7021 1366 2

PRINTED AND BOUND IN THE REPUBLIC OF SOUTH AFRICA BY
CREDA PRESS, ELIOT AVENUE, EPPINDUST 2, CAPE TOWN

CONTENTS

	Page
Hors d'oeuvres	7
Soups	10
Fish	18
Meat and poultry	25
Poultry and game	41
Meat sauce	44
Cold meats	47
Vegetables	50
Salads and salad dressings	58
Breakfast, luncheon and supper dishes	65
Vegetarian dishes	76
All kinds of pastry	80
Flaky pastry (foolproof)	93
Puddings: hot and cold	94
Pancakes and fritters	103
Gelatine mould	114
South African recipes	128
Bread, scones and buns	137
Cakes	148
Fillings and icings	173
Biscuits	179
Savouries and snacks	191
Savouries	198
Beverages	200
Jams, jellies and preserves	208
Chutney, pickles and sauces	221
Sweets	224
War-time recipes	232
A.B.C. of health	241
Household hints	243
Home nursing	248
The bride's corner	254
Suggested menus for two	262
Miscellaneous	271
Terms relating to cookery	277

METRIC MEASURE

TEMPERATURE EQUIVALENTS

For people with stoves marked only in degrees Fahrenheit, the following are conversions to Celsius.

	°C	°F	Gas Mark		°C	°F	Gas Mark
Very cool	110	225	¼	Moderately hot	190	375	5
	120	250	½		200	400	6
Cool	140	275	1	Hot	220	425	7
	150	300	2		230	450	8
Moderate	160	325	3	Very hot	240	475	9
	180	350	4		260	500	
					280	550	

Mass (Solids)

1 oz	30 g	(28 g)	4 lb	2,00 kg	(1,82 kg)
2 oz	60 g	(58 g)	5 lb	2,50 kg	(2,27 kg)
4 oz	125 g	(114 g)	6 lb	3,00 kg	(2,72 kg)
8 oz	250 g	(227 g)	7 lb	3,50 kg	(3,19 kg)
1 lb	500 g	(454 g)	8 lb	4,00 kg	(3,63 kg)
2 lb	1,00 kg	(908 g)	9 lb	4,50 kg	(4,09 kg)
3 lb	1,50 kg	(1,36 kg)	10 lb	5,00 kg	(4,54 kg)

As most kitchen scales omit finer metric graduations, the figures in the middle column show the figures normally found on scales, whilst that on the right shows a more exact conversion.

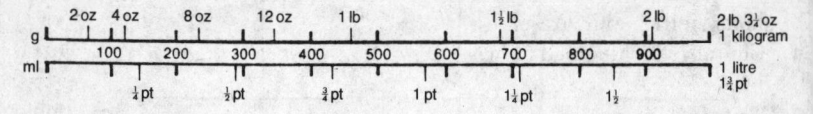

LIQUIDS

In Imperial measure the British cup was normally 10 fl ozs whilst for the past 50 years South Africans have used the American cup of 8 fl ozs. With metrication the standard South African cup measure is now 250 ml or ¼ litre. For your further information the old pint is approximately 560 ml.

¼ teaspoon	1 ml	⅓ cup	80 ml
½ teaspoon	2,5 ml	½ cup	125 ml
1 teaspoon	5 ml	¾ cup	190 ml
2 teaspoons	10 ml	1 cup	250 ml
1 tablespoon	15 ml	2 cups	500 ml
2 tablespoons	30 ml	3 cups	750 ml
¼ cup	60 ml	4 cups (1 litre)	1 000 ml

A fair start to dinner,
Like a fair start in life,
Depends very much,
On the right kind of wife.

HORS D'OEUVRES

The hors d'oeuvres course forms the prelude to the dinner. It is made up of little delicacies, nearly always cold and very daintily served in tiny portions as these dishes are meant to stimulate but never to satisfy the appetite. They may consist of fruit but seldom contain cheese, which is usually served, in some form or other, at the end of a dinner.

A variety of hors d'oeuvres may be placed in small dishes on a tray, but very often one dainty hors d'oeuvre is served to each person and should be placed on the table with special knife, fork or spoon before guests are seated.

Simple hors d'oeuvres may consist of the following: — Olives, sardines, anchovies, lax, caviare, stuffed hard boiled eggs, kippers, oysters, sliced tomato, potato or beetroot covered with mayonnaise, tiny sausages or salmon. Garnishes: Lettuce, parsley, aspic jelly, chopped hard boiled eggs and beetroot, various butters, canapes, biscuits and thin slices of brown bread are used.

The following recipes may have been slightly altered in the course of time but most of them came originally from Mrs. Slade.

ANCHOVY BUTTER

To ¼ lb. butter take 1 teaspoon anchovy paste or 1 teaspoon anchovy essence and a shake of cayenne pepper. Mix ingredients well together and add a few drops lemon or onion juice.

GREEN BUTTER

To ¼ lb. butter add finely chopped parsley, salt and pepper to taste, a tablespoon of lemon juice and a little anchovy essence or paste. Mix well and use as required.

PARSLEY BUTTER (Maitre d'Hotel Butter)

Mix finely chopped parsley, butter and lemon juice. Add salt and pepper to taste.

Any of these butters can be shaped into balls or pats and served on little squares of crisp toast or small lunch biscuits.

CANAPES

Take ¼ inch slices of stale white bread and cut into rounds or fancy shapes. Fry in very hot fat or butter until golden brown.

ANCHOVY CANAPES

Spread canapes with anchovy butter. Chop hard boiled eggs, whites and yolkes separately. Cover canapes with egg, alternating yolks and whites, dividing yolks from whites with anchovies. Border with anchovy butter.

OTHER CANAPES

(1) Caviare (the salted roe of the sturgeon) and finely mashed yolks of eggs.
(2) Olives, stoned, surrounded with anchovy fillets and garnished with chopped white of egg and parsley. Top olives with anchovy butter.
(3) Sardine. Cream butter and mashed sardines together with lemon juice, salt and pepper. Place on canapes with a stuffed olive in centre of each and garnish with chopped white of egg.
(4) Foie Gras. Pound the foie gras (goose liver) adding a little cream or sauce, pepper and salt. Pass through sieve and arrange daintily on canapes, garnishing with white of egg or any other suitable decoration.

ANCHOVY BISCUITS

Rub 2 tablespoons butter in ½ cup flour. Mix into firm dough with a little egg yolk beaten and mixed with one teaspoon anchovy essence, a little cayenne pepper, a few drops carmine, and 1 or 2 tablespoons water. Roll out thinly, cut into rounds and bake in hot oven till crisp.

FRUIT HORS D'OEUVRES

Sliced pawpaw and lemon.
Half avocado pear with vinegar or lemon juice.
Sliced melon or small portions of water melon.
Half grape fruit: remove centre and add one teaspoon sugar and dash of brandy just before serving. Place glace cherry in centre of grape fruit.
Fruit salad served in dainty glasses and flavoured with orange juice or liqueur.
Sliced raw apples spread with tasty sausage meat, sprinkled with chopped nuts.
Prunes stuffed with almonds or rolled in cooked bacon.
Sliced pineapple with cherry centre and grated nuts.

VEGETABLE HORS D'OEUVRES

Celery stuffed with cream cheese or cut into convenient pieces and rolled in mayonnaise and chopped nuts.
Tiny tomatoes, stuffed egg or sausage meat.
Radish roses.
Sliced tomatoes, beetroot, cucumber or potatoes.

―――――

He that never changed any of his opinions never corrected any of his mistakes.

I guessed my pepper, my soup was too hot.
I guessed my water, it dried in the pot.
I guessed my salt, and what do you think?
For the rest of the day we did nothing but drink.
I guessed my sugar, my sauce was too sweet,
And thus by guessing I spoilt our treat.
So now I guess nothing, for cooking by guesses
Will ruin all skill and produce only messes.

From an Old Cookery Book.

SOUPS

Soup is a most wholesome and digestible form of food and affords splendid opportunities for using material which would otherwise be wasted. Most left over meats can be made into nourishing soups. Pieces of ham, bacon, or bacon rinds should be saved for lentil or split pea soup. The remains of mutton roast make splendid potato soup. The remains of fowl make good rice soup.

Stock is the liquid in which meat has been cooked for several hours. Long, slow cooking is essential, about six hours. The usual quantities are 1 lb. of meat to a quart of water. The meat should be cut up and allowed to stand in cold water for some time, then very, very slowly brought to the boil. The vegetables should be added after stock has been brought to the boil and after scum has been removed.

Brown stock — made from beef and mutton.
White stock — made from veal and chicken.
Fish stock — made from bones and trimmings of fish.
First stock — made from fresh meat or bones.
Second stock — made from pre-cooked meat or bones.
It is well to make the stock some hours before it is required for use. Place in frig. for a time when all fat can easily be removed.
Soups can be divided into different classes:
Broths, such as mutton and Scotch broth.
Thick soups, such as chicken, giblet, gravy, hare, kindney and oxtail soup.
Purees — strained and thickened soups such as tomato, potato and vegetable soup.
Clear soup or consomme.
Fish soup and milk or cream soups.

TO CLARIFY SOUP

Add the crushed shell and slightly beaten white of one egg to liquid, stirring all the time till it boils. Simmer for twenty minutes, then strain through muslin.

Skim directly it begins to boil.
When soup is too salt add one or two unsalted potatoes. If soup is too greasy, strain and pass two or three times through a clean white cloth wrung out of very cold water, or a few ice cubes put into the soup will enable you to lift the grease from the surface.

CARROT AND POTATO SOUP

Take two quarts of second stock and add to it one chopped onion, 6 large potatoes diced, pepper and salt. Boil two hours, strain, see that nothing is wasted, and add two finely grated carrots, 1 tablespoon of chopped parsley, 2 cups milk and bring to boiling point. Made from roast mutton leftovers, this is delicious. *L.H.*

COCK-A-LEEKIE

One old fowl, 2 tablespoons rice, 6 leeks, salt and pepper. Cover fowl with water and boil for two or three hours. Wash leeks very well, cut up and add to stock with salt, pepper and rice. Boil one hour. When ready, remove fowl. Cut it in pieces, place in soup tureen and pour strained soup over it. *Mother.*

SCOTCH BROTH

2 lbs. neck of mutton, carrots, turnips, onion or leeks, green peas, greens — if any — parsley, pearl barley, salt and pepper. Put mutton into pot with 2 quarts of cold water, pepper and salt and barley. Simmer for two or three hours, then add diced vegetables and cook till soft. Before serving add chopped parsley and one grated carrot. Dried peas can be used but they must be soaked overnight. Use 2 tablespoons barley.
A good cut of mutton can be used and afterwards eaten accompanied by whole carrots, turnips, and onions boiled in the soup and served with a white sauce or caper sauce. *Mother.*

KIDNEY SOUP

Bones, 1 ox kidney, butter, pepper, salt, flour, carrot, turnip leeks, parsley, celery, sago.
Boil bones, salt and pepper in two quarts of water for three hours. Steep kidney in salt then wash, dry and cut up into small pieces. Roll in flour and fry in butter. When fried, add kidney to stock, add cut up vegetables and boil for another hour. Add a tablespoon sago if liked.
M.F.

BEAN SOUP

Have ready three pints stock and add it to 2 cups dry beans which have been soaked overnight, 2 carrots, 2 turnips, 1 onion — all diced — pepper and salt. Cook till beans are soft. Rub through sieve, thicken with a little flour and water, add chopped parsley and serve. Mint may be used in place of parsley. *J.H.*

TORONTO TOMATO SOUP

Skin and cook 1 lb. tomatoes till tender. Add ¼ teaspoon bicarbonate of soda — or just sufficient to nearly destroy the acid of the tomato. Thicken with 1 tablespoon sago or flour. Add a lump of butter, ¼ teaspoon sugar, salt and pepper to taste and milk to make it the consistency desired. Boil for a few minutes. Soak the sago.

Miss Hendrie, Johannesburg.

EMERGENCY SOUP

Grate 1 large potato and onion. Cook in a little water for five minutes and add a lump of butter, 1 spoonful chopped parsley, salt and pepper and milk as desired. Boil three minutes.

Miss Hendrie, Johannesburg.

FISH SOUP

Use fish stock or boil some pieces of fish (the cheaper pieces will do) in 1 pint of water for half an hour. Strain and add 2 sliced potatoes, 2 onions, a piece of butter, salt and pepper and boil half an hour more, then add milk and a little flaked fish.

Miss Hendrie, Johannesburg.

GIBLET SOUP

3 pint stock, the giblets of any fowl, carrots, onion, turnip, celery, macaroni, parsley.

Put the giblets into the stock and cook for 2 hours. Add the cut up vegetables, pepper and salt and cook till soft. Take out giblets, cut up fine and return to soup. Add one tablespoon macaroni, chopped parsley and serve. *M.B.K.*

GREEN OR SPLIT SOUP OR BEAN SOUP

1 lb. split peas, 2 quarts water or stock, 1 ham bone, 2 onions, pepper and salt.

Soak peas overnight. Put into stock with ham bone, onions, pepper and salt. Boil 3 or 4 hours, remove bone and rub peas, etc., through sieve. Reheat and serve with croutons of fried bread. Thicken with flour and water if necessary. *M.F.*

LENTIL SOUP

2 large cups lentils, ½ cup rice, onion, bacon, pepper and salt, 2 quarts stock or water.
Any pieces of old bacon or ham may be used.
Boil all together for three hours. Strain and rub through sieve. Reheat and serve with croutons of fried bread.   *J.H.*

ICED BEETROOT SOUP

Wash thoroughly and boil in the ordinary way about 8 young beetroots. When cooked plunge into cold water and rub the skins off.
When cool, grate the beetroots and put into an enamel saucepan with about 3 small cups water, add salt to season and level teaspoon tartaric acid. Boil for 5 minutes.
Remove from fire and let it cool. When quite cool add the beaten yolk of egg, which had been thoroughly mixed with a full tablespoon of sugar. More sugar can be added if necessary.
Put into frig. to chill.
Serve with cream and hot boiled potatoes.   *Mrs. J. Jacobson.*

OX TAIL SOUP

1 ox tail, 1½ quarts water, 1 onion, 2 carrots, 2 turnips, 2 strips celery, pepper, salt, flour and a small piece of butter.
Joint the ox tail, roll it in flour and fry in butter. Add water and vegetables, pepper and salt and boil for four hours. Let it cool, remove fat, trim the joints and serve with the soup. A little sherry may be added if liked.   *J.H.*

CLEAR SOUP

3 pints cold water, 1 lb. shin of beef, pepper and salt.
Bring slowly to boil and simmer for three or four hours. Add any diced vegetables and cook for another hour. Strain and cool. Remove all fat. Serve hot with diced vegetables or egg balls. Serve cold in cups with addition of a little wine or sherry. Add 2 ozs. vermicelli to this to make vermicelli soup.   *A.A.*

LEEK SOUP

2 pints second stock, ½ doz. leeks, 1 stick celery, 2 large potatoes, pepper and salt. Wash leeks carefully.
Heat stock, slice potatoes thinly, chop leeks and celery and boil all together for 2 hours.   *M.F.*

MULLIGATAWNY SOUP

3 pints stock, 3 slices ham, small piece butter, 1 turnip, 1 carrot, 1 apple, 1 teaspoon curry powder, 1 tablespoon flour, pepper and salt.

Fry onion in butter and add ham cut in pieces. Add diced vegetables, curry powder and stock. Simmer two hours then strain. Boil up again and thicken with flour. *R.M.B.*

CREAM SOUPS
CREAM OF ASPARAGUS

1 large tin asparagus, 1 tablespoon flour, 2 pints milk, 2 tablespoons cream, 1 tablespoon butter, salt, pepper and pinch sugar. Cut off asparagus tips. Boil remainder slowly with milk. Strain — press well through sieve. Return to pan, add butter, thicken with flour and milk and add pepper, salt, sugar and tips. Just before serving add the cream. *A. Archibald.*

CREAM OF RICE

1 quart second chicken stock (cooked chicken scraps boiled for two hours), ½ cup rice, yolks of 2 eggs, 2 tablespoons cream, salt and pepper and small onion.

Boil stock, rice and onion together for one hour. Press through sieve, reheat but do not bring to boiling point. Add cream and beaten egg yolks. Season and serve at once. *M.F.*

CREAM OF POTATO

6 potatoes, 2 leeks, 3 tablespoons sago, 1 pint milk, 2 ozs. butter or dripping, 2 pints water, pepper and salt.

Wash leeks thoroughly; pare and slice potatoes. Put dripping or butter into a pan and add the potatoes and leeks. Stir and cook for 5 minutes but do not brown; add water and boil 1 hour. Rub soup through sieve. Reheat, add milk and bring to the boil.

When boiling, sprinkle in the sago, stir well and cook for another fifteen minutes. Season and serve. *L. H. Durban.*

MEALIE SOUP

4 breakfast cups of water, 4 green mealie cobs, 1 cup of milk, 2 oz. flour, 2 oz. butter, salt and pepper.

Remove the young mealies from the cobs and mince. Boil the mealie cobs in water for twenty minutes, then strain off the liquid. Return to the saucepan, add the minced mealies and boil for twenty minutes. Blend the flour in the milk and add to the soup. Boil for 5 minutes. Add butter and seasoning and serve with dice of toasted bread.

CREAM OF SPINACH

Make a puree of 2 lbs. spinach and add to it a pint of white sauce and 1 pint second stock.

CREAM OF PEA SOUP

Make a puree of 2 cups green peas, and 1 teaspoon chopped mint. Add this to 1 pint thin white sauce (see white sauce under fish sauces), or use half sauce and half stock. Pepper and salt to taste.

CREAM OF CELERY SOUP

Use 2 cups or more chopped celery. Cook in half a pint of stock or water. Add 2 cups milk and a pat of butter. Thicken to taste with flour and milk and add seasoning.

ONION SOUP

Boil six chopped onions in 1 pint stock or vegetable water. Thicken with flour and milk, add a little cream and seasoning.

LEFT OVER STEWS MAKE EXCELLENT SOUPS FOR THE SMALL FAMILY, I.E.:

LEFT OVER VEGETABLE STEW

Cut remaining meat and vegetables very fine. Return to gravy, add a little stock or water, a freshly grated carrot and some parsley and boil for half an hour.

LEFT OVER STEAK AND KIDNEY OR OX TAIL STEW

Cut meat up finely. Add diced fresh vegetables — carrot, turnip, onion, etc. Mix all with gravy and extra stock or water and boil one hour.

LEFT OVER IRISH STEW

Strain potatoes and meat through colander. Add 2 cups milk, 2 tablespoons mashed potatoes, a little parsley and reheat. Season and thicken as desired.

LEFT OVER STEWED MINCE

Add stock or vegetable water, 1 or 2 diced potatoes and a grated onion and boil for one hour.

CHICKEN BROTH FOR INVALIDS

Fowl, onion, salt and pepper, water.

Cut up an old fowl and one small onion. Cover with 1 quart of water, pepper and salt and boil till fowl falls to pieces. When all nutriment is extracted, strain the broth, let it cool and remove fat before reheating for use.
E.C.

BEEF TEA

Take a large, juicy slice of steak. Shred it finely; removing skin and fat. Put into earthenware cooking vessel with four cups of water and a ½ teaspoon salt. Cover tightly and stand aside for 1 hour. Then cook in slow oven for three hours. Beef tea must never boil.
E.C.

WHAT TO SERVE WITH SOUP

Asparagus — Croutons of fried bread.
Barley Broth — Chopped parsley.
Beetroot — Croutons of fried bread.
Gravy Soup — Dry toast.
Carrot — Fried croutons of bread.
Celery — Fried croutons of bread.
Chicken Broth — Boiled rice. Forcemeat balls.
Consomme — Cooked vegetables (strips or cubes).
Giblet — Chopped parsley.
Split Pea — Powdered mint. Fried croutons of bread.
Bean — Parsley or mint.
Julienne — Stripped vegetables or egg balls.
Kidney — Dried toast. Parsley.
Lentil — Croutons of fried bread.
Mulligatawny — Cooked rice.
Macaroni — Grated cheese.
Mutton Broth — Chopped parsley.
Onion — Grated cheese.
Ox Tail — Dry toast.
Tomato — Croutons of fried bread.

SOUP ACCESSORIES

Croutons — Cut slices of bread ¼ inch thick. Cut into small fancy shapes and fry a golden brown in butter.

Egg Balls. — Boil two eggs hard and mash the yolks with 1 tablespoon butter; add sufficient flour to enable mixture to be formed into small balls. Cook in boiling water and add to clear soup before serving.

FORCEMEAT BALLS

2 tablespoons breadcrumbs, 1 teaspoon chopped parsley, pinch dried herbs, 1 oz. butter, pepper, salt and a little egg.
Rub butter into dry ingredients. Bind with sufficient egg and make into small balls. Drop into boiling water for 5 minutes.

CUSTARD ROYAL

Beat together 3 egg yolks and 1 egg white, add half a cup of beef stock, salt, pepper and a few grains cayenne. Pour mixture ½ inch deep into shallow pan. Set this inside a tin holding hot water and bake very lightly in moderate oven. When cold cut into fancy shapes. When placing in soup take care that they do not break.

Mrs. Slade.

BROWNING FOR SOUPS

½ lb. brown sugar, 1 tablespoon water.
Put into pan and stir over fire till it becomes a dark brown colour. Add 1 cup boiling water and 1 teaspoon salt. Bottle and keep corked. Use for soups, gravies and sauces.

From the East —
Put your faith in Allah, and work.

THE FISHERMAN'S PRAYER
Lord, grant this day I catch a fish,
So large that even I,
In telling of it afterwards,
Shall have no need to lie.

Anon.

FISH

SOME SOUTH AFRICAN FISH
Sole, Kabeljouw, Stockfish, Stumpnose, Kingklip, Cape Salmon, Seventy-four, Snoek, Silver Fish, Red Roman.

FISH
Boil fish very, very gently.
When boiling or steaming fish add a little salt and vinegar to the water — 1 teaspoon salt and 1 tablespoon vinegar to every 2 quarts water. Keep fish water for sauces and soups. Fish is cooked when bones separate easily.
To fry fish. — (1) Coat with egg and breadcrumbs, salt and pepper and fry in boiling fat. (2) Dip first in milk then in flour and salt and fry. (3) Dip in batter and fry.
Batter. — Beat 1 egg add 2 tablespoons flour, 3 tablespoons milk, salt and pepper. Good dripping or oil should be used for frying and when a faint blue smoke rises from the fat it is the right temperature for frying. Drain on cooking paper.
To grill fish. — After fish has been washed and dried brush over with a little oil or melted butter. Place on clean hot gridiron rubbed over with suet. Grill over clear fire or under electric grill.

FRIED SOLE
Wash and skin sole, cut off fins and head and dry. Shake flour, pepper and salt over sole, dip it into beaten egg and cover with fine breadcrumbs. Fry in deep, hot fat.

FILLETS OF SOLE IN MILK
Take some fillets of sole, roll and lay in a buttered pyrex dish. Season and cover with milk and a few drops vinegar and dab with butter. Cover dish with buttered paper and bake in moderate oven.

A. Archibald.

BAKED FISH IN TOMATO SAUCE
Clean a 3 lb. fish and put into baking dish with seasoning. Fry one large onion in slices and place on fish with a few slices of tomato. Make a good tomato sauce and pour over fish and bake in moderate oven for 40 minutes. Baste often.

M. Webb.

CREAMED FISH

One and a half pounds of any delicate fish. Remove skins and bones and pound meat very fine. Cook 1 cup stale breadcrumbs in 2 cups milk, add 2 tablespoons butter, 1 of cream, pepper and salt and, when cold, add to the fish. Beat thoroughly and add 2 well beaten eggs. Place mixture in buttered pyrex dish and stand in a baking dish filled with hot water, cover with cooking paper and bake 1 hour.
Serve with Hollandaise or tomato sauce. *M.B., Cape Town.*

FISH AND CHEESE

Any left over fish, mashed potatoes, white sauce, cheese, butter, pepper and salt.
Butter as many individual fireproof dishes as are required or one large dish. Put in a layer of flaked fish, cover with white sauce, spread well beaten, mashed potatoes on top, sprinkle with grated cheese, dab with butter and bake in oven for half an hour. Serve very hot. *J.H.*

FISH CAKES

Left over fish, mashed potatoes, parsley, butter, egg, pepper and salt. Salmon can be used.
Remove skin and bone from fish and mix with equal quantity of potatoes. Add pepper, salt, parsley and a little butter. Moisten with a portion of the egg, shape into cakes and dip in egg and breadcrumbs. Fry to a nice brown and serve with tomato sauce.
For the children put a cross of scrambled eggs on each cake. *J.H.*

SCALLOPED FISH

Six to eight ozs. cooked fish, half a pint white sauce, 2 ozs. breadcrumbs, 2 ozs. grated cheese, 2 hardboiled eggs, seasoning.
Flake fish, cover with sauce which has been mixed with cheese and eggs — keep back some egg to decorate. Put into greased piedish, cover with crumbs and heat thoroughly. Garnish with egg and parsley.
M.W.

BAKED STUFFED FISH

Wash and dry fish. Place on board and with sharp knife split from head to tail. Remove bones and fill with stuffing. Sew up and bake in moderate oven with greased paper on top.
Stuffing. — ½ lb. breadcrumbs, 2 ozs. suet, ½ teaspoon herbs, chopped parsley, 1 egg, pepper and salt, onion if liked. Mix all together, bind with egg and a little milk if necessary. *M.W.*

KEDGEREE

Any cold fish. — To 1 lb. fish allow ¼ lb. rice, 2 hard boiled eggs, 2 ozs. butter, salt and pepper.

Boil and dry the rice, divide fish into flakes, cut whites of eggs into slices and grate the yolks.

Melt butter in saucepan and add fish, rice, whites of eggs, salt and pepper. Stir till thoroughly hot. Heap mixture on hot dish and decorate with yolk of egg. Serve very hot.

MADRAS KEDGEREE

1½ cups cooked mealie rice, 1½ oz. butter, 2 tablespoons chopped onion, 1 lb. cooked fish, 1 dessertspoon curry powder, salt, 2 medium tomatoes, 1 teaspoon sugar, lemon juice or vinegar, 1 egg (hard-boiled).

Saute the onion in the butter. Stir in curry powder, cook for a few minutes. Add skinned, sliced tomatoes, sugar, salt and lemon juice. Flake the fish and add the curry sauce, stir in rice. Heat thoroughly. Turn the Kedgeree into a hot dish and garnish with slices of hard-boiled egg.

FINNAN HADDOCK

Soak a Finnan (really Findon from a village near Aberdeen) in cold water for half an hour. Dry, cut in large pieces and place in stewpan with two dessertspoons butter. Put lid on closely and steam for 10 to 15 minutes. Make a white sauce and pour over fish and butter, and boil for a few minutes. Serve very hot with toast.

FISH CUSTARD

Any white filleted fish, 1 dessertspoon flour, ½ oz. butter, 1 egg, 1 teacup milk, pepper and salt.

Cut fish into pieces and place in pyrex dish, sprinkle with pepper and salt. Put flour into a bowl and mix carefully with milk, egg, well beaten, and the melted butter. Pour over fish and bake in moderate oven 40 minutes. *M.H.*

SOLES AND OLIVE SAUCE

Have the soles filleted. Sprinkle with pepper and salt and add a squeeze of lemon juice.

Roll up each fillet with a stuffed olive inside it. Put the fillets into a buttered dish, dab with pieces of butter, cover with greased paper and bake in a moderate oven till tender. Make a white sauce and add to it a few chopped olives. Pour the sauce round the fillets and garnish with halved olives. *J.H.*

SOLE STEAMED

Skin sole and put the tail into the mouth. Place it on a well buttered plate, sprinkle lightly with salt, pepper and lemon juice and cover with a buttered paper. Place this on a saucepan containing boiling water and cover with another plate. Cook from 30 to 40 minutes turning the fish once. Make a little white sauce, pour over sole and serve. Garnish with parsley and lemon. *A.A.*

SALMON MOULD

1 small tin salmon, 1 heaped dessertspoon gelatine, pepper, salt, vinegar, cut-up pickles to taste.

Method. — Dissolve gelatine in cup hot water, put other ingredients in bowl and mix with gelatine. Line a wet mould with hard-boiled egg, beetroot and tomato, pour in mixture and allow to set. Turn out on dish, garnish with lettuce. *Mrs. A. Stevenson.*

CURRIED FISH

Fish, onions, curry powder, few orange leaves, vinegar, salt, 1 or 2 chillies or a little cayenne pepper.

Cut the fish into small slices about an inch in thickness, sprinkle with salt. Fry in boiling fat. Slice onions — 1 large onion to 1 lb. fish. Cook the onions in a little water, not too soft. Drain, then add the vinegar, enough to cover fish, chillies, curry powder, 1 dessertspoon to 1 lb. of fish, 1 teaspoon turmeric, 1 teaspoon of sugar. Boil for a few minutes. Allow to cool. Put the fish into a deep earthenware jar in layers with onions and curry sauce between each layer. Pour over the remaining sauce and cover closely. In two days it will be ready for use. A few orange leaves or bay leaves could be put on top of the fish. A little chutney added to the sauce improves the flavour. *Mrs. Withiel.*

STEAMED FISH FOR INVALIDS

1 slice of filleted fish, small piece of butter, salt and lemon. Wipe the fish, season with salt and lemon, place on greased plate and cover with buttered paper. Steam over boiling water till done — about half an hour. Serve with butter parsley and lemon or with a white sauce made with bones of fish.

FISH OMELETTE

Beat 2 eggs slightly and season with salt and pepper. Melt one tablespoon butter in frying pan and pour in the egg mixture together with 2 tablespoons cold flaked fish. Stir for a few seconds then leave until set and browned on bottom. Fold over and serve.

Mrs. Slade.

FISH PIE (Cape Dish)

Remains of cold boiled fish, 2 onions fried in dripping, salt, mustard, tomato sauce, mashed potato, 1 egg.

Clear fish from bones, break into small pieces, mix with onion, seasoning, butter, tomato sauce, half an egg and a little mashed potato. Pack in a buttered dish, cover with mashed potato, brush with the egg. Bake three-quarters of an hour (very good).

FISH BAKED IN CUSTARD

Take a small stock fish, remove the skin and bones and cut into fillets. Lay the fish in a greased baking dish, sprinkle over salt and pepper, 1 tablespoon finely chopped parsley, 2 tablespoons chopped onion, and 2 tablespoons grated cheese. Mix together, 2 eggs, slightly beaten, 2 tablespoons melted butter and 1 cup milk. Season with salt and pepper, then pour over fish, bake in a moderate oven until custard is set.

FISH SANDWICH

Thin slices of white fish, salt and pepper, 2 tablespoons onions (finely chopped), 1 egg, 1½ tablespoons butter, 1 teaspoon chopped parsley, 3 dessertspoons capers, tartar sauce, 3 ozs. soft breadcrumbs.

Saute onions lightly in butter. Mix breadcrumbs with onions and capers, and seasoning, and bind all with the egg. Place a little stuffing on a slice of fish and cover each with another slice. Put them in a buttered dish, cover and bake at 350 until the flesh is quite white. Time required about 25 minutes. Serve garnished with slices of olives or cucumber and tartar sauce.

A GOOD FISH DISH

1 lb. fish (cooked), ½ pint whipped sour cream, 2 cups breadcrumbs, salt and pepper.

Flake fish and season with salt and pepper. Place a layer of breadcrumbs on greased pyrex dish, follow with layer of fish and a layer of whipped cream. Repeat until the dish is full. Bake in a moderate oven to a golden brown (¾ hour). *Mrs. A. L. Ferguson.*

FISH SOUFFLE (Invalid Dish)

1 lb. white fish, steamed or boiled, 1 cup milk, tablespoon white breadcrumbs, nut of butter, squeeze lemon juice, whites of two eggs, seasoning.

Pound or flake fish finely. Boil milk and sprinkle in breadcrumbs. Cook till bread is absorbed. Add fish, nut of butter, lemon juice and seasoning. Cool slightly and add stiffly beaten whites of eggs. Pour into buttered casserole and bake ½ hour in moderate oven. Minced chicken may be used instead of fish. *Mrs. H. K. Lloyd, Ficksburg.*

FISH SOUFFLE

2 tablespoons butter, 4 eggs, 4 tablespoons flour, ½ lb. boiled or baked fish, 1 pint milk, juice of half a lemon.

Make a sauce of the butter, flour and milk. Add yolks of eggs and the fish flaked. Whip whites to a stiff froth and fold in. Flavour with salt and pepper. Bake till done, about 30 minutes, in a moderate oven. Serve at once or souffle will be tough.

Fish and visitors spoil after the third day.

FISH GARNISHES

Lemon, parsley, sliced tomato, lettuce.

FISH SAUCES

White, anchovy, bechamel, egg, Hollandaise, parsley, tartare, tomato.

WHITE SAUCE

1 oz. flour, 1 oz. butter, ½ pint milk, salt and pepper. Half milk and half stock can be used.

Melt butter in small saucepan, stir in the flour, cook for a few minutes but do not brown. Add milk and seasoning, stir till it boils and cook for a few minutes.

For cream sauce use cream in place of milk.

To make parsley sauce, add chopped parsley.

To make egg sauce, add chopped hard-boiled egg.

To make anchovy sauce, add 1 teaspoon anchovy essence, squeeze of lemon juice, cayenne pepper.

BECHAMEL SAUCE

1 oz. butter, 2 ozs. flour, 1 carrot, 1 onion, 1 bay leaf, ½ pint milk, 1 gill stock.

Melt butter, stir in flour and cook for a few minutes without browning. Pour in liquid and stir well till it boils, add vegetables, etc., simmer for three-quarters of an hour and strain.

TOMATO SAUCE

6 tomatoes, 1 onion, 1 gill stock, ½ teaspoon salt, 1 teaspoon sugar, cayenne pepper, pinch bicarbonate of soda.

Cut tomatoes into slices and stew with onion, salt and stock till quite soft. Pass through sieve, add cayenne, sugar and a squeeze of lemon juice. If necessary thicken with a little cornflour and add a dash of Worcester sauce.

TARTARE SAUCE

¼ pint mayonnaise sauce, 1 tablespoon finely chopped onion, 1 tablespoon chopped parsley, 1 tablespoon chopped capers, 1 tablespoon vinegar.

Stir all together and use as required.

MUSTARD SAUCE

Mix 2 tablespoons made mustard with 1 large cup white sauce or melted butter. Add a few grains cayenne. Use with fish or meat.

HOLLANDAISE SAUCE

½ cup butter, ½ cup boiling water, juice of ½ lemon, ¼ saltspoon pepper, 1 saltspoon salt, yolks of 3 eggs.
Beat butter to a cream with wooden spoon, add yolks of eggs one at a time and beat well, put in lemon juice and seasoning. Just before serving add the boiling water, a little at a time, stirring well. Place bowl in saucepan of boiling water and stir rapidly till sauce thickens.

It is better to remain silent than to speak the truth illhumoredly and so spoil an excellent dish by covering it with a bad sauce.

St. Francis.

KATY'S CURRIED OR PICKLED FISH

(An old Cape recipe modernised)
4 lbs. Hake, Cape Salmon or Kingklip, or any other firm fish, 4 large onions, 2 tablespoons water, 2 tablespoons vinegar.
Flour, salt and pepper, butter or dripping.
Clean and fillet the fish and cut into pieces convenient for serving. Dust with flour, salt and pepper. Peel onions and slice thinly. Place alternative layers of fish and onions in a fireproof dish. Pour vinegar and water over, dot with butter, cover and bake for one hour in a fairly hot oven (400 degrees). When fish is ready, pour off the liquid without disturbing the layers of fish and onion, then use the liquid for the following sauce:

Mix one cup liquid with one cup vinegar and bring to boil. Combine one heaped tablespoon curry powder with two tablespoons sugar, 1 teaspoon flour, salt and pepper to taste. Slake with a little extra vinegar, add to boiling liquid, stir well and cook for 15 minutes. (the addition of Chutney, Apricot jam or cooked apples to taste, is a great improvement). Sauce should be of consistency of thin cream.

Strain and pour sauce over fish and onions, taking care to cover every piece of fish, then return to oven for a few minutes.
Serve hot as curried fish with boiled rice or riced potatoes.
Serve cold as pickled fish, adding a few bay leaves if liked: cover well and keep for two or three days before serving. Serve with chutney or blatjang Chicken can be curried in the same way, using the liquid in which chicken has been freshly boiled, instead of fish stock for the curry sauce.

MEAT AND POULTRY

We may live without poetry, music and art,
We may live without conscience, and live without heart,
We may live without friends, we may live without books.
But civilised men cannot live without cooks.

CUTS OF MEAT

MUTTON AND LAMB

Gigot or Leg — Roasting and chops.
Loin — Roast or chops.
Flank — Boiling.
Breast — Boiling.
Runner — Boiling.
Shoulder — Roasting.
Neck — Boiling or stewing.

BEEF

Hough and Knuckle — Soups and stews.
Rump (silverside) — Steaks, boiling and pickling.
Fillet — Grilling and frying.
Flank — Boiling.
Nine Holes — Boiling.
Sirloin — Roasting.
Runner (thick end) — Stewing.
Shoulder — Stewing steaks, pie meat, etc.
Head — Cheek and tongue.

PORK

Flank — Rolled for boiling.
Breast — Streaky bacon.
Shoulder — Roast.
Loin — Roast.
Runner — Sliced bacon.
Leg — Roast. Rub skin with salad oil to make nice crackling.

VEAL

Leg — Roast and cutlets.
Loin — Roast or cutlets.
Shoulder — Stuffed and roasted.
Breast — Stewed.

SUITABLE JOINTS FOR GRILLING
Rump Steak — Fillet of beef or undercut of rump.
Loin Chops — Mutton or pork.
Chump Chops — Mutton.
Best End Neck — Mutton.
Joints of chicken.
Sheep kidneys.

SUITABLE JOINTS FOR SALTING
Silverside, topside, aitchbone, thick flank, tongue.

To Salt. — Rub meat well with salt and place in cold brine made from 1 lb. salt, 1½ oz. saltpetre, ½ lb. brown sugar, 1 quart boiling water. Immerse meat completely in the cold brine and leave for 3 or 4 days, turning daily.

To Cook Salt Meat. — Take out of brine and wash well. Cover with cold water and bring slowly to boil. Simmer, allowing 35 minutes to the lb. Long, gentle cooking is necessary. An hour before serving add some carrots, turnips and onions to boiling meat. Add suet dumplings half an hour before serving. Serve meat on hot dish, surrounded by vegetables and dumplings. If desired cold, allow meat to cool in liquid in which it was cooked.

RULES FOR COOKING

To Tenderise Meat. — Cover steak with a mixture of salad oil and vinegar. Soak chops in milk for half an hour.

Boiling. — Put fresh meat (other than soup meat) into boiling water and salt meat into cold. Simmer and skim well, allowing half an hour to each pound and half an hour over. Allow salt meat 1 hour over.

Stewing. — Cook long and slowly.

Baking and Roasting. — Wipe meat and dredge with flour, pepper and salt. Place in baking tin and cover with dripping. Cover poultry with strips of bacon. Place meat in hot oven for 15 minutes then lower heat and cook more slowly, turning often. Allow 20 minutes to the pound and 20 minutes over. Veal and pork half an hour to each pound and half an hour over.

Broiling and Grilling. — The fire must be clear and free from smoke or flame and the gridiron greased and heated.
Use a knife and spoon for turning. Turning every 2 minutes.
Time 10 to 15 minutes.

Braising or Pot Roasting. — This is a combination of roasting and stewing and is a splendid way to cook tough, lean meat. When tender remove meat and put into a quick oven to brown.

Frying. — The fat must be smoking hot. Turn meat with knife and

spoon. Drain on cooking paper. Put steak into very hot, dry pan. Sear on both sides then add fat and cook slowly.
To Stuff Leg of Pork or Mutton. — Take out the upper portion of the bone and fill with forcemeat. Skewer or tie firmly.
Shoulder can be boned, stuffed, rolled and roasted.

JUST STEWS

For the benefit of the "mere man" who promised to purchase this book if I would put in his Mother's stews. I may not be able to do that but I will do the next best thing and give him my Mother's.
Stewed Steak and Dumplings. — 1 lb. stewing steak, 2 carrots, 2 onions, 2 turnips, butter, seasoning and water.
Trim and cut up meat, dip in flour and seasoning and brown in butter or dripping. Pour off surplus fat, cover meat with hot water and stew very slowly for 2 hours. Add the prepared vegetables to the stew and cook for another hour. Thicken gravy if necessary.
Vary this by using tomatoes in place of carrots and turnips.
Dumplings. — ¼ lb. flour, 2 ozs, suet, ¼ teaspoon baking powder (optional), cold water, salt.
Mix dry ingredients, chop or grate suet very finely and add. Mix to a stiff dough with as little cold water as possible. Roll into balls and drop into the stew half an hour before serving.
For Norfolk dumplings omit the suet.
As a variation add kidney or giblets and leave out dumplings.
Shin of beef or hough stew from Aberdeen. — 2 lbs, shin of beef. Follow directions for stewed steak but cook for five hours very slowly.
Haricot or Stewed Mutton. — Add capers if liked. 2 lbs. neck of mutton, 2 onions, butter, flour, water, pepper and salt. Take away as much fat as possible.
Divide mutton into cutlets and roll in flour and seasoning. Brown lightly in butter, add boiling water and onions and stew gently for 2½ hours.
Lamb Stew. — 1 lb. lamb chops, onion, butter, flour, peas, pepper and salt. Sprinkle flour and seasoning over chops. Fry in butter and add onion and 1 cup of hot water and stew for 1 hour. Add 1 cup green peas and cook till tender. Just before serving add 1 cup tomato sauce. Serve with mashed potatoes.

IRISH STEW

1 lb. chops or 1 lb. neck of mutton, 6 large potatoes, 2 onions, water, salt and pepper.
Cut meat into pieces, slice potatoes and onions. Put into pan in layers, add seasoning and cover with cold water. Stew slowly for 2 or 3 hours.

OX TAIL STEW

1 ox tail, onion, carrots, water, butter, flour, salt and pepper.

Wash and dry tail and roll in flour, pepper and salt. Brown in butter with onion, cover with hot water and stew for 4 or 5 hours adding the carrots 1 hour before serving. Remove stew, allow to cool and remove fat. Reheat, thicken gravy and serve.

Better if made previous day and allowed to stand overnight.

BEEF OLIVES

1 lb. stewing steak cut into strips. Mix a little chopped suet, breadcrumbs, mixed herbs, salt and pepper with sufficient milk to bind. Place a little of this stuffing on each strip, roll up and tie with cotton. Sprinkle flour, pepper and salt over and brown lightly in a little fat. Have ready a little hot stock, put the rolled steak into this, add two small onions and stew gently for 2 hours. Can be cooked in casserole.

STUFFED STEAK

One very large slice of steak cut thin. Follow directions for beef olives but make one large roll instead of several small ones and cook a little longer.

HOT POT

1 lb. lean beef cut into pieces, 4 or 5 potatoes, 1 onion. Cut onion into slices and divide each potato into four or five pieces. Put layer of potato at bottom of pyrex dish, then a layer of meat and a few slices onion. Continue till all material is used. Fill dish 3 parts full with water. Cover and bake slowly for 3 hours, adding more water if necessary.

STEAK AND ONIONS

1 lb. steak, 2 large onions, dripping.

Cover 1 lb. fillet or rump steak with a mixture of 2 tablespoons olive oil and 1 of vinegar. Leave for 1 hour. Slice onions as thin as possible and fry in hot dripping. Put between two plates over pot of boiling water to keep hot. Make fat hot again and fry steak for 12 minutes, turning every 2 minutes. Serve with onions on top.

CARROT AND LIVER RISSOLE

One or 2 ozs. cooked liver, 4 ozs. cooked mashed carrot, 4 tablespoons breadcrumbs, 1 teaspoon chopped onion, pepper and salt. Mince the liver and mix with other ingredients. Add more breadcrumbs if mixture is too sloppy. Shape into balls and fry in hot fat. Serve with mashed potato, green peas and gravy.

ROLLED SHOULDER OF MUTTON
Shoulder of mutton.

Filling. — 2 cups breadcrumbs, 1 slice chopped ham or bacon, 6 nuts (pounded), 2 tablespoons lemon juice, 4 cloves, mixed spice, 1 egg, salt and pepper.

Mix dry ingredients, beat egg and add. Bone mutton, stuff, roll and tie with string or tape. Pot roast for 2 hours and serve with thick sauce.

STEAMED LIVER ROLL

Put through a mincer 1 sheep's liver, 2 slices of bacon and 1 onion. Add 1 cup breadcrumbs, 1 teaspoon salt, $\frac{1}{4}$ teaspoon pepper, a few gratings nutmeg and 2 slightly beaten eggs. Pour into a greased coffee tin and steam 1 hour. Serve with tomato sauce poured over. Instead of steaming, the liver may be put into a greased pie-dish, then placed in a pan of water and cooked in a slow oven of 300° until firm.
A. Friend, Johannesburg.

MEAT ROLL

1 lb. stewing steak, $\frac{1}{2}$ lb. salt pork (both minced), 1 egg, salt, pepper, 1 tablespoon lemon, $\frac{1}{2}$ cup breadcrumbs.

Method. — Mix meat, breadcrumbs and seasoning, add lemon juice and beaten egg, press well together and sprinkle with breadcrumbs. Bake in oven for 1 hour with dripping. Can be steamed for 3 or 4 hours in a jar or tin.
Mrs. Spence.

BOILED HAM

Soak the ham overnight, after scraping and cleaning it thoroughly. In the morning cover the ham with clean, cold water and bring to boil slowly. Skim and simmer till tender, allowing 25 minutes to each lb.

When ready allow to cool in the liquid, then remove and skin. Brush over with beaten egg and cover with browned breadcrumbs and set in oven for a few minutes. Garnish with parsley.

BAKED HAM

Scrub ham and soak overnight in cold water. Cover ham with a thick crust of paste made with 2 lbs. mealie meal and 2 lbs. of flour or boermeal and water. Cover ham entirely, put into hot oven with top switch off and leave for about 6 hours. Skin the ham and cover with browned breadcrumbs and put into oven for a few minutes. Serve either hot or cold.

STUFFED ROLLED VEAL
6 lbs. loin of veal (kidney end).

Have the loin carefully boned. Make a stuffing with 2 cups breadcrumbs, 2 slices chopped bacon, a little parsley, pepper and salt. Bind with an egg and spread over veal. Roll loin tightly and fasten with skewer or tie and roast in the ordinary way, allowing half an hour to the lb.

SUCKING PIG (A Favourite Cape Dish)

When piggy is ready, make a stuffing of breadcrumbs, suet, some dried sage leaves, pepper, salt and lemon peel. Moisten the whole with egg and water, stuff the pig, sew up with strong thread; truss it as a hare is trussed, with its forelegs skewered back and its hind legs forward. Lay it on a trivet, in a dripping pan with a pint of water in the pan. Rub the piggy all over with butter or fat and set it in a hot oven, (it will bake in about 2 hours) basting occasionally. If you rub the piggy with white of an egg before roasting, it will be nice and crip. Piggy may also be covered with cabbage leaves and basted with fat or butter; this will prevent it burning or becoming too hard.
Mrs. A. A.

LIVER AND BACON
½ lb. sheep's liver (as fresh as possible), ¼ lb. bacon, 1 tablespoon flour, salt and pepper. Small cup of boiling water.

Wash liver in salt and water and skin it. Cut into ½ inch slices and dip in seasoned flour. Fry bacon quickly and put into oven to keep hot. Fry liver in bacon fat for about 8 minutes or till tender. Place on hot dish and surround with cooked bacon. To make the gravy, add flour to fat and brown well, add boiling water and stir. Strain and pour round liver and bacon. Garnish with parsley and serve with fried tomatoes and creamed potatoes.

MIXED GRILL

Two or three sheep kidneys, 2 lamb cutlets, 2 slices fillet steak, 2 or 3 slices bacon, 2 tomatoes, sausages if liked, chip potatoes. Trim the cutlets and slices of fillet which should be about ½ inch thick. Skin, wash, split and core the kidneys. Before grilling brush the meat with melted fat or butter. Place kidneys, cutlets, steak and sausages on greased grid, place under hot grill for 10 to 15 minutes, turning every 2 minutes. The potatoes and tomatoes are fried separately. Place meat on hot dish with tiny dots of parsley butter on top, and garnish with bacon, potatoes and tomatoes.

VEAL CUTLETS

Cut 1 lb. of fillet of veal into neat pieces. Dust each piece with flour, pepper and salt. Dip into beaten egg and roll in breadcrumbs. Fry in hot fat for about 5 minutes. Serve with slices of lemon, mashed potato and spinach or green peas and a brown gravy or tomato puree.

BOILED BACON

Choose gammon or piece from back. Follow directions given for boiled ham.

PORTERHOUSE STEAK

A steak 1 inch thick cut from sirloin. Brush steak on both sides with melted butter and sprinkle with salt and pepper. Grill over a clear fire or under grill and serve with parsley butter. Serve with fried onions. *Mother.*

PORK OR VEAL AND HAM RAISED PIE

10 oz. flour, salt and pepper to taste. Melt 3 oz. lard in ½ teacup boiling water, and mix all to a dough, knead well.
Save a piece of dough for the lid, mould the remainder into a cake tin. *Filling.* — ½ lb. pork or veal, ½ lb. ham, minced coarsely and mixed with an egg, salt and pepper. Put into cake tin, cover with lid of pastry and decorate with leaves made from dough. Bake like a fruit cake. Stew any scraps of meat left over. When pie is cold dissolve a little gelatine in gravy and pour gently into pie through hole in lid.
Miss Jackson.

STUFFED OX HEART

Ox heart, flour, water, stuffing.
Wash the heart well. Remove the muscles from inside and all blood. Make a stuffing of 1 cup breadcrumbs, a little chopped onion, butter, pepper and salt and milk to bind. Stuff the heart cavities. Bind heart securely, place in stewpan, and simmer in stock for 3 hours. Thicken stock to make gravy.

BEEFSTEAK AND KIDNEY PUDDING

1½ lb. stewing steak, suet, 1 ox kidney, flour, water, salt and pepper.
Make a suet crust of ½ lb. flour, ¼ lb., finely chopped suet, ½ teaspoon baking powder, salt and a little cold water. Roll out two-thirds of paste and line a pudding basin. Cut meat into thin slices, place a small piece of kidney on each, roll and cover with flour and seasoning. Put meat into basin and cover with water. Roll out remainder of pastry, wet the edges and place on top. Cover basin and steam 6 hours. *M.F.*

BEEFSTEAK AND KIDNEY PIE

2 lbs. stewing steak, ½ ox kidney, flour, pepper and salt and cold water.

Soak kidney in salt and water for half an hour. Wash and dry and cut into small pieces. Cut steak into strips, place a piece of kidney on each and roll up. Dip each piece in flour and seasoning, brown and stew for 2 hours. Place in piedish with small pastry holder in centre and allow to cool. Make a puff or flaky pastry — see pastry making. Roll pastry to shape of piedish but rather larger. Measure and cut edges and place these on wetted edges of piedish. Wet these again and place crust on top. Pierce centre, decorate and bake in hot oven till well risen and nicely browned. Do not stretch pastry over pie and see that dish is full. *M.F.*

SALTED MUTTON RIBS

1 Medium-sized mutton rib, ½ cup prepared salt.

Method. — Bone rib, then rub thoroughly with salt on both sides and place in flat dish. Leave in brine for three days, turning meat every morning. Boil in plenty of water till tender. Serve hot with vegetables. This meat is at its best when it is re-heated by grilling on hot coals at an open fire and served with baked potatoes.

Salt for Dry Salting. — 2 lbs. salt, 1½ oz. ground saltpetre, ¼ lb. Demerara sugar, 1 dessertspoon crushed coriander seed.

Mix and put in bottle for use. *Mrs. Murray.*

BRAISED CHOPS

Sprinkle flour, pepper and salt over 1 lb. of chops. Brown in a little butter. Put into casserole with cut up carrots, turnips, parsnips and onions. Season and cover with stock or water. Cook for 2½ hours. When ready, thicken the gravy with a little flour and add a dash of Worcester sauce. Serve in casserole. *Mrs. Grant.*

TRIPE AND ONIONS

Clean tripe, cut into pieces and boil in four changes of water for 8 hours. An hour or two before serving put in onions. When ready, cut tripe into small pieces, thicken gravy with milk and flour, add salt and pepper and a good piece of butter. *M.B.*

TOAD IN THE HOLE

Can be made with sausages, cold cooked meat or slices of steak.

Meat, ¼ lb. flour, 1 egg and ½ pint milk, salt and pepper.

Make a batter by placing flour and salt in basin; break egg into centre and add ½ of the milk. Beat 10 minutes and add remainder of milk. Place meat or skinned sausages in piedish, season and pour batter over. Bake in moderate oven for half an hour.   *M.B.*

SAVOURY STEAK

Dredge a steak thickly with flour and sprinkle with pepper and salt. Well grease a casserole with dripping or butter and scatter chopped onion in bottom of dish. Put in the steak and cover with slices of onion; put on lid and cook slowly in oven for 1 hour. Add small skinned tomatoes a teaspoon curry powder and a teaspoon of flour mixed with a cup of stock or water. Cook for another 1½ hours or until tender. When cooked the steak can be lifted out and the gravy thickened if desired.   *Mrs. C. Griffith.*

SCOTCH MINCE COLLOPS (Savoury Mince)

1 lb. steak minced, 1 small onion, 2 tablespoons breadcrumbs, 1 oz. butter, 1 cup stock, pepper and salt.
Chop onion finely and mix thoroughly with mince, breadcrumbs and seasoning. Melt butter and fry the mixture well stirring thoroughly so that it does not lump. When well fried add the cup of stock and stew for about half an hour, stirring often. Serve very hot with mashed potatoes and garnish with croutons of bread. Add leeks to taste.   *J.H.*

STUFFED TOMATOES

As many tomatoes as required. Left over mince and parsley. Season and fill tomato cases with mixture, put a tiny piece of butter on each, replace tops and bake in moderate oven 20 minutes.

STUFFED ONIONS

Parboil onions, scoop out centres, fill cavities with mince. Bake 15 minutes and serve with gravy.

FRICADELLES — FATHER'S FAVOURITE

½ lb. steak and ½ lb. mutton minced, 1 onion finely chopped, ½ cup breadcrumbs, salt and pepper, 1 egg.
Moisten breadcrumbs with stock and add to minced meat, onion and seasoning. Mix well and shape into rounds, dredge with flour, dip in egg and coat with breadcrumbs. Fry in hot fat and serve with fried onions and gravy. Can be stewed gently in casserole for 1 hour if liked. For Hamburg steak use fresh minced beef only and serve with tomato sauce.   *J.H.*

SHEPHERD'S PIE

½ lb. minced cooked meat or, better still, ½ lb. fresh mince prepared as for mince collops with a dash of Worcester sauce. Put into piedish and cover with mashed potatoes. Brush over with egg, sprinkle with breadcrumbs and bake half an hour. Serve with gravy. Mince from left-overs must be moistened with gravy and sauce before being covered. *J.H.*

CRUMBED FILLET OR LAMB CHOPS

Cut some fillet into pieces 1 inch thick. Trim, season and dip into beaten egg and breadcrumbs. Fry a nice brown and serve with fried tomatoes. Cook chops in same way but serve with green peas and tomato sauce. *Mrs. Anderson.*

HAGGIS

Procure stomach bag of sheep and the pluck (lights, heart and liver), 1 lb. beef suet, 4 onions, 2 cups oatmeal, pepper, salt and cayenne.

Have the bag or paunch thoroughly cleaned and see that it is perfectly whole. Clean the pluck thoroughly, make incisions in heart and liver and boil the whole — let windpipe hang over edge of pot so that impurities may pass away. Boil for 2 hours and when cold cut away windpipe and any bits of skin or gristle. Mince half of the liver with the lights, heart, onions and suet very small, add oatmeal and seasoning and ½ pint of liquor in which pluck was boiled. Take the cleaned bag and ¾ fill it with mixture — if too full the contents will swell and burst the bag. Sew up with needle and thread. Put into a pot of boiling water and prick occasionally with a large darning needle. Boil for 3 hours with plate underneath. A double bag may be used if one is too thin. Serve on folded napkin without accompaniments other than the bagpipes. *M.F.*

SAUSAGE POTATOES

As many sausages as required, mashed potatoes, salt and pepper, dripping and parsley.

Prick sausages and fry in usual way. Boil and mash potatoes, adding a little milk. Take a spoonful of potatoes, lay a half sausage on it, cover with more potato leaving it quite rough. Put into greased baking tin and bake about half an hour or until nicely browned. Decorate each sausage potato with parsley.

SAUSAGE RISSOLES

¼ lb. sausage, 2 tablespoons breadcrumbs, 1 large cup cold mashed potatoes, salt and pepper, tomato sauce.

Mash potato and sausage meat together, add breadcrumbs and seasoning and sauce to bind mixture. Divide into five or six portions, shape into rolls, roll in toasted breadcrumbs and fry in hot fat. Apple sauce can be used instead of tomato and is delicious.

SAVOURY RICE RISSOLES

6 dessertspoonfuls minced meat or bacon, 6 dessertspoonfuls boiled rice, 2 teaspoons grated cheese, chopped parsley, pepper and salt, a little gravy.
Mix all ingredients together, shape into rissoles, roll in fine breadcrumbs and fry in hot fat till golden brown.

HAM CROQUETTES

½ lb. cooked ham, ¼ lb. cooked potatoes, 2 hard-boiled eggs, 1 yolk of egg, 1 tablespoon minced parsley.
Chop ham and eggs and mix with parsley, add potatoes and seasoning. Add yolk of egg and mix thoroughly. Flour the hand well and form into small balls. Fry in boiling fat.

HAM TOAST

2 eggs, 2 oz. butter, ¼ lb. cooked, minced ham, ¾ cup milk, 2 teaspoons chopped parsley, salt and pepper, slices of bread without crusts.
Beat 1 egg, add the milk and dip the bread into this. Fry till brown in 1 oz. butter. Place remaining butter in pan, beat egg with milk that is left and add ham, parsley, salt and pepper. Cook till thick. Pile on fried bread and garnish with parsley.

HAM DONE IN CASSEROLE

Take a slice of ham about 2 inches thick off gammon. Sprinkle lightly with sugar and brown. Spread some made mustard on each side, place in casserole, cover with milk. Put lid on dish, and bake in medium oven for 1½ hours. Serve with beans and tomato sauce.
For special occasions the ham can be cooked with mushroom soup (tinned) instead of milk.

MUTTON SLICES

Six to eight slices cooked mutton, 1 large onion, 2 tomatoes, gravy, pepper and salt, fat, potatoes.
Fry onion in a little fat. Remove from pan. Slice tomatoes and fry. Cut up 2 large potatoes and put a layer of sliced potatoes in bottom of pyrex dish. Put in the meat, onions and tomatoes in layers, season well, cover with gravy (kept from the roast) and put the remainder of potato slices on top. Bake half an hour in hot oven.   *J.H.*

COLD MEAT FRITTERS

Slices of mutton, lamb, pork or chicken. Dip in batter and fry lightly. Serve with tomato sauce.

Batter. — 4 oz. flour, 1 egg, salt, ¼ pint lukewarm water and 1 dessertspoon melted butter.

Mix flour, yolk of egg, salt and butter together. Add the water gradually and beat very well. Stand for a time and just before using beat egg white stiffly and fold into mixture. *America.*

CURRY

2 apples, 1 large onion, ½ oz. flour, 1 dessertspoon curry powder, raisins, bananas, chutney, lemon juice, stock.

Fry fruit and vegetables, etc., in 1 oz. butter. Add flour and curry powder and enough stock to make a sauce. Allow to simmer for 1 hour. Twenty minutes before serving add the meat, fish or eggs to be curried and the chutney. Serve with rice.

1 cup rice, salt, boiling water.

Wash rice thoroughly. Have the water boiling and salt added. Sprinkle in the rice but do not let water stop boiling. Boil hard for 15 to 20 minutes. Strain through colander, pour fresh boiling water over. Set the colander over a pot, cover with a cloth and steam until ready to serve. *Mrs. A. Mossop.*

TO COOK VENISON

The first thing to do is to wash the venison well in warm water to which a little vinegar has been added. Next lard it with fat, bacon, pork or spek, which you can obtain from your butcher; this is done by making incisions in the venison with a sharp-pointed knife and cutting the bacon or spek into lardons, narrow strips, about 1 inch by ½ inch, and forcing these in with a fork or larding needle. Now put the venison into a basin and pour 1 cup of vinegar over it, adding a few peppercorns and bay leaves. Turn every half hour and leave it in the vinegar for anything from 2 to 4 hours. Take out and drain. Spread a sheet of greaseproof paper on the table and moisten it with cold water, cover with another sheet and spread fat or butter over this, put the venison on the fat and cover with bacon rashers or any spek you have over, season with salt and pepper and rub flour on the meat. Wrap the paper round it. Put 1 cup of salted water into the roasting pan, put in the paper-covered meat. Place in a hot oven of 450° Fahr. or No. 9 for 10 or 15 minutes, then lower the heat to 400° Fahr., or No. 7 and allow 15 minutes to the lb. and 15 minutes over. Fifteen minutes before serving remove the paper and allow the venison to brown. Make a thick gravy and serve with red currant jelly. A little port wine added to the gravy is delicious. Another method of cooking

vension is to pot-roast it, using sour cream. The venison is larded and soaked in the vinegar as above, then placed in a saucepan and browned all over with 1 or 2 tablespoons of hot dripping, after which a cup of sour cream is added. Cover the saucepan closely and allow it to cook slowly until tender. Allow 20 minutes to the lb. and 30 minutes over. Sour cream may be used in roasting instead of dripping with good results.
"The Star."

BEEFSTEAK CAKE

Chop finely 1 lb. of raw beefsteak, add 2 tablespoonfuls of chopped suet, flavouring of chopped onion and parsley. Season with pepper and salt, bind with a beaten egg. Mix all together and make into small flat cakes. Dissolve some dripping in frying pan and when smoking hot put in cakes and fry a golden brown. Arrange mashed potatoes in the centre of a dish, with the steaks around it and over them pour a good, thick gravy. Braised onions should be served with this.
A. Friend, Johannesburg.

BREAKFAST ROLL

1 lb. lean gravy beef, ½ lb. bacon, ½ cup breadcrumbs, 1 egg, pepper, salt and a little nutmeg.
Mince beef and bacon together. Add egg and breadcrumbs, salt, pepper and small grating of nutmeg.
Form into roll, tie in a pudding cloth and boil about 2 hours.
Mrs. C. W. Smith.

DRY PICKLE

1 lb. brown sugar, 3½ lbs. salt, 1 oz. saltpetre, 1 oz. pickling spices. Mix well and rub into meat.

PICKLED MEAT (Dry)

Bone the meat if necessary and rub the pickle well into the meat. Make a hole in the centre of the pickle, put in meat and cover. Repeat this process daily, from three to eight days. Remove meat and wash and dry.

WET PICKLE

1½ lbs. coarse salt, ¾ lb. brown suggar, ¾ oz. saltpetre, 1 gallon water, 1 chili pod, 1 dozen peppercorns, 6 mustard seeds. Place all in pan and bring to boil.

PICKLED MEAT (Wet)

Bone the meat and place into the wet pickle. See that the pickle is cold. Cover and leave in pickle from three to ten days.

BAKED CORNED BEEF RING

5 cups cooked minced corned beef, 2 tablespoons chopped onion, 2 teaspoons horseradish, 1½ cups milk, 2 cups soft breadcrumbs, 3 tablespoons butter or dripping, 1½ teaspoons dry mustard, 2 eggs (slightly beaten).

Saute the onion in butter, add to the corned beef combined with breadcrumbs. Add horseradish and mustard. Add milk to beaten eggs and mix with corned beef. Pack mixture into a greased ring mould or individual moulds. Bake at 350° for about 30-40 minutes. Unmould, fill centre with cooked, chopped cabbage. Around the outside of the ring place new potatoes rolled in melted butter and sprinkled with chopped parsley, also boiled baby carrots.

LEFT OVERS

Rissoles. — Cold meat, flour, egg, breadcrumbs, parsley, onion, pepper and salt.

Mince meat, onion and parsley finely and season well. Bind with a little of the egg and form into rounds. Dip in flour, egg and breadcrumbs and fry in hot fat. Serve with tomato sauce or gravy.

Left over minced meat, mixed with mashed potatoes, chopped onion and parsley, formed into rolls, coated with egg and breadcrumbs and fried lightly is very good. *J.H.*

BAKED CUTLETS

Cut as many slices from a leg of lamb or mutton as desired. Coat each cutlet with a mixture of egg, breadcrumbs chopped onion and parsley. Pack into flat baking dish. Sprinkle with surplus breadcrumbs. Dot with fat and bake one hour — or until tender in moderate oven — about 400°.

To tenderise cutlets beat well and soak in milk for one hour.

Serve with peas, mashed potatoes and tomato sauce.

Pork cutlets may be used but substitute apple sauce for tomato.

CHICKEN PUFF

2 cups diced cooked chicken or other left-over poultry; 2 tablespoons finely-chopped parsley; ¼ cup mayonnaise; 8 slices white bread; 2 eggs (slightly beaten); ¼ teaspoon poultry seasoning; 2 cups milk; ¼ teaspoon salt.

Combine chicken with parsley and mayonnaise, and mix well: take 4 slices of buttered bread and place the chicken on each, then top with the other 4 slices: place in a large shallow casserole-dish. Combine eggs, milk, salt and poultry-seasoning, and pour over the sandwiches. Allow to stand for one hour in the 'fridge, or longer, if one is going out. Then bake in a moderate oven until puffed and a golden brown. Takes about one hour to bake.

RECOGNISED METHOD OF CUTTING UP MUTTON

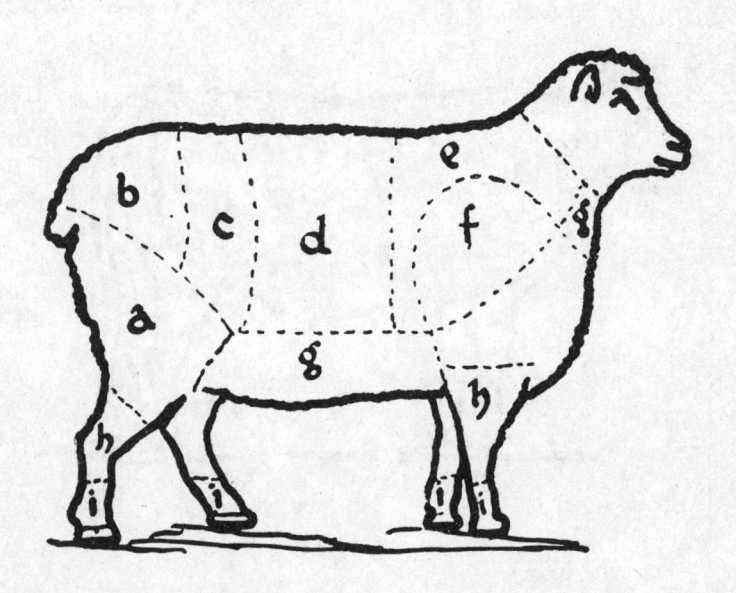

(a) Leg: For boiling or roasting and suitable for salting if to be kept for any length of time.
(b) Loin (chump end): For roasting, grilling or stewing.
(c) Loin (best end): For roasting and cutting as chops for grilling.
(d) Neck (best end): For roasting, boiling or braising, but generally divided into cutlets.
(e) Neck (scrag end): For boiling, stewing and broth.
(f) Shoulder: For roasting.
(g) Breast: For stewing or broth.
(h) The Shank: For soup.
(i) Trotters.

RECOGNIZED METHOD OF CUTTING UP BEEF

(a) Rump: For grilling, braising or entrées. May also be roasted.
(b) Sirloin: For roasting.
(c) Wing Rib: For roasting.
(d) Fore Rib: For roasting.
(e) Mid Rib: For roasting.
(f) Round (topside and silverside): For salting and boiling or pot roasting. Also used for gravy beef and sometimes used for stewing and beef steak puddings.
(g) Aitchbone: For salting, boiling and may be roasted.
(h) Thick Flank: For boiling, stewing or salting.
(i) Cheek: For entrées.
(j) Neck of Beef: For soup, stews, etc.
(k) Hough or Shin: For clear soup or stews.
(l) Brisket: For boiling or pickling.
(m) Thin Flank: For boiling or pickling.
(n) Leg: For soup or stews or servants' meat.
(o) Oxtail: For soup or stews.
(p) Cowheel: For brawn, stews or entrées.
(q) Chuck Steak: For soups and stews.

POULTRY AND GAME

Chickens. — Fried, grilled, boiled, roasted or pot roasted.
For roasting allow 1-1½ hours.
A large fowl will take from 1½ to 2½ hours.
A medium turkey or goose 2 to 3 hours.
A large turkey 3 to 4 hours.
Stuff fowl or crop of turkey with light bread stuffing using chopped onions or not as desired.
When birds have been cleaned and trussed ready for cooking, rub with cut lemon or vinegar, sprinkle with salt and pepper and dredge lightly with flour. Cover breast with thin slices of scored bacon, set in roasting pan and cover with fat. Put a small cup of water into pan. Put fowl into hot oven for few minutes then turn down to medium. For first hour or so cover breast of fowl with greaseproof paper, baste well.
Make gravy with giblets.

TO BOIL A FOWL

Truss as for roasting, rub with lemon, wrap in a cloth and plunge into boiling salted water. Simmer for 2 hours. When ready place on hot dish, cover with tasty white sauce garnish with lemon, sieved hard-boiled yolk of egg and parsley. A little boiled bacon or ham can be served with boiled fowl.

STUFFED ROAST CHICKEN

Stuffing. — 2 Slices bread, 2 eggs, 2 rashers of bacon chopped fine. Small quantity of parsley chopped fine.
Soak bread in 2 tablespoonfuls hot water, beat in eggs and bacon, add parsley, pepper and salt, then fill the inside of chicken.
Make a paste of 6 tablespoonfuls of flour with a little water and roll out. Smear chicken all over with fat and cover with the paste and bake in oven 375° for 2 hours. *Mrs. J. R. Runnals.*

ROAST TURKEY

Turkey, sausage-meat, stuffing, dripping, bacon, pepper and salt.
Prepare and truss turkey. Fill the crop with herb stuffing and put sausage-meat into body of bird. Lay turkey in baking tin with plenty of dripping. Cover the breast with bacon, baste well with hot fat and roast for 2 to 4 hours — according to size.

Before serving remove the bacon and allow the breast to brown. Serve with gravy made from the giblets and garnish with bacon rolls. To make these, remove rind, roll up rashers and stick on to a skewer. Cook for a few minutes under grill. *R.A.F.*

ROAST GOOSE OR DUCK

Stuff goose with sage and onion stuffing — see stuffings. Place on roasting tin, cover breast with butter paper and roast till tender, basting well.

Remove paper 20 minutes before serving. Dredge breast lightly with flour, baste and put back for final browning. Serve with apple sauce. Goose will take 2-3 hours to cook, according to size.

Duck will take 1-2 hours to cook, according to size.

CHICKEN IN CASSEROLE

Cut a chicken into joints, roll in flour, pepper and salt, fry in a little butter and put into casserole.

Make a gravy and pour over chicken, add a few slices fried onion and simmer gently for two or three hours.

A good way to cook an old bird.

FRIED CHICKEN

Cut slices from breast. Roll in flour, pepper and salt and fry gently in butter. Keep lid on pan till chicken is half done and then brown. To use left-over chicken re-heat it gently in mushroom sauce or thick mushroom soup (tinned). *Sent From America.*

ACCOMPANIMENTS TO MEAT AND POULTRY

Sirloin, Ribs of Beef and Roast Beef. — Horseradish sauce — Yorkshire pudding.
Hot Ox Tongue. — Red currant jelly.
Tripe — Onion sauce.
Roast Leg or Saddle of Mutton. — Red currant jelly and onion sauce.
Mutton Cutlets. — Tomato sauce.
Roast Lamb. — Mint sauce.
Roast Veal. — Tomato, onion and mushroom sauce.
Boiled Fowl. — Boiled ham, bacon or tongue, celery or parsley sauce.
Roast Turkey. — Bacon, cranberry sauce, sausages.
Roast Fowl. — Bread sauce.
Duck or Goose. — Apple sauce, sage and onion stuffing.
Roast Game. — Currant jelly sauce. Fried breadcrumbs.

YORKSHIRE PUDDING

1 cup milk, ½ cup flour, 2 eggs, ½ teaspoon salt.
Mix salt and flour, add milk gradually and form into a smooth paste, then add lightly beaten eggs.
Pour a little of the roast fat into a large, shallow pan — pour in the batter and bake 20 minutes in a hot oven. Baste well after it has risen and cut in squares for serving.   *Mrs. Slade.*

NOODLES

In making noodles, either whole eggs or the yolks of eggs may be used. Beat the eggs or egg yolks slightly, add ¼ teaspoon salt to each egg or to every 2 yolks and stir in sufficient flour to make a firm dough that will roll out easily. Roll out as thin as possible and leave to dry slightly for a few minutes, then sprinkle lightly with flour, roll up like a Swiss roll and with a sharp knife cut into shreds, thin or thick, as desired, or into fancy shapes with a vegetable cutter. Put on a sheet of paper and allow to dry, then when needed place in salted boiling water and let cook rapidly for 15 to 20 minutes.
Drain, return to saucepan and add 1 or 2 tablespoons butter, shaking until noodles are thoroughly coated. If liked, some grated cheese may also be added and any sauce, such as tomato sauce, sauce bechamel, etc. In making the noodle paste for clear soup, some grated cheese may be added to the flour, also a little cayenne pepper and, if liked, a little red colouring. On the other hand, instead of using only egg as the liquid, a little sherry may be substituted.
Noodles are similar in composition to what are known in South America as Tagerinas and there they are dished with gravy, cooked tomatoes and grated cheese.

NOODLE PIE

Put a layer of noodles in a pie dish, then a layer of tomatoes, peeled and sliced and the juice strained off, and sliced hard-boiled eggs, and next a layer of cheese sause. Repeat and have a last layer of sauce, sprinkle grated cheese on top and a few bits of butter, and bake in a hot oven until top is nice and brown.

COTSWOLD DUMPLINGS

4 ozs. grated cheese, 2 ozs. butter or margarine, 2 eggs, seasoning, breadcrumbs.
Mix cheese and margarine and add eggs and seasoning. Add sufficient breadcrumbs to make a stiff mixture. Roll in spare breadcrumbs and fry in hot fat.

"Friends" — *those relations one makes for oneself.*

MEAT SAUCES

ONION SAUCE

Boil 4 onions with a little salt. Drain and chop. Cover with white sauce. Add a little extra butter, stir and serve.
For white sauce see Fish Sauces.

MINT SAUCE

¼ cup finely chopped mint leaves, ½ cup vinegar, 1 teaspoon sugar, a little boiling water.
Cover leaves with water, add sugar and stand till cool. Add vinegar.

HORSERADISH SAUCE

2 tablespoons grated horseradish, 1 tablespoon vinegar, 1 teaspoon sugar, ½ teaspoon salt, ½ teaspoon made mustard, 3 tablespoons cream.
Mix thoroughly together adding cream last.
Bottled horseradish should be soaked in water first. *Mrs. Slade.*

SAUCE SUPREME

3 tablespoons butter, 1 tablespoon flour, 1 cup chicken gravy, 1 lemon, 1 teaspoon chopped parsley.
Place 2 tablespoons of the butter into a frying pan and, when hot, add the flour. Stir well and when turning brown add chicken gravy and boil for 4 minutes, stirring constantly. Add the juice of the lemon, parsley and remaining butter. Boil up again and serve.
Mrs. Slade.

APPLE SAUCE

4 apples, juice of 1 lemon, 2 tablespoons butter, 3 tablespoons sugar, 1 tablespoon water, pinch of salt.
Peel and slice apples and put into saucepan with other ingredients. When ready, rub through colander and re-heat.

SAUCE PIQUANTE

Put a tablespoon of butter into a saucepan and add 2 slices onion, 2 carrots, a little thyme, 2 cloves, 2 shallots, a bunch of parsley and, if liked, a clove of garlic, salt and pepper. Cook until carrot is soft, shake in a little flour, cook for another 5 minutes, add a cup of stock and ½ a cup of vinegar. Skim and strain through sieve.
Mrs. Slade.

CURRY SAUCE

1 tablespoon butter, 2 teaspoons chopped onion, 1 tablespoon flour, 1 teaspoon curry powder, 2 cups stock, salt. Fry the onion in the butter and add the curry powder. Simmer for 10 minutes then stir in the flour which has been slaked with 1 tablespoon cold water. When thick it is ready to use. *Mrs. Slade.*

FOR FLAVOURING ANY BOILED SALTED BEEF

2 tablespoons vinegar, 1 tablespoon sugar, 1 tablespoon Worcester sauce, 2 tablespoons dry mustard.
Add these to water in which beef is boiling. *Mrs. J. Knight.*

BREAD SAUCE

2 cups milk, ½ cup breadcrumbs, 1 onion, a few peppercorns, 2 tablespoons butter, ½ teaspoon salt and a few grains cayenne. Soak breadcrumbs in milk for quarter of an hour, place in saucepan with onion, pepper and salt. Cook 20 minutes, stir till smooth, remove onion and add seasoning. *A.A.*

PARSLEY BUTTER

Chop parsley very fine and work into butter — 1 tablespoon to every 2 of butter. Add a few drops lemon juice and a little salt. When well mixed form into balls and serve with grilled steak or fried fish. *A.A.*

CRANBERRY SAUCE

½ cup cold water, 1 tin cranberries, sugar to taste, 1 tablespoon red currant jelly, a dash of port wine.
Put cranberries into pan with water and bring to boil. Add sugar, wine and red currant jelly. Boil again and strain. *A.A.*

GRAVY FOR ROAST MEAT

After meat is cooked place on a hot dish and pour dripping into jar. Sprinkle a tablespoon of flour into roasting pan, add pepper and salt and stir, scraping up the brown particles which adhere to pan and which colour the gravy. Add half a pint hot water and strain.

ASPIC JELLY

1 quart stock, whites and shells of 3 eggs, 1 onion and carrot sliced, 1 tablespoon vinegar, 1 teaspoon salt, ½ teaspoon pepper, 2 ozs. gelatine, juice and rind of 1 lemon.

Slightly beat the eggs and add to the stock. Put everything into saucepan and whisk till it boils. Stand at side of stove for 10 minutes to clear, then strain through fine muslin.

GLAZE

Made from stock boiled down to a strong jelly or 1 tablespoon of gelatine in cup stock with 1 teaspoon Marmite or Bovril.

STUFFING FOR CHICKENS AND TURKEYS

2 cups stale breadcrumbs, 3 tablespoons butter, 1 teaspoon salt, 1 beaten egg, shake pepper, 1 chopped onion, 1 teaspoon mixed herbs, 1 tablespoon chopped parsley, sufficient milk to moisten. 2 tablespoons chopped suet may be used instead of butter. Beat the egg and add to other ingredients with sufficient milk to make fairly dry mixture.
J.H.

CHESTNUT STUFFING FOR TURKEY

Cook chestnuts in boiling water till skins are loosened. Remove the brown skins and put nuts back into boiling water and cook till tender. While still hot rub through a coarse sieve. Add a few breadcrumbs, 2 tablespoons melted butter, season with salt and pepper and moisten with a little cream. *Mrs Slade.*

SAUSAGE STUFFING

Mix 1 lb. of sausages with ½ lb. of breadcrumbs, a little minced onion, parsley and pepper and salt. Minced veal may be used. Bind with an egg. *J.H.*

GREEN MAIZE STUFFING

Take green maize cut from the cob, chop and add an equal amount of breadcrumbs, some finely chopped parsley, melted butter, salt and pepper and mix all together with an egg.

SAGE AND ONION STUFFING

Parboil 3 onions, chop them fine, add ½ cup breadcrumbs, 1 teaspoon sage, salt and pepper and 1 tablespoon melted butter.
M.B.

Wherever you are,
Whoever you are with,
Be yourself.

RECIPE FOR HAPPY FAMILY LIFE
In matters of principle stand like a rock.
In matters of taste swim with the current.

COLD MEATS

SCOTCH POTTED HEAD
Half an ox head and 2 calf's feet, salt pepper and water. Soak ox head and feet for several hours. Scald and clean thoroughly, removing as much of the fat and marrow as possible. Put into large pan and cover with cold water. Simmer for hours or till the meat leaves the bones easily. Take out head and feet, remove meat from them, cut up and return to liquid. Season highly with salt and pepper, boil for a few minutes and pour into moulds and allow to set. *Mother.*

SCOTCH POTTED MEAT OR BRAWN
Shin or hough, knuckle, water to cover, pepper and salt. 1 cow heel or a knuckle and 3 or 4 lbs. hough (shin).
Scald heel and clean very thoroughly. Put into pot with hough, cover with water and boil gently till meat falls away from bones, 6-8 hours. Cut up finely, season well, return to liquid, boil 10 minutes and put into moulds. *Mother.*

BRISKET OF BEEF
6-7 lbs. brisket boned. Put into pan with a little fat and brown on both sides; add 2 cups water salt and pepper and simmer for 6 or 7 hours. Lift into an oblong tin or piedish — it must fit tightly. Allow gravy to boil till reduced to ½ a cup, pour over meat, put grease-proof paper on top, press with weights and leave overnight.
To press flank of beef, have it boned and rolled and proceed as above. *Mother.*

BRAWN — PIG'S HEAD
Procure small pig's head and trotters. Get butcher to cut head in two, and clean, but finish process yourself by soaking in salted water for two hours. Remove nasal bones and eyes and any coarse skin with hair on it. Cover with cold water, add dessertspoonful salt and simmer for 6-7 hours until bones are free.
Lift meat into hot bowl with a little of the liquid. Skin tongue and replace. Cut meat up small, then cover bowl and place over pan of hot water until required.

Into the pan containing liquid and bones add one large chopped onion, 12 black peppercorns, 6 cloves, parsley, thyme, bayleaf or mace and 2 tablespoons vinegar. Boil for one hour, then strain and re-heat. Liquid must be well flavoured and seasoned and there should be about three pints in all.
Wet moulds, bowls or 2 lb. bread tins, half fill with meat, fill with liquid, and mix well. Allow to set. Should make 8-10 lbs. brawn.
Mrs. H. K. Lloyd.

SHEEP'S HEAD BRAWN

Follow directions for pig's head brawn but omit onion, herbs, cloves and vinegar. Season to taste. *Mrs. McNeil.*
Any remaining liquid from pig's head makes excellent split pea soup and liquid from sheep's head excellent Scotch broth.

HOLLANDSCH MEAT LOAF

½lb. minced pork, ½ lb. minced beef, 2 eggs, 1 large slice bread soaked in milk, ½ nutmeg, salt and pepper to taste.
Mix all well together and bake in bread tin for 1 hour in a slow oven. Very good cold. *Mrs. Simpson.*

GALANTINE OF TURKEY

Bone the turkey and lay it open. Put in a layer of sausage meat and a few strips bacon free of rind. Roll up turkey, tie in a cloth and boil or bake in large covered dish for 3 or 4 hours. Pour over a little aspic jelly and press under weights till next day. Glaze and use. *M.*

GALANTINE OF FOWL

Pick and singe the bird, remove the legs at the knee, wings at first joint, the head, neck, windpipe and crop. Cut down the centre of the back and bone the bird. Lay it out flat and season thoroughly, spread thickly with sausage meat and have ready some ham and 2 hard-boiled eggs. Arrange these in strips from head to tail. Roll up tightly, tie in a cloth and cook in stock with the bones, etc., for 3 hours. Tie tightly in the cloth and press lightly till cold. Brush with glaze. Dish and garnish with chopped aspic and salad. *L.M.*

GALANTINE OF VEAL

Proceed as above using 3 lbs. breast of veal instead of chicken. *L.M.*

PRESSED TONGUE (Salted)

Wash the tongue well and put into a pan with cold water. When boiling, put in a few slices of carrot and onion and, if liked, a few cloves and peppercorns. Boil for several hours and, when tender, lift from water and remove skin and roots. Press into a round pudding basin or cake tin. Melt 2 teaspoons of gelatine in 1 cup tongue stock, and pour this over the tongue. Cover with greaseproof paper, put a heavy weight on top and leave overnight. *Mother.*

JELLIED MEAT

Place a little aspic in bottom of mould. Cut any kind of cold meat into pieces and put loosely into the mould, garnished with slices of hard-boiled eggs, beetroot or tomato. Fill the dish with liquid aspic and place in frig. to set. Turn out and garnish with chopped aspic and green salad.

MEAT IN ASPIC

Any cooked meat may be set in aspic. For example: veal, chicken, ham, tongue, also hard-boiled eggs, etc.
For the Aspic. — Make a good stock by boiling very, very slowly 1 lb. of beef in 1 quart of water. Clear the stock and add 2 ozs. gelatine.

CHAUD FROIDS

A chaud froid is a sauce stiffened with aspic or gelatine and used for masking cold meat, etc. Any of the following sauces may be used: Bechamel, tomato, brown sauce or mayonnaise. Cut meat or chicken into neat slices and lay on a wire tray over a large plate. Have the sauce on the point of setting, carefully mask each piece and leave till set. Garnish the dish daintily with chopped aspic and salad. Aspic jelly can be whipped like ordinary jelly and used as garnish.

After all, depend upon it, it is better to be worn out with work in a thronged community, than to perish in inaction in a stagnant solitude. Take this into consideration when you tire of work and bustle.

VEGETABLES

COOKED VEGETABLES. Rules for Cooking

Put the vegetables that grow below the earth's surface (potatoes, carrots, etc.), into cold water, bring quickly to boiling point, then cook slowly. New potatoes — an exception to this rule — should be put into boiling water. The modern way is to cook all vegetables in boiling, salted water — the less water the better — and in the least possible time.

Put vegetables that grow above ground (cabbage, cauliflower, etc.), into boiling water to which salt has already been added. Use as little water as possible. Steamed vegetables are best. Before cooking cabbage, cauliflower, etc., place them in a bowl of cold water to draw out the insects. There should be no salt in this water, as this may kill the insects inside the vegetable.

Never use soda in cooking vegetables. It certainly preserves colour, but it destroys the mineral salts. A pinch of sugar in the water will help to keep the colour.

With the exception of turnips, which must be peeled, root vegetables should be washed, scrubbed or scraped.

NEW POTATOES

Cook 15 to 20 minutes. Drain and serve with oiled butter or dripping. Sprinkle with chopped mint or parsley.

OLD POTATOES

Cook in cold, salted water 20 to 25 minutes, or bake them, in their jackets, in a slow oven. For a change baked potatoes may be treated thus: Scoop out the centre, mix with grated cheese, herbs, butter, meat or fish. Pack into the jackets, and re-heat. To roast: Boil for 10 minutes, then place in roasting tin with nearly cooked joint.

TO USE COLD, COOKED POTATOES

Mash and mix with fish, chicken, or meat. Fashion into balls or cakes, and fry.
Slice up and fry in hot dripping.
Mash and blend with cold, cooked cabbage and meat, and fry, to make "Bubble and Squeak."

POTATO BALLS

Mash 4 large potatoes with 2 spoons butter, pepper and salt, a little parsley, and 1 beaten egg. Beat till creamy. Roll in flour. Dip in egg, and cover with breadcrumbs. Fry in hot fat.

POTATO PUFFS

Cook as for potato chips by drying, cutting into lengths, and frying in hot fat. When potatoes are nearly ready, drop the chips into a deep pot of very hot fat. When puffed, serve at once with fried meat, fish or omelette. *J.H.*

POTATOES AND CHEESE

2 cups mashed potatoes, 3 ozs. grated cheese, salt and pepper, 1 gill milk.

Mash potatoes, add salt, pepper, milk and cheese. Heat over gentle fire, beat with wooden spoon.

Grease piedish and pile in the mixture, sprinkle with cheese and put into oven until brown. *Mrs. Tibbits.*

STUFFED POTATOES

Bake potatoes in skins, cut length-ways, and scoop out, mash well, add a little butter and salt. Put a little mixture back into each skin, then place a sausage on each. Beat up 1 egg and add to the rest of the potatoes and pile on the top of sausages and bake for 15 minutes. *Mrs. Tibbits.*

SWEET POTATOES

Peel and boil in a little salted water for 20 minutes.

They are preferred by many either boiled or baked in their skins.

Bake 6 medium-sized sweet potatoes. Cut in halves, and scoop out insides. Mash, add 3 tablespoons butter and a little milk to moisten. Season with pepper and salt. Fold in beaten white of 1 egg. Refill the skins, brush tops with melted butter, and bake in moderate oven.

Sweet potatoes should be peeled, but not cut up, and boiled till tender. Drain off water and add 2 or 3 tablespoons golden syrup in place of sugar — also a lump of butter and a stick of cinnamon. Let the potatoes simmer gently until they have become nicely browned. Turn them over carefully so that they remain whole.

Parsnips (cut into strips) may be cooked in same way. The syrup gives a nicer flavour than sugar. *Mrs. J. F. Dick.*

EIGHTEENTH CENTURY POTATOES

Wash required number of potatoes, leaving the skins untouched. Put into saucepan with only enough water to keep them from burning. Add salt. Keep closely covered when cooking and when skins begin to crack drain off the water and let the potatoes stand covered for a few minutes, then peel them and place on gridiron. Brown on both sides, dab each potato with butter and send hot to table. If preferred crisp in oven instead of grilling.

CAULIFLOWER

Trim off outer leaves, cut off stump and plunge into cold water head downwards and leave for a few hours. May be cooked in stock or milk and a sauce made with the liquid. Steam and serve with tomato sauce or boil the cauliflower in the usual way, drain it and dish it with the flower standing upright. Pour a white sauce over the top and serve or cover with grated cheese and breadcrumbs, salt and pepper, put a few pieces of butter on top and bake for about 15 minutes.

ONIONS

Cook in cold water. They may be fried, stewed, baked, boiled, braised and when stuffed they are delicious. When boiled serve with white sauce and always parboil baked onions.

LEEKS

Must be thoroughly washed and cooked in boiling salted water. Serve with sauce or melted butter.

PEAS

Cook in boiling salted water with a sprig of mint and a pinch of sugar. No soda. Boil with lid off. To re-heat peas, put in a deep dish, pour boiling water over and stand 10 minutes, or place in covered dish with a little butter and heat over boiling water. Add left-over peas to soups, salads and stews.

PARSNIPS

Scrub and scrape, but if old peel. Boil in stock if possible 1 to 2 hours or parboil, cut in quarters, egg and breadcrumb, and fry. Another way is to mash the parsnips, add 2 tablespoons melted butter, 2 tablespoons milk, pepper and salt. Add a little beaten egg, form into balls, flour, egg and breadcrumb them, and fry in boiling fat.

CABBAGE
RED CABBAGE AS A HOT VEGETABLE

Cabbage thinly sliced, 2 onions, 2 cooking apples, few cloves, 2 teaspoons sugar, juice of 1 lemon or a little vinegar, 1 tablespoon rice and a lump of butter.

Put all into a saucepan with a little water and simmer for two hours. Mix well. *Mrs. Simpson.*

When cooking cabbage put a handful of breadcrumbs tied in a muslin cloth into the pan. The bread absorbs the bitter juice and makes the vegetable more digestible. *M.H.*

CABBAGE AU GRATIN

Quarter a white cabbage and cook rapidly in slightly salted water. Drain and put into a buttered oven dish. Pour over it a white sauce. Mix a tablespoonful of fine breadcrumbs with a tablespoonful of grated cheese. Spread over the top, dot with little lumps of butter, and bake until lightly browned. *Miss Hendrie, Johannesburg.*

WITH ONIONS

Boil the cabbage with two onions for half-an-hour. Drain. Melt 2 tablespoonfuls of butter in a frying pan, put in the cabbage. Pepper and salt. Fry for 10 minutes. *Miss Hendrie, Johannesburg.*

ANOTHER WAY WITH CABBAGE

Quarter the cabbage, and remove the core. Tie together, and boil for 20 minutes. Place 2 slices of bacon in a saucepan, put in the cabbage, add 1 finely sliced onion and 1 sliced green pepper, a teaspoonful chopped parsley, and a few bits of thyme or mint. Cover with thin meat stock, and simmer slowly for 1 hour. This is nice with corned beef. *Miss Hendrie, Johannesburg.*

ILLINOIS HOT SLAW

Shred the cabbage as for salad. Heat 2 spoonfuls butter in a frying pan. Put in the cabbage, add 2 tablespoons vinegar, salt and pepper. Cover with a close lid, and steam till nearly tender, then remove the lid, and fry. *Miss Hendrie, Johannesburg.*

CELERI A LA BOURGEOISIE

Blanch the celery for half an hour in boiling water, dip into cold water and press.
Have ready boiling a sauce of melted butter, flour and good brown stock. Cook celery in this for about an hour. Drain, reduce the sauce, pour over celery and serve very hot with grated cheese.
Mrs. W. Hamilton.

BEANS

BROAD BEANS

After boiling serve with rolls of stuffed bacon, and bacon fat poured over.

BEANS, FRENCH, KIDNEY AND SCARLET RUNNER

String, top, and tail, slice into strips. Boil in salted water, drain, and serve with butter, or serve with chopped, cooked onion and white sauce. Mix together and add 1 large spoonful finely chopped parsley.

HARICOT BEANS

Soak overnight in cold water. Put into saucepan with clean, cold water, boil 3 or 4 hours. Strain, season, and add a small piece of butter. Sprinkle with chopped parsley or mint.

BEETROOT AS A HOT VEGETABLE

Some cooked and sliced beetroot. Cook a large onion in a little water, add the sliced beet and bring to the boil. Mix a tablespoon of cornflour with a little vinegar and add to the beet with a good-sized lump of butter. Simmer for a little while and serve hot. An excellent blood-making vegetable. *Mrs. Simpson.*

CARROTS

When young, scrub and boil or steam in salted water.
When old, scrape and split. Put into cold water.
Serve with butter or white sauce, or mash as finely as possible.

SPINACH

Wash in several waters, and put into saucepan with salt but no additional water. Shake often. When done, squeeze quite dry, and beat well with a piece of butter.

TURNIPS

Young turnips are cooked whole in cold, salted water for 1 to 2 hours. Serve with white sauce, or mash with butter and sprinkle with parsley.
Swedes may be cut into slices and cooked in the same way.
Boil turnips with an equal quantity of carrots and onions. Cover with white sauce and serve with boiled beef.

MARROWS

Boil in very little water. Drain thoroughly, pour over melted butter or white sauce. Best steamed or sauted in a little butter or split lengthwise, filled with peas, carrots and chopped onion and baked in covered dish.

STUFFED MARROW

Peel the marrow, and halve lengthwise. Remove the seeds. Stuff with 2 chopped, boiled onions, 1 teaspoon sage, 2 slices soaked bread, 1 oz. butter, 1 egg, a little chopped ham, if liked. Salt and pepper. Put the halves together and bake half an hour, basting with butter.

Use a good-sized marrow. Cut in half lengthwise, take out pips and then make a mixture of 1 lb. steak (minced), 2 tomatoes peeled, and 2 onions cut fine. Mix together, add pepper and salt and fill both halves of marrow. Place together and tie a piece of clean string round each end to hold together. Place in baking tin. Heat oven to 450°, then switch off and put marrow in and cook for 2 hours.

To make a gravy, take marrow out of pan when cooked, add dessertspoonful of flour to liquid in pan, mix to smooth paste and add a little water with 1½ teaspoonfuls Queen's Gravy and salt and cook on top of stove until it thickens. *Mrs. J. P. Runnals.*

MUSHROOMS

Wash, peel and fry in hot butter, or put prepared mushrooms on a pyrex plate, pour over melted butter, place under grill, cook on both sides. Serve on hot toast.

TOMATOES

Cut large tomatoes into thick slices. Season with pepper and salt, dredge with flour, and fry, or

Cut tomatoes, and lay in flat pyrex dish. Cover with breadcrumbs. Pepper and salt. Dot with butter, and bake.

To peel tomatoes, dip into hot water.

TOMATO PIE

6 tomatoes, 1 teacup rice, 1 teaspoon chopped onion, 1 oz. butter, 1 cup breadcrumbs, seasoning to taste.

Boil rice well. Butter a piedish and arrange a layer of rice and a layer of sliced tomatoes, add seasoning and chopped onion. Cover the top with breadcrumbs, placing the butter in pieces on top. Bake until the crumbs are brown. *Mrs. W. Hamilton.*

PUMPKIN

Cut into slices, place in flat stewpan, sprinkle with salt and a little sugar. Add 2 spoons of butter and 2 of water. Stew very gently till tender. Brown on a quick plate before serving.

Slice pumpkin and put into roasting tin with joint ¾ of an hour before serving.

BAKED PUMPKIN

Cut into 1 inch slices. Dust with salt and sugar. Bake, basting with butter.

Pumpkin baked and sprinkled with cheese is very good.

BEETROOT

Boil, without peeling, in salt water with a little sugar. When tender remove from fire, peel, cut into thick slices. Put into Pyrex dish and dot butter all over. Cover dish and place in oven to re-heat.
Mrs. Carey.

STUFFED VEGETABLE MARROW

Take young marrows, the round ones are best. Pare, cut a slice off the top and take out the pips with a spoon. Take some cooked potatoes, cut small, some rice or breadcrumbs, a spoonful of minced onion, parsley, pepper and salt, and a slice of bacon or ham. Mix together with 1 beaten egg. Fill marrows with mixture and bake in a moderate oven until marrows are soft. Serve with a nicely flavoured sauce. Marrows stuffed with mincemeat make a very tasty dish.

SCALLOPED MARROW

Boil the marrow in the usual way and drain well. Cut up in pieces 2 inches in length and arrange in piedish. Coat well with white sauce and season carefully.
Sprinkle with breadcrumbs and cheese, put a little butter on and bake till nice and brown in rather a sharp oven.

FRIED BRINJALS

Pare and cut in thick slices, sprinkle with salt and pepper. Dip in butter, egg and breadcrumbs and fry in deep fat.

BEETROOT IN SAUCE

3 medium-sized beetroots, ½ teaspoon maizeko, ½ cup sugar, ½ cup vinegar, 2 tablespoons butter.
Boil beetroot until it is soft. Peel and cut in squares. Mix sugar and maizeko, add vinegar and boil mixture for 5 minutes.
Add beetroots and leave on cool part of stove for ½ hour. Add butter just before serving.

CREAMED TURNIPS

6 young turnips, 2 tablespoons cream, ½ teaspoon salt, 1/8 teaspoon pepper.
Peel turnips, then grate on the coarse side of a grater. Put into saucepan with a very little water, salt and pepper, and boil quickly for about 10 minutes, or until tender. Add cream just before serving. If liked, sprinkle a little finely chopped parsley on top.

FRIED ASPARAGUS SERVED WITH CHICKEN

Drain canned asparagus, roll in beaten egg and fine breadcrumbs and fry quickly in deep fat. Temperature of fat 400° F. Cauliflower flowerets parboiled in salted water can be cooked in a similar way.

SPINACH SOUFFLE

2 cups cooked, minced spinach, 2 eggs, 1 tablespoon onion juice, salt, 2 teaspoons lemon juice or vinegar, 2 tablespoons butter, 1 cup milk, 1 tablespoon flour.
Make a white sauce with butter, milk and flour. Add yolks of eggs, spinach and other ingredients. Lastly add stiffly beaten egg whites, bake in timbale cups in quick oven and serve with tomato sauce if liked.

BOILED GREEN MEALIES

Remove husks and silky threads. Cook 20 to 40 minutes in boiling salted water. Place on hot plate and serve with butter and salt.

JERUSALEM ARTICHOKES WITH BUTTER AND LEMON JUICE

1 lb. artichokes, 2 tablespoons lemon juice, 4 tablespoons butter, 2 tablespoons finely chopped parsley, a few grains cayenne. Scrub artichokes, pare and put at once into cold water ready to use. Cook until tender, 25 to 35 minutes, in boiling water, salt and a little vinegar. Cut into quarters, add remaining ingredients. Cook 3 minutes and serve.

SQUASH AND CARROT CASSEROLE

3-4 squashes, carrots, ¼ cup water, 1 dessertspoon butter, salt.
Cut squashes in halves. Place in casserole with carrots scraped and cut into quarters. Add water and salt. Cover dish and cook on lower shelf in oven. When cooked remove carrots, mash with butter, remove seeds from squashes and fill with mashed carrots.

An hour lost in the morning has to be run after all day.

SALADS AND SALAD DRESSINGS

To make a perfect salad four persons are needed. A miser for the vinegar, a spendthrift for the oil, a wise man for the salt and a madcap to mix the ingredients.

THE CACKLER
The hen so soon as she an egg doth lay,
Spreads the fame of her doing as she may,
About the yard she cackling now doth go,
To tell what 't was she at her nest did do.
Just this it is with some professing men;
If they do aught that good is, like our hen,
They can't but cackle on't, where'er they go;
What their right hand doth do their left must know.

Anon.

SALADS

EGG SALAD
4 hard-boiled eggs, 4 tomatoes, 1 lettuce, 1 small onion, 1 grated carrot, a little chopped beetroot, parsley.
Shred the lettuce and mix with chopped onion and put into salad bowl. Arrange slices of tomato round sides of bowl. On top of lettuce and just under tomato rings arrange a circle of grated carrots, then a circle of chopped whites of eggs, a small ring of chopped beetroot. Pile the grated yolks of eggs in centre and garnish with parsley. Serve with mayonnaise. *Mother.*

STUFFED EGGS
Boil 6 eggs, put into cold water for a few minutes. Shell and cut eggs crosswise, slicing off a piece from each end so that the eggs will stand firmly.
Remove the yolks and mix with either ham, chicken, sardines or salmon, season with salt and pepper and mix with a little mayonnaise. Fill egg whites and arrange on a bed of lettuce, dust with cayenne and sprinkle with parsley.

EGGS IN ASPIC
Anchovette, 6 hard-boiled eggs, parsley, salt, mayonnaise. After boiling cut eggs in halves, remove yolks and mix with chopped parsley, melted butter and 1 teaspoon anchovette. Fill egg whites with mixture and join Pour some aspic jelly into a mould and just before

it sets arrange the eggs in the mould and pour jelly around till mould is filled. Put into refrigerator and, when chilled, turn out on to crisp lettuce leaves and serve with mayonnaise.

LEMON ASPIC

1 tablespoon gelatine, ¼ cup cold water, 1¾ cups boiling water, 2 tablespoons lemon juice, 4 tablespoons vinegar and ¼ teaspoon salt.

Soak gelatine in cold water for 5 minutes and dissolve in boiling water. Add lemon juice, vinegar and salt and chill. Used as a basic jelly for vegetable salads.

AVOCADO PEAR AND BANANA SALAD

2 avocado pears, 6 bananas, 1 egg, salt and pepper.

Peel pears and cut across in slices. Cut bananas lengthwise, put a ring of pear over each. Lay daintily on bed of shredded lettuce, sprinkle grated egg lightly over and serve at once with light dressing.

BEETROOT AND PEA SALAD

Peel cooked beets and hollow out centre. Stand in vinegar till ready. Fill with cooked peas and diced, cooked carrot. Top with mayonnaise and parsley. Serve on lettuce leaves surrounded by sliced tomatoes.

TOMATO, CUCUMBER AND ONION SALAD

Place alternate slices of tomato, onion and cucumber on a bed of lettuce. Chill and serve with light salad dressing.

ORANGE AND DATE SALAD

Peel carefully 2 oranges. Slice and cut out centre. Place orange slices on lettuce leaves, place a prune, stuffed with walnut, in centre of each. Serve with duck. Cook, drain and stone prune.

CORN SALAD

Sweet corn, tomatoes, onion, mayonnaise, pepper and salt.

Choose firm tomatoes and scoop out half of the pulp. Mix sweetcorn with finely chopped onion, pepper and salt. Fill tomato cases, top with mayonnaise and parsley and serve on shredded lettuce or cress.

The pulp can be cooked with chopped onion, salt and pepper and a little sugar, set with a little gelatine, and chilled. Turn out on lettuce, top with cooked green peas and serve with mayonnaise.

CHILLED TOMATO SALAD

Put 4 large tomatoes in the oven to warm through, then pass through a sieve. Add equal quantity of water. Cook puree with 3 tablespoons grated onion, 1 clove garlic, salt and pepper. Strain and, to each breakfast cup of liquid add 1 dessertspoon of gelatine previously soaked in a little cold water. When cold, set in refrigerator. Cut into neat slices or cubes and serve on crisp lettuce leaves. *E.R.*

SALMON MAYONNAISE

Mayonnaise, 1 small tin salmon freed from bone and skin, 1 lettuce, 2 hard-boiled eggs, ½ cup cooked green peas, lemon.
Shred the lettuce and place in salad bowl. Pile salmon in centre of bowl, pour mayonnaise round, sprinkle peas over and decorate with sliced eggs and small pieces lemon.

Any cold dish can be done this way and parsley can always be used instead of peas. Top salmon and fish with parsley.

GOLDEN SALAD

Add 1 large cupful grated carrot to lemon aspic, which has thickened slightly. Turn into a mould and chill. Serve surrounded by shredded lettuce and sliced oranges. Top with mayonnaise.

From America.

CAULIFLOWER SALAD

1 cauliflower, lettuce, few capers, hard-boiled egg, cheese and mayonnaise.
Boil cauliflower in the usual way. Pick the best of the flower and, when cold, place on a bed of lettuce leaves. Pour mayonnaise over, garnish with grated cheese and capers and surround with slices of hard-boiled eggs.

STUFFED TOMATO SALAD

Skin medium-sized, firm tomatoes. Cut off top and scoop out centre. Mix tomato pulp with chopped chicken (ham, tongue, fish cheese) and parsley. Fill cases, top with mayonnaise and serve on bed of shredded lettuce. Chill.

ASPARAGUS SALAD

1 tin asparagus tips, lettuce, grated cheese, salt and cayenne pepper.
Drain the asparagus. Arrange daintly on lettuce leaves. Pour mayonnaise over lightly and on top sprinkle grated cheese, salt and cayenne.

POTATO SALAD

Slice 6 or 7 cold, boiled potatoes. Sprinkle with chopped celery or leek and cover with a good dressing.

BEETROOT AND ONIONS

Boil beetroot till tender, slice, add to it I sliced onion and cover with vinegar.

PINEAPPLE, CARROT AND PEA SALAD

Cook 1 pineapple, 2 or 3 carrots and as many peas as required. Cool and cut pineapple and carrots into cubes, mix with peas, pepper and salt and cover with mayonnaise.

HARICOT BEAN AND CARROT SALAD

Soak and boil the beans, and an hour before they are ready put in the carrots. Cool, dice the carrots, mix and serve with mayonnaise and parsley. Good with corned beef.

CHICKEN SALAD

Cut meat from cold chicken in strips. Mix with lettuce and a very little chopped celery. Cover with mayonnaise and put slices of hard-boiled egg and tomato on top. Any cold meat can be done this way, using chopped leek instead of celery.

PINEAPPLE SALAD

Cover a flat dish with shredded lettuce. Cut a pineapple into thin slices, core it and arrange on lettuce with slice of banana in centre of each ring. Top with halved cherries, sprinkle with grated nuts and serve with mayonnaise.

TOMATO AND BEAN SALAD

Eggs, 1 tin baked beans, ham, tomatoes, lettuce, parsley. Scoop out insides of tomatoes. Mix a little of the pulp with the baked beans, season to taste and refill tomato cases. Top with chopped ham and parsley, stand on bed of shredded lettuce, garnish with hard-boiled eggs. Chill and serve.

CHICKEN AND CELERY SALAD

Slice the breast of chicken. Cut the white part of celery into 1 inch lengths. Put on lettuce leaves, sprinkle with salt and cover with a thick mayonnaise dressing. Brown a few walnuts in oven, chop and sprinkle over salad.

MACEDOINE SALAD

Almost any left-over vegetables can be used.
Take 1 cup diced carrots, 1 cup diced turnips, 1 cup peas, a little cooked cauliflower.
Cut cauliflower into small pieces, mix with other vegetables. Place on lettuce leaves in individual dishes, cover with salad dressing and sprinkle with parsley

CABBAGE SALAD

Remove outside leaves of firm young cabbage. Halve and cut in very thin slices with sharp knife. Stand in cold water, drain well, mix with boiled salad dressing and chill.

CELERY SALAD

Cut into dice equal quantities of cooked celery, apples and potatoes. Pour a mayonnaise sauce over and garnish with lettuce and endives. *Mrs. W. Hamilton.*

MACEDOINE SALAD IN ASPIC

Take 1 cup each cooked carrots, turnips and peas. Have ready some lemon aspic and, just before it sets put the vegetables in in layers, mould and chill. Turn out on to crisp lettuce garnished with slices of tomato and top shape with grated carrot and parsley. Serve with mayonnaise. *J.H.*

SALAD DRESSING

MAYONNAISE

1 teaspoon mustard (level), 1 teaspoon sugar (level), 1 teaspoon salt (level), few grains cayenne pepper, 3 egg yolks 2 tablespoons vinegar, 2 tablespoons lemon juice, 1½ cups Epic oil.
Mix the dry ingredients. Stir the egg yolks in. When blended add a little of the acid. Add 3 teaspoons of the oil, dropping them in while beating vigorously. When the mixture thickens, slowly add a little acid again. Continue adding the oil and the acid alternately, beating all the time with an egg-beater. On a hot day stand the mixing bowl in a pan of cold water, to prevent the mixture curdling. Chilling the oil before beginning is a wise proceeding. When all the oil has been used, beat the mixture through thoroughly.
The more slowly the dressing is made, and the more it is beaten, the thicker the product will be. A thick dressing is very desirable. The above makes a large quantity which will keep indefinitely if stored in a cold place. Keep it covered. If a smaller amount is desired, halve the recipe. *Mrs. Beyers (M. J. Davidtsz.)*

MAYONNAISE

1 tablespoon butter, 1 teaspoon salt, ½ teaspoon pepper, ¼ teaspoon mustard, 1 egg, 4 tablespoons vinegar.
Put all the ingredients into basin. Mix well and place on side of stove to thicken. *Mr. S. Watson.*

MAYONNAISE

3 eggs, ½ cup vinegar, 1½ cups milk, ¼ cup sugar, 1 teaspoon mustard, 1 teaspoon salt, 1 tablespoon butter.
Beat eggs, add vinegar and milk. Mix sugar, mustard and salt and add to other mixture and butter. Cook in double cooker till it thickens, stirring constantly. *Mrs. Webb.*

QUICK MAYONNAISE

1 very hard-boiled egg. Crumb yolk of egg, mix with tablespoon of vinegar and sugar to taste; ½ teaspoon dry mustard. Mix ½ pint cream, slightly beaten, pinch salt.
Pour over salad, decorate with white of egg. *Mrs. S. Watson.*

UNCOOKED MAYONNAISE

¼ cup vinegar or lemon juice, ¼ cup Epic oil, 2 tablespoons condensed milk, 1 egg yolk, 1 teaspoon dry mustard, salt and pepper to taste. Put all ingredients into a jam jar in the order given. Shake for two minutes. *H. Michell.*

BOILED SALAD MAYONNAISE

1½ tablespoons flour, 1½ tablespoons butter, ¼ tablespoon salt, 1 teaspoon mustard, few grains cayenne, 2 egg yolks, ¾ cup milk, ¼ cup vinegar.
Mix the dry ingredients in a little saucepan. Stir in the butter and the egg yolks. When blended add the milk and lastly add the vinegar gradually, stirring very well so as not to curdle the mixture. Put on the stove and cook, stirring constantly till the mixture is thickened. Allow to come to the boil. Chill before using.
This dressing can be made and kept on hand as it does not spoil. Store in a cool place. *Mrs. Beyers (M. J. Davidtsz.)*

AMERICAN SALAD MAYONNAISE

1 teaspoon mustard, 1 teaspoon salt, 3 teaspoons flour, 6 teaspoons sugar, two-thirds cup vinegar, ¾ cup water.
Mix dry ingredients with egg, gradually add vinegar. Stir on fire to boil the mixture till thickened. When cool add cream or milk before serving. *M. Grove.*

A SPECIAL MAYONNAISE WITHOUT OIL

1 tablespoon flour, 1 teaspoon salt, 1 well beaten egg, ¼ pint milk, 2 tablespoons sugar, 1 teaspoon mustard, ¼ pint vinegar, ¼ pint cream, 3 ozs. butter.

Put flour, sugar, salt and mustard in a 2 lb. jar and mix to a smooth paste with beaten egg. Add milk and cream gradually. Stir in vinegar, add butter and stand jar in a pan of boiling water. Stir till thick.

For dressing add ¼ pint vinegar to above.

Mrs. E. W. Nicolson, Brooklyn.

HUMOROUS RECIPE

One of the Lecturers before the Cookery School of Baltimore recently gave this recipe: —

A good many husbands are spoiled by mismanagement. Some women go about as if their husbands were bladders, and blow them up. Others keep them constantly in hot water or let them freeze by their carelessness or indifference. Some keep them in pickle all their lives.

It cannot be supposed that any husband managed in this way will be tender and good, but they are really delicious if properly treated.

In selecting your husband you should not be guided by the silvery appearance as in buying mackerel, nor by the golden tint as if you wanted salmon. Be sure to select him yourself, as tastes differ. Do not go to market for him, as the best are always brought to your door. It is far better to have none unless you will patiently learn how to cook him. A preserving kettle of the finest porcelain is best, but if you have nothing but an earthenware or pipkin it will do with care. See that the linen in which you wrap him is nicely washed and mended, with the required number of buttons and strings tightly sewed on. Tie him in the kettle by a strong silk cord called comfort, as the one called duty is apt to be weak. They are apt to fly out of the kettle and be burned and crusty on the edges, since, like crabs and lobsters, you have to cook them while alive. Make a clear, steady fire of love, neatness and cheerfulness. Let him be as near this as seems to agree with him. If he splutters and frizzles do not be anxious, as some husbands do this until they are quite done. Add a little sugar in the form of what confectioners call kisses, but no vinegar or pepper on any account. A little spice improves them, but must be used with judgment. Do not stick any sharp instruments into him to see if he is becoming tender. Stir him gently, watching the while he does not lie too flat and close to the kettle, and so become useless. You cannot fail to know when he is done. If thus treated you will find him very digestible, agreeing nicely with you and the children, and he will keep as long as you want, unless you become carelass and set him in too cool a place.

A sense of humour is the oil of life's engine.

A MOTHER'S PRAYER

I must go softly, stay my pace,
Caring for things called commonplace,
Through shade or shine, this lot is mine,
Calm be my mien, imbued with grace.
I must go softly all my days,
Guard well my mind from frets and frays,
Ready to guide, aid, soothe or chide,
Kept be my feet in wisdom's ways.
I must go softly, heart alert,
Quick to relieve each fear and hurt,
All self to give, thus will I live,
So shall my feet with love be girt.

H.R.

BREAKFAST, LUNCHEON AND SUPPER DISHES

CHEESE SOUFFLE

When eggs are cheap, and meat bills soar like rockets,
Souffles are light and easy on our pockets.

1 oz. flour, 1 oz. butter, 1 large cup milk, 3 eggs, 3-4 ozs. grated cheese, pepper and salt.

Melt butter and stir in flour but do not brown. Gradually add warmed milk. Cool slightly and add egg yolks, cheese and seasoning. Beat egg whites very siffly and fold gently into mixture. Bake in greased pudding dish at 400 degrees for 30-40 minutes. Do not open oven door during baking and serve at once in dish in which it is baked. E.R.

This is a good basic recipe for other souffles.

Variations: 1 cup cooked spinach or cauliflower or sweetcorn, 1 cup chopped chicken, 1 cup savoury mince or minced ham, 1 cup pounded fish.

To save time: When making white sauce make a double quantity, keep half in frig. and use for souffles.

ANOTHER CHEESE SOUFFLE

1 oz. butter, 1 oz. flour, ½ pint milk, ½ cup breadcrumbs, 3 eggs, ¾ cup grated cheese, salt.

Melt butter in saucepan, stir in flour and cook till blended. Add milk gradually and then breadcrumbs. Cool slightly, add 3 beaten yolks of eggs, salt and grated cheese. Whisk whites of eggs very stiffly, fold into mixture, pour into buttered baking dish and bake 35 minutes in moderate oven. A.R.P.

CHICKEN FRITTERS

Cut cold cooked chicken in slices. Make batter of 1 cup flour, 1 beaten egg, 1 tablespoon melted butter, salt, 1 teaspoon baking powder and milk.

Season chicken, cover with batter and fry lightly. *Mrs. Gray.*

SALMON SOUFFLE

1 cup milk, 2 tablespoons flour, 1 tablespoon butter, salt, pepper, lemon juice, salmon, 3 eggs.

Make a white sauce of the milk, flour, butter, salt and pepper. Drain salmon and take out the skin and bones and mix with sauce. Add the beaten yolks of 2 eggs and the stiffly beaten whites of 3 eggs. Pour into a greased dish, sprinkle breadcrumbs on top and bake in a slow oven for 45 minutes.

Variations. — Chopped chicken, white fish, meat or vegetable puree.
Mrs. Robertson.

BRAINS ON TOAST

Brains, chopped cooked ham, salt and pepper and dessertspoon cream.

Soak brains in salt water. Drop into boiling water for 20 minutes. Dish, and remove skin. Chop and mix with other ingredients. Pile on buttered toast, sprinkle with toasted breadcrumbs and serve. *M.G.*

SWEET CORN SUPPER DISH

1 tin sweet corn, cooked bacon or ham, toast.

Have ready as many slices of toast as required. Heat a tin of sweet corn, thicken if necessary. Pile on toast and sprinkle finely chopped ham or bacon on top. Serve hot.

To thicken sweet corn and make it go further add ½ cup milk 1 teaspoon butter and 1 dessertspoon cornflour mixed with a little milk.
Mrs. Harris.

SWEETBREADS

Lay sweetbreads in salt and water for 2 hours. Wash well and put into boiling water and boil gently for 10 minutes, strain and cool, trim and cut into neat rounds. Put into stewpan with 2 ozs. butter and ½ cup of milk, and simmer gently for 2 hours.

Another Way. — Roll the sweetbreads in flour, fry in melted butter, add stock and seasoning and stew gently for 1½ hours. The sweetbreads may also be rolled in breadcrumbs or in batter and fried after being boiled for a short period. *M.C.*

SWEETBREADS (Suitable for Entree)

2 sweetbreads, slices of bacon, little parsley, a few mushrooms, breadcrumbs, pepper and salt to flavour, about 1 tablespoon of butter.

Wash and scald sweetbreads, cut into pieces and lard with the shreds of bacon. Chop mushrooms and herbs as fine as possible. Season with pepper and salt and stir together with butter. Put pieces of sweetbread into either pastry or paper cases, brush over with butter, put a layer of breadcrumbs and seasoning, place on this another piece of sweetbread and seasoning and bake a nice brown.

A. Friend, Johannesburg.

SALMON CROQUETTES

Mix some flaked salmon with mashed potatoes. Add finely chopped slice of onion and parsley and a little beaten egg, pepper and salt. Mix all well together, shape into rounds, and dip in remainder of egg and bread crumbs and fry. *A.L.M.*

SPINACH AND POACHED EGGS

Spinach, eggs, cream, butter, salt and pepper and cheese. Wash spinach thoroughly, put into dry saucepan with salt, cover closely and cook 15 minutes. Press through wire sieve. Melt butter and cream in pan, stir in spinach and make thoroughly hot. Place spinach on very hot dish, top with poached eggs, sprinkle grated cheese over and garnish with fried bread or toast. *R.R.C.*

MACARONI CHEESE

¼ lb. grated cheese, water, 2 cups milk, 3 tablespoons butter, ½ lb. macaroni, salt, pepper and breadcrumbs, 2 tablespoons flour.

Break macaroni into pieces and throw into boiling, salted water. Boil 20 minutes and drain. Put layer of macaroni in bottom of pyrex dish, then a layer of cheese. Repeat till dish is three-quarters filled. Season. Finish with layer of cheese on top. Pour over a white sauce made with butter, flour and milk, sprinkle breadcrumbs on top and bake till brown.

Variations. — (1) After cooking macaroni in boiling water make a custard with 2 cups of milk and 2 eggs, pepper and salt and grated cheese. Pour over macaroni, sprinkle breadcrumbs and grated cheese, on top and bake gently till set.

(2) Boil macaroni and place in alternate layers with grated cheese, pepper and salt. Cover with breadcrumbs and brown.

(3) Pour tomato sauce over boiled macaroni and grated cheese. Sprinkle breadcrumbs on top and bake 10 minutes. *R.R.C.*

SCRAMBLED EGGS

Put 2 tablespoons butter into frying pan. Use as many eggs as required and for every eggs use 1 or 2 tablespoons milk. Salt and pepper to taste. Beat eggs, add milk and seasoning and pour into pan. Stir continually till mixture is of a soft creamy consistency and serve at once. Vary this by adding herbs, chopped ham or bacon, cheese or parsley; or 1 cup cooked peas or cooked spinach. *R.M.T.*

SCRAMBLED EGGS WITH TOMATOES

Fry a small piece of onion with 2 sliced skinned tomatoes in butter. Season, and add 4 beaten eggs and keep stirring till mixture is set. Serve at once with fried bread.

SCOTCH EGGS

1 lb. skinned sausages, breadcrumbs, parsley, seasoning, eggs.

Boil eggs ¼ hour. Take off shells. Put sausage meat, breadcrumbs and seasoning into a bowl with parsley and mix together with a little egg. Coat boiled eggs with this mixture, roll in remainder of beaten egg and breadcrumbs and fry lightly. Halve and serve with tomato sauce or serve cold with lettuce and tomatoes.

FINNAN AND CHEESE SAVOURY

1 Finnan haddock, 2 ozs. grated cheese, tablespoon milk, a pinch of mustard and cayenne, 1 egg.

Scrape fish from bone and mix with everything but the egg. Cook for 10 minutes, add the beaten egg, stir till egg is cooked and serve at once on hot buttered toast.

TOMATO AND CHEESE

Put piece of butter size of walnut into saucepan and add ¼ lb. grated cheese, pepper and salt. Put large-sized tomato into boiling water for 5 minutes, peel and slice. Add this to the cheese and stir well till mixed, put in dash of Yorkshire relish. Pour on to thick buttered toast and serve very hot. *Mrs. Johnson.*

MINCE AND POACHED EGG

Cooked mince (see recipe for Scotch collops), eggs, pepper and salt.

Heat the mince, adding a little water or stock if necessary, and drop in as many eggs as required. Cook gently till set and lift carefully on to slices of buttered toast. Garnish with parsley and serve hot. *J.H.*

LIVER AND BACON SAVOURY

Left-over liver and bacon, 1 oz. butter, toast, pepper, salt and onion.

Mince liver and bacon very finely and add a very little grated onion. Mix and cook in butter for 10 minutes. Season and pile on slices of hot buttered toast. Serve very hot. If liked, top with a poached egg or sprinkle with chopped hardboiled eggs. *J.H.*

WELSH RAREBIT

½lb. cheese, 2 tablespoons milk or cream, salt and pepper, mustard, toast.

Grate or cut cheese finely and put into saucepan with cream, mustard and seasoning. Mix over fire till of a creamy consistency. Pour over toast, brown slightly under grill and serve at once. *M.R.*

DELICIOUS OMELETTE

4 eggs, 1 slice white bread soaked in milk (pulped), 1 spoon finely chopped parsley, dessertspoon chopped onion, salt and pepper.

Beat 4 egg yolks and white separately, add white bread and milk made into pulp, parsley, onion, salt and pepper.

Cook in frying pan until brown on one side, then bake in oven.

M. Grove.

GREEN MEALIE OMELETTE

3 eggs, 1 teaspoon flour, salt and pepper, 2 cups raw, young green mealies cut from the cob and minced.

Beat egg whites stiff, drop in the yolks and beat again. Stir in flour, seasoning and minced mealies. Fry in hot butter, about 1 teaspoonful; cook slowly till underside is nicely browned, then brown the top under a red-hot grill element. Serve quickly. *E.R.*

CHEESE CUSTARDS

Eggs, milk, cheese, salt, pepper, cayenne.

Beat 4 eggs, add 2 cupfuls hot milk with 4 tablespoons grated cheese and seasoning.

Pour into small, buttered moulds, place in a tin of water and bake gently till set — stirring occasionally so that the cheese will not settle. Fry some rounds of bread a golden brown, dish one custard on to each round and brown in oven. Garnish with parsley.

PLAIN OMELETTE

Break eggs into a bowl, beat well and add as many tablespoons of water or milk as there are eggs. Pepper and salt to taste. Have ready a hot frying pan with 1 tablespoon melted butter. Pour in the egg mixture and stand on stove till set, pricking with a fork occasionally. When omelette is brown underneath fold and turn on to hot plate.

PUFFY OMELETTE

For puffy omelette make as above but beat whites of eggs separately. Cut and fold the stiffly beaten whites into the yolk mixture. Turn it into a hot, buttered pan and let it stand en moderately warm cooking plate, then put into oven to brown. Fold and turn on to hot platter.

These omelettes may be varied by using different fillings. Herbs or grated cheese may be mixed with the omelette, or finely chopped ham, chicken, fish or meat may be sprinkled on to the surface of the omelette before it is folded. Fresh or canned peas, mushrooms and tomatoes all make nice fillings. Kidney omelette is very good. Dry and mashed pumpkin can be mixed into an omelette. Fried onions and potato wafers make a delicious filling.

TASTY SUPPER DISH

Take 3 sheep's kidneys, skin, cut up and lightly fry with a rasher of bacon. Remove from pan and chop up finely. Put into saucepan with seasoning and little water. Thicken and allow to cook for a few minutes.
Pile mixture on to hot buttered toast and add a spoonful of mashed prunes on top.
Makes a very attractive dish when surrounded with spinach or mashed potatoes. *M. Dunn, Johannesburg.*

NICE SUPPER SNACK

Have ready a slice of hot, buttered toast, on which place a piece of fried bacon, then 2 portions of fried banana cut lengthwise, a slice of tomato, seasoning and a sprinkling of grated cheese.
Place under grill for a few minutes and serve very hot.
Mrs. J. S. Fotheringham.

ONION AND CHEESE DISH

Put a layer of onions ½ an inch thick in a buttered dish. Sprinkle with pepper and salt. Cover with thinly sliced Cheddar cheese.

Continue putting alternate layers of sliced onions and cheese until dish is full. Put dots of butter on top and bake in a very hot oven.

Mrs. W. Hamilton.

LUNCHEON DISH

Cold, flaked fish, cooked macaroni, white sauce, grated cheese, browned breadcrumbs.

Flake fish and put into pyrex dish, with layers of cooked macaroni. Pour over prepared white sauce, to which a ½ cup of grated cheese has been added. Sprinkle with browned breadcrumbs on top, and put a few dabs of butter on the crumbs. Bake in a moderate oven.

Mrs. J. Jacobson.

OEUFS A LA PARISIENNE

Soak in hot milk as many slices of bread as you have guests. Butter a dish and place these slices at the bottom. Sprinkle with grated cheese and break an egg over each. Put into hot oven for about ½ hour.

Mrs. W. Hamilton.

SAVOURY MEALIE TOAST

2 cups cooked mealies (cut from the cob), 1 cup minced, cold meat, 1 tablespoon minced, cooked bacon, ½ cup white sauce, salt and pepper.

Mix all together and heat. Spread slices of toast first with a little butter, then with tomato sauce. Pile the hot mealie mixture on top.

TOMATO AND EGG

With a sharp knife cut the bottom part of a tomato and scoop out pulp with a teaspoon, sprinkle shell with salt. Break an egg in each and season. Place a piece of bacon on the top, bake in a fairly slow oven for egg to set. Cook pulp with a few drops of vinegar. Serve tomato shells on hot toast and pour pulp over.

Polony or minced meat can be used instead of egg. Mrs. J. Klopper.

CHEESE PUDDING (Supper Dish)

2 cups grated cheese, 2 cups breadcrumbs, 2 cups milk, 1 tablespoon butter, pinch of cayenne and salt, 2 eggs.

Grease dish well. Place layer of breadcrumbs, then layer of cheese. Continue till all is used. Beat up eggs, add milk and place over contents in dish. Put in butter and bake 20 minutes in moderate oven.

QUICK SUPPER DISH

Grate 1 medium-sized onion, chop 3 rashers of bacon up finely and put together and brown. Make ½ a pint of white sauce, mix with browned onion and bacon, and season. Pour into greased piedish and break as many eggs as required on top. Bake until set. Sprinkle with browned breadcrumbs and garnish with parsley.

CURRIED SALMON PIE

Boil 1 small cup of rice, add to contents of 1 tin of salmon. Mix 1 tablespoon curry powder with 2 tablespoons of tomato sauce. Add salt and pepper, mix throughly. Put mixture into a piedish with a few lumps of butter on top and bake in hot oven till brown.

Mrs. W. Hamilton.

SALMON SUPPER DISH

1 tin salmon, 5 slices toast, 3 hard-boiled eggs, 1 pint white sauce.

Butter pyrex dish, put in layer of diced toast and add layer of salmon. Slice up 1 egg. Cover with white sauce. Repeat till all has been used. Bake in oven till golden brown. (Any cold meats may be used in place of salmon).

MACARONI WITH TOMATOES

4 ozs. macaroni, 3 tomatoes, pepper and salt, 2-3 ozs. grated cheese, 1 teaspoon Bovril or Marmite melted in ¼ pint of hot water.

Break macaroni in short lengths and drop in boiling, salted water for 20 minutes or until soft. Drain and lay in greased piedish. Mix in tomatoes (skinned and cut up), cheese, stock, salt and plenty of pepper. Bake in moderate oven until brown. *Mrs. Harrison.*

STUFFED MUSHROOM EGGS

Hard-boiled eggs, butter for frying, mushrooms, white sauce, breadcrumbs.

Cut the tops off the eggs and take yolks out carefully, so as to keep whites whole. Chop yolks. Fry mushrooms in butter and chop. Mix with yolk and season highly, then stuff whites with the mixture. Put into fireproof dish, cut side down, and pour over them some good, fairly thick white sauce. Sprinkle with breadcrumbs, dot with butter and bake in good oven until browned. *Mrs. Harrison.*

BOSTON BAKED BEANS

1½ lbs. beans, ½ lb. bacon or pork, 3 dessertspoonfuls of treacle, 3 pints of water or more.

Boil beans for 4 hours, add bacon an hour before done. Empty into baking dish or casserole and add the treacle. Mix well and bake for an hour or longer or until the beans are brown on top. *Hazel Hawke.*

SALMON LOAF

2 cups salmon (flaked), 1½ cups grated cheese, 1 egg well beaten, 3 tablespoons milk, 1 tablespoon melted butter, salt, pepper, breadcrumbs.

Combine ingredients, using enough breadcrumbs to obtain stiff mixture. Shape in bread pan, bake, oven 375°, until brown. May be eaten hot or cold.

SCOTCH WOODCOCK

1 teaspoon anchovy paste, 2 tablespoons cream or milk, 1 tablespoon butter, yolk of egg, cayenne.

Put all into a saucepan and stir briskly with a spoon till thick. Spread on buttered toast or fried bread. Garnish with anchovy.

BANANAS AND BACON

Take 6 ripe bananas and encase in bacon. Bake in quick oven and serve with chicken or with fried egg for breakfast.

Mrs. W. Hamilton.

MUSHROOM AND SWEETBREAD PATTIES

Make cases of short pastry. Lay sweetbreads in salt water for 2 hours. Wash well and then put into boiling water and boil gently for 15 minutes. When cold trim and cut into dice. Put mushrooms and sweetbreads in a frying pan with a little butter and fry gently until tender. Add a little milk and thicken with yolk of egg or maizena. Fill pastry cases and serve very hot. *Mrs. D. K. Lawrie.*

POACHED EGGS WITH MUSHROOMS

Fry 1 shallot and few mushrooms cut into dice. Poach egg on toast and garnish with above.

CORN PANCAKES

1 small tin sweetcorn, ½ cup flour, 2 eggs, 1 teaspoon baking powder, 1 teaspoon chopped parsley, salt and pepper.

Drain corn into basin. Stir in flour, baking powder, salt and pepper and parsley. Mix well and add beaten eggs. Make some cooking fat smoking hot and into it drop the batter in dessertspoonfuls. Fry till golden brown on both sides. Serve with bacon.

CAULIFLOWER SNIPPETS

This is an excellent recipe for using up cold, cooked cauliflower. Two to three tablespoons grated cheese, ½ tablespoon dry breadcrumbs, salt, pepper, cayenne, 1 beaten egg, 1 or 2 rashers of bacon, 1 small head of cauliflower.

Pick off the flowerets of the cooked cauliflower, dip into the beaten egg, then roll in the grated cheese mixed with breadcrumbs, salt, pepper, cayenne. Have ready 2 or 3 rashers of bacon cut into short lengths. Fry until crisp and place on a hot dish. Cook the cauliflower snippets in the bacon fat to brown all over. Pile on to the bacon and pour the cheese which remains over in the frying pan over the cauliflower.

COLD CHEESE SOUFFLE (For Two or Three)

1 cup milk, 2 eggs, salt, pepper, pinch cayenne, ½ to ¾ cup grated cheese, 1 level dessertspoon gelatine, 1 tablespoon cold water.

Put the milk into a double saucepan and heat. Beat the egg yolks, pour the hot milk on the egg yolks and stir. Return to the saucepan and stir until it thickens. Remove and cool slightly. Add the grated cheese, salt, pepper and cayenne to taste, then stir in the gelatine mixed with the cold water and dissolved over hot water. Fold in the stiffly-beaten egg white. Pour into a rinsed mould and chill. Unmould and serve with tomato and lettuce.

MRS. FRANK'S CHEESE AND FISH PIE

1 lb. Kingklip or Cape salmon, 2 hard-boiled eggs, 1 cup grated cheese, 2 tomatoes, a little lemon rind, salt, pepper, 1 small onion.

Cook the fish in very little water with the thinly-sliced onion. When cooked remove from the stock and flake, putting a layer into a glass ovenproof dish. A little lemon rind and seasoning should be sprinkled over, then some slices of the hard-boiled egg and a layer of grated cheese. Continue until the ingredients are used, then cover with the following sauce: —

Sauce: — 1 dessertspoon flour, 1 dessertspoon butter, ½ cup milk, salt, pepper. Melt the butter, stir in the flour and cook a few minutes. Add the milk slowly and continue stirring while it boils a few minutes.

The sauce should not be too thick, so a little more milk may be added if necessary, season to taste with salt and pepper. Pour over the cheese and fish pie. Cover with dry breadcrumbs, then put slices of tomato over the top, sprinkling the tomato with salt, pepper and a pinch of sugar. Dab with butter and bake in a hot oven of 400° Fahr. for about 30 minutes.

TOMATO AND CHEESE RISSOLES

½ cup grated cheese, 1 cup cold, cooked potato, 1 medium-sized tomato, 2 tablespoons breadcrumbs, salt and pepper.

Mash the potato with the cheese, breadcrumbs and seasoning. Plunge tomato into boiling water and remove skin. Pass remainder through a coarse sieve and add to mixture. Divide into four and shape into flat cakes. Roll in browned breadcrumbs and fry in hot fat till golden brown. Good with fried bacon.

EGG AND BACON PIE

Line a sandwich tin with flaky pastry. Break 3 or 4 eggs into centre of pastry, sprinkle with 3 rashers of chopped bacon, salt and pepper. Cover with a lid of pastry and bake in a hot oven (400-450°) for 30 minutes. If liked, the eggs can be separated by rows of chopped parsley. A good luncheon dish.

OATMEAL RISSOLES

2 tablespoons fine oatmeal, 2 tablespoons grated cheese, 3 tablespoons cold, cooked potato, 1 dessertspoon minced cooked ham or bacon, pepper, salt and a little milk.

Mash the potato and mix it with the bacon. Add the other ingredients, mix thoroughly and add enough milk to bind. Divide and make into rissoles, roll in oatmeal and fry in hot fat.

TASTY LUNCH DISH

4 small potatoes, 1 medium onion, 2 slices bacon, 4 eggs, 1 tablespoon cream or top of milk.

Cut bacon and onion into small pieces and fry with a little fat in a wide frying-pan. Remove and fry potatoes cut into small cubes. When cooked, mix with onion and bacon previously fried. Now fry eggs on top of this mixture and add cream or top of milk. Cover pan and allow eggs to settle. Serve with sliced tomato or tomato sauce.
This serves four persons.

My home is full of little joys —
The joy of work to do,
Of shining pewter, gleaming brass,
The joy of nankeen blue.
The patterned sunlight on the floor,
The wafted scent of flowers.
The hum of bees upon the sill
Through summer's sunny hours.
                              Anon.

VEGETARIAN DISHES
(Mrs. W. K. McLoughlin)

VEGETARIAN PIE
Boil 5 large potatoes and 3 onions. When soft leave onions to simmer. Mash potatoes, add salt, butter and a little milk. Put a layer of potatoes in a dish and 3 hard-boiled eggs, cut up, then more potatoes. Heat in oven.

Sauce. — Add to onions a dessertspoon flour, ¾ cup milk, salt and a piece of butter. Stir till it thickens and serve with pie.
                              D. Johnson.

VEGETARIAN SOUPS
CLEAR VEGETABLE BOUILLON
Take turnips, carrots, parsnips, onions, cabbage, parsley, leek, tomatoes, celery, or any other vegetable you may have. Wash and cut into small pieces. Add sufficient water and a cup of lentils, cook for 2 to 3 hours. Strain, add a little butter and Marmite and seasoning to taste.

VEGETARIAN BROTH
½ cup dried green peas, soaked overnight, 1 small cup pearl barley, 1 small cabbage shredded finely, 2 large carrots, 1 turnip, 1 Spanish onion and 2 leeks all cut into very small pieces.
Add about 3 quarts of water and allow to boil until vegetables are very soft. Add a generous piece of butter, salt and, if the flavour of Marmite is liked, a little may be added.

CREAM OF ONION
Peel, wash and slice 3 Spanish onions; gently stew in a little water for half an hour, then add a quart of milk and allow to cook for another half hour. Thicken with a little soya bean flour. Add salt to taste.

MARROW SOUP

1 small marrow, 1 onion, several sprigs fresh mint, 2 tomatoes, celery salt, ½ pint milk, soya bean flour or pea flour; 1 teaspoon butter.

Scrub and cut up marrow, including peel and seeds, slightly brown the onion in the butter, add the marrow, tomatoes, mint and salt. Bring this to the boil in about 2 pints of water, and let simmer for a further 40-50 minutes. Rub through a coarse sieve. Mix the flour to a paste with the milk and gradually pour on the soup. Pour back into the saucepan and re-heat.

SPINACH CLEAR SOUP

Boil a good handful spinach in about 1½ pints of water. Rub spinach through a fine sieve. Brown a finely chopped onion in butter and add to spinach water. Salt and Marmite are added to taste.

NUT LOAF

2 cups wholewheat breadcrumbs, 1 cup finely ground walnuts, 1 egg (well beaten with a pinch of salt), 2 cups milk, 1 small onion (finely chopped), ½ teaspoon sage (powdered).

Mix ingredients thoroughly. Put into a loaf pan, dot with butter. Bake in a moderate oven 30 minutes.

SPINACH FRITTERS

Spinach, ½ tablespoon butter, 1 egg, breadcrumbs, salt, pepper.

Cook spinach gently with a little salt (do not add water). When tender chop finely. Melt the butter in the saucepan, return spinach to the pan and mix thoroughly. Beat egg well, add spinach and enough breadcrumbs to bind, season with salt and pepper, form into cakes or balls and fry in boiling fat. Drain well and serve hot.

POTATO RISSOLES

3 large cooked potatoes, ¼ lb. mixed nuts, 1 tablespoon butter, pepper and salt, 2 tablespoons milk, 1 tablespoon grated cheese, egg and breadcrumbs.

Roast the nuts slightly and put through the mill. Melt the butter in a small saucepan, sieve the potatoes and add with the prepared nuts, milk and seasoning. Mix thoroughly and turn on to plate to cool. Form into balls, dip in egg and breadcrumbs and fry in boiling fat. Drain well and serve hot.

HARICOT BEANS

¼ lb. haricot beans, 1 small onion, 1 teaspoon butter, parsley (finely chopped), salt and pepper.

Soak haricot beans overnight to soften them. Next day put in saucepan with plenty of cold water and the onion cut in four. Boil from 2 to 2½ hours, or until they feel quite soft. When ready drain in a colander and lift out the pieces of onion. Return to the pan and add the butter, parsley, pepper and salt. Shake the beans over the fire for a minute or two and serve them hot. A squeeze of lemon may be added, or they may be served with parsley sauce poured over them.

CARROTS EN CASSEROLE

6 young carrots, 2 level tablespoons butter, ½ cup cream, 1 egg yolk, little chopped parsley, pepper and salt.

Place carrots, which have been cut into thin slices, in the casserole with the butter, salt and pepper. Just cover with water. Put on the lid of the casserole and simmer for 30 minutes. When the carrots are tender add the yolks of the egg and cream, beaten together, and the chopped parsley, stir carefully over the fire until thick, but do not boil. Serve hot en casserole.

EGGPLANTS (BRINJALS) AND BANANA SAVOURY

Wash and split open brinjals, take out a small quantity of the centre and stuff the centre with mashed bananas mixed with a little butter and paprika. Butter the baking dish and sprinkle lightly with breadcrumbs, place brinjals on this and bake in a moderate oven until tender.

Take some tomatoes and some cauliflower chopped into sprigs and a few finely chopped shallots, add the centres which were taken from the brinjals, mix altogether in a saucepan with ½ cup water. Cook gently until tender. Pour on to brinjals and serve hot.

CURRIED BEANS AND TOMATOES

½ lb. Soya beans, 1 small apple, 1 small onion, 1 dessertspoon curry powder, 1 tablespoon sultanas, 6 tomatoes.

Soak beans overnight and cook in same water for 2 hours. Melt a little butter in a saucepan, grate in the onion and when partly cooked grate in the apple and add the sultanas. Mix the curry powder with a small cup of vegetable stock or water and pour into the pan. Mix well then add the cooked beans. Draw all this into the middle of the pan — put the tomatoes around. When the tomatoes are cooked, turn it onto a fireproof dish, with the beans in the middle and the tomatoes arranged carefully around. Garnish with sprigs of parsley. Serve hot.

LEEKS ON TOAST

Wash and trim leeks, cook in a very little boiling water until soft. Season lightly and arrange on buttered wholewheat toast.

LENTIL "SAUSAGES"

½ lb. red lentils, ¼ lb. grated cheese, 1 tablespoon grated onion, little salt.

Cook lentils until soft. Mix together all ingredients, form into the shape of sausages, dip in beaten egg and breadcrumbs and fry in deep fat. Drain well.

ONION AND TOMATO PIE

2 Spanish onions, 1 lb. tomatoes, 1 tablespoon butter, breadcrumbs.

Peel onions and cover with boiling water for a few moments, drain and wipe dry. Cut in slices and cook in butter until tender. Slice tomatoes, butter a fireproof dish and put a layer of tomato, then a layer of onion and a few breadcrumbs. Continue until dish is full. Sprinkle crumbs on top, adding a few bits of butter. Bake in a moderate oven until brown.

WALNUT PIE

Cooked unpolished rice, ground walnuts, tomatoes, onion, breadcrumbs.

Butter and sprinkle a few breadcrumbs in a piedish. Place a layer of rice, then a layer of walnuts, a layer of tomato and a little grated onion. Repeat the process until the piedish is full. Cover fairly thickly with wholewheat breadcrumbs. Place a few pieces of butter on top and bake until brown in a moderate oven. Serve with tomato sauce.

NUT ROAST

1 cup of ground, mixed nuts, 1 cup cold mashed potatoes, 1 teacup breadcrumbs, 1 onion finely chopped, Marmite and seasoning.

Mix all the ingredients together thoroughly, add the Marmite, mixed with a little water if desired, bind with an egg. Place in a buttered casserole and bake until brown.

Make what you can make — be it symphonies or pullovers, epics or mince-pies — and sweet content will be yours.   Francis Brett Young.

LITTLE THINGS

We sometimes get impatient doing simple little things, like stitching buttons, washing gloves — the trifling tasks life brings — we think we're wasting precious time and grumble terribly — because we think we're fitted for a higher destiny ... But God did not despise the doing of the tiny things — He must have spent a lot of time on making flowers and wings — He made the mountains and the seas, the whirling worlds on high — and yet He deigned to make the ant, the bee, the butterfly — the spider and the snowflake and the smallest bird that sings — so surely we with grace and care can do — the little things.
Patience Strong.

ALL KINDS OF PASTRY

PUFF PASTRY

Use a knife for mixing all pastry

½ lb. flour, ½ lb. butter, 1 teaspoon lemon juice, salt. Very cold water (as little as possible).

Squeeze and flatten the butter in a floured cloth to remove any moisture. Put flour into bowl with salt, make a hole in the centre, add lemon juice and sufficient water to make a firm dough. Work till smooth then roll out. Place the butter, which must be the same thickness as pastry, on one half of paste, fold the other over and press edges together. Let it stand in refrigerator for 10 minutes. Now roll it out into a long piece — always rolling away from you — fold in three, turn the edges towards you, roll again, fold in three and set aside for 15 minutes. Repeat till pastry has been rolled seven times. Hot oven.   *J.H.*

FLAKY PASTRY

9 oz. flour, 6 oz. butter, pinch salt, lemon, cold water.

Add salt to flour and rub quarter of the butter in. Mix to a stiff paste with cold water. Roll out in a long strip on floured board and dab small pieces of the butter on to pastry. Fold in three, turn open edges towards you, press the edges and roll out again. Repeat till butter is finished. Hot oven.   *J.H.*

PLAIN SHORT CRUST

½ lb. flour, 4 oz. butter, lemon juice, salt, water.

Rub butter into dry ingredients, add the water and work into smooth paste. Roll out and use at once. If liked, the yolk of an egg can be added to the water in making this pastry. Medium oven.   *J.H.*

RICH SHORT PASTRY FOR TARTS, FLANS, ETC.

½ lb. flour, 6 oz. butter, 1 oz. castor sugar, yolk of 1 egg, water, salt.

Mix dry ingredients, rub in butter, add egg and as little water as possible to make a stiff paste. Roll out and use. Medium oven.

SUET CRUST, FOR BOILED PUDDINGS, ETC.

½ lb. flour, ¼ lb. suet, teaspoon salt, ½ teaspoon baking powder, water.

Chop suet very fine with a little of the flour. Add flour, salt, baking powder and water and make into fairly stiff dough.

ANOTHER SUET CRUST

8 oz. flour, 3 oz. breadcrumbs, 6 oz. suet, 1 teaspoon baking powder, salt, ½ pint water. Same method as above.

BOILED PASTE FOR PIES

4 oz. good beef dripping, ½ pint water, 1 lb. flour, ½ teaspoon salt.

Boil water and melt dripping in it. Sieve the flour and salt into bowl, make a well in centre and pour in hot liquid. Mix with knife, but when cool use the hands and form quickly into one lump. Turn out on floured board, knead lightly. Keep pastry warm while working. Use for meat pies, etc. *J.H.*

A QUICKLY MADE PASTRY

½ lb. flour, 6 oz. butter, squeeze of lemon juice, water, salt.

Sieve flour and salt, cut butter in thin slices, cut it roughly into the flour with a knife. Add lemon juice and water and make into firm paste. Roll out four times very lightly and use. *J.H.*

GERMAN PASTRY

1 lb. flour, ½ lb. butter, ¼ lb. sugar, 2 eggs, pinch salt.

Cream butter and sugar, add eggs, sift in flour and salt and mix well together. Roll out and use for flans and tarts. *Mrs. Watson.*

SHORT PASTRY

½ lb. flour, 2 oz. cornflour, ½ cup castor sugar, ¼ lb. butter, 1 egg, 1 tablespoon lemon juice, ¼ teaspoon soda, ½ teaspoon salt.

Mix flour, cornflour, salt and soda. Put on board, make a well in the centre, put in butter and sugar, break egg on top, then mix into a soft dough, adding lemon juice and a little milk if necessary. Knead well.
Mrs. Slade.

CHOUX PASTE

2 oz. butter, 4 oz. flour, 3 eggs, ½ pint water, pinch salt and vanilla essence.

Put butter and water into saucepan, bring to boil and gradually sift in flour. Beat till smooth and boil for 3 or 4 minutes, cool and add beaten eggs and vanilla. Spoon mixture on to baking sheet in rounds or oblong pieces. Bake half an hour.

A FAVOURITE MINCEMEAT PIE
(Meaning Steak Minced)

Follow the recipe for savoury mince, using only half cup water. Have the mince very cold. Use either the plain short crust recipe or the quickly made pastry. Grease an ordinary sandwich tin. Line with pastry, pour in mince. Dot with butter. Put pastry cover on top. Prick well and brush over with egg. Bake ½ hour in hot oven.

CORNISH PASTIES

Quickly made pastry, ½ lb. mutton or beef, 2 large potatoes, 1 small onion, a little stock, pepper and salt.

Cut mutton and onion into tiny pieces and potatoes a little larger. Put into a bowl, season, and pour over ½ a cup of stock. Cut the pastry into rounds the size of a saucer, put a spoonful of the mixture into centre of each, moisten the edges and join together on the top to form an upstanding frill. Bake 1 hour in moderate oven. *J.H.*

CORNISH PASTIES

Rich, firm pastry, ½ lb. rump steak with fat, 3 large potatoes, 1 small onion, 1 small turnip (if liked), pepper and salt.

Cut meat into very small pieces and potatoes very small and thin, chop onions and turnips finely. Divide pastry and cut into rounds size of a large saucer.

Arrange across centre of each round a layer of potatoes with little onion and turnip on top, then of meat and lastly of potatoes with onion, seasoning each layer and adding small dabs of butter if no fat is on the meat.

Pick up sides of pastry and press together and roll over with the two forefingers and thumbs to form a twist. Be sure to pack well to keep pastry firm and in good shape. Slit holes on top with knife.

Place on greaseproof paper and bake in shallow baking tin in very hot oven for 45 minutes, reducing heat the last 15 minutes.
Mrs. D. Murdoch.

SCOTCH MUTTON PIES

Use plain or boiled paste, mutton, gravy, pepper and salt. Remove all gristle and fat from meat, cut into small pieces and season. Line small pie or patty tins with pastry, fill with meat, moistened with gravy. Cut rounds of pastry for the tops, wet edges, place over pies and press the two edges firmly together. Make a hole in the centre of each pie. Brush over with a little milk or egg. Bake 1 hour in a moderate oven. When ready fill up with a little more gravy and serve either very hot or cold. *Mrs. Fotheringham.*

SAUSAGE ROLLS

Use flaky or quickly made pastry, 1 lb. sausages.
Skin sausages and roll them into as many small sausages as required. Roll out pastry very thinly and cut into 3-inch squares. Moisten edges, place sausage on each piece, roll, brush over with beaten egg and bake 20 minutes in hot oven. *J.H.*

CHICKEN PATTIES

Use puff pastry. Roll out pastry and cut into rounds with cutters about the size of a tumbler top. Cut centres out of half of the rounds, moisten the edges with egg and place on top of uncut rounds. Brush over with egg and bake in hot oven. When baked fill with following mixture: —
1 cup very finely chopped, cooked chicken, salt, pepper, butter, 1 slice onion grated, parsley, 1 tablespoon gravy or stock. Melt butter in pan. Mix other ingredients thoroughly and heat through in melted butter. Split pastry cases, remove some of the inside, fill with mixture and replace tops.

APPLE TART
(Make Rhubarb Tart in same way)

Rich short pastry, 5 large apples, 6 tablespoons sugar, butter, pinch salt.
Line a sandwich tin with two-thirds of the pastry. Peel the apples and cut in rather thick slices — they cook better than thin ones. Place on pastry in two layers with sugar between. Dot small pieces of butter on top and cover with remainder of pastry. Brush with egg, prick and bake in moderate oven for 35 minutes. When ready, dust with sugar and serve with cream. *J.H.*

DEEP APPLE PIE

Short crust pastry, 6 apples, 1 cup sugar, butter, a shake of mixed spice or ginger, 2 tablespoons water.

Peel and cut apples and fill a piedish with them, putting sugar in centre. Sprinkle with spice, dot with butter and add water. Cover piedish with rich, short crust ¼ inch thick, prick and bake in a medium oven about 40 minutes. Serve with custard or cream. *J.H.*

APPLE CRUSTY PUDDING

6 tablespoons flour, 4 tablespoons sugar, 2 tablespoons butter, ½ teaspoon baking powder, pinch salt.

Mix dry ingredients and rub in butter and put roughly on top of apples as prepared for deep apple pie. *J.H.*

AMERICAN RAISIN PIE

1 packet seeded raisins, ¼ lb. butter, ¼ lb. sugar, rind and juice of 1 lemon, 1 cup water, 2 eggs, Post Toasties, short crust. Sufficient for 1 very large or 2 smaller pies.

Cook raisins, butter, sugar, lemon and water together for 5 minutes. Cool slightly and add beaten eggs and cook in double boiler till it begins to thicken. Set aside to cool.

Line sandwich tins with rich short crust pastry. Sprinkle a handful of crushed Post Toasties on bottom, put in raisin mixture, cover with pastry, prick, brush over with egg and bake in moderate oven 40 minutes.

Serve hot with cream for dinner, or, when cold, cut into slices for tea. Dust with sugar. *J.H.*

PINEAPPLE MERINGUE PIE

Line a sandwich tin with short pastry and cake crumbs. Grate 1 large or 2 small pineapples, drain off as much juice as possible, add the yolks of 2 eggs, ½ cup sugar and 1 tablespoon butter. Place this on pastry and cook for 25 minutes. Beat whites of eggs very stiffly with 2 tablespoons castor sugar and return to oven till meringue is set. *L.H.*

GERMAN APPLE TART

Cream ¼ lb. butter with ¼ lb. castor sugar, add 1 egg. Mix in ½ lb. flour. Roll and line a sandwich tin, prick and bake in medium oven.

Stew 6 large apples with 1 cup sugar, rind and juice of 1 lemon and large piece of butter; cook as dry as possible. Pour over pastry shell and top with cream. Very good. *From Australia.*

LEMON PIE

1 cup breadcrumbs, 1 cup sugar, 1 cup water, yolks of 3 eggs, 1 oz. butter, juice and grated rind of 3 lemons. Mix all together

and bake in a tin lined with rich short crust. Beat whites of eggs with 3 tablespoons castor sugar till quite stiff.
When pie is baked, remove from oven, top with meringue and return, when oven is cool, to brown and set. *From Australia.*

PUMPKIN PIE

1½ cups mashed pumpkin, 1 cup boiling water, ½ cup sugar, salt, ½ teaspoon each ginger, cinnamon and nutmeg and 2 beaten eggs.
Line a pyrex plate with short crust and spread over it the pumpkin mixture. Cover with remainder of pastry and bake 20 to 30 minutes. Top with sugar and cinnamon. Pie can be left open. *M.L., Cape.*

BUTTERSCOTCH PIE

Line a tin with rich short pastry and bake.
For the Filling. — Boil 2 tablespoons syrup, 1 oz. butter and a teacup of milk. Thicken with 1 teaspoon cornflour and the yolks of 2 eggs and add a squeeze of lemon juice. Pour into the pastry shell and serve with or without meringue top.
Another Filling. — ¾ cup sugar, ¼ lb. butter, 2 lemons (juice and rind), 4 well beaten eggs. Put all into a double boiler, stir occasionally, until the mixture is thick.
Will keep for months if bottled. Use for large or small tarts.

ALMOND CUT

Line shallow tin with pastry and spread thinly with jam. On this place a mixture of 3 ozs. butter, 3 tablespoons sugar, 6 tablespoons Tiger Oats, 4 tablespoons milk, almond essence. Bake and when cold cut into fingers. *Mrs. Roos.*

BAKEWELL TART

Line a tin with pastry and spread with jam. Put into this a mixture of 3 egg yolks, 3 ozs. ground almonds, 3 ozs. breadcrumbs, 3 ozs. sugar and the grated rind and juice of a lemon. Whisk up the whites of eggs and stir in. Bake in hot oven 20 to 30 minutes.
From Lincoln.

ANOTHER BAKEWELL TART

Line a plate with pastry, cover with jam and pour on the filling.
1 oz. butter, 1 egg, ½ teacup hot milk, 1½ oz. sugar, 1 dessertspoon flour, ½ teaspoon essence of lemon.
Melt butter, add flour and sugar, add beaten egg, milk and lemon. Pour over pastry. Bake about ½ hour. *Mrs. J. Inglis.*

SWISS TART

4 heaped tablespoons flour, 2 tablespoons sugar, 1 slice butter, 1½ teaspoon baking powder, 1 egg, pinch salt.
Cream butter and sugar; mix dry ingredients and add with sufficient milk to make a fairly thin batter. When baked cover with apricot jam.

Mrs. G. Butterfield.

CHOCOLATE TARTS

About ½ lb. short or flaky pastry, cut in rounds and put in patty tins. Fill with 1 dessertspoon chocolate or cocoa, 1½ oz. butter, 1 egg, 2 ozs. castor sugar, 1 oz. ground rice, 1 oz. flour, 1 oz. almonds or walnuts, apricot jam.

Sieve flour, ground rice and chocolate: blanche and chop almonds. Beat sugar and butter to cream, stir in egg, add dry ingredients and nuts, add a few drops of vanilla, put a little jam at the bottom of each tartlet, and on top put a teaspoon of chocolate mixture. *Mrs. Murphy.*

SANDRINGHAM TARTLETS

Short or flaky pastry, cut in rounds and put into patty tins.
Filling. — 1 egg, its weight in sugar, butter and ground rice, almond flavouring.
Cream butter and sugar, add egg, beat well, add flavouring and dry ingredients.
Place a little raspberry jam at the bottom of each tart, place a teaspoon of the mixture on top. Bake 10 minutes (oven 400°).

Mrs. Murphy.

PIONEER TART

Line a plate with rich short crust pastry, cover the centre with thinly sliced banana, then pour 1 to 1½ tablespoons golden syrup or honey over the top. Sprinkle with Tiger Oats and bake at 400° F. until well baked. Serve with cream or custard. *Mrs. W. Hamilton.*

GERMAN TART

½ cup sugar, 1 egg, 1 teaspoon vanilla, 2 teaspoons baking powder, ¼ lb. butter, 2 cups flour.
Cream butter and sugar, beat egg with vanilla and add to butter mixture; add flour and baking powder.
Roll and press half the dough in cake tin and spread with raspberry jam, grate the other half of dough on top of jam.
Bake in a medium oven till golden brown.
Use apple puree as alternative to jam. *Mrs. H. Mill.*

STRAWBERRY CHIFFON PIE

4 eggs, ⅔ cup sugar, ½ teaspoon salt, 1 tablespoon (level) gelatine, ¼ cup cold water, 1 tablespoon lemon juice, 1 cup mashed strawberries, red colouring, whipped cream.

Beat the yolks of the eggs with half the sugar, add the salt and the lemon juice. Cook over hot water till the mixture thickens. Soak the gelatine in the cold water and pour over it the thickened egg. Add the strawberry pulp and add a few drops of the red vegetable colouring till a soft pink is obtained. Cool. When the mixture begins to set, fold in the egg whites beaten stiffly with the remaining sugar. Pile this mixture lightly into a baked pie-shell, made of very thin puff pastry. Let the filling set. Then decorate with whipped cream and a few of the whole strawberries.   *Mrs. Beyers (M. J. Davidtsz.)*

SPICED APPLE TART

Mix 1 teacup of flour with 3 tablespoons butter, 1 teaspoon mixed spice and 1 teaspoon baking powder. Beat up 1 egg with 2 tablespoons sugar, add to flour and knead into a soft dough. Line a sandwich tin with two-thirds of the pastry, fill with stewed apples and cover with the remaining pastry. Bake in a hot oven for 20 minutes.

Mrs. W. Hamilton.

SWISS SACHER TART

¼ lb. butter, ¼ lb. sugar, well creamed. Mix ¼ lb. grated chocolate and 1 tablespoon water, make slightly warm, and add gradually to the creamed butter and sugar. Add 7 egg yolks and beat well. Slightly warm ¼ lb. flour, add to mixture and lastly fold in stiffly beaten whites of 7 eggs. Put mixture in buttered round cake tin and bake in moderate oven 30-40 minutes. Don't open oven during baking. Leave for a day or two before using, then spread with apricot jam and ice with chocolate icing.   *Mrs. W. Hamilton.*

LEMON-CURD TART

6 tablespoons flour (rather heaped), 1 level teaspoon baking powder, pinch of salt, 3 teaspoons sugar (heaped), 2 teaspoons butter.

Rub butter into dry ingredients. Beat up 2 egg yolks and 1 white, ¼ cup milk.

Roll out, spread over breakfast plates and bake in moderate oven for ¼ hour.

Filling. — Beat the yolks of 3 eggs well. Add 3 teaspoons sugar, beat well, add 1 tin condensed milk, beat well and add ½ cup lemon juice,

stirring all the time. Whip up 3 whites of eggs and add 6 level teaspoons sugar.
Spread tart with filling and cover with beaten up whites of egg. Bake ¼ hour or less. *M. S. Malan.*

CHOCOLATE SMALL TARTS OR LARGE TARTS
(Short Pastry)

Filling. — ¾ cup ground almonds (3 ozs.), ⅓ cup castor sugar (2 ozs.), 2 tablespoons butter (1 oz.), 1 egg, 3 teaspoons cocoa, raspberry jam, 10 drops vanilla essence.
Cream butter and sugar lightly and add beaten egg and beat well together. Mix cocoa and ground almonds together and stir in, adding flavouring.
If for small tarts line patty tins with pastry. Put ½ teaspoon jam in bottom of each and put 1 teaspoon of mixture on top.
Bake in a hot oven 450° for 10 to 15 minutes. Makes 16 tarts. If a big tart is required line dish with pastry and put about ¼ inch jam and the mixture on top. *Mrs. C. Kaplan, Balfour.*

NOUGAT TART

Line tin with short crust pastry and fill with the following mixture: —
½ cup ground almonds, 1 cup cocoanut, 1 cup sugar, ½ cup currants, 1 egg, 2 level teaspoons cinnamon. Add enough milk to make the mixture soft. Bake slowly from 20 to 30 minutes. *Mrs. J. McMillan.*

DATE TART

Line tin with short crust pastry, prick and partly cook. Then add a layer of chopped dates and cover with the following mixture: —
½ breakfast cup cocoanut, ⅓ breakfast cup castor sugar, 1 oz. butter, 1 egg, little milk.
Return to oven to brown. *Mrs. J. McMillan.*

SPONGE TART

1 tablespoon cornflour, 2 tablespoons butter, 2 teaspoons baking powder, 3 tablespoons flour, 3 tablespoons sugar, 2 eggs.
Mix butter and 1½ tablespoons sugar to cream. Add egg yolks (well beaten), then cornflour, flour and baking powder. Mix well, then roll on to a buttered plate and bake. When done spread with jam. Beat up the whites of eggs and sugar and spread on top of the jam. Put back into oven and bake until pale golden brown.

LEMON MERINGUE PIE

1¼ cups boiling water, 1¼ cups sugar, 5 tablespoons pastry flour, 1 tablespoon butter, 3 eggs, pinch salt, juice of 2 lemons, grated rind of ½ lemon.

Mix flour and sugar together with a little cold water and add to the boiling water, stirring constantly until mixture thickens. Add butter, salt, lemon juice and rind and pour on to well-beaten egg yolks. Return to heat and cook for 2 minutes. Pour into a baked pie-shell and cover with meringue, made by beating egg whites stiff and adding 3 tablespoons powdered sugar and ¼ teaspoon lemon essence. Bake in a slow oven until the meringue is a golden brown — about 20 minutes.

Mrs. Blake.

CHEESE TARTLETS

Make short pastry and line your patty tins. Take ½ oz. butter, 1 teaspoon cornflour, 4 tablespoons milk, 2 tablespoons grated cheese, 1 egg and a little cayenne. Mix all together to a paste and fill pastry cases and cook in a moderate oven until brown. *Mrs. Tibbits.*

GINGER TART

Line pan with short crust as follows: 5 ozs. flour, 1 oz. castor sugar, 3 ozs. butter, yolk of 1 egg, little water if required.

Filling. — Melt 1 oz. butter. Add 1 oz. flour and cook for a few seconds, then add ½ cup of milk and stir until boiling. Remove from fire and add another ½ cup of milk, 2 ozs. blanched and chopped almonds, 2 ozs. chopped glacé cherries, 2 ozs. cut up ginger (glacé or crystallised), 1 oz. castor sugar, yolks of 2 eggs (beaten) and grated lemon rind. (A little cooked apple may be added to mixture if liked). Pour mixture into raw crust and bake in oven at about 400°.

May be covered with meringue, browned, or served with cream. Excellent. *Mrs. W. J. Kennedy, Johannesburg.*

SHORTBREAD PASTRY

4 oz. sugar, ½ lb. butter, 1 lb. flour (sifted), 2 eggs, pinch of salt.

Cream butter and sugar, add eggs, mix in flour with salt, mix all well together, roll out and use as required.

APPLE TART

Can be made with the above pastry. Line a sandwich tin with pastry, fill with prepared apple, wet edges with water, cover with pastry, prick with a fork. Bake 30 minutes in moderate oven, cover with icing sugar, when cold, or can be iced with lemon icing.

Mrs. S. Watson.

BUTTER-SCOTCH TART
Line a plate with rich short crust.
Filling. — 1 cup yellow sugar, 1 lump butter (size of an egg), 1½ teaspoons flour, 1 cup *warm water*, 2 eggs, 1 teaspoon vanilla essence. Melt butter and sugar in saucepan, add flour slowly and mix well. Add the warm water slowly, stirring all the time until thick. Add the well-beaten yolks of the eggs and allow to thicken. Add the vanilla essence. Cool the mixture. Put thin layer apricot jam on the pastry and pour on the mixture. Bake. Beat the egg whites stiffly with 2 tablespoons sugar and put on to the tart in spoonfuls. Put into a slow oven to set whites. *Mrs. C. Griffith.*

SUMMER FRUIT FLANS
Flans consist of short pastry cases filled with fruit (fresh or tinned) set in jelly. Sliced cooked apples, cherries, apricots, pineapples, gooseberries and pears can all be used. Line a sandwich tin with very rich short pastry, put a little rice on paper or bread in bottom to keep it flat and bake in medium oven for about 20 minutes. Before it is quite cooked remove the bread or rice and finish baking. Drain the fruit well before putting into pastry case. Boil up the syrup and add ½ packet of lemon jelly to it. When jelly is on the point of setting, pour it over the fruit. Top with cream or, when using peaches or apricots, surround the jellied fruit with lemon snow, to resemble fried eggs, and serve with cream or custard. The lemon snow can be made by incorporating the stiffly beaten white of egg with the other half of the lemon jelly. The egg white is beaten in just before jelly sets. This is a pretty sweet. *J.H.*

MOCK MINCE PIE
Rough puff pastry, 1½ cups seeded raisins, 3 large cooking apples, grated rind and juice of 1 orange, ½ cup any "leftover" fruit juice, 1½ cup sugar, pinch salt, ½ teaspoon cinnamon, 2-3 tablespoons crushed biscuits, 1 or 2 tablespoons brandy (optional).
Combine and cook raisins, pared, cored and sliced apples, rind and juice of orange, fruit juice and sugar. Cook until apples are very soft. Add cinnamon, crushed biscuits and brandy. Line a 9 inch pie plate with pastry, fill with mincemeat, cover it with an upper crust or with a latice of pastry. Bake at 435-450° for about 30 minutes.

CRUMBLY FRUIT TART
½ lb. flour, ¼ lb. butter, 3 ozs. sugar, 1 egg (beaten), 1 teaspoon baking powder, salt.
Filling. — 2 cooking apples, 2 tablespoons water, ½ cup currants,

½ cup raisins (stoned), ½ cup sultanas, ¼ cup mixed peel, sugar to taste (about 2 tablespoons), pinch salt, dessertspoon butter. Combine filling and cook. Sift flour, salt and baking powder together. Rub in butter, add egg to make a crumbly mixture. Pack half of crumbly mixture into lined, loose base tin. Spread cooled fruit mixture on top. Top with remaining crumb mixture. Bake at about 400° for about 30 minutes.

BANANA PIE

1 9 inch pie shell, 2 egg whites, 1 cup sugar, 1 teaspoon vanilla, pinch salt, 3 bananas (mashed), ½ cup crushed peaches or other fruit, ½ cup finely chopped nuts.

German Pastry. — ½ lb. flour; ¼ lb. butter, 2 ozs. castor sugar, creamed together; 1 egg, 1 teaspoon baking powder, salt.

Line a 9 inch pie plate with pastry, prick well and bake at 400° for about 20 minutes. Beat egg whites, add sugar gradually. Add mashed bananas and continue beating until smooth. Add salt and flavouring. Pile into baked shell and bake at 350° for 20 minutes. Cool, top with whipped cream. Put crushed peaches over top and sprinkle with chopped nuts. Fresh or canned peaches can be used.

APPLE SAUCE CHEESE PIE

Short sweet pastry, 1 cup apple sauce, 1 tin condensed milk, rind and juice of 1 lemon, 3 eggs, pinch salt, cinnamon.

Sweet Short Pastry. — ½ lb. flour, ¼ lb. butter, 2 ozs. castor sugar, ¼ teaspoon baking powder, pinch salt, 1 egg and about 2 tablespoons iced water.

Line deep pie plate with pastry. Combine apple sauce, milk, juice and rind of lemon and egg yolks. Beat egg whites with salt. Fold into apple mixture. Fill pie shell with mixture, sprinkle top with cinnamon, if liked. Bake at 375° for about 50 minutes.

MERINGUE FRUIT TART

Ginger snap crumb crust, stewed or canned pears or a mixture of fruit, 2 egg whites, 3 tablespoons sugar (for meringue).

Crumb Crust. — 1½ cups crushed ginger snaps, 1 tablespoon icing sugar, ⅓ cup butter (melted).

Combine crushed biscuit crumbs, icing sugar and melted butter. Pat firmly with the palm of the hand or spoon against the bottom and sides of the pan or plate to make a shell. Chill the crust thoroughly. Fill with cooked sweetened fruit, top with meringue. Bake at 300° until meringue is crisp.

SAVOURY FLAN

½ lb. boiled ham, 1 hard boiled egg, 3 ozs. grated cheese, 2 raw eggs, lump of butter, little milk, salt, pepper and mustard to taste.

Mince ham and hard-boiled egg and mix with other ingredients, using well-beaten eggs with sufficient milk to make fairly thick mixture. Line a sandwich tin with short crust, put in above filling and bake in moderate oven for about 35 minutes.   *Mrs. T. J. Faurie, Ficksburg.*

LEMON CHIFFON PIE

1 tablespoon gelatine, 3 eggs, 1 teacup castor sugar. 1 cup lemon juice, pinch salt, grated rind of one lemon, raspberry or sieved strawberry jam, baked pastry flan.

Line a sandwich cake tin with short crust pastry. Prick well and bake in moderate oven. (Slices of stale bread, placed on cooking paper will keep the shape of the flan and the bread can be used for crumbing later). Soak gelatine for a few minutes in two tablespoons water. Beat egg yolks with half of the sugar, add lemon juice and salt and cook in double boiler till mixture thickens slightly. Stir in rind and soaked gelatine and leave till cold. Beat egg whites till stiff and add remainder of sugar. Fold into cold lemon mixture. Cover bottom of pastry case with jam; pour lemon mixture on top and chill. Sprinkle with chopped nuts and decorate or serve with cream.

CAPE GOOSEBERRY FLAN

Rich short crust, jam, ground almonds, sugar, gooseberries and jelly, egg yolk. Stew as many gooseberries as required with sugar to taste. When cooked, drain off the juice and add to it a little lemon jelly powder. While this is cooling line your flan or sandwich tin with rich short crust. Into a basin put 4 tablespoons raspberry jam, 2 tablespoons ground almonds, and 2 tablespoons cakecrumbs and egg. Put this mixture into pastry case and bake in medium oven for 20 minutes. When cold, put in the gooseberries and the partly set jelly. Chill and serve with cream.

ANOTHER FILLING FOR LEMON MERINGUE PIE

2 large cups milk, 2 level tablespoons custard powder, ½ cup sugar, yolks of 3 eggs, grated rind and juice of 2 lemons.

Slake custard powder with a little of the milk. Add the remainder of milk, sugar and salt. Stir till boiling, cool slightly, and add beaten yolks of eggs, lemon juice and grated rind. Pour on to baked pie-shell. *Meringue.* — Beat egg whites till stiff and dry, add 3 tablespoons castor sugar and beat again. Spread over custard and bake till golden brown. Use rich short crust recipe for pie crust.

CANNED PEACH TART

Pastry. — ¼ lb. flour, not quite ¼ lb. butter, ¼ lb. sugar, ½ teaspoon baking powder, 1 egg beaten.

Mix dry ingredients, then add egg. If not moist enough, add a little brandy and water.

Filling. — Take 1 tin canned fruit and separate syrup from fruit. Boil syrup and add 2 teaspoons maizena and 1 teaspoon custard powder, mixed with a little milk. Boil for a few minutes, then take off stove and stir in well-beaten yolks of 2 eggs. Beat whites to a stiff froth and add to finished mixture. Pour over the peaches after they have been placed on the uncooked pie-crust and bake in a slow oven for about 1 hour.

Mrs. J. C. Smuts.

FLAKY PASTRY (Foolproof)

1 lb. butter or vegetable-fat, 2 large breakfastcups (piled) of flour, ½ teaspoon salt, 1 large breakfastcup boiling water.

Place fat in bowl, break up into pieces with fork, and pour boiling water over. Stand for few minutes, then stir in the flour and salt, mixing thoroughly. Place bowl in 'fridge until mixture hardens. Turn out onto well-floured board and roll out once.

May be kept in 'fridge in greaseproof paper.

APPLE PIE

2 lbs. cooking apples or 1 tin pie apples, 2 oz. ground almonds (or nuts), 1 egg, 2 ozs. butter or margarine, 2 ozs. sugar, A few almonds or nuts. About 1 cup breadcrumbs.

Stew apples to a pulp, sweeten to taste and allow to cool. Mix in the breadcrumbs and place in a buttered pie-dish. Beat butter and sugar to a cream, add ground almonds and well-beaten egg. Spread this mixture over the apples, decorate with split nuts, and bake to a light golden brown.

Serve with cream.

I'm quite ashamed, 'tis mighty rude
to eat so much, but all so good.

Pope.

FOUND IN AN OLD CATHEDRAL

*Give us a good digestion, Lord,
And also something to digest,
But when or how that something comes,
We leave to Thee, who knowest best.*

*Give us a healthy body, Lord,
Give us the sense to keep it so,
Also a heart that is not bored,
Whatever work we have to do.*

*Give us a sense of humour, Lord,
Give us the power to see a joke,
To get some happiness from life.
And pass it on to other folk.*

PUDDINGS: HOT AND COLD

DATE PUDDING

1 cup dates, 2 tablespoons butter, 1 good cup breadcrumbs, 3 eggs, 1 teaspoon cream of tartar, 1 cup flour, ½ cup syrup, 2 tablespoons sugar, 1 teaspoon mixed spice, ½ teaspoon heaped soda, mixed in a little milk.

Mix butter, crumbs, spice and cream of tartar and flour. Then pour in syrup, beat eggs and sugar together and add to mixture; add dates and lastly mix bi-carbonate of soda and milk (you must judge quantity of milk). Fairly stiff mixture.

Put in greased basin. Steam 3 hours.

Figs or raisins can be used in place of dates. *Mrs. S. Watson.*

SAUCE FOR DATE PUDDING

1 cup yellow sugar, 1 teaspoon maizena, 1 cup wine, 1 cup water, 1 tablespoon butter.

Boil sugar and water. Add maizena mixed with water and butter to boiling syrup, lastly add wine. *Mrs. S. Watson.*

CANARY PUDDING

4 oz. flour, 3 oz. sugar, 2 oz. butter, 2 eggs, salt, 1 teaspoon baking powder, ¼ cup milk.

Cream butter and sugar and add each egg separately. Beat well, then stir in flour and baking powder and milk. Pour into a buttered mould and steam 1 to 2 hours. Serve with syrup or jam. Syrup can be put into bottom of mould and cooked with pudding.

If dark pudding is desired, leave out baking powder and mix with ½ teaspoon bicarbonate soda and 1 teaspoon cream of tartar and put strawberry jam in bottom of mould. *J.H.*

TREACLE PUDDING

½ lb. breadcrumbs, 2 eggs, ¼ lb. butter, 2 oz. sugar, 4 tablespoons treacle or syrup.

Rub butter and breadcrumbs together, add sugar, well beaten eggs and treacle. Butter a mould, put in the mixture and steam 4 or 5 hours. Serve with melted treacle or syrup. *Mrs. Gray.*

BROWN BETTY

2 cups breadcrumbs, ½ cup sugar, ¼ cup melted butter, ¼ teaspoon nutmeg, 4 cooking apples. Grated rind and juice ½ lemon, ½ cup hot water.

Mix crumbs and butter lightly. Cover bottom of buttered pudding dish with crumb mixture and spread over half the apples, sprinkle with some of the sugar, nutmeg, lemon juice and rind mixed together, repeat. Spread remaining crumbs on surface, put in water, cover with buttered paper at first and bake in moderate oven 40 minutes. Serve with cream.

From California.

RAISIN PIE

Crumb ½ lb. digestive biscuits, mix with ¼ lb. melted butter. Now take ¾ of a ½ lb. packet of seedless raisins, cover with water (only just) and put on stove. Stir 3 level dessertspoons maizena blended with water, add 1 teaspoon ground ginger, lemon juice and sugar to taste to the boiling raisins, and cook for a few minutes. Line a pyrex plate bottom with nearly half the crumbed biscuits, pour over the raisin filling, then put the rest of biscuits over the filling and bake in oven about 3-5 minutes to brown. Serve with cream or custard.

Mrs. W. Hamilton.

PLUM PUDDING

1 cup flour, 1 cup breadcrumbs, 1 cup sugar, 1 teaspoon salt, 1 cup finely chopped suet, 1 cup currants, 1 teaspoon bi-carbonate of soda, 1 cup raisins, 1 cup sultanas, 2 ozs. almonds, 1 grated carrot, 1 grated apple, 1 tablespoon treacle, 1 tablespoon marmalade, grated rind of 1 lemon, 1 packet mixed spice, 6 eggs, 1 glass brandy.

Have fruit cleaned and floured night before. Mix fruit with dry ingredients, grated carrot and apple. Beat eggs and add to them the marmalade, treacle and brandy. Mix all together, stir well and cook for 6 or 7 hours in mould or pudding cloth. *Mother.*

FAVOURITE PLUM PUDDING

2 cups flour, 1 teaspoon soda, 3 cups cake crumbs, 1 cup sugar, 1 cup shortening, 1 cup raisins, 1 cup currants, 1 cup chopped dates, ½ cup chopped crystallised ginger, 2 teaspoons ginger, 2 teaspoons cinnamon, ½ teaspoon nutmeg, ½ teaspoon cloves, 2 eggs.

Mix all together with sufficient *sour* milk to form a stiff dough. Put into a well greased bowl and boil steadily for 6 hours.

Violet R. Hendrie.

DUTCH APPLE PUDDING

½ cup sugar, 2 tablespoons butter, 1 cup milk, 1 egg, ¼ teaspoon nutmeg, 1¾ cups flour, 3 teaspoons baking powder, ½ teaspoon salt, 6 sour apples.

Cream butter, add sugar, beaten egg and milk. Sift flour, salt and baking powder, add to liquid. Mix into soft dough. Spread mixture into shallow dish. Peel and quarter apples, press pieces into batter, sprinkle with 3 tablespoons sugar and grated nutmeg over top. Serve with foamy sauce.

A lovely pudding this. Mrs. Murray.

FOAMY SAUCE

1 cup sugar, 2 tablespoons butter, 1 egg, ½ teaspoon nutmeg.

Cream butter and sugar, add egg, whip till foamy. Serve on hot pudding. Mrs. E. Murray.

VINEGAR PUDDING

Take 2 eggs, weigh them, then take the same weight in flour, butter and sugar. Cream butter and sugar and add 1 tablespoon golden syrup, then eggs well beaten, flour and 1 teaspoon of baking powder, lastly 1 dessertspoon of vinegar. Mix well and place in a cloth wrung out of hot water and well floured, leaving enough room for a little rising, then place it in a pot of boiling water in which has been placed a small plate to prevent burning, now boil for about 2 hours. May be steamed. Mrs. Mill.

VINEGAR PUDDING (Excellent)

Combine 1½ cups flour, ¾ cup milk, ½ cup sugar, 1 tablespoon apricot jam or golden syrup and dates, 1 tablespoon butter or fat, 1 teaspoon soda, ½ teapsoon ginger, ½ teaspoon cinnamon, 1 egg.

Rub butter into flour before combining.

Butter the mould and put in ½ cup water, ½ cup sugar, ¼ cup vinegar and put the dough into it. Don't stir again. Steam for 2½ hours.

Mrs. T. Reinicke.

SAUCE FOR VINEGAR PUDDING

1 tablespoon butter, 1 tablespoon jam. Maizena. 2 cups water, 1 cup sugar, a little ginger and cinnamon.

Boil water. Put in tablespoon butter and apricot jam, and thicken with a little maizena. Mrs. T. Reinicke.

AUNTY A's APPLE DUMPLING

Use suet crust recipe No. 1. 4 large apples, ½ cup sugar, ¼ cup water, 2 cloves or ¼ teaspoon ground ginger.

Peel and core the apples and put into the steamer with the sugar, spice and water and a dab or two of butter.

Roll out suet crust to fit top of dish, cover carefully and steam 3 or 4 hours. If liked, the pudding basin can be lined, and in that case use suet crust recipe as given, but this makes rather a large pudding. If pastry is used for top cover only use half quantity of suet crust. This makes the better pudding. Cape gooseberries or any dried fruits can be used.

A DIFFERENT ROLY-POLY

2 cups flour, 1½ dessertspoons baking powder, 2 dessert spoons butter, 1 egg well beaten, a little milk, and a pinch of salt.

For the Syrup. — 1½ cups water, 1½ cups sugar, 12 cloves.

Put sugar, water and cloves into a saucepan to heat and dissolve while preparing for pudding.

Rub the butter into the flour and salt. Add egg and milk and form into a stiff dough. Roll out, spread with jam and roll up. Put into an oblong dish, cover with hot syrup and bake at 375° for about 25 minutes. Sufficient for 8 persons. The pudding gradually absorbs the syrup.
Mrs. B. Mills.

For ordinary roly-poly use suet crust No. 1. Roll out to ¼ of an inch thick. Spread jam to within 1 inch of edge, moisten sides and far end with water and roll up, sealing the edges. Wrap roll in scalded and floured pudding cloth and secure ends firmly with string. Boil for 2 hours or bake for 1 hour. Instead of jam Christmas mince meat can be used or finely chopped apples, honey and cinnamon. Serve with jam sauce or apple syrup.
J.H.

SAVOURY ROLY-POLY

For savoury roly-poly follow above recipe, but use Scotch mince collops (see recipe) instead of sweet filling. Serve with gravy and green vegetables.

Variations. — Minced chicken and bacon, veal and ham.

APPLE DUMPLINGS BAKED

Use the short crust recipe. Use as many apples as required. Peel and core the apples and fill the centres with raisins, spice, sugar and a tiny piece of butter. Roll the pastry out and cut it into rounds large enough to cover apples. Place one in the centre of each round, wet the edges and cover the apple, being careful to join the paste completely. Put them join downwards, on a baking sheet and bake 20 to 30 minutes in a fairly hot oven. When nearly done, brush over with water and sprinkle with sugar. J.H.

GRANNY'S RAISIN DUMPLING (Spotted Dick)

8 oz. flour, 4 ozs. suet, ½ teaspoon baking powder, 4 ozs. large seeded raisins, salt, water.

Chop suet and mix with dry ingredients and fruit. Use just enough water to make a stiff paste. Roll out and fold over and over. Put into pudding cloth, tie securely and boil for 2 or 3 hours. Serve with fruit syrup or sauce. J.H.

STEAMED BROWN PUDDING

5 heaped tablespoons flour, 3 tablespoons fat, Purene or butter, 3 tablespoons jam or syrup, level teaspoon bi-carbonate, 2 or 3 eggs, according to size, pinch salt.

Butter pudding basin well. Line bottom of basin with jam. Mix flour, soda, salt and fat, then add jam and, lastly, the beaten eggs. Steam for 2½ to 3 hours. Serve with custard or wine sauce. This pudding can be varied by adding fruit, marmalade or dates. Mrs. J. Jacobson.

LEMON CURD PUDDING OR LEMON DELICACY

2 tablespoons butter, ¾ cup sugar, juice of 1 lemon, grated rind 1 lemon, 1 cup milk, 2 tablespoons flour, 2 eggs.

Cream butter, add sugar gradually and cream well together — add well-beaten egg yolks, flour, lemon juice and rind. Mix thoroughly — add milk and fold in stiffly beaten egg whites. Pour into greased baking dish. Set in pan of hot water and bake in slow oven 350° about 45 minutes. A delicate crust will form on top and this pudding supplies its own sauce. Mrs. N. Taylor, Durban.
Mrs. Tibbits, Pretoria.

STUFFED APPLES

3 large apples, 15 dates, desiccated cocoanut, water, jam, or jelly.

Peel the apples and remove the cores. Stone the dates and cut up 9 and stuff them inside the apples, keeping aside the remainder of the dates whole. Bake the apples until almost tender, brush with melted jam or jelly and sprinkle with cocoanut. Return to oven and finish cooking and slightly brown the cocoanut.

Serve either hot or cold and decorate with whole dates. Mrs. J.S.F.

VELVET PUDDING

4 cups milk, ¾ cup flour, ½ cup sugar, 3 eggs, 2 tablespoons butter, 1 teaspoon salt, 1 teaspoon vanilla.

Scald the milk. Mix the dry ingredients. Gradually add a little of the hot milk. Stir till well blended. Return to the heat. Stir while cooking till the mixture is thicker, add the butter and vanilla. Then stir it gradually into the well-beaten egg yolks. Pour into a greased pudding dish. Bake in a moderate oven till it slightly browns. Cool, and place a layer of apricot jam thinly over the top. On the top of this pile a meringue made with the 3 egg whites and 3 tablespoons of sugar. Place in an oven of 300° for 15 minutes to set the meringue.

Mrs. Beyers (M. J. Davidtsz.)

CAKE AND FRUIT PUDDING

Have fruit (gooseberry, apple, rhubarb, etc.), boiling hot before adding the cake mixture.

1 teacup flour, 3 ozs. butter, pinch salt, ¾ teacup sugar, 1 teaspoon baking powder, 1 egg.

Cream butter and sugar, add well beaten egg; beat well together; add sifted flour, baking powder and salt. Pour on to hot fruit and bake in oven. Bake 20 minutes. Serve with cream or custard. Mrs. S. Culbert.

SPICE PUDDING

1 breakfast cup flour, 2 teaspoons spice, 2 ozs. dripping, ¼ pint milk, ¾ teaspoon baking powder, ½ teacup syrup, 2 ozs. sugar. Serve with custard.

Sift dry ingredients into basin. Melt together dripping and syrup, and allow to cool. Add to flour and mix well, add milk. Turn into small, greased moulds and steam for about 40 minutes. Mrs. Harrison.

APPLE "POFFERTJIES"

4 ozs. flour, 4 ozs. sugar, 6 cooked, sieved apples, 2 ozs. seeded, chopped raisins, 1 egg, salt and ¼ pint milk.

Mix all ingredients together to a stiff batter. Fry in small spoonfuls in smoking hot dripping (deep fat frying.) Drain on brown paper and serve with cinnamon and sugar or hot syrup.

BANANA BATTER

Use 1 pint of milk, 2 eggs and 6 ozs. of self-raising flour to make a creamy batter. When the batter is well beaten and full of air-bubbles, let it stand for ½ hour or so. Meanwhile skin 6 bananas and coat them with castor sugar. Put a knob of lard in a baking dish, and when it is smoking hot pour in the batter over the bananas and bake for 20-30 minutes. A fairly deep dish should be used for this sweet so that the bananas are covered with batter whilst they are cooking. Sprinkle with castor sugar and serve at once.

BANANA PUDDING

This is an ideal dish for children. Pour 1 pint of very hot milk over 4 ozs. of broken bread. When cool, add a beaten egg and the grated rind of a small lemon. Sweeten with sugar and pour this mixture over 6 sliced bananas in a buttered pie dish. Bake for 30 minutes and serve hot with sifted sugar.

APPLE PUDDING

2 cups breadcrumbs, 2 cups coarsely chopped apples, ½ lb. finely chopped suet, 1 cup sugar, 4 eggs, 1 cup milk, ¼ teaspoon salt, ¼ teaspoon grated nutmeg.

Mix all dry ingredients together, add beaten eggs and milk and let stand 1 hour for the bread to soak. Pour mixture into a well greased basin and steam for 2 hour. *A. Friend, Johannesburg.*

GINGER AND APPLE PUDDING (Steamed)

2 cups breadcrumbs, ½ cup butter, 2 eggs, ½ cup sugar, 2 large apples grated, 1 cup flour, 1½ teaspoons baking powder, 1½ teaspoonfuls ginger, 1 tablespoon syrup, pinch of salt.

Take all dry ingredients, mix well, rub in butter, add well beaten eggs, apple and syrup. Mix moderately stiff — use a little milk to thin down. Steam for 2 hours. Can be served with any sweet sauce.

Mrs. E. C. Coleman.

ASHFIELD PUDDING

¼ lb. flour, 2 ozs. butter, 1 egg, 3 ozs. sugar, 1 teaspoon baking powder, ¾ cup milk.

Rub butter into dry ingredients. Add egg and milk. Butter pudding basin and put 2 tablespoons jam at bottom, pour in mixture and steam for 2 hours.

URNEY PUDDING

2 eggs, ¼ lb. butter, 1 tablespoon raspberry jam, ¼ lb. flour, 2 ozs. sugar, ½ teaspoon bi-carbonate of soda.

Cream butter and sugar, add egg then flour and soda. Lastly add jam. Steam 1½ hours. Serve with cream, custard or jam juice. *Mrs. Smith.*

APPLE CAKE PUDDING

Peel and core 4 apples, cook in saucepan with little water and sugar to taste and cook until tender.

Put 5 tablespoons flour into basin, add 2 tablespoons dripping or butter and rub well into flour. Add 3 tablespoons sugar and grated rind of lemon; break in 1 or 2 eggs — stir well with wooden spoon and add a little milk and beat to a smooth cake mixture. Add 2 teaspoons baking powder.

Pour apples into a piedish and cover with mixture, cook in oven which has been brought up to 450° and switched off; cook pudding for about ½ hour. *Mrs. J. P. Runnals.*

LAST-MINUTE PUDDING

As many slices of white bread as are required, 1 egg, 1 cup of milk, sugar to sweeten, jam.

Beat egg very well, add to milk and sugar. Place in a deep plate. Have a pan ready with a small piece of melted butter. Soak bread in egg mixture, place in hot pan, when browned on one side turn and repeat. While still hot spread with jam, and if cream can be dotted on top this makes a big improvement. *Mrs. P. W. Gaines, Durban.*

FAVOURITE PUDDING

2 eggs, 2 cups water, pinch salt, 1 cup sugar, 2 tablespoons maizena, juice of 3 lemons.

Boil the sugar, lemon juice and water together. Add the maizena and salt, mixed with a little cold water, and allow to boil for 5 minutes, stirring all the time. Remove from the fire and add the well-beaten egg whites. Place in mould and set. The egg yolks can be slightly beaten and added to 2 small cups of milk, with sugar to taste, placed in a jug or basin, and stood in a saucepan of boiling water, until the custard thickens. The saucepan can be left on a cool part of the stove, with just sufficient heat to keep the water hot.

SPONGE DUMPLINGS

1 gill milk, 1 oz. butter, 1 tablespoon sugar, 3 ozs. flour, 2 eggs, pinch of salt.

Put milk and butter into a saucepan, bring to the boil. Add flour and salt, stir over the fire until the mixture leaves the side of the pan. Cool slightly, stir in sugar and beaten yolks of eggs. Beat whites to a stiff froth and fold into other ingredients.

Drop spoonfuls into boiling salted water and boil 10 to 15 minutes. Serve with syrup or jam. *Mrs. C. M. Smith.*

RUSSIAN APPLE PUDDING

2½ ozs. butter, 3 ozs. sugar, 4 ozs. flour, 2 eggs, 3 teaspoons baking powder, 2 teacups milk, pinch of salt, stewed apples.

Sift flour, sugar and salt together, rub in butter, then add eggs and milk. Mix thoroughly, then add baking powder. Pour mixture over stewed apples and bake in hot oven 20-30 minutes. Serve with sweet sauce or cream. *Mrs. W. J. Kennedy, Johannesburg.*

APPLE CHARLOTTE

2 lbs. cooking apples, 4 tablespoons sugar, ½ lb. breadcrumbs, ¼ lb. finely shredded suet, 1 teaspoon cinnamon, 1 oz. butter.
Peel and core apples and cut in thick slices. Butter a piedish and coat with some of the breadcrumbs. Mix rest of breadcrumbs with cinnamon and suet and put a layer of this in bottom of dish, add a layer of apple sprinkled with sugar then another layer of crumbs and suet. Fill up the dish having a top layer of suet and breadcrumbs. Press down firmly, dab with butter and bake in moderate oven for at least 1 hour or until nicely browned. *J.H.*

GOLDEN PUDDING

4 ozs. flour, 4 ozs. breadcrumbs, 4 ozs. suet, 3 ozs. sugar, 4 ozs. golden syrup, ½ teaspoon baking powder, ½ cup milk, 1 egg. Chop suet and mix with dry ingredients. Beat egg and add to milk and syrup. Mix and steam for 2½ hours.
Serve with fruit sauce or syrup. *Mrs. Jamieson.*

DATE PUDDING

Soak 4 tablespoons sago in 1 large cup milk, or ½ milk and water, overnight. Next morning mix with 1 teacup of breadcrumbs, 1½ cups dates (cut fine), 1 tablespoon melted butter, 1 egg, 1 oz. sugar and a little lemon rind. Lastly, a teaspoon soda mixed with a little boiling water. Mix thoroughly. Tie up in a well-floured cloth and boil 4 hours. Serve with a custard sauce. *Mrs. D. Ogilvie.*

SAGO PUDDING

¾ cup sago, 1 pint milk, 2 eggs, 2 tablespoons sugar, a little butter.
Soak sago and sugar in milk for some hours. Boil up and when sago in clear, cool slightly, add beaten eggs and flavouring and bake in oven.
Use this recipe for vermicilli, rice or semolina.
Sago Cream. — Use above recipe but add yolks and whites of eggs separately. The whites beaten to a stiff froth before adding. Bake for 20 minutes and serve, or chill and serve without baking. *Mrs. Johnson.*

QUEEN OF PUDDINGS

2 teacups breadcrumbs, 1 pint milk, 1 cup sugar, grated rind of 1 lemon, 2 eggs, salt.
Mix the crumbs, milk, sugar, lemon and yolks of eggs together. Bake in slow oven till set. When done spread jam over surface of pudding. Beat whites of eggs with a little sugar, spread over pudding and put back into oven to brown slightly. *Mrs. Johnson.*

CREAM PUDDING

4 cups cornflakes, ¼ cup melted butter, 6 tablespoons flour, 2 cups hot water, ¼ teaspoon salt, 2 eggs, separated, cup sweetened condensed milk, 1 teaspoon vanilla essence, 1 tablespoon syrup, Squeeze of half a lemon.

Crush cornflakes into fine crumbs: add butter and mix well. Press gently and firmly in bottom of pan, reserving 2 tablespoons for topping: chill.

Mix flour and salt: add condensed milk gradually, stirring until well mixed. Stir in hot water. Cook over hot water until thick and smooth, stirring occasionally. Continue to cook for about 15 minutes.

Beat egg-yolks, stir slowly in small amount of hot mixture. Return to remaining mixture and cook for about 2 minutes. Cool, then add vanilla. Pour onto crumb-lined pan.

Beat egg-whites until frothy, gradually add syrup, beating until stiff. Spread meringue over pudding, sprinkle crumbs on top, place in oven and slightly brown.

Nine servings.

PARADISE PUDDING

Pare, core and mince 3 apples, and mix with ¼ lb. breadcrumbs, 3 ozs. sugar, 2 ozs. currants, salt and nutmeg to taste, grated rind of ½ a lemon and 3 well beaten eggs.

Put into a buttered pudding basin and steam for 2 hours. Serve with sweet sauce. *Mrs. Johnson.*

PANCAKES AND FRITTERS

FRITTER BATTER

1½ cups flour, 2 teaspoon baking powder, ¼ teaspoon salt, ⅔ cup milk, 1 well beaten egg, 1 tablespoon melted butter.

Mix and sift dry ingredients, add milk gradually, egg and butter; 2 eggs and one teaspoon baking powder may be used.

For sweet fritters add 2 tablespoons castor sugar.

PINEAPPLE AND APPLE FRITTERS

Peel and core apples. Cut in ½ inch rings. Dip into batter and fry lightly. Drain on paper and sprinkle with castor sugar. Pineapple same as apple.

BANANA FRITTERS

Cut bananas lengthwise, squeeze lemon juice over. Dip in batter and fry.

OATMEAL FRITTERS

To left-over cooked oats (say 2 cups) add 2 well beaten eggs, sift 1 teaspoon baking powder, little salt and sufficient flour (¾ cup) to make a loose mixture. If you find mixture rather thick add a little milk. Fry in deep fat (oil perferably) and serve hot with cinnamon and castor sugar and stewed fruit if desired.

PUMPKIN FRITTERS

Cold mashed pumpkin, flour, egg, cinnamon or lemon juice, baking powder, salt.

To 1 cup of pumpkin use 1 egg, about ¼ cup of flour, ½ teaspoon of baking powder, pinch salt. Mix all well together. Fry in hot lard or vegetable fat. Serve with cinnamon and sugar or lemon juice and sugar. *Mrs. Withel.*

PANCAKES

¼ lb. flour, ½ teaspoon baking powder, pinch salt, 1 egg ½ pint milk.

Sieve flour and salt into mixing bowl. Make a well in centre, break the egg into this and stir in a little of the milk. Add remainder of milk very gradually. Beat well and stand aside for 1 hour. When ready beat batter again and pour into a jug. Melt a small piece of pastrine in frying pan, just sufficient to cover the bottom of pan. Fry gently to a golden brown then toss or turn with palette knife. Have ready a sheet of cooking paper sprinkled with castor sugar, turn pancake on to this, squeezing a little lemon juice over and roll up.

Use any fillings, sweet or savoury.

SOME SWEET AND SAVOURY FILLINGS FOR PANCAKES

Sweet. — Spread lightly with warmed marmalade or jam. Pounded bananas and lemon juice warmed before spreading. Chopped nuts and raisins bound together with honey. Stewed and pounded prunes and nuts, sprinkled with cinnamon.

Savoury. — Minced chicken, ham or cold meat mixed with sauce. Scrambled egg and cheese. Pounded liver and bacon.

A puree of fish and sauce.

Cooked kidney diced. Chicken livers, seasoned.

COLD PUDDINGS

MOTTLED JELLY

1 red and 1 yellow jelly.

Make a raspberry jelly as directed on packet, pour into shallow dish and leave to set. Then make a lemon jelly as directed. About ¾ fill a mould.

When cool and on the point of setting, cut part of the red jelly into dice and drop into the mould, giving, a gentle stir to distribute them and leave to set.

Garnish with the remainder of the jelly chopped.   *Mrs. Harrison.*

A QUICKLY PREPARED SWEET

Allow ½ Spaanspek per person: scoop out the pips of each half and place a ball of ice-cream in each: finish with a spoonful of strained Granadilla pulp.

APRICOT DELIGHT

1 cup apricot pulp, 2 cups marshmallows, 1 cup chopped nuts, 1 cup cream, 1 teaspoon gelatine in a little warm water.

Cut marshmallows in quarters and combine with apricot pulp and ¾ nuts; add gelatine (cooled and melted). Let mixture stand for an hour and when it thickens fold in the stiffly whipped cream. Pile into crystal dish and sprinkle with remaining nuts. Place in frig. till firm and serve with apricot juice.

CHOCOLATE SPECIAL

1 tin evaporated milk, 2 ozs. chocolate, ½ lb. marshmallows, 4 ozs. castor sugar, pinch salt.

Chill ⅔ milk. Grate chocolate and mix with salt and sugar, remainder of the milk and half teacup water. Cook in double boiler, stirring constantly, add marshmallows and stir till smooth. Whip chilled milk till stiff and fold into marshmallow mixture — freeze.

PAW-PAW MOULD

1 paw-paw, 4 bananas, juice of four oranges, 2 heaped tablespoons sugar, 1 packet jelly.

Dice paw-paw and slice bananas, add orange juice and sugar and boil together for ten minutes. Add jelly to above mixture and when cool fold in whites of two eggs. Set in mould and serve with cream or custard.

MARSHMALLOW MERINGUE

3 whites of eggs, 6 tablespoons castor sugar, 1 teaspoon vinegar, flavouring.

Beat whites of eggs, add sugar gradually, and continue beating until very stiff. Add vinegar and flavouring. Line loose-bottomed cake tin with greaseproof paper (extra thickness on bottom), pour in merinque and bake in slow oven (about 300°) for one hour and leave in cooling oven for one hour. Serve with fruit and cream.   *Mrs. L. Malan.*

ORANGE SPONGE CREAM

Place one tin Ideal Milk in can of boiling water and boil for twenty minutes. Chill overnight. Combine chilled milk with one small cup sugar, and whip to a cream. Melt one packet jelly in two cups orange or granadilla juice, combine with cream and pour into crystal dish. Serve with canned fruit.   *Mrs. L. Malan.*

STONE CREAM

Dissolve 2 level tablespoons gelatine in 2 cups of hot water, allow to stand for about 3 minutes, add 1 teaspoon vanilla essence and 2 tablespoons wine, then add 1 tin condensed milk, stirring all the time. Pour in mould and allow to set. The stiffly beaten white of 1 egg may be added just as it begins to set. Serve with custard.
   Mrs. J. Klopper.

CITROEN CREAM

2 tablespoons sugar and the yolks of 2 eggs, well beaten together, add grated rind of ½ and juice of 1 lemon, 2 dessertspoons gelatine melted in a little boiling water. When slightly set, stir in very lightly well beaten whites of eggs. This sweet is not cooked.
   Mrs. Jackson, Maritzburg.

ORANGE SWEET

1 cup orange juice, 2 eggs, pinch salt, ¼ cup sugar, 1 dessertspoon gelatine.

Beat egg whites very stiffly, beat egg yolks separately and add sugar to yolks, also salt. Mix gelatine with ½ cup hot water, and orange juice, when cool add to yolks, beat again. Lastly add egg whites and beat all thoroughly. Set in wet moulds.   *Mrs. A. Stevenson.*

BANANA MOUSSE

½ pint banana pulp, 1 lemon, ½ pint milk, ½ oz. gelatine, ¼ lb. icing sugar, ½ pint cream.

Mix banana, juice of ½ lemon and cream (whipped), dissolve gelatine first in a little cold, then hot water. Mix icing sugar with milk. Mix all together, mould. Set in refrigerator, decorate with slices of banana dipped in lemon juice and whipped cream.   *E.R.*

APRICOT SOUFFLE

1 tin apricots, 1 dessertspoon gelatine, 2 ozs. castor sugar, 2 eggs, 1 cup milk.

Make a boiled custard with milk, sugar and egg yolk. Cool. Sieve apricots and add to custard. Heat ½ cup syrup of the fruit and in this dissolve the gelatine. Whip egg whites stiff and mix all together. Cool to the point of setting, whip, mould and chill. *E.R.*

COLD PUDDING

2 cups water, 2 tablespoons maizena, 1 cup sugar, juice of 1 lemon, whites of 2 eggs, fruit.

Boil water, sugar and slaked maizena well with lemon juice. Add either 4 grenadillas or 1 grated pineapple, and lastly the whites of eggs well beaten. Use yolks for custard sauce to serve. *Mrs. R. W. Carlisle.*

JELLY PUDDING

Dissolve ½ flavoured jelly in ½ cup boiling water. Make custard with 2 egg yolks and ½ cup milk. When cool add to jelly. When starting to set, fold stiffly beaten egg whites in. Set in frig. Delicious served with cream. *Mrs. G. Poole.*

MUSHROOMS IN THE FIELD

1 packet green jelly, 6 round, smooth meringues, 3 bananas, ¼ pint cream, 1 tablespoon icing sugar, 1 tablespoon cocoa.

Prepare jelly in the usual way and pour ¼ of it into a shallow dish. When nearly set stand half bananas upright in it. Whip cream and sweeten and spread on underside of meringues. Mark with a fork and dust with cocoa. Set meringues on banana stalks to form mushrooms. Chop remaining jelly and sprinkle between them. *E.R.*

NOUGAT CREAM

1 packet lemon jelly, ¾ pint hot water, ¼ pint cream, 2 tablespoons castor sugar, ¾ oz. blanched almonds, ½ oz. ratafia biscuits, 8 marshmallows, 6 ozs. glacé cherries.

Cut up marshmallows, cherries, nuts and ratafias.
When jelly is beginning to set, whisk until frothy, stir in prepared ingredients, then whipped cream and sugar.
Whisk slightly and pour into mould. Place in refrigerator to set, and serve with cream. *A. Friend, Johannesburg.*

ORANGE CUSTARD

1 or 2 eggs, 1 large ripe orange, 1 breakfast cup water, 1 heaped teaspoon butter, 1 heaped tablespoon sugar, 1 dessertspoon cornflour.

Place the water, sugar and butter in a saucepan with the grated rind of the orange. Bring to the boil and thicken with the cornflour. When the mixture is cooked, beat in the yolks only of the eggs and cook for 1 minute.

Remove from stove and whip in the juice of the orange and more sugar if orange is not sweet. Whip the whites of the eggs separately and either fold in or place on top of the mixture and brown in oven very quickly.
Mrs. C. Sayce, Johannesburg.

EGG JELLY

Make a lemon jelly, use less water when making. Beat up 1 egg with cup of milk and sugar. Just bring to boil and mix with jelly already made. Put in frig. to set.
M. Grove.

JELLY SNOW

2½ cups milk (put on to boil), add 1 tablespoonful of custard powder, 2 yolks of eggs, small teaspoon butter, 1 tablespoon sugar and pinch of salt.

Make above into custard and cool.

Beat up whites of egg and slowly add ½ packet jelly. Beat stiff, pile in heaps on custard pudding.

ORANGE PUDDING

1 tablespoon rounded with gelatine to be dissolved in 1 cup hot water. Beat yolks of 4 eggs with 1 lb. sugar, add juice of 4 large oranges. Add dissolved gelatine, stir well. Add stiff beaten whites of eggs. Set. Serve with custard or cream.

PAWPAW AND PASSION FRUIT MOULD

3 dessertspoons gelatine, ½ cup hot water, 2 cups diced pawpaw, 2 cups passion fruit (Granadilla), 1½ cups cold water, 1 teaspoon grated lemon rind, ¼ cup sugar.

Dissolve gelatine in hot water: bring sugar, lemon rind and cold water to the boil: strain and stir in the gelatine. Cool mixture until it thickens, then fold in the pawpaw and granadilla. Turn into mould and chill. Serve with cream or custard.

CARAMEL BANANAS

2 eggs, 1 pint of milk, 1 dessertspoon castor sugar, 2 ozs. lump sugar, ½ gill water, 3 or 4 bananas.

Put the lump sugar and water into a saucepan. Cook slowly until syrup is a golden brown. Allow to cool, then add milk and stir over low heat to dissolve caramel. Beat up eggs and put in double cooker with caramel milk, stirring until custard thickens.

Remove at once from the hot water and add sugar. Allow to cool, then pour mixture into custard glasses, filling about two-thirds full. Fill glasses up with slices of bananas and decorate with whipped cream and slice of banana on top.

Sufficient for six persons.
Mrs. J. S. F.

CREAM RICE

3 ozs. rice, 1 pint milk, ½ pint of cream, 1 tablespoon castor sugar, 2 tablespoons of sherry, glacé cherries.

Simmer the rice in the milk until tender, drain well and allow to cool. Whip the cream stiffly, stir in the rice, add the sherry, and sugar, and serve in individual glasses decorated with glacé cherries. Mrs. J. S. F.

PEAR CREAM

Small tin of pears (pint size), 2 ozs. butter, 1½ ozs. flour, milk, 2 dessertspoons castor sugar, 2 yolks of eggs.

Strain the syrup off the pears and make it up to 1 pint with milk. Save a few pears for the top and cut the remainder into small portions. Melt the butter, add the flour and when blended stir in the pear juice and milk. Cook gently for a few minutes and when cool add the sugar and beaten yolks of eggs.

Put the cut pears into a buttered pyrex dish and pour custard over. Bake in oven for about 20 minutes in a pan with a little water to prevent custard from boiling. Serve cold with remainder of pears arranged on top of custard.
Mrs. J. S. F.

CHOCOLATE MOUSSE

Into a double pan break a ½ lb. slab of plain chocolate, stir over gentle heat and allow contents to become liquid and smooth, stirring occasionally. Don't put lid on pan. Remove chocolate from heat and stir in the yolks of 6 eggs, beat whites very stiff and fold into chocolate mixture, pour into individual glasses and set aside to cool, decorate with whipped cream.
Miss Jackson.

PINEAPPLE MOULD

Grate 2 pineapples. Add ½ cup of sugar, 2 cups of water and boil for about 15 minutes.

Dilute 1 packet of pineapple jelly in a cup of boiling water; add to pineapple, mix together and allow to cool. When on point of setting, stir in lightly the stiffly beaten whites of 2 eggs. Serve with thin custard made from 2 egg yolks.
Mrs. S. Warne, Kopjes.

APPLE MOULDS

1 lb. cooking apples, ½ gill water, 2 ozs. sugar, 2 ozs. glacé cherries, rind of ½ a lemon, 1 egg, 1 oz. butter, ¼ oz. gelatine, 2 tablespoons water.

Cook the apples in ½ gill of water and the sugar until tender, then rub through sieve. Add the butter, beaten egg and grated lemon rind to the puree and stir over low heat but do not allow to boil. Add the gelatine dissolved in 2 tablespoons of water, and 1 oz. of the cherries cut up into small pieces.

Pour into custard cups. When set decorate with remainder of cherries and serve with cream. Sufficient for four persons. *Mrs. J. S. F.*

VANILLA CREAM

½ oz. gelatine, ½ pint cream, 3 eggs, 2 tablespoons water, pinch salt, ½ pint milk, 2 ozs. sugar, ½ teaspoon vanilla essence.

Dissolve gelatine in water. Make a custard of milk, egg yolks and sugar. Cook gently until it thickens. Add gelatine and mix well. When custard is on point of setting add it to the half-whipped cream and stiffly beaten egg whites. Mould and chill. To vary add 2 ozs. grated chocolate. *Mrs. Blake.*

BANANA SPONGE

2 ozs. sugar, ¾ oz. gelatine, 2 egg whites, 2 large lemons, 6 bananas.

Rub 3 bananas through a sieve and add sugar and lemon juice. Dissolve gelatine in ½ pint of cold water and add to banana puree. Stir in stiffly beaten egg whites and whisk all together till frothy and solid. Pour mixture in a mould to set, and decorate with glacé cherries and sliced bananas.

This quantity is sufficient for three or four persons. *Mrs. J.S.F.*

GOLDEN CREAM PUDDING

3 eggs, 4 ozs. sugar, ¾ oz. gelatine, 1½ pints of milk, pinch of salt, 1 teaspoon vanilla essence, ¼ wineglassful of white wine.

Dissolve gelatine slowly in milk, then add sugar and yolks of eggs well beaten. Stir over fire for 10 minutes but do not allow to boil. When cool add vanilla, salt and the wine, and stir in the stiffly beaten whites of eggs. Whisk all together and pour into wet mould to set.

Mrs. J. S. F.

COLD DATE PUDDING

Boil 1 lb. of stoned dates with 1 tablespoon of sugar and 3 cups of water for about ¼ hour. Stir thoroughly and then pass through strainer to make puree.

Dilute 1 packet of red jelly in 1 cup of water; add to date puree and mix together. When on point of setting whip in lightly the stiffly beaten whites of 3 eggs. Pour into mould and set.

A thin custard may be made with the yolks of eggs to serve with pudding.   *Mrs. S. Warne, Kopjes.*

COLD CHOCOLATE PUDDING

4 eggs, 4 ozs. castor sugar, 1/4 oz. gelatine (1 level dessertspoon), 1 gill milk, 1 gill water, 1/4 lb. plain chocolate, vanilla.

Dissolve the gelatine in water and chocolate in milk. Beat yolks and sugar slightly — add chocolate gradually and gelatine, then stir in stiffly beaten egg whites and vanilla flavouring. Half of this quantity makes five individual glasses.   *Mrs. R. Cruickshank, Johannesburg.*

BANANA DELICIOUS

Slice some ripe bananas thinly. Sprinkle well with castor sugar. Arrange in individual pudding dishes or glasses. Place a tablespoonful of clear honey over the bananas in each glass. On top of this put a large spoonful of whipped cream flavoured with vanilla, but left unsweetened. Sprinkle the top with chopped walnuts or almonds. For variation, pour a little sherry over the bananas for extra flavour.

                                                    Mrs. Beyers (M. J. Davidtsz).

CHOCOLATE PUDDING

4 tablespoons (rounded) flour, 2 tablespoons butter, 2 cups milk, 1 tablespoon cocoa, 5 tablespoons sugar, 2 eggs, 1 teaspoon vanilla, pinch salt.

Melt butter in a saucepan, stir in the flour, then gradually add milk, then sugar. Stir until thick and smooth. Allow to cook in double boiler gently for 5 minutes. Then add beaten egg yolk and stir until egg is sufficiently cooked (do not boil). Remove from fire and add salt, vanilla, cocoa and egg whites (stiffly beaten). Pour into mould and when set decorate with blanched almonds and cream.   *Mrs. Reeler.*

CREAM ORANGE

1 pint milk, 4 ozs. sugar, 1 oz. gelatine, 3 eggs, rind of 2 oranges, juice of 1 lemon.

Make custard of eggs, milk and sugar. Stir till it thickens. Dissolve gelatine in a little warm water; add orange and lemon. Stir into custard. Pour into buttered mould and set on ice.

APPLE SAGO

6 cooking apples, 1/2 cup sago, 3/4 cup sugar, rind and juice of 1 lemon. Make a puree with the apples; sugar and lemon. Soak

sago for 2 hours in water. When swollen add to puree, turn into a double boiler and cook till clear. Top with cream and serve with custard.
J.H.

APPLE CUSTARD

Put remains of apple sago into pyrex dish. Make a custard of 1 egg, 1 cup milk, 1 tablespoon sugar, pour over apple sago, dust with cinnamon, nutmeg or cocoanut and bake in very slow oven for 1 hour. Serve with cream.
J.H.

ORANGE SAGO

Follow directions for apple sago, but instead of apples use 1 pint pure orange juice. Serve with custard and top with ratafias. Almost any fruit puree can be used.
J.H.

CREAM GINGER (A Quickly Made Sweet)

Whip cream and crumb some ginger nuts. Put in layers in glasses. Finish with cream and top with nuts and cherries.
Mrs. W. Hamilton.

TRIFLE

6 small spongecakes, 12 maccaroons, 24 ratafias, 2 ozs. almonds, raspberry jam, rich custard, green and red jellies, whipped cream.

Cut sponge cakes in slices and spread with jam. Place in a deep dish with the maccaroons and ratafias and soak with sherry. Pour the custard over and chill. Have the jellies made and set, chop and place on top of custard and decorate with almonds (blanched) and button ratafias. Serve with cream.
J.H.

HONEYCOMB CREAM

Make a boiled custard of the yolks of 3 eggs, 2 cups milk, 3 level tablespoons sugar, add 2 teaspoons gelatine and 1 teaspoon vanilla. Just before it sets whip in the stiffly beaten whites of eggs and put into refrigerator to set. Serve with custard.

Custard. — 2 cups milk, 2 tablespoons sugar, yolks of 2 eggs, 1 teaspoon vanilla essence. Heat milk and sugar and pour on to beaten yolks. Heat again and add essence.

For the Children. — 1 packet jelly, ½ pint boiling water, ½ pint orange juice, whites of 2 eggs. Melt the jelly in the boiling water and orange juice. Whip up whites of eggs very stiffly and, when jelly is beginning to set, beat the whites into it and chill. Serve with above custard.
Mrs. D. Hawke.

PEACH PARFAIT

½ cup sugar boiled with ¼ cup orange juice and 2 tablespoons water until it spins a thread.

Whisk the whites of 2 eggs stiffly. Add the orange juice slowly and then ¼ pint whipped cream and lastly ½ cup mashed peaches either fresh or canned. Freeze and decorate with sliced peaches. *Mrs. B. Mills.*

BANANA PUDDING

5 bananas, 1 cup orange juice, 2 egg whites, 2 tablespoons lemon juice, 1 dessertspoon gelatine, ½ cup sugar.

Stew bananas sugar, orange juice and lemon juice, till bananas are "pappy,", add gelatine, stir until gelatine is dissolved, put in dish when ready — add 2 stiff whipped egg whites. *Mrs. T. Reinicke.*

STRAWBERRY TRIFLE

⅓ cup sugar, 2 cups sliced strawberries, cream, 1 packet strawberry jelly, 2¼ cups hot water.

Sprinkle sugar over strawberries and allow to stand 30 minutes. Dissolve jelly in hot water; chill until syrupy, fold in strawberries. Chill until thickened. Pile in sherbert glasses. Serve with cream.

Mrs. Harrison.

BANANA WHIP

6 ripe bananas, 2 tablespoons lemon juice, 3 tablespoons sugar, whites of 2 eggs or ½ cup cream, ½ cup chopped nuts or cherries.

Mash bananas, mix with lemon juice, sugar and nuts (or cherries). Beat cream (or egg whites) stiffly and fold into mixture. Serve in individual glasses. *Mrs. D. K. Lawrie.*

CHOCOLATE MOULD

1 pint milk, ¼ lb. plain slab chocolate, ¼ cup sugar, ¼ teaspoon salt, 1 tablespoon granulated gelatine (soaked in 2 tablespoons cold water until dissolved), 1 egg white may be added.

Scald milk with chocolate and beat until smooth. Add sugar, salt and soaked gelatine, beat well and mould. If egg white is to be added, chill until mixture begins to thicken, then beat until smooth and fold in stiffly beaten white of egg before moulding. Make custard with yolk of egg. *Mrs. D. Hawke.*

PRUNE SOUFFLE

Soak ½ lb. prunes overnight. Cook till soft with very little water, add ¼ lb. brown sugar.

Remove stones and press prunes through sieve, add the beaten whites of 2 eggs and pour into buttered pyrex dish. Cook in fairly hot oven for 30 minutes.

CHILLED PEARS (With Hot Chocolate Sauce)

Drain a tin of pears, chop the pears up and mix with 1 cup chopped, preserved ginger or chopped cherries, add the juice from the pears, mix well together. Line a glass dish with a layer of sponge fingers or tennis biscuits, moisten slightly with sherry, cover with a layer of the pear mixture and juice, put in more biscuits and more of the pear mixture until the dish is full. (Finish with a layer of fruit). Chill thoroughly. Serve with the following sauce: —

Chocolate Sauce. — 1 cup milk, 2 ozs. plain milk chocolate grated, 1 teaspoon cornflour, 2 teaspoons castor sugar, vanilla essence.

Mix the cornflour and sugar to a paste with a little of the milk, heat the rest of the milk with the chocolate, stirring until it is dissolved, pour on to the cornflour mixture, return to the saucepan and stir until it has cooked 3 to 4 minutes. Cool slightly. Add the vanilla and serve hot with the chilled pears, or with ice cream.

GELATINE MOULD

BASIC RECIPE FOR FRUIT JELLIES
(Mrs. Slade)

The following recipe for lemon jelly can be used as a base for fruit moulds and fruit jellies of all kinds: —

1½ cups water, ¼ cup lemon juice, thinly peeled rind of lemon, 1 cup sugar, ¼ cup sherry, ¼-inch stick cinnamon, 2 or three cloves, 1 tablespoon gelatine.

Put all ingredients in a saucepan over the fire, excepting the sherry and gelatine, and bring to the boil, then add gelatine and stir until dissolved. Remove from fire, then strain through a wire sieve lined with a piece of muslin. Lastly add the sherry.

LEMON SPONGE

Put 2 cups plain lemon jelly in cool place. Just as it begins to thicken, beat with an egg whisk until white and frothy, then add the stiffly beaten whites of 2 eggs. Beat until nice and smooth, pour into wet mould and leave until set.

LEMON CREAM

Prepare the same way as lemon sponge, substituting 1 cup half-whipped cream for egg whites.

FRUIT CREAMS

Stewed dried fruits, soft fresh fruits, or canned fruits may be used. Rub through a coarse sieve. Dissolve 2 tablespoons gelatine in 4 tablespoons boiling water, then stir in 2 cups fruit pulp. Leave in a cool place and when on point of congealing, fold in 1 cup half-whipped cream or, if liked, the stiffly beaten whites of 2 eggs may be substituted for the cream, or half and half.

MACEDOINE OF FRUIT

Make a wine or lemon jelly, fill a mould to the depth of ¼ inch with this, allow it to become firm, then lay sliced bananas, diced pineapple (cooked), sliced oranges, etc., in alternate layers until mould is full, then pour in jelly to come to the top of the mould. Leave in a cold place until set. Turn out and garnish with whipped cream.

JELLY SUNDAES

Take plain lemon jelly and when on point of setting add any kind of fruit, such as strawberries, grapes, pineapples, cherries, etc., and half fill custard glasses. Take some more lemon or orange jelly, colour yellow or red, and pour half of the mixture into a wet square pan until set, then turn on to a wet board and chop. The other half should be poured into a basin and when on point of setting whipped to a light froth. Fill up glasses, some with whipped and some with chopped jelly. Decorate with cherries and chopped nuts.

JELLY TRIFLE

Spread slices of sponge cake with jam or mashed stewed apples or bananas, arrange in a dish, and pour a little sherry over. Next pour over some plain jelly and leave till firm. Decorate top with jelly sponge and chopped jelly, glacé cherries and whipped cream.

CUSTARD FRUIT CREAMS OR FRUIT FOOLS
CUSTARD BASE

3 cups milk, ½ cup sugar, 4 eggs, 1½ teaspoons vanilla, pinch of salt, 1½ tablespoons gelatine.

Warm milk, beat eggs slightly and pour milk over, add sugar and cook over gentle heat or in double boiler till thick. Remove from fire, add vanilla essence and salt, and leave to cool down a little, then add gelatine dissolved in 3 tablespoons boiling water.

VANILLA CREAM

Take 2 cups plain custard base and when on point of setting, fold in 1 cup half-whipped cream. If liked, ½ cup cream may be used and the stiffly beaten whites of 2 eggs. Pour into a wet mould lined with ¼ inch plain lemon jelly, and garnished with cherries, angelica, etc.

CHARLOTTE RUSSE

Line a mould with ¼-inch plain lemon jelly and garnish attractively. Set the decorations with little plain jelly, then line sides of mould with lady fingers. Fill the mould with vanilla cream.

CHOCOLATE CREAM

To 2 cups plain custard base add 2 tablespoons cocoa dissolved in 2 tablespoons boiling water. When on point of setting, add ½ cup whipped cream. Garnish bottom of mould with slices of bananas.

CUSTARD FRUIT CREAMS

To 1 cup plain custard base add 1 cup fruit puree using fresh fruits, canned fruits or dried, stewed fruits pressed through a coarse sieve. When on point of setting, add ½ cup half-whipped cream or, if liked, the stiffly beaten whites of 2 eggs may be substituted for the cream.

DATE CREAM

Prepare the same was as Custard Fruit Cream, using stewed dates.

AMERICAN OR HONEYCOMB CREAM

Prepare a custard as for Custard Base, add the gelatine and allow to come to the boil. As soon as it comes to the boil and the mixture has curdled, remove from the fire, allow to cool slightly, then pour on to the stiffly beaten whites of eggs, allowing 2 egg whites to 2 cups custard. When cold, there will be a clear layer on top.

SWISS ROLL MOULD

Take a round cake tin and line with a layer of plain jelly and when set garnish with slices of Swiss Roll. Take 2 cups custard base and when on the point of setting pour on to stiffly beaten whites of 2 eggs, then pour into mould and leave until set.

GRENADILLA MOULD

To 2 cups custard base add 1 cup grenadilla pulp, When on point of setting, add ½ cup whipped cream and stiffly beaten whites of 2 eggs.

COFFEE CREAM

2 cups milk, 3 tablespoons coffee, 3 eggs, ½ cup sugar, pinch salt, 2 level dessertspoons gelatine, ¼ cup water, 1 cup cream, vanilla essence, 1 cup chopped nuts.

Heat 1 cup milk, add the coffee and let it boil 5 minutes, then strain through butter muslin. Put the strained coffee into a saucepan with the rest of the milk. Stand over hot water. Beat the egg yolks with the sugar and pour the hot mixture on to it, return to the saucepan and stir over the heat until it coats the back of a spoon, turn into a basin, stand over ice cubes until cold. Mix the gelatine with the cold water and dissolve over hot water, then add to the other mixture, which should not be too cold. Stir until it commences to thicken, fold in the whipped cream, chopped nuts, vanilla and lastly the stiffly beaten egg whites, which should be beaten with a pinch of salt. Turn into a rinsed mould and chill. Serve with chilled, stewed fruit.

APPLE MARSHMALLOW

3 large cooking apples, ¾ cup brown sugar, juice of 1 lemon, 1/3 cup melted butter, 1½ cups crushed gingersnaps, ½ teaspoon cinnamon, 6 marshmallows.

Peel, core, quarter and slice the apples thinly, sprinkle with the lemon juice. Mix the sugar, melted butter, cinnamon and gingersnap crumbs well together. Fill a baking dish with alternate layers of apples and the crumb mixture, cover and bake in a moderate oven of No. 5, or 375° Fahr., for 1 to 1½ hours. About 5 minutes before the pudding is cooked, put the marshmallows over the top and allow them to melt over. Serve hot or cold with custard, whipped cream or ice cream.

PRUNE MOULD

½ lb. prunes, 1 cup milk, 2 eggs, 1 tablespoon sugar, lemon rind, vanilla, 1 level tablespoon gelatine, ¼ cup cold water.

Wash the prunes and if they are hard, cover with water and soak overnight. Next day stew with 1 or 2 tablespoons honey or sugar to taste, the thinly peeled rind of a lemon and the water in which they were soaked. Cool, remove the prunes from the juice and take out the stones, and chop or mince. Remove the lemon rind. Make a custard with the milk, egg yolks and sugar, remove from the stove and cool. Melt the gelatine in ¼ cup water over hot water and add to the cooled custard, add the prunes, 1 cup prune juice and, if liked, ½ cup of chopped nuts. Stir over ice cubes until they commence to thicken, then fold in the stiffly beaten egg whites. Pour into a rinsed mould and chill. Unmould and serve with whipped cream.

PEANUT MOULD

1 cup peanuts, 1 pint milk, 1 cup sugar, 1 cup cream, 2 eggs, 1 teaspoon vanilla, 1 level tablespoon gelatine, ¼ cup cold water.

Roast the peanuts and chop finely. Put ½ cup of sugar into a saucepan and allow to melt slowly until it is a brown syrup, pour in the milk and heat. Beat the egg yolks with the sugar until creamy, pour the hot milk on to it, return to the saucepan and stir over hot water until it coats the back of the spoon. Remove and cool. Melt the gelatine in the cold water over hot water, stir into the custard, stand over ice cubes and stir until it begins to thicken, then fold in the whipped cream, the chopped peanuts and vanilla. Lastly, fold in the stiffly beaten egg whites and pour into a rinsed mould. Chill. Unmould and serve garnished with cherries.

N.B. — This recipe may be made into an excellent ice cream if the gelatine is omitted.

STRAWBERRY ICEBOX CAKE

The cake. Beat 3 eggs with 5 tablespoons castor sugar until creamy, then fold in 4 tablespoons flour sifted with 2 tablespoons cornflour and 1½ teaspoons baking powder. Melt 1½ tablespoons butter in 4 tablespoons hot water and fold into the mixture. Have ready a deep cake tin lined with ungreased paper, pour in the mixture, and bake in a moderate oven of 375° Fahr., or No. 5, for 40 to 50 minutes. Turn on to a wire sieve and leave until cold. Then split into 3 or 4 layers.

Melt 1 packet of strawberry jelly in 1 cup boiling water and when dissolved, stir in 1 cup cold water or orange juice. Cool over ice until it commences to thicken, then stir in 1 cup mashed and sweetened strawberries. Line a deep cake tin with waxed paper, put the top layer of the cake in face downwards, cover with a thick layer of the almost set jelly, a layer of cake, more jelly, and continue until the cake is used up, finishing with the bottom layer of the cake. Leave to chill. Turn out on to a serving dish, remove the paper. Whip 1 cup of cream until stiff, flavour with vanilla and castor sugar, spread some of the cream on top of the cake, and use the rest in a bag with fancy tube to decorate the top, finish with strawberries and green cherries. Chill before serving.

GOOSEBERRY DE LUXE

1 deep sponge cake, 3 egg whites, 8 ozs. sugar, ½ cup water, 3 to 4 cups gooseberries, 1 oz. blanched and shredded almonds, whipped cream.

Wash the gooseberries and put into a saucepan without water, pressing some of the gooseberries with a wooden spoon to extract their juice. Mix the sugar with the water, stir over a gentle heat until dissolved, then boil together until thick; rub the cooked gooseberries through a sieve. Beat the whites of the eggs until very stiff, pour the mixed gooseberry pulp and syrup on to the egg whites and beat until frothy. Cut the top of the cake off, hollow it out so that a shell remains, moisten the inside with sherry, heap the gooseberry mixture into the centre decorate with whipped cream, the almonds and cherries. Chill and serve.

BAKED CHEESE CUSTARD

2 cup milk, 1 cup grated Cheddar cheese, ½ teaspoon salt, 2 eggs slightly beaten, 1 tablespoon melted butter, few gratings nutmeg.

Bring milk to the boil, then gradually pour on to the slightly beaten eggs. Add seasoning, melted butter and grated cheese, then pour into a buttered baking dish. Sprinkle a few gratings nutmeg on top, stand in a pan of hot water, then bake in a moderate oven of 350° for 50 minutes or until set.

APPLE CUSTARD PUDDING

2 cups stewed apple puree, 1 cup stale cake crumbs, 1 cup milk, 2 eggs, 2 tablespoons sugar, ¼ teaspoon lemon essence, 1 tablespoon butter.

Put stewed apple puree into a greased piedish, sprinkle cake crumbs on top, then pour custard over prepared in the same way as Baked Cup Custards. Put little dabs of butter on top and bake in a moderate oven to a nice golden brown.

BOILED CUSTARD

2 cups milk, 2 eggs, $1/8$ teaspoon salt, 2 tablespoons sugar, ½ teaspoon vanilla essence.

Beat eggs, sugar and salt for a few seconds, then gradually pour on the milk brought to boiling point. Return to the saucepan and stir over boiling water until the mixture thickens and coats a wooden spoon, stirring constantly. Remove from the fire and add the flavouring.

SILVER AND GOLD CUSTARD
SILVER CUSTARD

4 egg whites, 1 pint milk, 4 tablespoons sugar, ½ teaspoon almond essence, ½ teaspoon vanilla essence, few grains of salt.

GOLD CUSTARD

4 egg yolks, 1 pint milk, 2 tablespoons sugar, ½ teaspoon vanilla essence.

Prepare the Silver Custard by beating the egg whites together with sugar and a teaspoon of milk (the milk is necessary to make the mixture smooth). Beat slightly until well blended, add salt and essences, then strain into small greased tinbale moulds. Set in a pan of hot water and cook in a slow oven until firm. Turn out and serve with gold custard poured around and prepared in the same way as Boiled Custard.

PAWPAW CUSTARD DE LUXE

1 pint milk, 2 tablespoons cornflour, 3 eggs, ⅛ teaspoon salt, ½ cup thick cream, ½ cup sugar, 1 cup pawpaw puree, 1 tablespoon lemon juice, ¼ teaspoon ground ginger.

Prepare a custard with the milk, cornflour, eggs and sugar and leave to cool, then add pawpaw puree passed through a sieve, and season with lemon juice and ginger. Lastly, fold in the cream whipped until thick but not stiff. Serve in longstemmed glasses and garnish with a little whipped cream, glacé cherries and angelica.

FRUIT CUSTARD FOAM

1 pint milk, 2 tablespoons cornflour, 3 eggs, ½ cup sugar, 1 cup stewed, dried or fresh fruit puree, ½ teaspoon salt.

Mix together sugar, cornflour, salt and beaten egg yolks, then gradually pour on boiling milk. Return to saucepan over the fire and stir until thick and smooth. Allow to cook 3 to 5 minutes, then remove from the fire and mix with the stewed fruit passed through a sieve. Lastly, fold in the stiffly beaten whites of the eggs. Continue beating until well blended. Serve in tall glasses and garnish with a cherry.

QUAKING CUSTARD

1 pint milk, 2 tablespoons cornflour, 3 eggs, ½ cup sugar, 1 tablespoon powdered gelatine, ½ teaspoon vanilla essence, ⅛ teaspoon salt.

Prepare a custard from the milk, cornflour, eggs and sugar and leave to cool, then add powdered gelatine dissolved in ¼ cup of boiling water. Pour into individual moulds and leave until set, then turn out and surround with strawberry sauce, prepared with strawberry jam thinned down with a little boiling water, then strained through a sieve. If liked, the custard may be poured into a large mould, lined with jelly in the bottom.

CHOCOLATE CUSTARD

1 pint milk, 3 eggs, ¼ cup sugar, 1 square chocolate or 2 tablespoons cocoa, ½ teaspoon vanilla essence, 1/8 teaspoon salt.

Add chocolate to the milk or the cocoa dissolved in a little hot water, and bring to the boil, then pour on to the well beaten eggs and sugar. Return to saucepan over the fire and cook over boiling water until thick. Allow to cool, then add vanilla essence.

COFFEE CUSTARD

Prepare in the same way as Chocolate Custard, adding strong coffee instead of chocolate or cocoa.

MOCK BUTTERSCOTCH CUSTARD

1 cup yellow sugar, 6 tablespoons flour, 1/8 teaspoon salt, 3 cups milk, 3 eggs, ½ teaspoon vanilla essence.

Mix sugar thoroughly with beaten egg yolks, then gradually pour on the milk brought to boiling point. Return to the saucepan over the fire and stir until thick and smooth, then continue to boil for 5 to 10 minutes. Add to the beaten yolks of eggs and cook 2 minutes longer, stirring constantly. Remove from the fire and fold in the stiffly beaten whites of eggs. Lastly add salt and vanilla essence.

COCOANUT CUSTARD PIE

1 pint milk, 3 eggs, 4 tablespoons sugar, ½ teaspoon vanilla essence, pinch of salt, grated nutmeg, short pastry crust.

Make custard in the same way as Baked Cup Custards, then strain into a pie plate lined with short pastry, first sprinkling the cocoanut over the crust before filling it with custard. Grate nutmeg on top and put the pie into a hot oven of 400° F. to cook the crust quickly, then reduce the heat after 10 minutes and leave until custard is set.

VARIATIONS OF BAKED CUSTARD
BAKED HONEY CUSTARD

Instead of sugar, sweeten with honey, and substitute cinnamon for nutmeg.

CHOCOLATE CUSTARD

Add 2 squares of chocolate to milk, heat until melted, then pour on to beaten eggs.

CARAMEL CUSTARD

Add 2 tablespoons caramel to milk. (To prepare caramel, put 2 tablespoons sugar into a frying pan over the fire and leave until a dark amber colour, then gradually add 2 tablespoons boiling water and stir until dissolved).

CREME BRULEE

1 cup cream, 1 cup milk, ¼ teaspoon vanilla essence, 1 cup caramellised sugar, 4 level tablespoons sugar, 6 egg yolks, pinch of salt.

Put cream, milk, sugar and salt into a saucepan and bring to the boil, then gradually pour on to the beaten yolks of eggs. Add vanilla flavouring, then pour into a buttered piedish. Stand in a pan of hot water and bake in a slow oven until firm. Leave in a cool place until cold, and, if possible, put into a refrigerator to get ice cold. Just before serving, prepare the caramellised sugar as follows: — Melt 1 cup castor sugar in a frying pan over a slow fire, and when light brown pour evenly on top of cold custard, when it will set immediately. When serving, tap lightly with the back of spoon in order to crack the transparent film of caramellised sugar.

COOL CUSTARD FOR WARM DAYS

Generally speaking, custards may be divided into three classes. The simplest is the baked or steamed custard, which is mixed and strained into cups, a pudding dish or a pie plate lined with crust, and baked in a moderate oven.

Another type is the "boiled" custard, which, however, should never be allowed to reach boiling point, otherwise it will curdle.

A third type of custard, although it is not a proper custard in the true sense of the word, is one in which less egg is used and a little starchy material in the form of cornflour or flour substitute as part of the thickening.

The usual proportions for a baked custard are: 3 eggs to a pint of milk; and for a boiled custard, 2 eggs together with a sweetening of sugar and a little flavouring. Variations are made to produce different effects.

BAKED CUP CUSTARDS

1 pint milk, 3 eggs, pinch of salt, few gratings nutmeg, 4 tablespoons sugar.

Beat eggs, sugar and salt for a few seconds, then pour on the milk brought to the boil. Strain into buttered cups, grate a little nutmeg on top, then stand the cups in a pan of hot water. Cook 20 to 30 minutes in a moderate oven until set and a nice golden brown on top. If liked, a little vanilla essence may be used for flavouring, and instead of pouring into cups, a small baking dish may be used.

ICES
CUSTARD FOUNDATIONS FOR ICE CREAM
1. FRESH MILK

Warm 1 pint milk, but do not boil. Beat 2 eggs well and pour on the hot milk, add sugar. Pour mixture into a double saucepan and stir until it thickens but do not boil.

Use any flavouring desired and add cream to this custard before it freezes.

2. CONDENSED MILK

1 pint water, 1 tin condensed milk, 3 dessertspoons cornflour, 2 eggs.

Heat water and condensed milk. Mix cornflour with a little cold water and stir into milk. Continue stirring until it boils, cool and add the well beaten eggs. Cook again for 1 or 2 minutes, then flavour and freeze. Add cream.

CARAMEL ICE CREAM

1 pint custard No. 1, 2 tablespoons cream, 2 ozs. loaf sugar.

Boil sugar with a little water until it becomes brown. Stir this into the cream, heat gently and continue to stir until it boils, then add to the custard. Mix and freeze.

CHOCOLATE ICE CREAM

1 pint custard, No. 1, 4 ozs. chocolate, ½ teacup milk, ¼ lb. castor sugar.

Prepare custard and allow to cool. Grate chocolate and stir into milk, add the sugar. Mix well and add custard. Freeze.

Coffee Ice Cream. — As above, using coffee essence and hot water in place of chocolate and milk.

PEACH CREAM SUNDAE

Vanilla ice cream, peaches, whipped cream.

Put some vanilla ice cream into a long glass, on it lay half a peach and cover with whipped cream.

Pineapple Sundae as above. Top with cherry.

Raspberry. — As above, using bottled raspberries and topping with pistachio nuts.

ICE CREAM (Needs no Cooking)

1 tin condensed milk, 2 tins of fresh milk, 2 eggs, 2 teaspoons vanilla or any essence, 1 tablespoon powdered gelatine dissolved in a small cup of boiling water.

Empty condensed milk into basin, fill up tin twice with fresh milk, break in eggs, add essence, also gelatine already dissolved. Beat all together with beater, put in tray for about one hour or until hard. Take out and beat up again in basin until creamy consistency. Put back to freeze. Refrigerator must be turned on to freeze quickly to get best results.
Mrs. G. Poole.

CUSTARD ICE CREAM

To 1 pint milk which has been brought to the boil, add ¼ lb. sugar, stir well, let this boil up again and add a pinch of salt. Now mix together ¼ pint fresh cream (or 1 small tin Nestle's cream), ½ tablespoon custard powder and 1 egg. Beat very well. Add this to the milk and sugar mixture (which has cooled in the meantime). Now put into double boiler and stir over heat until thick, but do not allow the mixture to boil. Add 1 teaspoon vanilla or almond essence. Allow to cool, pour into trays and freeze — stir up often, so that crystals do not form.
Mrs. J. F. Dick.

DELICIOUS ICE CREAM

½ tin condensed milk, ¼ pint cream, 2 egg whites (beaten dry), vanilla essence.

Mix all together well and freeze. Egg yolks made into custard with 1 cup milk (no sugar) and added to above improves it.
Mrs. A. Stevenson.

FRENCH VANILLA ICE CREAM

2 cups milk, 3 eggs, 1 dessertspoon corn starch, ½ cup sugar, 1 tablespoon cold water, 1 cup cream, ¾ teaspoon vanilla, 1 teaspoon gelatine, pinch of salt.

Scald the milk, add corn starch creamed with a little milk, add sugar. Cook for 10 minutes. Cool slightly. Pour over beaten egg yolks. Add gelatine which has soaked in 1 tablespoon cold water. Chill, add flavouring, whipped cream and stiffly beaten egg whites. Chill in basin on floor of refrigerator; when nearly set, beat well and pour into freezing trays. Freeze quickly.
E.R.

ECONOMICAL ICE CREAM

Scald unopened tin Ideal Milk by standing it in a saucepan of cold water, bring to boil, and continue boiling for about 20 minutes. Cool. Thoroughly chill in refrigerator overnight. Open tin; whip milk (about 10 minutes), add icing sugar and flavouring to taste. Freeze for about 1 hour.

Note. — Several tins may be scalded at a time and stored in refrigerator for immediate use at any time.
E.R.

CONDENSED MILK ICE CREAM

¾ tin condensed milk, 1½ breakfast cups milk, ½ teaspoon vanilla, ½ pint cream, 2 whites of eggs, pinch of salt.

Mix together condensed milk, milk, salt and vanilla. Stir in the whipped cream and stiffly beaten whites of eggs. Freeze for 1 hour, turn into a basin and stir well. Return to freezing trays and continue freezing.

E.R.

MARSHMALLOW ICE CREAM

20 marshmallows, 1 pint of milk, ¼ pint cream, 1 teaspoon vanilla.

Scald the milk and dissolve the mallows in it. Allow to cool, then add the cream lightly beaten with the vanilla. Pour into a tray. Turn out once to stir. Return and finish freezing. *E.R.*

SWEET SAUCES
CUSTARD SAUCE

2 cups hot milk, 2 egg yolks, 2 tablespoons sugar, pinch of salt, ½ teaspoon vanilla.

Beat egg yolks with sugar and salt. Pour hot milk on to this and stir. Put into double boiler and cook, stirring all the time until the mixture thickens. Cool and add vanilla. *M.*

SOFT CUSTARD

2 cups milk, 2 tablespoons (level) custard powder or cornflour, ½ cup sugar, 2 eggs, 1 teaspoon vanilla.

Boil milk and sugar. Blend the powder with a little milk, add to the hot milk, stirring well, and cook for 5 minutes. Cool slightly and pour over beaten egg yolks and return to double boiler till custard thickens. Beat whites of eggs and pour custard over. Add vanilla. *California.*

BRANDY SAUCE. I.

Cream ¼ cup butter and 1 cup castor sugar, add 2 tablespoons brandy, and the well beaten yolks of 2 eggs. When mixed, add ½ cup rich milk, cook in double boiler until thick, then pour on to beaten whites of 2 eggs. *Mrs. Slade.*

BRANDY SAUCE. II.

¼ pint water, 1 wineglass brandy, 2 ozs. sugar, 1 tablespoon (level) custard powder. Mix powder into a smooth paste and add to the boiling water and sugar. Stir in the brandy and serve.

Mrs. Slade.

CHOCOLATE SAUCE

2 cups milk, 1½ tablespoons maizena, 2 squares chocolate, 4 tablespoons castor sugar, 2 tablespoons hot water, 2 eggs, ²/₃ cup powdered sugar, 1 teaspoon vanilla.

Blend the maizena with a little of the milk. Bring remainder of milk to boiling point, add maizena and cook 8 minutes in double boiler. Melt chocolate over hot water, stir until smooth and add to cooked mixture. Beat whites of eggs with powdered sugar, add unbeaten yolks and stir into cooked mixture. Cook 1 minute.

FOAMY SAUCE

½ cup butter, 1 cup castor sugar, 1 egg, vanilla essence. Cream butter and sugar, add well beaten egg and vanilla. No cooking.

Mrs. Murray.

LEMON SAUCE

1 cup sugar, ¼ cup water, 2 teaspoons butter, 1 tablespoon lemon juice.

Make a syrup by boiling sugar and water. Remove from fire and add butter and lemon juice.

Mrs. Slade.

HARD SAUCE

⅓ cup butter, 1 cup castor sugar, ½ teaspoon lemon essence, ½ teaspoon vanilla.

Cream butter and sugar and add flavouring.

CHOCOLATE SAUCE

1 cup milk, 2 ozs. plain milk chocolate grated, 1 teaspoon cornflour, 2 teaspoons castor sugar, vanilla essence.

Mix the cornflour and sugar to a paste with a little of the milk, heat the rest of the milk with the chocolate, stirring until it is dissolved, pour on to the cornflour mixture, return to saucepan and stir until it has cooked 3 to 4 minutes. Cool slightly. Add the vanilla and serve hot with chilled pears or with ice cream.

MRS HUMPHREY'S CHOCOLATE FUDGE SAUCE

1 cup sugar, 2 ozs. plain chocolate, 1 tablespoon butter, 1 tablespoon syrup, ½ cup boiling water, ½ teaspoon vanilla.

Melt chocolate over hot water. Add other ingredients, stirring constantly. Boil for a few minutes over direct heat. Use for ice creams or puddings, hot or cold.

FRUIT SAUCE

1 cup fruit pulp and juice, ½ cup jelly, ½ cup sugar, 1 dessertspoon maizena, 1 tablespoon hot water.

Mix fruit with jelly and sugar. Bring to boiling point and add maizena mixed with water. Stir till mixture clears. Strain and serve.

APRICOT SAUCE

¾ cup apricot pulp, ¾ cup whipped cream. Mix the two together and sweeten to taste.

CARAMEL SAUCE

1 cup sugar, 1 tablespoon cold water, 1½ cups hot water, 1 tablespoon cornflour, 1 tablespoon butter, 1 teaspoon vanilla essence. Put sugar and cold water into pan and stir till syrup is a clear brown, then add hot water very carefully and stir well. Add cornflour mixed with a little cold water and boil 5 minutes. Continue cooking in double boiler for 15 minutes then beat in butter and vanilla.

No thoroughly occupied man was ever yet very miserable.

IRONING

I love to iron my silken things and smooth them out like new — It's quite the most delightful task of all the jobs I do — To change a crumpled heap of stuff into a perfect dress — To watch the creases disappear, as patiently I press. And sometimes as I'm doing this I wish that I could find — A magic iron that would erase the creases from my mind — The sadness and the worry and the marks of human strife — The scars of all the sorrows that we take with us through life — And so I wish that I could smooth my troubles all away — Just clear them from my mind — and make a fresh start every day.   *Patience Strong.*

To the land of the sun,
Frae the land of the heather,
Our food, like our folks,
Go very well together.

SOUTH AFRICAN RECIPES

YELLOW RICE

1 cup rice, 4 cups water, 2 tablespoons sugar, 1 teaspoon salt, 1 tablespoon butter, ½ teaspoon turmeric, ¼ cup raisins.

Wash the rice well. When the water boils rapidly add the other ingredients except the raisins. Boil rapidly when the rice is swollen out and soft, push aside to a cooler part of the stove. Put the washed raisins on top and allow the rice to steam for about an hour.

Mrs. Beyers (M. J. Davidtsz).

TOMATO BREDEE

Cut up about two pounds of the ribs of mutton in pieces large enough for individual servings. Slice a large onion. Melt some soft fat or dripping in a saucepan. Add the onion and stir till the onion is a golden yellow. Add the meat. Cover the saucepan and let the meat and onion cook slowly for about an hour. Slice about eight tomatoes and add to the meat. Also salt and pepper to taste and one teaspoon of sugar. A small piece of red chilli may be added if desired. Stew for another hour. Add some peeled potatoes cut in quarters. Continue cooking till the potatoes are soft.
Serve with boiled rice.

Mrs. Beyers (M. J. Davidtsz).

STRING BEAN BREDEE

Wash the beans. String and slice crosswise very thinly. Put in a saucepan. Barely cover with water. Add ribs of mutton cut into individual servings. Season with pepper and salt. Slice and add one large onion. Cover and stew for about three hours. During the last half hour add some peeled potatoes cut into quarters. Serve with boiled rice.

If desired the onion may first be fried in hot fat as for tomato bredee. Then add the meat, beans and water to cover.

Mrs. Beyers (M. J. Davidtsz).

CABBAGE BREDEE

Fry a large sliced onion in hot fat in a saucepan, till golden in colour. Add mutton ribs cut in small pieces. Then add one head of cabbage shredded, and a little water. Season cover and stew for about three hours, adding some peeled potatoes during the last half an hour of cooking. *Mrs. Beyers (M. J. Davidtsz).*

CABBAGE FRIKKADEL

Use minced leg of mutton. To about two pounds add half an onion finely chopped, one thick slice of bread soaked in milk, pepper, salt, a little chopped parsley, half a grated nutmeg, one or two eggs. Mix well. Form into balls. Heat some fat in saucepan and lay the frikkadels in this. Cover and allow to brown well. Remove from the fire. In the meantime remove the outer leaves of a head of cabbage gently to keep them whole. Pour some boiling water over them. Roll a cabbage leaf round each frikkadel and return to the hot fat in the pot. Fry in the open pot till well browned underneath. Turn and brown the other side. Serve with boiled rice. *Mrs. Beyers (M. J. Davidtsz).*

SOSATIES

Take a leg of mutton. Cut the meat off the bone and cut in about one and a half inch cubes. There must be some fat similarly cut up, either from the mutton or spek. Slice an onion finely. Fry in hot fat till of a golden colour. Put this over the meat which has been placed in a basin.

Mix 2 ozs. of curry powder with half a cup of vinegar. If tamarind is obtainable pour a cup of boiling water over about an ounce of it and let it steep and use this instead of the vinegar. Lemon juice may also be used. Add one heaped tablespoon sugar, season with salt and pepper. Stir in one cup milk. Place a few lemon or orange leaves in between the meat. Pour the curry mixture over it. Cover and leave in a cool place for a day or two. Then use skewers, and skewer the meat, putting pieces of fat in between. Grill over coals or in a griller. They may be pan grilled. Heat the sauce and add 2 tablespoons of butter. Serve with the sosaties which should be accompanied by boiled rice.

Mrs. Beyers (M. J. Davidtsz).

KOEKSISTERS

7 cups flour, ½ cup sugar, ½ cup butter, 2 eggs, 2½ teaspoons baking powder, ½ cup milk, 4 tablespoons cream, 1 teaspoon salt.

Method. Cream the butter. Add the sugar gradually and the eggs well beaten. Sift in the flour with the baking powder and salt, alternately with the milk and cream. Toss on a floured board. Sprinkle lightly with a little flour and roll to about a quarter of an inch thick. Cut in strips about 4 inches long and plait together three bits. Fry in deep fat at 360° F. till a golden brown. Drain on paper to remove surplus fat and then dip in a thick syrup which was previously prepared and allowed to get cold.

SYRUP FOR KOEKSISTERS

3 cups water, 3 cups sugar, ¼ teaspoon cream of tartar. Dissolve the sugar in the water. Bring to the boil. Wash down the crystals at the side of the pot, or put the lid on for three minutes to allow the steam to wash the crystals down. This is to prevent the syrup from becoming sugary. Do not shake the pot when removing it from the fire but handle gently, also to prevent crystals.

Mrs. Beyers (M. J. Davidtsz).

BILTONG

To every 5 lbs. Swartkop salt add ¼ lb. saltpetre and ¼ lb. ground coriander seed, well mixed. Rub into dry meat and shake off surplus. Place in wooden tub, leave for 48 hours if pieces of meat are small and for larger pieces leave further 24 hours. After removing, wash in brine and hang up. To make brine, use 1 lb. salt to 3 gallons water.

Mr. A. B. Marais, Ficksburg.

WHEN GREEN MEALIES ARE TOO OLD TO EAT ON THE COB

By Mrs. H. M. Slade.

GREEN MAIZE DISHES

It often happens that those of us who are dependent on the markets or greengrocers sometimes find ourselves landed with maize much too old and hard for serving on the cob, but if cut off the cobs and put through the mincing machine, it can be used in a variety of delicious ways, as the following recipes will indicate: —

STEAM MAIZE BREAD

3 cups green maize cut from the cobs, 1 teaspoon salt, 1 level tablespoon sugar, 1 level teaspoon baking powder.

Put the maize through the mincing machines, add the other ingredients, mix well, then pour into a well-greased coffee-tin or pudding mould, about three-quarters full. Put into saucepan of boiling water and allow to boil for 1½ hours. Remove from the tin and serve hot or cold, cut into slices and spread with butter. This also makes a nice vegetable served with roast meat.

If liked, the mixture may be made richer by adding an egg, some melted butter, cocoa, preserved fruits, chopped raisins and various spices.

GREEN MAIZE FRITTERS

1 cup green maize, ¼ cup flour, 1 teaspoon baking powder, 1 egg, ½ teaspoon salt, ⅛ teaspoon pepper, few gratings nutmeg, fat for frying.

Cut the maize off the cobs and put through the mincing machine. Mix together with flour, well beaten egg yolk, and seasonings. Lastly fold in the stiffly beaten white of egg. Drop by spoonfuls into smoking hot fat, preferably lard, and fry to a nice golden brown. Drain on paper. Serve as a vegetable, also with fried bacon. If liked, the fritters may be served as a sweet with hot golden syrup or rolled in sugar and cinnamon, but in that case pepper must be omitted.

MAIZE CREAM TOAST

1 cup green maize cut off the cobs, 1 medium onion finely chopped, 1 cup cream, 2 tablespoons butter, 1 hard-boiled egg, ½ teaspoon salt, 1/8 teaspoon pepper, 6 slices buttered toast, parsley.

Put butter into frying pan, add the onion and cook to a golden brown, then add maize (if on the hard side, put through mincing machine), cream, salt and pepper. Allow to simmer gently for 5 minutes, then pour over toast from which the crusts have been removed. Sprinkle on top the finely chopped white of egg and the egg yolk rubbed through a sieve. Garnish with a sprig of parsley.

SCRAMBLED MAIZE TOAST

1 cup green maize cut off the cobs, 1 small onion finely chopped, 2 tablespoons butter, 1 tablespoon flour, 3 or 4 eggs, 6 slices buttered toast, salt, pepper and parsley, 2 cups milk.

Cut the maize off the cobs and put through a mincing machine. Cook the onion in butter to a golden brown, then stir in the flour. Blend well, then gradually add the milk or cream. Cook until thick and smooth, stirring constantly, then add the maize and seasonings and simmer gently for about 5 minutes. Beat eggs slightly, add to the creamed maize and keep on folding over and over until the egg is cooked and the scramble is done. Serve on buttered toast and garnish with a sprig of parsley. If liked a little grated cheese may be added to the scramble.

GREEN MAIZE PUDDING

2 cups green maize cut off the cobs, 2 eggs, 2 tablespoons melted butter, ½ teaspoon salt, few gratings nutmeg, 2 cups boiling milk, 1 small onion finely chopped, 1 teaspoon dried mixed herbs.

Put maize through a mincing machine, then combine with well-beaten eggs and the rest of ingredients. Pour into a buttered piedish and bake in a slow oven of 325° F. until firm and a nice golden brown on top. Serve with roast chicken.

If liked the onion and herbs may be omitted and 4 tablespoons sugar added, then served as a dessert with the following sauce: —

Caramel Sauce. — Put 1 cup sugar into a frying pan over a gentle heat and allow to melt, stirring constantly with the blade of a knife. When of a nice golden brown colour remove from the fire, add 1 cup boiling water gradually, and stir over the fire until a thick syrup has formed. Remove from the fire, add 1 tablespoon butter and stir until melted.

GREEN MAIZE CHEESE CUSTARD AND TOMATO SAUCE

2 cups green maize cut off the cob, 1 cup grated cheese, 1 teaspoon onion juice, 1 cup milk, 3 eggs, 6 ripe tomatoes, 1 bay leaf, 2 slices onion, 2 cloves, salt and pepper.

Cut enough maize off the cobs to make 2 cupfuls, then put through the mincing machine. Beat eggs thoroughly, stir into the maize pulp, together with milk, onion juice, grated cheese and a seasoning of salt and pepper. Pour into well-greased custard cups or timbale moulds, stand them in a pan of hot water and cover with a sheet of greaseproof paper. Put into a moderate oven of 350° F. for 30 minutes, or until firm, then turn out on to a warm dish and pour the following sauce around: —

TOMATO SAUCE

Cut up tomatoes roughly, add onion, bay leaf, cloves and 1 teaspoon sugar. Cook until tender, rub through a sieve. Melt 1 tablespoon butter in a saucepan, blend in 1 tablespoon flour, then gradually add tomato puree. Stir until thick and smooth, add a seasoning of salt and pepper and, if liked, a little grated cheese.

GREEN MAIZE CHOWDER

2 cups green maize cut off the cobs, 1 cup milk, 1 cup green maize stock, 1 chopped onion, 1 large potato, 1 tablespoon butter, 2 tablespoons flour, 1 egg, salt and pepper.

After the maize has been cut off the cobs, take the cobs and place in a saucepan, together with 2 cups water and allow to cook gently for 10 to 15 minutes, then strain off the water and use as stock. Put the maize through a mincing machine and peel and dice the potato. Put a layer of potato in the bottom of saucepan then a sprinkling of finely chopped onion, a little salt and pepper, then a layer of maize. Add the stock, cover the saucepan and allow to simmer gently over a moderate fire for about 30 minutes. Melt the butter in a saucepan, blend in the flour, then gradually add the milk. Stir until thick and smooth, add to the chowder and cook five minutes longer. Remove from the fire and stir in the well-beaten egg.

GREEN MAIZE SOUFFLE

1 cup minced green maize pulp, 1 cup milk, 1 tablespoon butter, 2 tablespoons cornflour, 3 eggs, ½ teaspoon salt, ¼ teaspoon pepper, few gratings nutmeg.

To the minced maize pulp add the milk, salt, pepper and nutmeg and cook over a gentle fire for 10 minutes. Blend butter and cornflour together, then stir into the creamed mixture, together with well-beaten yolks of eggs. Cook until smooth and creamy, remove from the fire, allow to cool slightly, then fold in the stiffly beaten whites of eggs. Pour into a well-buttered souffle dish, stand in a pan of hot water, cover over with a sheet of greaseproof paper and bake in moderate oven of 350° F. for 30 minutes, or until a nice golden brown. Serve immediately.

BOERWORS

3 lbs. mutton, 3 lbs. pork, 3 lbs. beef, 1½ lbs. tail, 1½ lbs. pork fat (fat to be cut in small cubes and added last to mince).

Mince and add seasoning comprising 2 tablespoons vinegar, 2 tablespoons salt, 1 tablespoon pepper, 4 tablespoons ground coriander, 1 dessertspoon ground cloves, 1 tablespoon allspice. Mix seasoning well with mince and fill sausage skins. *A.L.A.*

PAMPOEN MOES

Take a marrow, peel it and slice thinly. Put a layer in an oven dish, cover with a layer of thinly cut white bread spread with butter. Sprinkle over a little sugar, a few pieces of cinnamon and three or four cloves. Repeat the layers until the dish is full. A small glass of wine can be added if liked. Bake in a moderate oven.

Mrs. J. C. Smuts.

KRAKELINGE

6-8 ozs. butter, ¼ lb. sugar, 1 egg, ¾ lb. flour, 1 teaspoon baking powder.

Cream butter and sugar, add beaten egg, then flour and baking powder sifted together. Roll into strips about the thickness of a pencil, form into biscuits the shape of an 8. Brush with egg yolk, dip in sugar and chopped almonds (blanched) and bake in quick oven.

Mrs. J. C. Smuts.

POFFERTJIES

1 lb. flour, 4 to 5 eggs, 1½ pints milk, ¼ lb. sugar, 2 spoons well risen yeast.

Beat eggs, add sugar, yeast, then milk and flour; mix all well and leave to rise for an hour. Drop by spoonfuls into a pot of deep, hot fat. Cook until brown and puffed up. *Mrs. J. C. Smuts.*

SOET KOEKIES

6 lbs. meal (seconds), 2 lbs. lard, 3 lbs. Government sugar, 1 packet mixed spice, 1 teaspoon ground cloves, 1 teaspoon ground ginger, 1 teaspoon ground cinnamon, pinch of salt.

Mix all the above together well. Lastly add 1 packet bi-carbonate soda in about 1 cup hot water. Knead well. Roll out and bake.

Mrs. J. C. Smuts.

SOET KOEKIES

12 cups flour, 1 lb. butter, ½ lb. ground almonds, 5 cups sugar, 1 packet bi-carbonate of soda, 1 teaspoon salt, ½ tumbler port wine, 6 eggs, 1 packet mixed spice.

Rub butter in flour, add sugar, almonds, spice and salt. Beat eggs and add to the mixture, then wine and lastly soda mixed with a little milk.

U.C.

CABBAGE AND FRIKKADEL

Select a firm cabbage, cut out the hard core and all hard parts of leaves to make a nice basket. Tie the leaves to prevent their becoming loose, cut off a small portion at the end so that the basket will stand. Place in salted water while the meat is being prepared.

1½ lbs. minced mutton, 1 slice white bread soaked in milk, salt and pepper to taste, 1 egg, 1 small onion, a grating of nutmeg. Mix make into balls and fill the cabbage with them. Pour over 1 cup of stock and cover with cabbage leaves. Place cabbage basket in saucepan in which 1 onion has been browned, add 1 cup of water and simmer till cabbage is tender. Serve hot with rice.

Mrs. E. Murray.

BOBOTIE

2 lbs. of meat, 2 onions, 1 large slice of white bread, 1 cup of milk, 3 or 4 eggs, 2 tablespoons of curry powder, 1 dessertspoon of sugar, juice of a lemon, or 2 tablespoons of vinegar, lump of butter.

Method. — Mince the meat. Soak the bread in water and squeeze out dry. Fry onions in butter. Mix all the ingredients — curry powder, sugar, salt, vinegar, etc., with the meat and soaked bread. Mix two eggs (or three) with cup of milk and add to meat. Lastly beat one egg with a little milk and pour on top. Put 2 or 3 lemon or bay leaves on top and bake.

Mrs. R. C. Harris.

BOBOTIE

1 lb. of raw or cooked, minced mutton, 2 tablespoons butter. 12 pounded almonds (1 dessertspoon ground almonds), 1 slice white bread, 1 cup milk, juice of 1 lemon, 1 onion, 1 dessertspoon curry powder, 2 eggs, pepper and salt.

Soak bread in a little gravy or water, squeeze dry and add to the minced meat. Chop the onion finely and fry in the butter. Mix the curry powder with the lemon juice. Add the onion, curry powder and almonds to the meat and season to taste. Place the mixture in piedish with here and there a bay or orange leaf. Bake in moderate oven 350°, for about 20 minutes. Then beat up eggs with the milk, add a pinch of salt and pour over the mixture. Bake till custard on top has set. Serve with rice and blatjang. *Mrs. Withiel.*

BLATJANG

1 lb. dried apricots, 1 lb. stoned raisins or sultanas, 2 ozs. pounded and sifted chillies or 1 dessertspoonful cayenne pepper, 2 ozs. ground almonds, 3 or 4 large onions, 1 garlic (minced), ½ lb. salt, 2 teaspoons ground ginger, 2 bottles vinegar.

Soak the apricots overnight and boil until soft. Mince the raisins and parboil onions. Add all the other ingredients and boil to right consistency, stirring continually about half an hour. Must be a nice, smooth paste that will not flow when tested on a plate. *Mrs. Withiel.*

STEWED SWEET POTATOES

Sweet potatoes, yellow sugar, butter, cinnamon sticks or ginger, pinch of salt, little sherry (optional).

Peel and cut the potatoes into small chips. To 1 lb. of potatoes allow 2 ozs. yellow sugar, and 1 tablespoon of butter. Put a layer of sweet potatoes in a saucepan, then sugar, bits of butter and a sprinkling of salt, proceed until all potatoes are used up. Cover with water, put in a stick of cinnamon or one or two pieces of bruised ginger. Stew gently. When potatoes are cooked add a little sherry and thicken the sauce with a little maizeko. *Mrs. Withiel.*

OLD FASHIONED MILK TART

Rich pastry, 1 pint of milk, ¼ teaspoon salt, yolks of 4 eggs, 2 heaped tablespoons flour, 4 tablespoons sugar, ground cinnamon. Almond essence if liked.

Method. — Line 2 plates with rich pastry, set aside to cool. Boil milk, add flour which has been mixed to a smooth paste with a little cold milk, salt and sugar. Cook in double boiler. It should be a smooth, thick cream; when done cool slightly, add beaten egg yolks (or whole beaten eggs). Some like the whites whipped and added to the cream. Fill the lined plate and sprinkle cinnamon on top. Bake in a hot oven, having greater heat at bottom. When pastry is a nice brown remove from oven. If cinnamon is not liked, use a few drops of almond essence.

The secret of a good milk tart lies in using rich pastry and making a filling rich, smooth and thick. If well baked the lower crust should not be soggy. *Mrs. Murray.*

MILK TART

For puff pastry, made out of 1 lb. butter and 1 lb. flour, which will make 6 milk tarts in dinnerplates, 1 give you the following filling: —

6 cups milk, 7 tablespoons flour, 1 tablespoon butter, 1½ cups sugar, 1 teaspoon almond essence, 4 eggs.

Method. — Boil milk. Beat yolks of eggs well, add ¾ cup cold milk; mix flour and sugar and add to egg yolks and milk; stir in boiling milk, then add butter, take off fire and let cool down, put in stiffly beaten whites of eggs and essence. Then it is ready to be put into plates lined with pastry. Do not let filling get too cold before putting in the pastry. Bake in hot oven from 450-500°. If desired, put over some powdered cinnamon. *M. L. Malan.*

QUINCE MEBOS

1½ lb. quinces, 1½ lb. sugar, 2 packets red jelly crystals.

Method. — Peel and grate quinces, put in pot with sugar. Stir all the time, boil 20 minutes. Take off fire, stir in jelly crystals. Pour into wetted tin and leave to set, cut into pieces, roll in sugar and pack in wooden box. *Mrs. R. W. Carlisle.*

She was distinguished for that perfect good breeding which is the result of nature and not education; for it may be found in a cottage and missed in a palace. 'Tis a quiet regard for the feelings of others that springs from absolute absence of selfishness. Lord Beaconsfield.

> So many things that simply must be done —
> The cleaning and the mending,
> The dusting, never ending.
> The cooking and the washing — not much fun.
> So many things to fill the busy day —
> The telephone still ringing,
> The door bell ting-a-linging,
> So little while to come apart and pray.
> And so I stand besided the kitchen sink,
> And washing dishes there,
> Breathe out my little prayer,
> And surely He will hear my prayer, I think.
>
> *D.V.*

BREAD, SCONES AND BUNS

BREAD

To make good bread follow the directions carefully. See that the water is just warm and the bread put in a warm place to rise. Cold will prevent fermentation of yeast and too much heat kills it. Kneading is necessary to make a smooth dough and to distribute the yeast evenly.

WHITE BREAD (Quick Method)

3½ lbs. flour, 1 oz. yeast, 1 teaspoon sugar, 3 teaspoons salt, 1½ pints lukewarm water.

Sift the flour and salt into a bowl, make a well in the centre. Cream the yeast and sugar, stir in about ¾ pint of lukewarm water, pour into the well in the flour, sprinkle dry flour over to cover. Cover with a dry cloth and stand in a warm place for 20 minutes. Then work in all the flour with a knife, adding more warm water to form a dough. Knead 5 to 10 minutes. Cover and stand in a warm place for about 1½ hours, until it doubles its bulk. Turn on to a floured board and knead lightly, then form into loaves and put into greased tins, making them about half full. Stand in a warm place for about 15 minutes or until risen to the top of the tins. Heat the oven to 400° Fahr. or the gas oven for 10 minutes at full, then lower to No. 7. Bake the bread from 45 to 60 minutes in the middle of an electric oven or on upper shelf in the gas oven. When the loaf is browned and rings hollow on top when rapped with the knuckles, turn out and cook upside down until the bottom rings hollow. The electric oven may be switched off for the last 15 minutes.

The Star.

WHITE BREAD (Overnight Rising Method)

3 lbs. flour, 1 tablespoon butter or fat (optional), lukewarm water (about 1 pint), 1 tablespoon salt.

For the Sponge. — 1 cup lukewarm water or potato water, 3 teaspoons sugar, pinch salt, ½ yeast cake.

Stir sufficient flour into potato water to make a soft batter. Add half a yeast cake and sugar and cover and leave in warm place for about half an hour, until fermentation starts. Warm basin flour, add salt and rub in butter or fat if desired. Add sponge and sufficient lukewarm water to make into a fairly stiff dough. Knead well for 10 minutes or longer. Cover and leave in a warm place overnight. Re-knead in the morning. Grease bread tins slightly and leave again to rise until double in bulk. Pre-heat oven to 400-425°. Place bread just below centre, turn top off, leave bottom element on high for 10-15 minutes, then low. Bake for at least one hour, large loaves for 1½ hours.

BROWN BREAD

5 lbs. No. 1 Boer Meal, 1 tablespoon of salt, 1 of sugar, 2 handfuls (large) of bran, 1 square Thistle yeast, 9 cups of water.

This quantity makes two large loaves and 16 small bread buns. That is little bits of dough made round with the hands allowed to rise and baked before the bread while it is rising. Put buns into oven (electric) after they have risen, then turn on oven and when heat reaches 400° they are done and bread can be put in then for one hour without even looking at it.

Method. — Place yeast broken into small pieces in bowl, add sugar and one handful of flour, 1 cup of luke warm water and mix with the hand until yeast is dissolved. Then add rest of water and salt. (Never forget salt). Then flour and bran. With one hand work all together until it is all well worked. Clean sides of bowl and hand with dry flour — the bowl must not be left at all messy. Leave in same bowl overnight and cover with another bowl.

Next morning take out of bowl leaving not a speck behind and put onto well floured board or table. Cut in two, using lots of dry flour all the time. Then take a piece off each and make the buns.

Well grease two loaf tins (gallon paraffin tins cut open) place dough inside and press well down with fist. Prick with fork and let rise in warm place for 1 hour. Then place in oven at 400° heat. Turn top off, leave bottom on low all the time, 1 hour. Sometimes heat varies. If after one hour the bread doesn't seem brown enough turn off heat and leave on oven shelf for a little while longer.

Half of this quantity can be used for small family. *Mrs. S. J. Paxton.*

NUT BREAD

½ cup sugar, 1 egg, 1 cup milk, 2 cups flour, 2 teaspoons baking powder, ½ cup chopped walnuts, little salt.

Cream eggs and sugar, add milk, then flour, baking powder and salt sifted together. Lastly chopped walnuts. Let rise for 20 minutes. Cover with greased paper and bake in moderate oven about ¾ hour.

Mrs. Shaw.

RAISIN BREAD

6 cups flour (1½ lbs. flour), ½ oz. yeast, 1 tablespoon sugar, 1 cup lukewarm water, 1 cup scalded and cooled milk, 4 ozs. butter, ¾ cup sugar, 1 cup stoned and floured raisins, 1 teaspoon salt.

Cream the yeast with the tablespoon sugar and mix with the lukewarm water, add the lukewarm milk and 2 cups of sifted flour. Cream the butter with the ¾ cup of sugar, mix with the yeast, cover and leave in a warm place for 1 hour. Then add the raisins, salt and the rest of the sifted flour to make a soft dough. Knead lightly, put into a greased bowl, cover and leave to double its bulk. Break down, form into two loaves, half filling the greased pans, cover and leave for 20 minutes. Brush over with beaten egg to which 2 teaspoons water have been added. Bake at 400° Fahr. or No. 7 in a gas oven for 40 to 60 minutes.

The Star.

FRIG. BREAD ROLLS

Prepare overnight:

1 lb. flour (4 cups), 1 level teaspoon salt, 1½ cakes yeast, ¼ cup lukewarm water, 1 level tablespoon sugar, 2 ozs. lard or margarine, 1 cup boiling water, 1 egg.

Dissolve yeast in ¼ cup warm water.

Place lard, salt and sugar in bowl and pour over one cup boiling water. When lukewarm add dissolved yeast and beaten egg. Stir in flour to make soft dough. Place in frig., cover with grease-proof paper and plate and chill for 12 hours.

Spoon into greased patty pans, ½ full. Set to rise in warm place for one hour. Brush over with egg and bake in hot oven — good bottom heat — for about 20 minutes. Remove from patty pans at once.

Keep remainder of dough in frig, well covered, and use as required. Will keep at least one week.

DINNER ROLLS

1 lb. flour (4 cups), 1 level teaspoon salt, 1 medium teaspoon baking powder, 1 heaped teaspoon sugar, 1 cake yeast, 1 cup warm milk and water — half each.

Dissolve yeast in sugar and add to warm milk and water.

Mix dry ingredients and add liquid, knead to a smooth dough, place dough in bowl and cover tightly, leave till double in bulk, turn on to floured board and shape into rolls — about two dozen, place on baking tray and allow to rise for at least half an hour, brush over with beaten egg before baking or with melted butter after baking, bake at 400° 20 minutes to half an hour.

BOSTON BREAD

1 cup unsifted boermeal, 1 cup mealie meal, 1 cup flour, 1 teaspoon bicarbonate of soda, ½ teaspoon salt, ½ teaspoon allspice, 1 cup treacle or honey, 1½ cups sour milk, 1 cup fruit or fruit and nuts.

Sift the dry ingredients together, mix in the unsifted boermeal, add the treacle or honey and the milk, add the fruit and mix well. Have ready 2 coffee tins greased with vegetable fat, fill the tins two-thirds full and cover with a piece of greased paper, then the lids. Steam in boiling water for 3½ hours. *The Star.*

FANCY BREAD

Fancy breads are made by the addition of a little fat such as butter or pastrine, etc. Rub this into the flour or melt and mix with liquid. Milk can be used instead of water and an egg added sometimes. One to 2 ozs. of fat to a pound of flour is sufficient. In making sweet bread with fruit and sugar use 2 ozs. of each to 1 lb. of flour. Glaze after cooking and return to oven to dry.

HOT CROSS BUNS (Scotch Fashion)

Salt, 2 lbs. flour, 6 ozs. butter, 1 breakfast cup yeast, 3 eggs, water, ½ lb. sugar, 1 oz. spice, pastry, dry yeast, 2 cakes, may be used.

Rub six ounces of butter into 2 lbs. of flour and break in three eggs. Add one breakfast cup yeast and mix all together with sufficient tepid water to make a thin batter. Cover and stand all night in warm place. Mix next morning with half a pound of sugar and 1 oz. mixed spice. Mix all well together with as much flour as will keep the dough from sticking to the hands. Shape into buns and stand for one hour in warm place. Cut scraps of pastry into narrow strips and place these on the buns in shape of cross. Bake in quick oven and glaze with sugar and water. *Mrs. Mac.*

HOT CROSS BUNS

1 lb. flour, ½ teaspoon salt, 2 yeast cakes, 3 tablespoons sugar, 1 level teaspoon powdered cinnamon, 1 level teaspoon mixed spice, 3 ozs. margarine, 2 ozs. mixed peel, 3-4 ozs. currants, 3-4 ozs. sultanas, 1 egg, about ½ pint milk.

Sift flour with salt and spices. Rub in margarine and add fruit and sugar. Mix the yeast with 1 teaspoon of sugar until they liquefy, then stir in the warm milk. Strain this mixture into the centre of the dry ingredients and mix them to a soft dough, adding the beaten egg. Leave to rise overnight or a few hours. Turn the dough on to a floured board; divide into small portions and shape into buns, placing them on a baking sheet at least 3 inches apart. Mark a cross with the back of a knife on each bun. Leave to rise until double their size. Bake in a hot oven for 15-20 minutes. When cooked brush the buns with a glaze of sugar and milk.

MOS BOLLETJIES

12½ lbs. flour, 1 lb. raisins, 1½ lbs. butter (or butter and lard), 2¾ lbs. sugar, 3 tablespoons aniseed, 1 tablespoon cinnamon, 2 or 3 eggs, 1 pint milk.

Cut the raisins or mince them, put them into a jar or calabash with 6 cups lukewarm water; put in a warm place for 24 hours until they ferment. If jar or calabash is unseasoned, that is, if not previously used for "Mos", fermentation will take longer. When raisins rise to the top yeast is ready.

Mix flour with the sugar, spices, etc., and make a hollow in the centre; into this strain the fermented juice of the raisins, sprinkle some flour over the top and set to rise for some hours in a warm place.

Melt the butter and fat, warm the milk and mix the whole well together into a stiff dough and knead well. Let it stand overnight to rise and in the morning roll into buns, put in greased pans in a warm place, and let rise again until double in bulk. Brush with the yolk of an egg and some milk and sugar. Bake for half an hour in a hot oven.

The aniseed may be omitted if desired and 1 grated nutmeg added instead. *Mrs. Slade.*

RUSKS

Make as above and when cold cut into two or three pieces and put into a cool oven overnight to dry. *Mrs. Slade.*

ALMOND CRESCENTS

1 cup scalded milk, ½ cup sugar, 2 yeast cakes, about 5 cups flour, 3 ozs. butter or margarine, 1 teaspoon salt, ¼ cup lukewarm water, 2 eggs beaten.

Filling. — 3 tablespoons butter, ½ cup sugar, ½ cup almonds (blanched), chopped or ground, lemon rind, 1 egg.

Combine scalded milk, shortening, sugar and salt. Soften yeast in lukewarm water, stir and combine with cooled milk mixture, add about half the flour, add beaten eggs and beat well. Add enough flour to make a soft dough. Knead lightly for 10 minutes or until smooth and satiny. Place the dough in a warm place and let rise until double in bulk — about 2 hours. Roll it on floured board to the thickness of ¼-inch, cut the dough into 4-inch squares. Cut across the squares making 2 triangles out of every square. Spread with filling. Start with the long end and roll the triangles into little rolls. Twist the rolls into half circles (crescent shaped). Place the crescents on a greased baking sheet. Permit them to rise in a warm place for ½-¾ hour. Brush tops lightly with butter. Bake at 350° for about 30 minutes.

STREUSEL COFFEE CAKE

1 cup scalded milk, 2 ozs. butter or margarine, ½ cup sugar, 1 teaspoon salt, 2 cakes yeast, ¼ cup lukewarm water, about 5 cups flour, 2 eggs beaten.

Topping. — ½ cup sugar, 3 ozs. butter, 1 tablespoon ground almonds (optional), 1 cup dry cake crumbs.

Combine scalded milk, shortening, sugar and salt. Soften yeast in lukewarm water, stir and combine with cooled milk mixture, add about half the flour, add beaten eggs and beat well. Add enough flour to make a soft dough. Knead lightly for 10 minutes or until smooth and satiny. Place the dough in a warm place and let rise until double in bulk — about 2 hours. When dough is light, roll into a circle 1-inch thick. Place in a 9-inch or 10-inch greased cake pan. Spread the top with a topping made by creaming together 3 tablespoons butter, ½ cup Government sugar and cake crumbs. Let rise again until doubled in bulk. Bake at 375° for about 30-35 minutes.

PLAIN SCONES. Standard Recipe

2 cups flour, 4 teaspoons (level) baking powder, 2 ozs. butter, ¾ cup milk, 1 teaspoon salt.

Sift dry ingredients together, rub in butter and add liquid to make a soft dough. Turn out on to floured board and knead very lightly. Roll out to ½-inch thick, cut with cutter or floured knife and bake in hot oven 10 to 15 minutes.

RICH SCONES

To above recipe add one beaten egg and 2 tablespoons sugar. This scone can be varied by adding ½ cup dates, currants or sultanas.

For oven treacle scones leave out the sugar and add 2 tablespoons treacle. *J.H.*

BUTTER ROLLS

Use standard recipe. Roll out scones to ¼-inch thickness, cut with floured cutter, put a dab of butter in centre of each scone, wet edges and fold over. Brush with egg and bake 12 minutes.   *J.H.*

FAIRY SCONES

1½ cups flour, 1½ teaspoons baking powder, 2 tablespoons sugar, 1 egg, 1 teaspoon salt, 1 heaped tablespoon butter (melted), ⅔ cup milk.

Beat sugar and egg, add milk and melted butter and dry ingredients. Lift a spoonful at a time roll lightly in flour with tips of fingers and drop on to baking tin. Bake 15 minutes.   *Mrs. W. Godfrey.*

BROWN SCONES

Use standard recipe and substitute unsifted boermeal for flour and add one egg. Good with dates and sugar.   *J.H.*

CHEESE SCONES

2 cups flour, 4 teaspoons baking powder, 1 teaspoon salt, 3 tablespoons butter, ¾ cup grated cheese, ½ cup milk.

Mix dry ingredients, rub in butter and add cheese and milk Roll out to ½-inch thickness, cut into rounds, brush over with egg and bake 15 minutes in hot oven.   *J.H.*

CHEESE SCONES

½ teacup flour, ½ cup grated cheese, 1 dessertspoon butter, 1 dessertspoon baking powder, 1 egg, little salt, about 1 tablespoon milk.

Method. — Mix flour and butter together first. Bake at 450° for about 6 minutes with elements turned off.   *Mrs. J. Klopper.*

DATE OR RAISIN SCONES

2 cups flour, 4 teaspoons baking powder, 3 ozs. butter, ½ cup milk, 2 tablespoons sugar, 1 teaspoon salt, 1 egg, ¾ cup chopped seeded raisins or stoned dates.

Mix dry ingredients together, add raisins or dates. Mix with beaten egg and milk. Roll out lightly, cut with a sharp knife brush over with egg and bake in hot oven 15 minutes.   *Mrs. Morgan.*

CREAM SCONES

2 cups flour, 4 teaspoons baking powder, 2 ozs. butter, ½ cup milk, 1 teaspoon salt, 2 tablespoons sugar, 1 egg, 2 tablespoons cream.

Proceed as for standard recipe.   *J.H.*

DROP SCONES

Ingredients: 7 heaped tablespoons flour, 4 level tablespoons sugar, 2 eggs, 1 cup (large) milk, 1 heaped teaspoon cream of tartar, ½ teaspoon bicarbonate of soda, 1 tablespoon butter (melted), pinch of salt.

Method: Whisk eggs and add milk, put flour, cream of tartar, salt and soda into sieve and gradually sieve them into the egg and milk, beating with a fork. Next beat in sugar and lastly the hot melted butter. Drop by spoonfuls on to hot girdle, previously greased, and when little holes appear, turn them over. When cooked put on to plate and cover with cloth. Pack immediately into tin while warm. Keep tin closed.

Mrs. C. Griffith.

SCOTCH PANCAKES

1 cup flour, pinch of salt, 1 egg, 2 tablespoons sugar, 1 tablespoon golden syrup, 1 tablespoon Epic oil, ½ pint milk, 1 teaspoon vanilla essence, 1 teaspoon baking powder.

Mix flour, salt and sugar in large bowl, make a well in the middle, add egg, syrup, oil, vanilla and milk slowly, stirring all the time working the flour in gradually to make a mixture the consistency of thin cream. Have girdle or hot-plate moderately hot, wipe over with a piece of cloth dipped in oil. Just before beginning to cook, add baking powder to mixture.

H. Michell.

BUTTER SCOTCH COOKIES (Biscuits)

2 cups brown sugar, 2 eggs, ½ cup shortening, 4 cups flour, 1 teaspoon bicarbonate soda, ⅛ teaspoon salt, 1 teaspoon vanilla, 1 teaspoon cream of tartar.

Method. — Cream shortening with sugar, add beaten eggs and vanilla, sift salt, soda and cream of tartar with flour and add gradually to the mixture. No other liquid should be added. Mix at night and make into a long roll. In the morning cut into slices and bake in a moderate oven 350°.

Mrs. R. W. Carlisle.

SWEET CORN SCONES

2 cups flour, 1 level tablespoonful baking powder, 1½ teaspoons salt, 2 tablespoons butter, 1 tin sweet corn.

Method. — Sift flour, salt and baking powder together, rub in butter, lastly mix the sweet corn in. If desired 1 egg may be added. Bake 15 minutes. These make good breakfast scones.

Mrs. R. C. Harris.

SPICED TEA SCONES

½ lb. flour, 2 ozs. butter, ½ level teaspoon ground cinnamon, 4 level teaspoons baking powder, ½ cup currants and sultanas, 2 tablespoons castor sugar, milk and pinch of salt.
Sift the flour, baking powder and cinnamon into a basin. Rub in the butter and add the sugar and fruit. Mix well and stir in sufficient milk to make a soft dough. Pat flat with hand — do not roll — cut out and bake in hot oven, 450°, for about seven minutes.   *Mrs. Withiel.*

DATE SCONES

4 cups flour, 4 tablespoons butter, 2 eggs, ¾ cup sugar, 6 teaspoons baking powder, 1 cup dates.
Mix all dry ingredients and rub butter and dates into mixture. Add eggs and enough milk to make soft dough. Roll out and bake at 400° for 15 minutes. Also very nice made into loaf and baked 375° for ¾ hour.

STANDARD MUFFINS

2 cups flour, 4 tablespoons butter, 4 teaspoons baking powder, 4 tablespoons sugar, ½ teaspoon salt, 1 egg, about 1 cup milk. Cream butter, add salt and sugar gradually and well-beaten egg. Sift in dry ingredients alternately with the milk. Bake at 400° for 18 minutes.   *Mrs. Beyers.*

BREAKFAST ROLLS

2 large cups flour, or brown meal, 1 teaspoon salt, 1 dessertspoon sugar, 1 cake "Thistle Brand" yeast, 2 tablespoons butter or Purene.
Set yeast with teaspoon sugar and ½ cup lukewarm water. Let stand for 20 minutes. Then dissolve butter with ½ cup hot water and cool down with milk to make 1 cup liquid. Add liquid and yeast to dry ingredients and beat with wooden spoon until dough forms a ball. Mixture must be softer than for bread. Cover and let stand until dough is double in size. Then make into rolls about 2 in. long and let rise again and bake in a quick oven.   *Mrs. A. Daines.*

GIRDLE SCONES

Flour, butter, salt, bicarbonate of soda, cream of tartar, sour milk.
Mix together 1 lb. flour, 1 teaspoon salt, 1 teaspoon bicarbonate of soda and 1 teaspoon cream of tartar.
Rub in 2 ozs. of butter and stir in gradually half a pint sour milk. Turn out on to a floured board, knead as little as possible — divide

into four. Flatten each piece into a round scone ½ in. in thickness. Cut each in quarters, flour them and place on hot girdle. Cook for about five minutes, then turn with a knife and cook on other side for same length of time. When edges are dry they are ready. Flour the girdle. *Mother.*

For treacle scones add two or three tablespoons treacle to above mixture, mixing treacle with milk.

SOFT BISCUITS

To every pound of bread-dough add 3 ozs. of melted butter and a tablespoon of sugar. Turn into flat rounds about size of saucer and bake in good oven. *Mrs. Mac.*

BAPS (Scotch Breakfast Rolls)

Sift 1 lb. of flour into a warm bowl and mix with it a teaspoon of salt. Rub in 2 ozs. butter. Add 1 oz. yeast and a teaspoon sugar, ½ pint of tepid milk and water and mix. Make into a soft dough and set to rise for one hour in a warm place. Knead lightly and divide into pieces of equal size and form into oval shapes three or four inches long and two wide. Brush with milk and dust with flour. Place on a greased tin and set aside for 15 minutes. Press a finger into centre of each before baking. Bake in a hot oven from 10 to 20 minutes.

Mrs. Mac.

ROCK BUNS

2 cups flour, 3 teaspoons baking powder, ½ teaspoon salt, 3 ozs. sugar, 4 ozs. butter, ¼ cup currants, a little grated lemon peel, 1 egg, ¼ cup milk.

Mix dry ingredients, rub in butter and add fruit. Make into stiff dough with beaten egg and milk. Drop in rocky piles on to a greased baking tray and bake in hot oven 15 to 20 minutes. *J.H.*

RICE BUNS

¼ lb. butter, ¼ lb. sugar, ¼ lb. rice flour, ½ lb. flour, 2 teaspoons baking powder, 2 eggs, grated rind of lemon.

Beat butter and sugar to a cream. Put in the well-beaten eggs, add the rice flour and other ingredients. Place a dessertspoonful at a time on well-greased baking sheet, brush over with egg and sift a little sugar on each. Bake in hot oven 10 or 15 minutes. *From Australia.*

COFFEE BUNS

8 ozs. flour, 4 ozs. butter, 2 ozs. currants, 4 ozs. sugar, 1 teaspoon baking powder, pinch of salt, 1 teaspoon mixed spice, 1 tablespoon coffee essence, 1 egg.

Proceed as for Rock Buns. *J.H.*

YEAST COOKIES

2 large cups flour, little salt (½ teaspoon), ½ cup (teacup) sugar, ½ cup butter, Pastrine or Purene, milk, ½ cup currants, 1 cake "Thistle Brand" yeast.

Set yeast with little sugar and ½ cup lukewarm water. Let stand for 20 minutes. Take butter and melt with little boiling water, and then cool with milk to make large cup liquid. Add liquid and yeast to dry ingredients and beat with wooden spoon until a ball is formed, or dough comes off spoon easily. Add currants and mix again. Cover and let stand until risen double in size. Make into small, round buns and let rise again. When risen brush with beaten egg and fire in a quick oven.

Mrs. A. Daines.

QUICK LUNCHEON ROLLS

4 cups flour, 2 tablespoons butter, 6 level teaspoons baking powder, 1 teaspoon salt, 1½ cups milk or milk and water.

Sift dry ingredients into bowl: rub in butter: add milk to form smooth soft dough easy to handle on floured board. Knead for a few minutes until smooth, then divide into small pieces. Form into tapered rolls, place on greased baking-sheet in warm place for 10 minutes. Brush with milk and bake in hot oven (450 degrees) for 15 to 20 minutes. When almost baked, brush again with melted butter. (Serve hot in napkins).

Nature gives enough for all. But Man, with arrogant selfishness, proud of his heaps, hoards up superflous stores — robbed from his fellows. Starves the poor, or gives to pity what he owes to justice!

Robert Southey.

HER FIRST CAKE

She measured out the butter, with a very solemn air,
The milk and sugar also, and she took the greatest care
To count the eggs correctly, and to add the little bit
Of baking powder, which, you know, beginners oft omit,
Then she mixed it all together, and she baked it full an hour,
But she never quite forgave herself for leaving out the flour.

Anon.

CAKES
TABLE OF WEIGHTS AND MEASURES

1 lb. flour = 4 cups.
1 lb. sugar, white = 2 cups.
1 lb. brown sugar = 2²/₃ cups.
1 lb. butter = 2 cups.
1 lb. raisins = 2 cups (tightly packed).
1 lb. castor sugar = 2²/₃ cups.
1 lb. icing sugar = 3½ cups.
1 lb. egg = 9 large eggs.
1 oz. almonds = ⅓ cup blanched and chopped.
1 oz. liquid = 2 tablespoons.
1 oz. butter = 2 tablespoons.
1 oz. sugar = 2 tablespoons.
1 oz. grated chocolate = 3½ tablespoons.

N.B. — The cup referred to should be a measuring cup, which is about the size of a large coffee cup. An ordinary cup, or tea cup, holds about ¾ cup.

The tablespoon which will give the above measures is the deep, medium-sized tablespoon, not the very large nor the very shallow spoon.

1 pint = 2 cups — 16 tablespoons (breakfast cups).
1 quart = 4 cups.
1 gallon = 16 cups.
1 gill = ½ cup.
All measurements level.

Mrs. Beyers (M. J. Davidtsz).

WEIGHTS AND MEASUREMENTS
TABLE OF LIQUID EQUIVALENTS

1 saltspoon = ½ teaspoon.
1 teaspoon = ½ dessertspoon.
1 dessertspoon = ½ tablespoon.
1 breakfast cup of liquid = ½ pint.
1 teacup liquid = ¼ pint.

Almonds, ground, 1 tablespoon = 1 oz.
Barley, pearl, 1 tablespoon = ¾ oz.
Beans, haricot, 1 breakfast cup = 6 ozs.
Breadcrumbs, fresh, 1 breakfast cup = 4 ozs.
Breadcrumbs, crisp, 1 breakfast cup = 5 ozs.
Butter (heaped), 1 breakfast cup = 7 ozs.
Butter, 1 tablespoon = 1 oz.
Butter, piece the size of a walnut = ½ oz.
Cream of tartar, 1 teaspoon = ¼ oz.
Cheese, grated, 1 tablespoon = ½ oz.
Cocoa — 1 tablespoon = ½ oz.
Cocoanut, desiccated, 1 breakfast cup = 2 ozs.
Cornflour, 1 breakfast cup = 4 ozs.
Currants, 1 breakfast cup = 5 ozs.
Eggs, 3 average size = 5 ozs.
Flour, 1 breakfast cup = 4 ozs.
Lentils, 1 breakfast cup = 5 ozs.
Margarine, 1 breakfast cup = 7 ozs.
Oatmeal, 1 breakfast cup = 5 ozs.
Raisins, 1 breakfast cup = 6 ozs.
Rice, 1 breakfast cup = 7 ozs.
Rice, ground, 1 breakfast cup = 5 ozs.
Salt (rough), 1 tablespoon = 1 oz.
Soda, bicarbonate, 1 teaspoon = ¼ oz.
Suet (chopped), 1 breakfast cup = 4 ozs.
Sugar, 1 breakfast cup = 7 ozs.
Sugar, moist, 1 breakfast cup = 8 ozs.
Semolina, 1 breakfast cup = 4 ozs.
Sago, 1 breakfast cup = 4 ozs.
Tapioca, 1 breakfast cup = 4 ozs.
(With acknowledgments to the Nestle Powdered Milk Recipe Book).

HINTS

Measure ingredients carefully and have them ready and pans greased before mixing cake.
Grease pans with lard or pastrine — never butter — and sprinkle lightly with flour. Look to your oven.
Bake large cakes in moderate oven and small cakes in a hot oven.
The success of a cake depends largely on the creaming. Creaming consists of beating butter and sugar together till they become like thick cream. Always use a wooden spoon. When adding eggs to butter and sugar they should be dropped in one at a time, stirred very quickly and well beaten before next egg is added.
An alternative method is to whisk the eggs first in a separate basin and add alternately with the flour to the creamed butter and sugar.

If baking powder is used, the cake must be baked directly it is mixed. Bicarbonate of soda darkens cake.

Two teaspoons baking powder are equal to one teaspoon baking soda and 2 cream of tartar.

1 cup sour milk equals 1 teaspoon cream of tartar, and may be used as a substitute.

When a recipe calls for treacle, soda should be used. If cake is put into too cold an oven it rises over the pan and is of a coarse texture. If oven is too hot, a crust will form on top before cake is sufficiently risen and the mixture will break through. Too much flour will also cause cakes to crack on top.

In making sponge cakes, beat egg yolks till thick and lemon coloured, beat in the sugar, then fold in the whites beaten until stiff and dry. Layer and chocolate cakes should have a slightly thinner mixture than the ordinary cake. Fruit cake, especially cherry, should have a stiff mixture and the fruit should always be rolled in flour.

Should the butter be very hard, cut in pieces, put in mixing bowl and stand in sun or near fire, but do not allow it to become oily.

When making small cakes, grease the tins well and sprinkle flour and castor sugar lightly over.

For large cakes, grease tins lightly and line with greaseproof, or kitchen paper and see that the paper stands at least 2 inches higher than the tin. For the first half-hour of baking, cover top of cake with paper. Do not open oven door for first half-hour after putting in the cake, and never bang the door.

Cool cakes on pastry tray or sieve, out of a draught.

GUIDE TO OVEN TEMPERATURES

Ovens vary, so it is not always wise to give set temperatures, but the following may help: —

500 — very hot — puff pastries.
450 — very hot — scones.
425 — hot — small cakes.
400 — moderate — sandwich and layer cakes.
350 — moderate — biscuits.
325 — slow — shortbread.
325-275 — slow — large fruit cakes.
250-225 — very slow — meringues.

STANDARD CAKE MIXTURES
(1) PLAIN

2 cups (8 ozs.) flour, ½ cup (4 ozs.) castor sugar, ½ cup (4 ozs.) butter, 2 eggs, 2 teaspoons baking powder, ¼ cup of milk or milk and water, pinch salt.

(2) MEDIUM

2 cups flour, 2 tablespoons milk, $2/3$ cup butter (6 ozs.), 3 eggs, 2 teaspoons baking powder, $2/3$ cup sugar (6 ozs.), pinch of salt.

(3) RICH BUTTER CAKE

2 cups flour, 1 cup (8 ozs.) sugar, 1 cup (8 ozs.) butter, 4 eggs, 2 teaspoons baking powder, pinch of salt.

CHOCOLATE CAKE

Use quantities No. 2, adding 2 tablespoons cocoa dissolved in hot milk and cooled. Add ½ teaspoon cinnamon and 1 teaspoon vanilla.

ORANGE CAKE

Use quantites No. 2, substituting orange juice for milk and adding grated rind of orange.
Both Chocolate and Orange Cakes can be baked in sandwich tins and joined together with butter icing. Use vanilla essence for Chocolate Cake butter icing (see butter filling) and orange juice for Orange Cake filling.

CHERRY CAKE

Use quantities No. 2, adding ¼ lb. cherries which have been rolled in flour.

CURRANT, SULTANA, RAISIN OR DATE CAKE

Use recipe No. 1, adding 2 tablespoons sugar, 1 cup currants, sultanas, raisins or dates.

MADEIRA CAKE

Use recipe No. 3 and flavour with grated rind of lemon. Put citron peel on top.

MARBLE CAKE

Use recipe No. 2. Divide mixture into three portions. To one add 1 tablespoon cocoa dissolved in a spoonful of hot water. To second add a few drops of cochineal and leave third portion plain. Put into tin in alternate spoonfuls.

WALNUT CAKE

Use recipe No. 2, adding a cup of chopped walnuts and pinch of cinnamon.

COCOANUT CAKE

Use recipe No. 1, adding 2 ozs. castor sugar and 1 cup desiccated cocoanut. Use 3 eggs.

MOCHA CAKE

Use recipe No. 2, substituting strong coffee (cold) for milk and adding ½ cup of sugar.

SEED CAKE

Use recipe 1 or 2 and add 1 teaspoon carraway seed.

GINGER LOAF

¼ lb. sugar (small cup), ½ lb. flour, 2 ozs. butter, 2 dessertspoons syrup, 1 teaspoon cinnamon, 1 teaspoon mixed spice, 1 teaspoon ground ginger, 1 teaspoon bicarbonate soda, 1 egg, 1 teacup milk, ¼ teaspoon salt.

Method. — Cream butter and sugar. Add syrup, egg and milk and 1 cup flour. Add soda and spices, then the rest of the flour. Bake for 1 hour 400—300°. *Mrs. Burke.*

GRANNY'S GINGERBREAD

1 lb. flour, ¼ lb. sugar, 1 teaspoon salt, 2 teaspoons mixed spice, 2 teaspoons ground ginger, 1 teaspoon cinnamon, 1 teaspoon bicarbonate soda, 6 ozs. butter, 4 tablespoons syrup, 2 tablespoons treacle, 1 cup hot water, 2 eggs.

If very dark gingerbread is required, reverse the amount of syrup and treacle.

Put butter, syrup, treacle, hot water and soda into pan and mix till butter is melted — do not boil. Put aside to cool. Mix dry ingredients together very thoroughly. Beat eggs and add to the cold butter and syrup mixture and then mix with other ingredients. Beat well, pour into a greased and lined tin and bake in slow oven for 1¼ hours. Do not open oven door during baking. *J.H.*

GINGER CAKE

1 lb. flour or No. 1 Boermeal, 3 ozs. sugar, 1 oz. candied peel, good pinch of salt, 1 teaspoon of soda bicarbonate, 3 ozs. butter, ¾ lb. treacle or syrup, 1 egg, 2 heaped teaspoons of ginger, 1 teacupful of boiling water.

Method. — Put syrup to warm. Mix all dry ingredients together, rub butter into flour. Add beaten egg, pour boiling water over soda and syrup, mix and bake in rather cool oven for 1 hour. For electric stove put in oven at 400° and leave for 1 hour. If not done leave longer and turn over to cook top and bottom. *A. Paxton.*

DATE AND WALNUT CAKE

1 tablespoon butter, ¾ cup sugar, 1 egg, 1½ cups flour, 1 teaspoon baking powder, pinch salt, 1 teaspoon bicarbonate soda, ½ cup chopped dates, ½ cup chopped walnuts, ¾ cup boiling water, 1 teaspoon vanilla.

Cream butter and sugar and add egg. Pour boiling water (with soda dissolved in it) over dates and allow to cool. Sift flour, baking powder and salt together and add this alternately with date mixture to creamed butter. Add nuts and bake one hour at 350°. Mixture should be quite soft. *Mrs. Thatcher, Durban.*

SOME SMALL CAKES

6 ozs. flour, 4 ozs. butter, 3 ozs. castor sugar, 2 eggs, 2 teaspoons (level) baking powder, salt, ¼ cup milk.

Beat butter and castor sugar to a cream. Add eggs one at a time and beat well. Sift in baking powder and salt and add milk. Bake in patty pans in quick oven 15 minutes.

Ice and decorate when cold, or roll cakes in jam and coat with cocoanut.

Coburg Cakes. Use above recipe, but add ½ teaspoon spice, ½ teaspoon ground ginger, ½ teaspoon cinnamon and one dessertspoon treacle.

Queen Cakes. Add a few currants.

Chocolate Cakes. Add 2 teaspoons chocolate or cocoa and 1 teaspoon vanilla essence. *J.H.*

ALMOND CHEESE CAKES

Short crust pastry. Filling: 2 ozs. butter, 1 tablespoon rice flour, 2 ozs. castor sugar, 2 ozs. ground almonds, a little grated lemon rind, 1 egg, almond essence. Milk if necessary. Beat butter and sugar, add beaten egg, then other ingredients, and fill pastry cases or open tart and bake. *Mrs. B. Mills.*

WALNUT FILLING

3 ozs. butter, 3 ozs. sugar, 3 ozs. chopped walnuts, 1 egg, vanilla essence. Proceed as above. *Mrs. B. Mills.*

SCOTCH BLACK BUN. A Very Old Recipe

2 lbs. seeded raisins, 2 lbs. currants, ½ lb. almonds (blanched and chopped), ½ lb. chopped mixed peel.

Sift a pound of flour and mix it with 4 ozs. sugar, ½ oz. ground cloves or cinnamon, ½ oz, ground ginger, a teaspoon Jamaica pepper and ½ teaspoon black pepper and a small teaspoon bicarbonate of soda.

Add to these the prepared fruits. Add just enough milk or beaten egg with a tablespoon of brandy to moisten the mixture.

Make a paste by lightly rubbing half a pound of butter into a pound of flour and mixing in quickly enough water to make a stiff dough. Roll out thinly. Grease a large cake tin and line it evenly with the paste, retaining enough to cover the top. Trim the edges, put the mixture in and make the surface flat and smooth. Moisten edges of pastry with cold water and place on the round top. With a skewer make four holes right down to the bottom of the cake. Prick all over with a fork, brush with beaten egg and bake in a moderate oven for about four hours.

Mrs. Mac.

SELKIRK BANNOCK

Bread dough, butter, lard, sugar, sultanas, orange peel. Into 2 lbs. of bread dough rub 4 ozs. butter and 4 ozs. lard. Work in half a pound of sugar, ¾ lb. sultanas (or half a pound sultanas and a ¼ lb. currants) and ¼ lb. finely chopped orange peel. Put the dough into a buttered tin, let it stand in a warm place for half an hour to rise and then bake in a good steady oven 1 hour.

Mrs. Mac.

CUMBERLAND BUN LOAF

2 lbs. flour, ½ lb. butter, 1 lb. sugar, 2 lbs. currants, ½ lb. raisins, ¼ lb. peel, 1 teaspoon bicarbonate soda, 2 eggs, 1 pint milk, 4 tablespoons black treacle, ½ teaspoon salt, 2 teaspoons spice.

Method. — Sieve together flour, soda, spice and salt, rub in butter and add other ingredients. Bake in a slow oven about 3 hours. Keep a month before cutting.

Miss Jackson.

SHORTBREAD

¾ lb. flour, ¼ lb. cornflour, ½ lb. butter, ¼ lb. icing sugar. Put butter and sugar on to a board and work with the hand until thoroughly incorporated. Mix flour and cornflour together and work gradually into the butter and sugar until dough is of the consistency of short crust. Do not roll it out, but press with the hands into 2 or 3 round cakes on a sheet of baking paper, making the cakes about ¾ inch in thickness. Pinch the edges neatly all round with finger and thumb and prick all over with a fork. Bake to a light golden brown in a rather slow oven 30 to 40 minutes. Cut into convenient pieces while hot.

Mrs. John Hendrie.

SHORTBREAD (Easy Method)

2 teacupfuls flour, 1 teacupful (¼ lb.) butter, 2 tablespoons castor sugar, pinch salt.

Put flour, sugar and salt in a basin. Melt butter and pour on to the dry ingredients. Mix with the hand until a solid lump. Put into a sandwich tin and make flat with a knife. Prick it all over with a fork and bake in a cool oven. *B. C. Cleghorn.*

GRETNA GREEN SHORTBREAD

¾ lb. flour, ½ lb. butter, ½ lb. soft brown sugar, 2 level teaspoon ground ginger, small teaspoon bicarbonate soda, ¼ teaspoon cream of tartar.

Method. — Cream butter and sugar, add flour, etc. Finish same as for shortbread, roughen on top with a fork. Bake until a golden brown. Cut into squares while warm. *Mrs. L. Malan.*

JAM CAKES

2 ozs. butter, 2 ozs. castor sugar, 1 egg, 3 ozs. flour, ½ teaspoon baking powder, 3 teaspoons strawberry jam, 2 tablespoons water, 1 tablespoon chopped nuts or peanuts.

Cream butter and sugar, beat in the egg, and when well mixed fold in the sifted flour, baking powder and salt. Put into small, greased patty tins, greased and dusted with castor sugar and flour. Bake at 350° or No. 4 for 25 minutes. Mix the jam with 2 tablespoons hot water, brush over the cakes, roll in chopped nuts. *The Star.*

FAIRY CAKES

2 ozs. butter, 2 ozs. castor sugar, 2 ozs. flour, ½ teaspoon baking powder, ½ teaspoon lemon essence, 1 egg, 2 ozs. cornflour, 2 tablespoons milk.

Cream butter and sugar, work in egg and beat well. Mix the sifted flour, baking powder and cornflour lightly into egg mixture, adding milk alternately with it. Put into greased patty tins and bake in quick oven 400° or No. 7 for 10 minutes. *The Star.*

SMALL GINGER CAKES

4 ozs. butter, 4 ozs. castor sugar, grated rind of ½ a lemon, 2 ozs. chopped, preserved ginger, 4½ ozs. flour, 2 small eggs, ½ teaspoon baking powder, 1 teaspoon milk if required.

Cream butter and sugar, add the chopped ginger and grated lemon rind. Stir in the well-beaten eggs, sift flour and baking powder, and if the mixture is too dry, the milk. Drop into greased patty tins and bake in a moderate oven of 375° or No. 5 for 15 to 20 minutes. Cool on a wire rack, cover with ginger butter icing, and decorate with crystallised ginger and angelica. *The Star.*

GINGER BUTTER ICING

Cream 2 ozs. butter with 3 or 4 ozs. sifted icing sugar until creamy, then flavour with a little ground ginger to your own taste.

Spread smoothly over the cakes and glaze by dipping a knife in hot water and smoothing it over the cakes. Decorate as desired. *The Star.*

SPONGE SANDWICH

3 eggs, ¾ teacup castor sugar (beat together until thick), 1 breakfast cup flour, ½ teaspoon cream of tartar, ¼ teaspoon bicarbonate of soda, pinch of salt, 3 tablespoons boiling water.
Bake at 400° for about 12 minutes. *Mrs. J. McMillan.*

MILE-A-MINUTE SANDWICH CAKE

(So called because of speed in making)

1½ cups flour, 2 heaped teaspoons baking powder, 1 cup sugar, ¼ cup melted butter, 2 eggs, milk.

Method. — Mix dry ingredients thoroughly. Break the unbeaten eggs into melted butter and fill up the cup with milk. Pour into the dry ingredients and mix well. Add a little more milk as the mixture must be fairly thin.

Bake in two sandwich tins in a moderate oven (350°) for 15-20 minutes.
Mrs. E. Pyper.

BOILING WATER SPONGE

3 eggs, ¾ cup sugar, 1 cup flour, 2 teaspoons baking powder, 1 dessertspoon butter, 4 tablespoons water.

Filling. — Whipped cream.

Method. — Beat eggs and sugar until thick and creamy, sift in flour, add butter to water and bring to boil. While still boiling add to above mixture, then lightly stir in baking powder. Bake 12 minutes, oven 400°.
Mrs. A. Stevenson.

CAKE MIXTURE (SANDWICH CAKE)

4 ozs. butter, 4 ozs. flour, pinch of salt, 4 ozs. sugar, 1 teaspoon baking powder, 2 eggs, flavouring if desired.

Cream butter and sugar. Beat up eggs well, add to butter and sugar. Beat up well, fold in sifted flour, baking powder and salt gradually. If mixture seems too stiff thin down with milk. Bake in swiss roll tin for 15 minutes.

When cold cut in half, spread one half with any desired jam, place the other half on top and sprinkle with icing sugar. Cut in small fingers. *Mrs. S. Gilbert.*

SANDWICH CAKE WITH MARSHMALLOW FROSTING

2 heaped tablespoons butter, 4 heaped tablespoons sugar, 6 heaped tablespoons flour, 2 eggs, 2 heaped teaspoons baking powder, pinch of salt, milk.

Method. — Cream butter and sugar, beat eggs and add. Sift in flour with salt alternately with a little milk. Beat well. Lastly add baking powder, beat again lightly and put in greased tins. Bake 15 minutes.
Filling and Frosting. — 1 unbeaten egg white, 3 tablespoons cold water, ⁷⁄₈ cup sugar, ½ teaspoon baking powder.
Method. — Place all ingredients except baking powder in top of double cooker. Place over boiling water and beat with egg beater for 7 minutes, then add baking powder and beat again. Cut 8 marshmallows fine and add after frosting becomes thick; then beat until marshmallows melt.
Mrs. A. Stevenson.

JELLY CAKE (made with powdered milk)

3 eggs, ½ cup castor sugar, 1 cup flour, 1 teaspoon milk powder, 1 teaspoon baking powder, 1 tablespoon water.
Method. — Beat egg yolks and sugar until creamy and lemon coloured. Sift flour, baking powder and milk powder. Beat the eggs, butter and water again and add the flour mixture, and lastly the stiffly beaten egg whites. Put into greased sandwich tins and bake at 400° for 10-15 minutes until cooked and brown.
Filling. — Any jelly such as quince, currant or apple, etc., may be used for filling the cake. Sandwich the two cakes and cover with butter icing.
Mrs. W. Hamilton.

AMERICAN CREAM LAYER CAKE

1 cup flour, 1 cup sugar, 3 eggs, 1 tablespoon baking powder, 2 tablespoons milk.
Beat yolks of eggs, add sugar, beat again, add milk, sift in flour and fold in beaten whites. Divide mixture into 3 or 4 parts, 4 for preference. Bake in layer tins adding 1 level teaspoon baking powder to each part just before mixture is put into tins, beat well. Bake 7-10 minutes in fairly hot oven. Fill with cream while it is warm.

For the Cream:
Stir into ½ pint of boiling milk 1½ tablespoons maizena, wet with a little milk and mixed with 1 beaten egg, 2 tablespoons white sugar. Stir until mixture thickens, take off stove and stir in ½ teaspoon vanilla. Spread between layers while still hot, ice with white icing and sprinkle with fine cocoanut on top. *Hazel Hawke.*

ORANGE SANDWICH

6 ozs. flour, 1 tablespoon orange juice, 4 ozs. sugar, 3 ozs. butter, ½ teaspoonful bicarbonate of soda, 1 teaspoonful cream of tartar, 2 or 3 tablespoonfuls milk, grated rind of ½ orange, 2 eggs.
Method. — Cream butter and sugar, add eggs beaten and flavouring. Sift bicarbonate soda, cream of tartar and flour together, mix in lightly

with milk, spread in a flat tin and bake in moderate oven. When cold, split open and spread the following mixture: —
Filling. — Put 1 dessertspoonful butter in a pan with 1 dessertspoonful cornflour and mix over heat, add ¼ pint of orange juice, heated, 1 tablespoonful lemon juice and 1 oz. or 2 ozs. sugar, let boil 5 minutes, use when cold. Cover with water icing if liked. *Mrs. Spence.*

SANDWICH CAKE

1 tablespoon butter, 4 tablespoons water, 2 eggs, 1 cup sugar, 1 cup flour, 1 teaspoon baking powder, essence to taste.
Boil butter and water together. Beat eggs and sugar very well together. Add flour and baking powder to eggs and sugar, and add butter and water (boiling). Divide mixture between two sandwich tins (medium size) and bake in moderate oven for ½ hour.
For Chocolate Sandwich. — Add 1 tablespoon grated chocolate or cocoa to butter and water.
For orange Flavour. — Add rind (grated) of orange to eggs and sugar and juice to butter and water. *Mrs. Reeler.*

QUEEN MARY'S SPONGE CAKE

3 eggs, pinch of salt, weight 3 eggs in castor sugar, weight 2 eggs in self-raising flour.
Beat egg whites until stiff with a pinch of salt; add yolks one by one and beat well together, then add the sifted castor sugar and again beat. Fold in the sifted flour. Bake in oven 350°. *Mrs. Withiel.*

SWISS ROLL

2 eggs, 3 tablespoons flour, 3 tablespoons sugar, 1 teaspoon baking powder, 2 tablespoons boiling water.
Method. — Beat eggs and sugar until a thick cream and fold in flour after sifting twice with the baking powder. Add the boiling water. Bake in moderate oven. Sprinkle greaseproof paper with sugar, turn out and spread jam. Roll up while hot. *Mrs. S. Watson.*

ORANGE CAKE

3 eggs, ½ cup butter, 2 cups flour, ½ cup milk, 1 teaspoon cream of tartar, 1 cup sugar, rind of 2 oranges, ½ teaspoon soda.
Method. — Beat butter and sugar to cream, add eggs; beat well. Add flour and grated rind of orange mixed with cream of tartar. Add soda to milk. Mix all well together and bake in a moderate oven for ½ hour.
Icing. — ½ lb. icing sugar, juice of one orange. Mix to smooth paste. Decorate cake with sprinkle of orange rind. *Mrs. S. Watson.*

LAYER CAKE

1 cup flour, ½ cup sugar, 2 eggs, 1 dessertspoon baking powder, 1 tablespoon butter, milk to mix.

Method. — Cream butter and sugar, add eggs, beat well, then add flour sifted with baking powder, and enough milk to make a soft dough. Pour into layer cake tins, bake 20 minutes in a moderate oven.

For Brown Cake add spices and cut up ginger or dates.

For Coffee Cake add coffee essence to taste and make coffee filling.
Mrs. L. Malan.

GRANADILLA LAYER CAKE

Use fine butter cake recipe and spread a layer of whipped cream on the bottom layer and spread lightly with grenadilla pulp. Put top layer on — spread a thin layer of cream over the top, spread a layer granadilla, and over this layer pipe whipped cream through a pastry tube, using a paper bag (folded from butter paper).

If the grenadilla is too liquid, drain a little of the juice off, to prevent making the cake soggy. *Mrs. Beyers (M. J. Davidtsz).*

STRAWBERRY LAYER CAKE

Proceed as for grenadilla layer cake, using strawberries for the fruit. Leave a few berries whole to decorate the top.
Mrs. Beyers (M. J. Davidtsz).

FINE BUTTER CAKE (Excellent Layer Cake)

⅓ cup butter, ⅞ cup sugar, 2 eggs, ½ cup milk, 1¾ cups flour, ½ teaspoon salt, 2 teaspoons baking powder, ½ teaspoon vanilla.

Cream the butter well, adding the sugar gradually. Beat the eggs thoroughly and add gradually to the butter mixture. Sift in the flour with the salt and baking powder, alternately with the milk. Bake in a greased pan for 30 minutes at 350°.

For Layer Cake. — Bake in two layers at 380° for 20 minutes. When cold put together with cream filling. Sprinkle the top lightly with castor sugar. *Mrs. Beyers (M. J. Davidtsz).*

CREAM FILLING FOR ABOVE

½ cup sugar, ⅓ cup flour, ⅛ teaspoon salt, 2 eggs, 1 cup scalded milk, 1 teaspoon vanilla.

Mix the dry ingredients well. Gradually stir the scalded milk into them. When smooth, return to heat and cook, stirring constantly until the mixture is thick. Add the beaten eggs, and cook again stirring all the time till the egg is thickened. Cool, add vanilla.

The above makes a thick layer which is delicious. Place the other layer gently on top. *Mrs. Beyers (M. J. Davidtsz.)*

ORANGE LAYER CAKE

Use fine butter cake recipe. Substitute one teaspoon grated orange rind in both the cake and the filling, for the vanilla essence.

Mrs. Beyers (M. J. Davidtsz).

PINEAPPLE LAYER CAKE

Use fine butter cake recipe. Put a layer of grated pineapple cooked with very little sugar for two minutes. It must not be too syrupy. Leave a few pieces of pineapple whole (core removed) to garnish the top.
Decorate the top of the cake with whipped cream and the cooked pieces of pineapple.

Mrs. Beyers (M. J. Davidtsz).

HAZELNUT CAKE

½ lb. butter, ½ lb. castor sugar, 1 teaspoon vanilla, ¼ lb. flour, 1 teaspoon baking powder, 1/8 lb. minced hazelnuts, 8 egg whites. Cream butter and sugar and add vanilla. Sift flour and baking powder and mix with nuts. Beat egg whites stiff. Mix all together. Bake at 375° for 1¼ hours.

E.R.

RASPBERRY BUNS

½ lb. flour, 4 ozs. sugar, 1 teaspoon cream of tartar, 1 teaspoon bicarbonate soda, 1 egg, 4 ozs. butter.
Method. — Sieve flour, cream of tartar and bicarbonate soda, add sugar, rub in butter, add egg and a little milk.
Roll out pastry, line patty tins with rounds, place a teaspoon raspberry jam in each, and cover with smaller rounds.
Bake 10 minutes to 15 minutes (oven 370°).

Mrs. Murphy.

RASPBERRY BUNS

1 large cup flour, ¼ lb. butter, 1½ teaspoons baking powder, 1 egg, pinch of salt, 2 tablespoons sugar, ½ teaspoon vanilla essence.
Method. — Rub butter into dry ingredients, add beaten egg, essence, and enough milk to make a fairly soft dough, roll and cut into rounds. Drop a little raspberry jam in centre of each round, and pinch up into a ball.
Bake upside down at 400°.

Mrs. Atherton.

RICE CAKE

Ingredients. — 3 ozs. butter, 2 ozs. ground rice, 1 egg, 3 ozs. sugar, 2 ozs. flour, ½ teaspoon baking powder.
Method. — Beat butter and sugar; add egg and dry ingredients, and

I tablespoon milk if mixture is too stiff. Bake in moderate oven (350°). When cold, split and spread with raspberry jam, or spread the top with jam.
Mrs. W. I. Christie.

BACHELOR'S BUTTONS

Ingredients. — 5 ozs. flour, 3 ozs. sugar, ½ teaspoon baking powder, 3 ozs. butter, 1 egg.

Method. — Beat butter, sugar and egg to a cream. Stir in flour, adding baking powder. Roll pieces in the hands to form little balls, and place on greased tin. Bake in moderate oven for 10 minutes.
Mrs. W. I. Christie.

BANANA LOAF

2 cups flour, ¾ cup sugar, ½ cup butter, 2 eggs, ½ cup shelled walnuts (chopped), 1 teaspoon bicarbonate soda, 3 tablespoons sour milk, 1 teaspoon vanilla, ½ teaspoon salt, 3 large bananas well mashed.

Method. — Cream butter well, add sugar gradually and well beaten eggs with sour milk, also bananas. Sift in the soda with the flour alternately with above liquid. Bake in a loaf tin in moderate oven for 45 minutes. Spread slices thinly with butter when serving.
Mrs. L. Malan.

MADEIRA CAKE

Ingredients. — 3 ozs. flour, 2 ozs. butter, ½ teaspoon baking powder, 3 ozs. castor sugar, 2 eggs.

Method. — Beat butter and sugar to a cream, add egg and beat, a little flour folded in, another egg beaten in, then more flour until well mixed; if mixture is too stiff, add little water, but mixture must be thick; add baking powder last. Spread evenly in loaf tin and bake in 300° to 400° oven for ¾ hour.
Mrs. W. I. Christie.

BANANA BREAD

2 cups flour, ¼ lb. butter, 2 eggs, 3 or 4 ripe bananas, 1 cup sugar, 1 heaped teaspoon baking powder, 1 level teaspoon baking soda, pinch salt.

Cream butter and sugar, add mashed bananas, beat well, add beaten eggs. Sift flour and salt and add to mixture with ¼ cup water in which the soda has been dissolved, beat well and lastly add baking powder. Bake in moderate oven for 1 hour.
Mrs. H. C. Lake, Maritzburg.

DATE AND WALNUT LOAF

3 cups wholemeal flour, 4 teaspoons baking powder, 1 cup sugar, 1 saltspoon salt, 3 ozs. butter, ½ lb. chopped and stoned dates, 1 cup chopped walnuts, 1 egg, 1 cup milk.

Method. — Mix together wholemeal flour, baking powder, salt, sugar. Rub in butter. Add chopped dates and walnuts. Beat up egg and add cup milk. Gradually stir this into dry ingredients and when well mixed place in a greased bread tin and leave to rise (20 minutes).
Bake in a moderate oven about 1 hour. *M. Grove.*

DATE AND NUT LOAF

Ingredients. — ¾lb. stoneless dates, 1 cup walnuts, 1 cup boiling water, 3 tablespoons butter, 1 teaspoon bicarbonate of soda, 3 eggs, 2½ cups flour, 1 teaspoon baking powder, pinch salt, 1 cup sugar, 1 teaspoon vanilla essence.

Method. — Chop up the dates and walnuts. Put the boiling water into a basin and add the butter and bicarbonate of soda; mix well. Stir in the chopped dates and leave to cool. Stir in the beaten eggs. Sieve together the flour, baking powder and salt and stir into the mixture. Finally add the nuts and flavouring. Pour into a greased baking tin and bake in a moderate oven (350 degrees) for 1 hour and 10 minutes. (The pan should be of the loaf variety and measure 9 in. by 3½ in.
Mrs. C. Griffith.

LIGHT FRUIT CAKE

6 ozs. butter, 6 ozs. castor sugar, 3 eggs, 8 ozs. flour, 1 teaspoon baking powder, about 1 cup mixed cherries and sultanas.
Bake about 65 minutes at 370°. *Mrs. J. McMillan.*

DARK FRUIT CAKE

½ lb. butter, ½ lb. sugar, ¾ lb. flour, 5 eggs, 1½ lbs. fruit (currants, sultanas, raisins), ½ lb. cherries, 2 ozs. candied peel (if liked), 3 tablespoons brandy, 1 level teaspoon bicarbonate soda (dissolved in 1 dessertspoon cold water).

Method. — Usual method creaming butter and sugar, etc. Bake 1 hour at 300°, then 2 hours at 250°, then 1 hour at 200°. *Mrs. J. Mc.Millan.*

FRUIT CAKE

1¼ lbs. butter, 1¼ lbs. sugar, 1¼ lbs. flour, 10 eggs, ¼ lb. lemon peel, ½ lb. chopped almonds, 2½ lbs. currants, wineglass rum.

Method. — Cream butter and sugar, and continue to mix like any other pound cake. *Miss Jackson.*

POUND CAKE

¾ lb. flour, ½ lb. butter, ½ lb. sugar, ¼ lb. lemon peel, ¾ lb. currants, 5 eggs, lemon essence to taste.

Method. — Cream butter and sugar. Add well-beaten eggs and other ingredients alternately. Mix well together.
Bake in moderate oven about 2¾ hours. *Mrs. C. C. Harrison.*

YORK CHERRY CAKE

½ lb. butter, ½ lb. sugar, 4 eggs, 10 ozs. flour, 2 ozs. cherries, 1 teaspoon baking powder.

Method. — Cream butter and sugar. Add well-beaten eggs and flour (to which cherries and baking powder have been added) alternately. Bake in moderate oven about 1¾ hours. *Mrs. C. C. Harrison.*

MRS. R. HAMILTON'S CAKE

½ lb. butter, 1½ cups sugar, 5 eggs, 1 cup milk, 3 cups flour, 2 teaspoons cream of tartar, 1 teaspoon bicarbonate soda.

Method. — Cream butter and sugar, add eggs gradually, well beaten. Dissolve soda in milk. Add cream of tartar to flour. Sift flour in with milk and soda. Beat all ingredients well for ¼ hour. Put mixture into greased round cake tin and bake 1 to 1½ hours in a moderate oven.
 Mrs. R. Hamilton.

MEG'S FRUIT CAKE

1 lb. flour, 1 lb. currants, ½ lb. sultanas, ½ lb. raisins (stoned), 1 lb. sugar, ½ lb. candied peel, ½ lb. chopped almonds, ¾ lb. butter, 1 dozen eggs, half a nutmeg, ½ teaspoon bicarbonate of soda, 2 teaspoon cream of tartar, ¼ teaspoon each of cloves, allspice, mace and ginger (mixed), ¼ tumbler of brandy, rosewater with almonds.

Beat butter to a cream. Add sugar then the yolks beaten well; add the whites beaten to a stiff froth then the fruits and lastly flour and brandy. Makes two large cakes. *M. Dunn, Johannesburg.*

RICH FRUIT CAKE

¾ lb. flour, ½ lb. butter, ½ lb. sultanas, ½ lb. raisins, ¼ lb. mixed peel, ½ teaspoon ground nutmeg, 1 teaspoon baking powder, 1 teaspoon mixed spice, 2 ozs. ground almonds, 6 eggs, ½ lb. sugar, 3 ozs. cherries, ¾ lb. currants, 2 tablespoons Morton's browning essence, ½ whisky glass of brandy.

Cream butter and sugar, add eggs one at a time, beat well, then add essence and brandy, then flour mixed with baking powder (sifted), then ground almonds and fruit. Bake 3½ hours. This can also be steamed for 3 hours then baked for 2½ hours in moderate oven.
 Mrs. S. Watson.

CHRISTMAS CAKE

12 eggs, 1 lb. butter, 1 lb. castor sugar, 1 lb. currants, 1 lb. sultanas, 1 lb. raisins, ¼ lb. peel, ¼ lb. almonds, ½ lb. cherries, 1½ lbs. flour, 1 tablespoon caramel, 1 teaspoon mixed spice, 1 gill brandy, ½ teaspoon bicarbonate of soda, ¼ teaspoon salt.

Cream butter and sugar, beat in eggs one at a time with the hand, then stir in the other ingredients. Flour all fruits before mixing in. Line cake tin with four to six thicknesses of paper, and have equal thickness to cover the top.

Turn top and bottom elements on high until thermometer registers 500° for one large cake or 450° for half size. Place cake in oven and turn both switches off until the heat drops to 300°. Then maintain an even heat of 300° with the bottom element only, on medium, or low, whichever is necessary. A large cake takes 4½ hours to bake; a half size one 3½ hours. *E.R.*

CHRISTMAS CAKE

1 lb. flour, ¾ lb. butter, ½ lb. mixed peel, ¾ lb. raisins, ¾ lb. currants, ¾ lb. sultanas, ¾ lb. sugar, ¼ lb. sweet almonds, ¼ lb. glacé cherries, 1½ teaspoons cinnamon, 1½ teaspoons ginger, 1 teaspoon mixed spice, 8 eggs, little salt.

Method. — Cream butter and sugar. Sift flour and spices. Prepare the fruit. Blanch, peel and chop almonds. Beat eggs. Add flour and eggs alternately to creamed butter and sugar, add fruit and mix well. Put into tin lined with double greased paper. Bake in a moderate oven for 4 hours. *Mrs. L. Malan.*

LUNCH CAKE

1 lb. flour, 6 ozs. butter, ¾ tumble milk, 2 tablespoons vinegar, 8 ozs. sugar, 8 ozs. sultanas, ½ teaspoon bicarbonate soda, 4 eggs.

Method. — Beat butter and sugar to a cream, add eggs with a little flour one by one, beating well. Mix milk, soda and vinegar together, add first flour then liquid till all is used. Cover with halved almonds before baking in moderate oven 350°. *Miss. Jackson, Maritzburg.*

CHINESE CAKE

Pastry. — 6 ozs. flour, 3 ozs. butter, 1 egg yolk, 1 teaspoon castor sugar, a little lemon juice.

Rub butter into flour. Add sugar and egg, then mix to a stiff paste with lemon juice and water.

Line a shallow, round tin with the pastry, leaving some for crossbars.

Filling. — 2 ozs. castor, sugar, 2 ozs. butter, 1 oz. ground almonds, 1 oz. cake crumbs, ½ teaspoon vanilla essence.

Cream butter and sugar, add egg, crumbs, ground almonds and flavouring.
Pour on to pastry. Trim with crossbars, bake for about 35 to 40 minutes in a fairly hot oven.
When cooked spread a thin layer of apricot jam between the bars and run a very little thin water icing over. *Mrs. C. M. Smith.*

DANISH APPLE CAKE

1 lb. flour, ½ lb. butter, ½ lb. white sugar, 2 eggs, 1 teaspoon ammonia powder, ¾ lb. apple rings or 6 fresh apples.
Method. — Mix flour and ammonia powder, rub in butter, add sugar and beaten eggs. Knead well, divide into 4 portions and roll out. Bake in 4 round tins, slightly greased. Prick well with fork as for shortbread. Bake about 10 minutes. Oven 400°.
Filling. — If apple rings are used, soak first, then stew with very little liquid, sweeten to taste. When soft, rub through coarse sieve. If fresh apples are used cook with very little juice. Leave cooked apple, spread on dish to dry, until following day. Spread a generous layer of apple between cakes. *Mrs. Swemmer.*

KISSES

Take the weight of 2 eggs in butter, flour, castor sugar and maizena. Beat butter and sugar to a cream, add eggs one at a time, beat well, sift in flour and maizena and add 1 teaspoon baking powder. Drop on well greased paper, in small round pieces size of a small nut. Bake quickly, put two together with raspberry jam or butter filling. Sprinkle with icing sugar or ice lightly. *Hazel Hawke.*

CHOCOLATE CAKE

¼ lb. butter, 1 cup sugar, 2 cups flour, 2 eggs, 1 large tablespoon cocoa, vanilla essence.
Cream butter and sugar. Add cocoa and essence, whisk eggs separately and fold in. Add flour gradually with baking powder. If too thick add little milk. Put into 2 sandwich tins and bake for 15 minutes.
Filling. — Cream about 1 tablespoon butter with 3 or 4 tablespoons icing sugar. Add vanilla essence. If too stiff and a drop of milk. If too thin, add more icing sugar. Place between layers and dust with icing sugar. *Mrs. C. Kaplan, Balfour.*

LAMINGTON SQUARES

Make a Genoese sponge with 4 eggs, 3 ozs. flour, 3 ozs. butter, ½ teaspoon Royal baking powder, 4 ozs. castor sugar, salt.
Line a small baking tray with paper. Brush the paper with melted pastrine. Beat eggs and sugar for 15 minutes melt butter very carefully

and add it to eggs and sugar alternately with flour and baking powder, taking care to fold it in lightly. Pour into baking tin and bake in medium oven for 15 minutes. When cold cut into squares and coat with chocolate sauce and roll in cocoanut.

Chocolate Sauce.

2 ozs. sweet chocolate, 2 tablespoons butter, 1 tablespoon sugar, ¼ cup icing sugar, 1 cup milk, 1 teaspoon vanilla, 1 teaspoon arrowroot, pinch salt.

Heat milk, sugar and chocolate and add the arrowroot, which has been slaked with a little milk. Cook for ten minutes, stirring constantly. Melt butter and icing sugar and cook till well caramelised. Add and flavour with vanilla.

CHOCOLATE CAKE

1½ cups sugar, ½ cup milk, ¼ cup chocolate or cocoa, 1 teaspoon cream of tartar, ½ cup butter, 1¾ cups flour, ½ teaspoon bicarbonate of soda, 3 eggs.

Beat butter to cream, gradually adding sugar. Add 3 tablespoons boiling water to cocoa and add to butter and sugar, then milk mixed with bicarbonate of soda and cream of tartar, then eggs well beaten, and lastly the flour sifted in.

Bake ¾ or 1 hour at 400°. *M. L. Malan.*

COCOA ALMOND FILLING AND FROSTING

(This goes with the chocolate cake)

6 tablespoons butter, 3 cups confectioner's sugar, 8 tablespoons cocoa, ½ teaspoon almond extract, ⅓ cup cream.

Method. — Cream butter, add sugar and cocoa, a little at a time, beating until very light and creamy. Add flavouring and cream. More cream if necessary. Spread thickly between layers and put a thin layer on top and sides of cake. With icing tube (rose border) put the icing up and down sides of cake to represent the bark of a tree. *M. L. Malan.*

RICH FRUIT CAKE

1 lb. flour, ½ lb. butter, ½ lb. castor sugar, ½ teaspoon salt, 8 eggs, ½ lb. raisins, ½ lb. currants, 1 lb. sultanas, 4 ozs. mixed peel (optional), 4 ozs. glacé cherries, 4 ozs. ground almonds, 1 teaspoon each vanilla and almond essence, 2 tablespoons coffee essence, 1 level teaspoonful bicarbonate soda dissolved in 2 tablespoons brandy.

Cream butter and sugar and add coffee essence. Beat eggs and add flour and eggs alternately to butter and sugar mixture. Add floured fruit, peel and almonds, essences and brandy and soda last of all. Drop halved cherries in at intervals. Line a 4 lb. cake tin with brown paper and then with greaseproof paper, and tie brown paper round the outside. Place sandwich tin on top of cake tin and asbestos mat on top of that. Bake 4 hours in moderate oven. *Mrs. McElrath.*

HILDA'S CAKE
1 teacup white sugar, 1 teacup cornflour, ½ teacup milk, whites of 2 eggs, 1 teacup flour, ½ teacup butter, 2 teaspoonfuls baking powder, 2 teaspoons essence, any flavour.

Beat the butter and sugar to a cream, add the other ingredients, lastly add the egg whites, very well beaten. Bake at once in a moderate oven.
Mrs. E. C. Coleman.

WALNUT MAPLE CAKE
1 cup brown or yellow sugar (preferably yellow), ½ cup butter, 1⅓ cups flour, 2 eggs, 1 cup chopped walnuts, ½ cup cherries, ½ cup milk, 2 teaspoons baking powder, 1 teaspoon vanilla essence, pinch salt.

Cream together sugar and butter. Add yolks of eggs and milk. Then add flour, which has been sifted twice, adding 2 teaspoons baking powder before the second sifting. Add 1 teaspoon vanilla essence and salt, walnuts and cherries. Lastly the egg whites beaten stiff.
Bake in a well greased and papered angel tin for 4-5 minutes at 375°. Cover with icing and sprinkle sides with chopped nuts and decorate top with half walnuts and cherries. *Mrs. Blake.*

WALNUT TART
7 eggs, 2 tablespoons breadcrumbs, 3 tablespoons sugar, ½ lb. shelled walnuts, vanilla and pinch of salt.

Method. — Beat egg yolks and sugar very well, add walnuts, crumbs, salt and vanilla and fold in stiffly-beaten egg whites, bake in a hot oven.
Trim on top at intervals with half-walnuts. *Mrs. Kaplan, Balfour.*

CREAM CRACKER CAKE
2 heaped tablespoons butter, 3 eggs, ½ lb. cream crackers, ½ teaspoon salt, 1 cup sugar, 1 small cup milk, 2 teaspoons baking powder, ½ cup chopped nuts.

Method. — Cream sugar and butter and yolks of eggs together, then add milk. Next add cream crackers (rolled fine like crumbs) and mix baking powder, then add to other ingredients. Add salt and chopped nuts, lastly fold in whites of eggs well beaten.
Filling (or cream can be used).
2 tablespoons butter, 1 yolk egg, 3 tablespoons icing sugar, essence. Mix all well together. *Mrs. S. Watson.*

APPLE CAKE

Makes two cakes, 2 eggs, 2 level cups flour, 2 teaspoons baking powder, ¼ lb. butter, 5 apples (sweet), ½ cup sugar.

Method. — Cream butter and sugar, add eggs, then flour, sifted with baking powder. This batter can be mixed with juice from the apples or a little milk and water; batter must not be too thin. Core and peel apples, cook until soft with ¼ cup sugar, little water and little butter. Pour cake mixture into sandwich tins, arrange apples on top of batter, sprinkle nuts and little ground cinnamon and sugar, put small pats of butter on top.

Bake 1 hour. Oven 400°. When cold, can be decorated with cream.

Mrs. S. Watson.

CHEESE CAKES

Sponge. — 1 egg, 1½ tablespoons castor sugar, 1 teaspoon baking powder, 1 tablespoon butter, essence to taste, 1½ tablespoons milk, 2 tablespoons heaped flour.

Short Paste. — 6 ozs. flour, 4 ozs. butter, pinch salt, cold water.

Method (Short Paste). — Rub butter into flour and salt. Cold water to make soft dough to roll out. Put dough in patty tins. Put small spoon jam, then add sponge mixture, on top, put cross of dough on top of sponge mixture. Bake in 450° oven.

MADEIRA CAKE

5 ozs. butter, ¾ cup sugar (castor), 2 cups flour, 3 eggs, 1 level teaspoon baking powder, ½ cup milk and water mixed.

Method. — Beat butter and sugar to cream, add eggs, one at a time. Mix well. Add milk and water, flour sieved with baking powder. Bake ¾ hour in moderate oven.

Mr. S. Watson.

WALNUT CAKE

3 tablespoons butter, 7 tablespoons flour, 6 tablespoons sugar, 3 eggs, 1 teaspoon baking powder level, ½ teacup milk, ½ teacup walnuts, ½ tablespoon coffee essence.

Method. — Cream butter and sugar. Add eggs, one at a time, then flour which has been sifted with baking powder, then walnuts and lastly essence and milk. Bake 1 hour.

Put whipped cream on top, sprinkle with chopped walnuts. Cake can be cut through the middle and cream fillling put in.

Mr. S. Watson.

COCOANUT SQUARES

¼ lb. butter, ½ cup sugar, 3 egg yolks, 2 cups flour, 2 teaspoons baking powder, ¼ cup milk.

Method. — Beat butter and sugar to cream. Add beaten yolks, then milk, lastly baking powder and flour that have been sifted together. Roll into a thin paste. Use half paste for small tarts and fill with jam. Balance of paste put on scone pan and spread with raspberry jam, then spread with the following mixture: —
Filling. — 1 cup cocoanut, 1 small cup sugar, whites of three eggs.
Method. — Beat whites of eggs stiffly, then add sugar and cocoanut. Spread on paste.
Bake ¼ hour in slow oven. Cut in squares when nearly cold.
Mr. S. Watson.

MAIDS OF HONOUR

½ lb. short pastry made with 4 ozs. of shortening, 8 ozs. flour, pinch of salt, small teaspoon baking powder, mix with water.
Method. — Roll out pastry, cut into rounds, place in patty pans. Put a little jam in each, then rest of filling. Place a thin strip of pastry on top making a cross. Bake in quick oven.
Filling. — 2 eggs, 4 ozs. ground rice, 3 ozs. of sugar, 3 ozs. of butter, almond flavouring. Mix all well together. *A. Paxton.*

SPICE CAKE

6 tablespoons Epic oil, 6 tablespoons castor sugar, 2 cups sifted flour, 1 teaspoon Bournville cocoa, ½ teaspoon mixed spices (nutmeg, cinnamon, cloves, etc.), 3 teaspoons Royal baking powder, ¼ teaspoon salt, 3 eggs and a little vanilla essence.
Method. — Add Epic oil to castor sugar and beat slightly. Sift flour, baking powder, salt, spices and cocoa. Add a little flour and one egg to oil and sugar. Beat thoroughly till frothy, then add next egg and a little more flour and beat well again. Continue till last egg is used. Add remainder of flour and enough cold water to make a soft, dropping consistency. Pour mixture into greased sandwich tins (large) bake 20 minutes in hot oven 400°.
Filling. — A spiced butter filling may be used or a cooked apple and date filling.
Cook together a few dates (stoned), apple chips, sultanas and raisins, with a little of the spice, sugar and lemon juice till the mixture is soft and pulpy and thick. Allow to cool, and spread between the sandwich cakes.
Icing. — Make an ordinary butter icing and add 1 teaspoon cocoa and ½ teaspoon mixed spices and a few drops of vanilla essence. Spread roughly on top of cake. Draw a fork through icing in rough, wavy lines, and decorate with whole dates and walnuts.
Mrs. P. J. Foot.

MADELINE CAKES

2 eggs, their weight in castor sugar, 4 ozs. flour, 2½ ozs. butter, ½ teaspoon baking powder, ½ gill milk.

Method. — Sieve flour and baking powder, cream butter and sugar, add eggs (one at a time) beating well, add flour etc. Pour into greased moulds, three parts full; bake 10 minutes (oven 400°).

When cooked, roll in jam, apricot or raspberry, thinned with a little boiling water, then roll in desiccated cocoanut. *Mrs. Murphy.*

COCOANUT CAKE

Bottom Layer:

5 tablespoons flour, 2 tablespoons sugar, 1 tablespoon butter, ½ teaspoon baking powder, yolks of 2 eggs.

Method. — Cream butter and sugar, add yolks of eggs well beaten. Little warm water, if necessary, then add flour and baking powder.

Top Layer:

1 cup desiccated cocoanut, ½ cup sugar, whites of 2 eggs.

Method. — Mix cocoanut and sugar, add whites of eggs well beaten. Bake in one sandwich cake tin. Put cake in oven at 400° and turn elements right off. Bake for 25 minutes. *Mrs. J. Klopper.*

SHORTBREAD

1½ lbs. flour, ¼ lb. maizena, 1 lb. butter, ½ lb. castor sugar.

Mix dry ingredients and combine with butter. Mould into two round, flat cakes. Place these on grease proof paper and with hands press out to half inch thickness. Pinch edges and prick all over with fork. Bake to biscuit colour in cool oven one hour. *Mrs. Mackenzie.*

TEA RUSKS

6 cupfuls of flour, 2 eggs, 2 teaspoonfuls of cream of tartar, piece of butter size of an egg, 1 cupful of sugar, 2 teaspoonfuls of soda, 2 cupfuls milk.

This makes a large quantity, but they keep well.

Method. — Mix all dry ingredients together. Rub in butter. Mix with milk. Roll out, cut in any shape and bake in quick oven. *A. Paxton.*

CINNAMON SPONGE

Beat 1 dessertspoonful of butter with ½ cup of sugar. Add 1 egg and beat well. Add 1 tablespoon golden syrup and ½ cup milk to which ½ teaspoon of bicarbonate of soda has been added. Sift together 1 cup flour, 1 teaspoon baking powder, 2 level teaspoons spice

of cinnamon and pinch of salt. Beat all together. Bake 15 minutes in moderate oven.
Date filling. *M. Grove.*

QUICK CAKE

Beat 2 eggs with ½ cup sugar into cream for 10 minutes. Sift 1 cup flour with 2 teaspoons baking powder and pinch of salt. Then boil ½ cup milk with lump of butter size of egg.

Add flour to beaten eggs alternately with boiling milk. Bake in layer tins well greased and floured for 15-20 minutes. Put in filling. This cake may be made into Chocolate Cake by adding 1 tablespoon cocoa to dry ingredients.

COCOANUT MACAROON CAKES

Short pastry cut into rounds and placed in pastry-pans, ¼ teaspoon of apricot jam in each, then a heaped teaspoon of the following mixture: 2 eggs, 2 cups cocoanut, 1 cup castor sugar. Decorate with strips of pastry and cook in moderate oven until browned nicely.
Mrs. H. C. Lake, Maritzburg.

FRENCH CAKE

2 cups flour, 3 eggs, ½ teaspoon soda, lemon essence, 1 cup sugar, 2 tablespoons butter, 1 teaspoon cream of tartar, pinch of salt.

Beat sugar and butter to a cream. Add eggs (one by one). Add flour, salt and cream of tartar (which have been sifted together), then soda dissolved in 1 cup milk. Bake for 1 hour. *Mrs. Blake.*

WELSH CAKES

1 lb. flour, ¼ lb. lard, ¼ lb. butter, 2 ozs. currants, 3 ozs. sultanas, 2 eggs, ¼ lb. sugar, 2 ozs. peel, ½ teaspoon salt, 2 teaspoons baking powder.

Sift flour, baking powder and salt and rub in fat. Add sugar and fruit. Make into stiff dough with beaten eggs; if necessary add a very little milk, but mixture must be stiff. Knead and roll out $1/3$ in. thick, cut into rounds and bake on hot, ungreased girdle, turning when brown.
Mrs. Linton.

CHOCOLATE FANCIES
(No Baking)

Melt coolly as possible ½ lb. plain Bournville chocolate, add 1 dessertspoon boiled milk and 2 ozs. rice crispies. Put in rocky heaps on rice paper. Will keep well. *Mrs. D. K. Lawrie, Johannesburg.*

RIBBON CAKE

2 cups flour, 1½ cups castor sugar, 4 eggs, 6 ozs. butter, 3 teaspoons baking powder, ⅓ cup milk, pinch of salt.

Cream butter and sugar together, add the beaten eggs and mix well. Mix and sift flour, baking powder and salt and add alternately with the milk to the first mixture. Divide batter into three parts. To one part add pink colouring, and to another 3 tablespoons of melted chocolate and one part plain. Bake in three layers in a hot oven, 400° for 20 minutes. Put together with any filling preferred. The above mixture could be baked in a large square tin and cut up into fancy shapes for small cakes and iced. *Mrs. Withiel.*

FRIG. CAKE

½ lb. butter, 1 lb. castor sugar, 2 tablespoons cocoa, 2 eggs, well beaten, 1 packet Marie biscuits.

Method. — Melt butter with sugar in coca. Stir in beaten eggs. Break biscuits and stir all together. Pour mixture into ice tray and leave for six hours. *Mrs. T. Reinecke.*

FRUIT CAKE

1 lb. mixed fruit. Wash, then cover with 1 breakfastcup water and ¾ cup sugar and 3 ozs. butter. Boil together for five minutes, and when cold, add one beaten egg, 2 cups meal or flour, spices, dates, etc., and 1 tablespoon Brandy, into which mix 1 teaspoon bi-carb.

Bake in slow oven for 2 hours.

A real friend is one who walks in when the rest of the world walks out.

FILLINGS AND ICINGS

FRENCH CREAM FILLING

Add the stiffly-beaten white of an egg to ½ cup cream beaten until thick. Flavour and sweeten. *Mrs. W. T.*

CONFECTIONER'S LEMON CURD FILLING

Put into saucepan 1 cup sugar, 4 eggs, ½ lb. butter, the rind and juice of 4 lemons. Stir constantly over the fire until it thickens.
Mrs. W. T.

PRUNE FILLING

1 cup sugar and ¼ cup prune liquid (in which ¼ lb. prunes have been cooked to soft ball stage, that is when syrup begins to thread when dropped from spoon or fork). Then pour the boiling sugar on to stiffly-beaten whites of 2 eggs, add ¼ cup cooked prunes cut up, and ¼ lb. almonds, blanched and chopped. Add 1 or 2 tablespoons sherry or juice of a lemon. *Mrs. W. T.*

FONDANT ICING

Put 1 cup of sugar on the fire with ¼ cup cold water, and stir until all the sugar grains have dissolved. Just as it commences to boil stir in quickly ⅛ of a teaspoon cream of tartar, dissolved in ½ teaspoon of water, then allow to cook undisturbed and fairly rapidly until it reaches the soft ball stage (that is when the syrup forms hair-like threads when dropped from the tip of the spoon). Another way to test is to drop a little in cold water, and when the syrup can be taken up between the finger and thumb and formed into a little soft ball. Then remove from the fire and gently pour without shaking into a flat meat dish rinsed in cold water. Leave until luke warm, then beat until it thickens and turns creamy and knead until smooth. To use, melt over hot water and pour over cake, adding any colouring and flavouring desired.

JELLY ICING

½ cup cream, ⅓ cup boiling water, ¾ tablespoon powdered gelatine, juice of a half lemon, colouring.

Dissolve gelatine in boiling water, add lemon juice, cream and any colouring desired. Stir until thick and pour over cakes.

LEMON PIE MIXTURE

Beat up an egg very lightly, add ¼ lb. sugar and the juice of a small lemon, mix all well together.

Line plate with short pastry, pour in mixture, cover with pastry.
Miss Jackson.

MOCK WHIPPED CREAM FILLING

Dissolve 1 teaspoon powdered gelatine in 3 tablespoons hot water. Put ¼ lb. butter, 1½ tablespoons sugar, and a pinch of salt into a basin, together with a ¼ teaspoon cream of tartar, then add hot gelatine and beat well for 10 minutes until the mixture looks like whipped cream. Add any flavouring desired.

FRUIT JUICE FILLING

Dissolve 1 level tablespoon gelatine in half a cup of hot water, add 2 tablespoons sugar, then stir in ½ cup of any kind of fruit juice. Pour into a wet sandwich tin, the same size as the cake. When set, warm the tin slightly, and the jelly will slip out on to the cake.

BUTTER ICING

Mix 12 tablespoons sifted icing sugar with 4 tablespoons of butter, until smooth, adding a little milk if necessary to make it of a consistency to spread. Flavour with vanilla, brandy or Van der Hum liqueur.

FIG FILLING

To ½ cup custard filling add ¼ cup stewed figs rubbed through a sieve.

CONFECTIONER'S CUSTARD FILLING

Put into saucepan 3 eggs, ¾ cup sugar, ¼ teaspoon salt, 1 cup flour and about 2 cups water.

Stir constantly over the fire until it thickens and loses its raw taste, then remove and add ¼ lb. butter and 1 teaspoon vanilla essence. This custard makes a very nice filling for cakes, and can be mixed with the syrup and any finely-chopped up preserves, coffee essence, chocolate, cocoa, mashed fruits, etc.

CHOCOLATE FILLING

Add to custard filling one square baker's chocolate (or 2 tablespoons Bournville cocoa) melted over hot water, and use ¼ cup more sugar.

COCOANUT ICING

2 eggs whites, 2 ozs. desiccated cocoanut, 4 ozs. castor. Whip the whites of eggs to a stiff froth, then mix in lightly the sugar and cocoanut. After spreading it on top of the cake, place in a cool oven for 5 minutes to set.

CHOCOLATE ICING

2 squares finelly-grated chocolate (or 2 tablespoons Bournville cocoa), 1 teaspoon butter, 4 tablespoons hot water, ¼ teaspoon vanilla, icing sugar.

Melt chocolate over boiling water, add butter and hot water. Cool, and add sufficient icing sugar to make right consistency to spread. Add flavouring.

ORANGE ICING

Grated rind of 1 orange, 1 teaspoon brandy, ½ teaspoon lemon juice, 1 tablespoon orange juice, yolk of 1 egg, icing sugar.

Add rind to brandy, and fruit juices, and leave 15 minutes. Strain and add gradually to egg yolk slightly beaten, then add sufficient icing sugar (sifted) to make the right consistency to spread.

GELATINE ICING

Dissolve 1 teaspoon powdered gelatine in 3 teaspoons hot water, then stir in ½ cup icing sugar and any desired flavouring. Beat until smooth and then pour over cake.

FRUIT GLACE ICING

To every ¼ lb. icing sugar allow 1 teaspoon orange juice or water flavoured with lemon juice, or fruit essences, or any liquid desired, such as coffee, liqueur, etc. Pour the sugar and liquid into a bowl, and mix, then allow to get warm over boiling water, but do not let the mixture get hot, otherwise it will be dull. Any fruit juice may be used, and any colouring liked, then pour over cake.

MOCHA ICING

Two-thirds of a cup of butter, 2½ cups icing sugar, yolk of 1 egg, coffee extract, 1 teaspoon vanilla.

Rub the butter to a cream, add beaten yolk of egg and gradually the sugar, vanilla and enough coffee extract to give the desired flavour. Colour should be that of a strong cup of coffee with cream in it. The egg yolk may be omitted if desired. One tablespoon cocoa may also be added.

LEMON ICING

Squeeze and strain the juice of 2 lemons, 2 tablespoons melted butter. Then stir in as much sifted icing sugar as will make a paste.

ALMOND PASTE

1 lb. castor sugar, 1 lb. sifted icing sugar, 1 lb. ground almonds, 2 eggs, 2 teaspoons strained lemon juice, 2 teaspoons rose water, ½ teaspoon orange flower water, ½ teaspoon vanilla essence, ½ teaspoon almond essence.

Mix sugar and almonds together, make hole in the centre and add eggs one at a time, mix well and add flavouring ingredients. Knead well on a pastry board sprinkled with castor sugar, till smooth. Roll out and place on cake, previously brushed over with melted jelly.

WATER ICING

Mix icing sugar with sufficient warm water to make it just thick enough to run smooth. Instead of water, any liquid may be used, such as fruit juices, coffee essence, etc., and any flavouring added.

COFFEE ICING

Make a water icing and add enough coffee essence to colour. Flavour with vanilla.

BUTTER ICING

Cream together ¼ lb. butter and 6 ozs. icing sugar. Add any flavouring and colouring desired, and decorate with chopped nuts, desiccated cocoanut slightly browned in a cool oven, crystallised cherries, pistachio nuts, angelica, etc. Smooth with a knife dipped in hot water.

YELLOW ICING

Make same as Butter Icing, adding 1 egg yolk.

CARAMEL ICING

Make as Mocha Icing, using caramel or burnt sugar instead of coffee extract.

WHITE MOUNTAIN CREAM OR BOILED ICING

1 cup sugar, ⅓ cup boiling water, white of 1 egg, 1 teaspoon vanilla or ½ teaspoon lemon juice, ⅛ teaspoon cream of tartar. Put sugar and water in a saucepan, and stir to prevent sugar from adhering to saucepan. Heat gradually to boiling point, then add cream of tartar and stop stirring. Continue boiling until it threads when dropped from a spoon. Then pour syrup gradually on stiffly-beaten white of egg, beating constantly. Continue beating until of right consistency to spread, then add flavouring, and pour over cake, spreading evenly with knife dipped in warm water.

BUTTERSCOTCH FILLING

¾ cup brown sugar, 4 tablespoons butter, ⅓ cup flour, ½ teaspoon salt, 2 beaten eggs, 2 cups milk, ¼ teaspoon vanilla.

Mix butter and sugar. Cook 2 minutes or until syrup is brown. Add ⅓-⅔ cup cold milk and cook over hot water. Mix flour and salt with remaining milk, add to hot mixture and cook 15 minutes, add eggs, cook 2 minutes. Cool and flavour. *Mrs. L. Malan.*

CHOCOLATE FILLING
(For immediate use)

Whip ¼ pint cream stiffly, then first add 2 ozs. grated chocolate, then 2 ozs. ground almonds and ¼ lb. icing sugar.

Mrs. Withiel.

YELLOW BOILED ICING

Proceed as for White Mountain Cream, using egg yolk instead of white. *Mrs. W. Travers.*

ALMOND FILLING

Mix together 2 tablespoons ground almonds, 2 tablespoons apricot jam, 1 tablespoon whipped cream and 1 teaspoon of vanilla essence. *Mrs. Withiel.*

LEMON CURD

4 tablespoons lemon juice, 1 tablespoon lemon rind, ½ lb. white sugar, 2 ozs. butter, 3 egg yolks and one whole egg.

Boil lemon juice and rind together for a few minutes. Put hot juice, butter and sugar into top of double saucepan and when butter and sugar are melted pour over beaten egg and yolks. Return to double saucepan and stir all the time until mixture is smooth and thickens.

GRANADILLA CHEESE

3 eggs, 2 ozs. butter, ½ lb. sugar, ½ cup strained granadilla juice.

Put butter, sugar and juice into saucepan and stir over a slow heat until sugar is melted. Beat eggs and add to mixture. Stir until thick and mixture reaches boiling point. Bottle and use like lemon curd.

Mrs. H. C. Lake, Maritzburg.

MINCEMEAT 1

1 lb. each currants, sultanas, raisins, apples, sugar, a little brandy, ½ lb. mixed peel, rind and juice of 1 lemon.

Put through mincer and mix together. Steam 3 hours and while hot stir in 3 tablespoons butter. Bottle and store till needed. *M.L.B.*

MINCEMEAT 2

2 lbs. each currants, raisins, apples, suet, 1½ lbs. sugar, ½ pint brandy, 1 lb. peel, juice 2 lemons.

Put all through mincer, mix well, put in bottles and keep until needed. *M.L.B.*

ECONOMICAL MINCEMEAT

4 ozs. suet, 4 ozs. raisins, 4 ozs. sultanas, 6 ozs. currants, ½ lb. sugar, 3 ozs. candied peel, juice and grated yellow rind of 1 lemon, ½ lb. apples (peeled and cored), 1 teaspoon mixed spice, ½ teaspoon cinnamon, pinch of salt, ½ wine glass brandy.

Shred and chop the suet, stone the raisins, clean the sultanas and currants, chop the peel very finely, grate the lemon rind and chop the apples. Mix all ingredients well together and press into jars.

ECONOMICAL LEMON CURD

Juice of 2 and most of the finely grated yellow rind of 1 lemon, 2 eggs, butter the size of a walnut, ¾ of a breakfast cup of sugar.

Melt the sugar in the juice of lemons with the grated rind and butter, cool a little and then add eggs slightly beaten. Put in double cooker or stand a basin in hot water till the mixture thickens. *Mrs. Shaw.*

LEMON CURD 1

6 lemons (rind and juice), ½ lb. sugar, ½ lb. butter, 4 eggs, a pinch of salt.

Mix all together and cook in double cooker until thick. *J.H.*

LEMON CURD 2 (Sweeter)

6 lemons (rind and juice), 1 lb. sugar, 6 eggs, 6 ozs. butter, a pinch of salt.

Boil the butter, sugar and lemon juice and grated rind, pour in the eggs and cook in double saucepan. *M.L.B.*

If you want an obligement, ask a busy woman. — *M.A.W.*

SILENCE

If you stand very still in the heart of a wood — you will hear many wonderful things — the snap of a twig and the wind in the trees and the whir of invisible wings... if you stand very still in the turmoil of life — and you wait for the voice from within — you'll be led down the quiet ways of wisdom and peace — in a mad world of chaos and din... if you stand very still and you hold to your faith — you will get all the help that you ask — you will draw from the Silence the things that you need — Hope and courage, and strength for your task.   *Patience Strong.*

BISCUITS

FOUNDATION RECIPE

1 lb. flour, ½ lb. butter, 2 eggs, 6 ozs. sugar.

Cream the butter and sugar very thoroughly, then beat in the eggs one at a time, gradually add the flour sifted with a good pinch of salt and knead the whole very thoroughly. Roll out thinly and cut into shapes. Bake in a quick oven until golden brown.

VARIATIONS

Divide the paste into several portions and add the following: —

(1) ¼ of the paste, 3 ozs. chopped cherries and dates, knead fruit into the paste. Roll out and cook as above.

(2) ¼ of the paste, 1 oz. melted chocolate, 1 oz. chopped walnuts, vanilla. Melt chocolate over boiling water, mix with the paste, then knead in vanilla and walnuts, adding a little more flour if necessary.

(3) ¼ of the paste, ½ teaspoon coffee essence, 1 oz. chopped walnuts. Mix in the coffee essence and knead in chopped nuts.

(4) ¼ of the paste, 1 heaped tablespoon cocoanut, a little grated lemon rind. Knead in cocoanut and lemon rind.

OUBLIETJIES

8 tablespoons flour, 3 eggs, 4 tablespoons sugar, 1 tablespoon melted butter.

Mix all together and add enough water to make a thin batter.

Bake in "oublietjie" pan — ½ tablespoon butter to each biscuit.

Mrs. J.C. Smuts.

CORNFLAKE CREAMS

Whites of 2 eggs, ½ cup castor sugar, 2 cups of cornflakes or Post Toasties.

Method. — Beat egg whites stiffly, stir in sugar, then cornflakes. Place in teaspoonfuls on tray, bake for 10 minutes till crisp and brown, put two together with whipped cream.

FAIRY SHORTBREAD (Biscuits)

1½ cups icing sugar, 3 cups flour, 1 cup clarified butter. Boil butter, let it cool. Remove the pure fat from the sediment and cream well. Alternately add icing sugar and flour, and beat well. Knead well. Break off into pieces the size of a walnut, shape into fingers and score with a knife. Place a half almond on each biscuit and bake in moderate oven. *Mrs. Sorour, Ficksburg.*

COCOANUT MACAROONS

½ cup condensed milk, 2 cups shredded cocoanut, 1 teaspoon vanilla (optional).

Mix condensed milk and shredded cocoanut together. Drop by spoonfuls on a buttered pan, about an inch apart, bake in a moderate oven until a delicate brown. These macaroons are delicious. *"The Star".*

DATE BISCUITS

1 lb. flour, ½ lb. butter, ½ lb. sugar, 1 teaspoon cream of tartar, ½ teaspoon soda, 2 eggs, milk, pinch salt.

Mix dry ingredients and rub in butter. Drop in eggs whole and mix thoroughly, using a little milk if necessary. Roll out ¼ inch thick. Put a layer of mashed dates on ½ of the paste, fold over and cut into fingers. Bake in moderate oven until a pale brown. *Mrs. D. Hawke.*

DATE TURN-OVERS

1 lb flour, 1 teaspoon baking powder, ¼ lb. butter, 2 eggs dates.

Make the pastry into strips about three inches wide, lay a date on each strip and roll, then dip into egg. Roll in sugar and put into well greased pans. Bake in a quick oven. *Mrs. E. C. Coleman.*

PARKINS

½ lb. oatmeal, ½ lb. flour, 6 ozs. granulated sugar, ¼ lb. lard or butter, 6 ozs. syrup = 2 tablespoons, 1 egg, 1½ teaspoons bicarbonate of soda, 1 teaspoon ground ginger, 1 teaspoon ground cinnamon, ½ teaspoon mixed spice.

Mix dry ingredients and rub in lard or butter, switch egg and add to golden syrup and mix well, work all into a stiff dough. I break little bits off the dough and form into a ball with my hands, just exactly the size of a small marble, and grease a baking tin and lay on the marbles, not too close together as they spread in the baking and go flat, and bake in the middle of the oven for a few minutes as they brown very quickly. Be sure to take them out before they are too dark. Lift them out with a broad knife, and lay on a cool dish to harden. Place a blanched almond on centre of each parkin before baking.

Mrs. Duncan (late Rose Deep, Germiston).

ALMOND BISCUITS

½ lb. flour, 7 ozs. sugar, 7 ozs. butter, ½ lb. ground almonds, 2 eggs, pinch of cinnamon, white of egg to brush over.

Rub butter into flour. Beat yolks and one white of egg together and add. Roll out and cut. Brush over with white of egg and place almond on top. Bake in moderate oven till pale brown. *J.H.*

ABERNETHY BISCUITS

1 lb. flour, 6 ozs. butter, 3 ozs. sugar, 1 level teaspoon soda, 2 level teaspoons cream of tartar, milk sufficient to make a stiff dough, cut into rounds ⅛ inch in thickness.

Rub in butter. Bake about 30 minutes in moderate oven. *J.H.*

MEALIE BISCUITS

1 cup flour, 1½ cups mealie meal, ¾ cup butter, 1 cup sugar (barely), 1 teaspoon baking powder, 1 egg, essence of lemon.

Mix butter and sugar to cream, add other ingredients and a little milk if necessary. Bake 20 minutes. Slow oven. *L. Hendrie.*

SHORTBREAD BISCUITS

4 ozs. butter, 4 ozs. flour, 1 oz. cornflour, 2 ozs. castor sugar.

Cream the butter. Sift the flour with a pinch of salt, cornflour and sugar. Turn on to the board and gradually knead the butter into it to make a workable dough. Dust the board lightly with sifted flour, roll out the mixture to ½ inch thickness, cut into fancy shapes and fingers. Prick with a fork and place on greased baking sheet. Bake at 375° or No. 5 for 20 to 25 minutes until golden brown. Remove from oven and brush over with water icing, sprinkle with chopped walnuts or blanched and chopped almonds. *"The Star".*

BUTTERSCOTCH BISCUITS

½ lb. flour, ½ teaspoon salt, 4 level tablespoons brown sugar, 1 beaten egg, vanilla essence, milk to mix, ¼ lb. butter.

Cream the butter and sugar, add the beaten egg, then gradually work in the sifted flour and salt, adding a little milk if necessary. Chill thoroughly. Turn on to a floured board. Roll out and cut into shapes. Put on a greased baking sheet, sprinkle with brown sugar and bake at 400° Fahr. or No. 7 for 10-15 minutes. *"The Star".*

CHOCOLATE BISCUITS

1 lb. flour, ½ teaspoon mixed spice, ½ teaspoon salt, 2 ozs. cocoa or melted chocolate, ¼ lb. butter, vanilla essence, 6 ozs. castor sugar, 1 well-beaten egg, 1 teaspoon baking powder, 1 tablespoon milk.

Cream the butter and work the melted chocolate or cocoa into it, add the sugar and cream very thoroughly, then add egg, milk and vanilla essence. Sift half the flour with the baking powder and salt and work it well together, then gradually work in as much of the rest of the flour as it will take. Chill thoroughly, roll out on a board lightly dusted with flour to ¼ inch thickness. Cut into fingers and put on a greased baking sheet, sprinkle with castor sugar. Bake at 400° Fahr. or No. 5 for 10-15 minutes. When cold cover with a water icing, either plain or mixed with chocolate. *"The Star".*

GINGER SNAPS

¼ butter or Purene, ⅔ cup Demarara sugar, ⅓ cup treacle or syrup, 2½ cups flour, ½ teaspoon salt, ½ teaspoon bicarbonate of soda, 1½ teaspoons ground ginger, about ½ cup milk.

Cream the butter and sugar, add the treacle or syrup. Add the sifted, dry ingredients, mixing the bicarbonate of soda with the milk and adding it last, then form into a roll. Wrap in paper and chill for 1 hour. Roll and cut into rounds. Bake at 350° or No. 4 for 8 to 10 minutes on a greased baking sheet. Leave until just warm before removing from the pan. *"The Star".*

COCOANUT BISCUITS

¼ lb. butter, 4 ozs. castor sugar, 1 egg, 5 tablespoons flour, 3 heaped tablespoons cocoanut, 1 tablespoon finely-chopped cherries.

Cream the butter and sugar, beat in 1 small egg, then fold in the sifted flour and salt and the cocoanut and cherries. Roll out and cut into rounds. Bake at 400° Fahr. or No. 7 until delicately browned.
"The Star".

CHEESE BISCUITS

4 ozs. flour, 3 ozs. grated cheese, 2 ozs. butter, 1 egg yolk, pepper, salt and cayenne.

Sift the flour, pepper, salt, with the cayenne pepper, rub in the butter, then add the grated cheese and make to a stiff paste with the beaten yolk and 2 teaspoons milk or water. Roll out thinly, cut into fingers or rounds and serve hot with any savoury filling. *"The Star".*

DATE DAINTIES

1 lb. stoned and chopped dates, ¾ cup sugar, 1 cup chopped nuts, 5 tablespoons flour, 2 teaspoons baking powder, 3 eggs, pinch of salt, vanilla essence.

Sift flour, salt and baking powder into a basin. Add nuts, dates, sugar and vanilla essence, then drop in eggs without previously beating them and mix all the ingredients well together. Spread the mixture on a greased baking tin and bake in a moderate oven for 40 minutes. When done remove and cool, cut into squares and sprinkle with castor or icing sugar. *"The Star"*.

DATE CRACKERS

¼ lb. stoned dates, 1¼ cups rolled oats, 1¼ cups flour, ½ cup brown sugar, ½ cup white sugar, ½ cup butter, ¼ cup hot water, ¼ cup cold water, 1 teaspoon baking powder.

Put dates, white sugar and cold water into a saucepan and bring to the boil. Allow to simmer gently until the dates are quite soft, then remove from stove and cool.

Cream the butter and brown sugar, then add oats which have been mixed with the sifted flour and baking powder and the hot water. Divide the mixture into two equal parts and roll out thinly. Spread the date mixture on the one half and cover with the other half of the rolled out mixture. Press down firmly and cut into small squares. Put on a greased baking tin and bake for about twenty minutes. *"The Star"*.

MACAROONS

½ lb. castor sugar, ¼ lb. ground almonds, 2 egg whites, few drops almond essence, few blanched almonds.

Mix together sugar, ground almonds, almond essence and unbeaten egg whites to form a fairly stiff paste. Line a baking sheet with rice paper and put macaroon mixture on in small mounds. Place half a blanched almond or glacé cherry on each biscuit. *"The Star"*.

HAZELNUT BISCUITS

¼ lb. butter, ¼ lb. castor sugar, 1 egg, ¾ lb. flour, few drops vanilla essence, 3 ozs. chopped hazelnuts, water icing.

Cream together butter and sugar, beat in the egg, then add sifted flour alternately with nuts, beating the mixture all the time until it resembles a smooth paste that can be rolled out. Turn on to floured board and roll out thinly. Cut into fancy shapes, put on to a baking tin and bake in a slow oven of 325° Fahr. or No. 3 for about 30 minutes. When done remove and cool then brush over the tops with water icing and decorate with a glacé cherry. *"The Star"*.

SHERRY STICKS

6 ozs. flour, 4 ozs. butter, 3 ozs. sugar, 1 egg yolk, 1 tablespoon sherry, chopped, blanched almonds, or chopped cherries.

Sift flour and rub in the butter, add sugar, then egg yolk and sherry. Mix all together to form a firm paste. Turn on to a floured board and roll out thinly. Cut into narrow fingers; brush over with the white of egg and sprinkle thickly with chopped, blanched almods or cherries. Bake in a moderate oven till firm and brown, about 12-15 minutes.

"The Star".

DATE SLICES

¾ cup rolled oats, ¾ cup flour, 2 ozs. butter, ¼ cup brown sugar, ⅛ cup warm water, ¼ teaspoon bicarbonate of soda.

Cream butter and sugar. Mix bicarbonate with the warm water. Mix all dry ingredients and make to a stiff dough with cold water or milk. Roll out and cut into fingers about 3 inches by 1 inch. Cook in moderate oven for 20 to 25 minutes. Remove and cool. Put ¼ lb. dates into a saucepan with ¼ cup of sugar and ⅛ cup cold water or lemon juice. Cook until tender. Beat up with a fork and use to sandwich biscuits together.

"The Star".

DIGESTIVE WHOLEMEAL BISCUITS

¼ lb. butter, ¼ lb. moist sugar, 1 lb. unsifted boermeal, 4 level teaspoons baking powder, ⅓ teaspoon bicarbonate of soda, ⅓ teaspoon salt, ⅓ pint of sour milk.

Mix boermeal with salt and baking powder, rub in butter until like fine breadcrumbs. Mix in the sugar, make into a stiff dough with the bicarbonate of soda mixed with the milk. Roll out to ⅛ of an inch, cut into shapes and bake in a moderate oven for 15 to 20 minutes or until a pale brown. Cool and coat with chocolate.

"The Star".

LADY FINGERS

3 egg whites, 6 tablespoons castor sugar, 2 egg yolks, 6 tablespoons flour, ⅛ teaspoon salt, ½ teaspoon vanilla.

Beat egg whites, stiff, add sugar gradually, beating all the time. Add egg yolks, and beat until thick and lemon coloured, then add flavouring. Sift flour with salt. Gradually cut and fold it into the egg mixture with a knife. Put into a forcing bag with a hole tube and force in shapes about 1 inch by 4 inches long on to ungreased paper on baking sheet. Sprinkle with castor sugar and bake in a moderate oven till delicately brown — about 12 to 15 minutes.

"The Star".

MABELA BISCUITS

½ lb. flour, ½ lb. mabela, 4 ozs. butter, 1 teaspoon baking powder, ½ lb. chopped dates, 1 tablespoon sugar, 1 egg and little milk or water to mix.

Sift flour, salt and baking powder, rub in the butter and mix in the mabela and sugar, add the dates. Mix to a soft dough with 1 egg beaten in about ¾ cup water. Roll out to ¼ inch thickness, cut into small rounds, brush with beaten egg and bake for 10 minutes or till lightly browned. Slit open and fill with butter icing when cold.   *"The Star"*.

SHORTBREAD BISCUITS

Ingredients. — 10 ozs. flour, 4 ozs. sugar, 1 egg, 6 ozs. butter, 1 teaspoon baking powder.

Method. — Mix all ingredients and knead like shortbread. Roll thinly, cut into shapes, sprinkle with ground almonds. Bake in medium oven, turn down to low when biscuits are put in.   *Mrs. C. Griffith*.

GERMAN BISCUITS

2 ozs. butter, 2 ozs. castor sugar, ½ teaspoon baking powder, 3½ ozs. flour, 1 egg yolk, ¼ teaspoon ground cinnamon, pinch of salt.

Method. — Mix the dry ingredients. Rub in butter and mix to a firm paste with egg yolk and water if necessary.

Knead, roll out and cut into rounds ¼ inch thick.

Bake in moderate oven 15 minutes. Cool. Sandwich two biscuits together with apricot jam. Ice with glacé icing or chocolate icing and decorate with a cherry.   *Mrs. G. Poole*.

NUT WAFERS

Ingredients. — Two egg whites, ½ cup castor sugar, 1 cup nuts (flaked almonds), 2 cups Post Toasties.

Method. — Beat egg whites well, add sugar then nuts, then Post Toasties. Put in greased tin in spoonfuls. Bake for 20 minutes.

CRUNCHIES

1 teacup flour, 1 teacup sugar, 1 teacup Quaker or Tiger Oats, 1 teacup cocoanut, 1 tablespoon golden syrup, 2 tablespoons boiling water, 4 ozs. butter, 1 teaspoon bicarbonate of soda.

Method. — Rub the butter into flour, add sugar, oats and cocoanut. Put the soda and syrup in a cup and pour over them the boiling water. Mix and allow to cool a little, then add to the dry ingredients. Place in spoonfuls (large teaspoon) on a greased, shallow pan and bake for 30 minutes. Allow plenty of room for the biscuits to spread. Or the mixture can be put in the tins and cut into fingers when baked.

Violet R. Hendrie.

MEALIE MEAL BISCUITS

3 cups flour, 1½ cups sugar, 1 teaspoonful salt, 2 large eggs, 2 cups mealie meal, 1½ cups good beef dripping, 2 teaspoonfuls baking powder, water.

Rub the dripping into the flour and meal. Add the remainder. Roll into thin biscuits. Bake in a moderate oven.

Very good children's biscuits. *Mrs. E. Loveday.*

GROUND RICE BISCUITS

½ lb. butter, 2 cups flour, ½ teaspoon baking powder, 1 egg, ½ teaspoon salt, 1 cup sugar, 1 cup ground rice.

Rub flour, butter, baking powder, salt, sugar, ground rice all together, then mix with egg to stiff paste, roll out, cut and bake for about 10 minutes. *Mrs. N. Taylor, Durban.*

GINGER CRISPIES

3 ozs. butter, 3 ozs. castor sugar, 1 oz. chopped, crystallised ginger, pinch of salt, 4 ozs. flour, ½ teaspoon ground ginger, 1 yolk of egg, milk, corn flakes.

Method. — Cream butter and sugar, add the crystallised ginger. Sieve the flour, salt and ground ginger together. Add these to the creamed mixture with sufficient egg yolk and milk to make a stiff paste. Knead and shape the mixture into small balls and roll each in cornflakes, pressing them in lightly. Place on a greased baking sheet and bake for 20 minutes in a moderate oven, until golden brown and crisp.

Mrs. Atherton.

BISCUITS

4 ozs. butter, 4 ozs. castor sugar, 1 egg yolk, 6 ozs. flour, ½ teaspoon baking powder, few almonds or cherries.

Method. — Cream butter and sugar, beat in egg, add sifted dry ingredients. Knead well until smooth. Cut out in any shapes and place on oven tray with ½ almond (or cherry) on each.

Bake in slow oven for about 10 minutes. *Mrs. G. R. Poole.*

GINGERNUTS

1 lb. flour, 5 ozs. butter, 8 ozs. golden syrup (¾ cup), 10 ozs. brown sugar (1½ cups), a little salt, 1½ teaspoons ginger, 1 egg, 2 tablespoons bicarbonate soda, 1-10th teaspoon Rodibolus (colouring).

Mix dry ingredients, rub in butter, moisten with beaten egg and golden syrup and leave mixed overnight.

Pinch off small pieces the size of a marble and make into a round ball, flatten a little, and place apart on greased tins. Leave on the tins till they harden. Not too hot oven. *Mrs. C. Kaplan, Balfour.*

ALMOND ROLLS

½ lb. butter, 3 eggs, ½ lb. chopped almonds or walnuts, 1 cup sugar, 1 teaspoon vanilla, 1 teaspoon baking powder, flour to stiffen dough.

Mix butter and sugar, add eggs well beaten, add other dry ingredients, roll out into long rolls to fit pan. Spread egg on top and bake. When baked cut into desired shapes and put back into oven to dry and get crisp.
Mrs. C. Kaplan, Balfour.

BISCUITS WHICH KEEP WELL

½ lb. flour, ½ lb. arrowroot, ½ lb. butter, 6 ozs. sugar, 1 egg, 2 teaspoons baking powder, milk to mix into soft dough.

Cream butter and sugar. Add beaten egg, then baking powder, sifted with flour and arrowroot and pinch salt, alternately with the milk. Roll out and cut into shapes. Bake in quick oven until brown.
Mrs. H. C. Lake, Maritzburg.

ALMOND BISCUITS

¼ lb. butter, ½ cup sugar, 1½ cups flour, 2 tablespoons ground almonds, 1 teaspoon baking powder, 1 egg, pinch salt.

Rub flour, butter, baking powder, salt, sugar, ground almonds all together, then mix with egg to stiff paste — roll out, cut and bake for about 10 minutes.
Mrs. N. Taylor, Durban.

DATE FINGERS

Put into a saucepan: ½ lb. of white sugar, ½ cup water and 1 lb. stoned dates, and cook until soft (not over flame as the mixture burns). Cool.

Cream together: 6 ozs. butter, ½ lb. yellow sugar. Add ¾ lb. flour and ½ lb. Tiger Oats. Mix well. Add quickly 1 teaspoon bicarbonate of soda dissolved in ½ cup hot water.

Roll out as ordinary pastry thinly and divide into two. Put one layer in shallow tin (greased), spread filling over; cover with other layer; roll flat lightly; cut slightly into fingers. Bake in moderate oven (brown at bottom first, then finish above).
Mrs. C. Griffith.

WINE FINGERS

3 ozs. flour, 2 ozs. butter, 1½ ozs. sugar, ½ yolk egg, ½ tablespoon sherry.

Method. — Rub the butter into the flour, add sugar and mix to a firm paste with the egg yolk and sherry. Roll out thinly and cut into fingers. Brush with white of egg and sprinkle with chopped almonds. Bake in a fairly hot oven till brown and firm, 12 to 15 minutes.

N.B. — These biscuits may be decorated with small pieces of cherry, angelica, etc.
Mrs. L. Malan.

OAT SQUARES

1 cup oats, 1½ cups flour, 1 egg, ¼ lb. butter, 3 tablespoons sugar, 2 teaspoons baking powder, pinch salt.

Method. — Beat egg, melt butter, and pour both on to dry ingredients. Flatten mixture out on a greased tray with palm of hand until you can get the required thickness. Cut into squares while hot, and put on a cake cooler. (Serve hot or cold). Bake in moderate oven. *M. Grove.*

CHEESE BISCUITS

8 ozs. flour, 4 ozs. butter, 4 ozs. grated cheese, seasoning to taste.

Rub butter and cheese into flour, knead as for shortbread. Roll out fairly thin and cut into rounds. Bake in a moderate oven.

Mrs. G. W. Nelson, Johannesburg.

TRU-WEAT DIGESTIVE BISCUITS

2 cups Tru-Weat, 1 tablespoon brown sugar, 1 teaspoon baking powder, 4 ozs. shortening, pinch of salt, ¼ cup milk.

Method. — Mix dry ingredients, rub in shortening, mix to a stiff dough with milk. Roll out to quarter inch thickness, into shapes. Bake in a moderate oven for 10-15 minutes.

CHOCOLATE TOASTIES

1 oz. plain chocolate, 1 oz. milk, 1 oz. Pastrine, ½ packet Post Toasties.

Combine three first ingredients, melt over hot water, then stir in half a packet of Post Toasties. Stir thoroughly, then drop by spoonfuls into cake cases. They will harden at once, and are delicious for tea.

Mrs. J. C. Smuts.

BITTER AMANDEL KOEKIES

½ lb. bitter almonds (pounded), ½ lb. sweet almonds, ½ lb. sugar, whites of 3 eggs (stiffly beaten).

Mix all well together, put in small rough heaps in pan lined with buttered paper. Bake about 10 minutes in not too hot oven.

Mrs. J. C. Smuts.

COCOANUT FINGERS

¼ lb. butter, ½ cup sugar, 1 egg, 1 teaspoon baking powder, 1¾ cups flour, little salt.

Cream butter and sugar, add beaten egg, then dry ingredients. Roll out. Fill large biscuit tin, spread with jam, then add filling.

Filling. — 1 tablespoon butter, 2 tablespoons sugar, 1 egg, 1 large cup cocoanut.

Mix together, place on top of jam and sprinkle with chopped almonds and sliced cherries. Bake at 400° 25 minutes. Cut while hot.

W. E. Rowse.

SHORTBREAD BISCUITS

2 scant breakfast cups flour, 4 tablespoons Maizena or cornflour, ½ lb. butter, 6 tablespoons castor sugar, 1 egg.

Knead all dry ingredients together and add beaten egg last. Bake in cool oven till light brown. *Mrs. Shaw.*

NUTTY WONDERS

Ingredients. — ¼ lb. butter, 1 egg, 1 teaspoon baking powder, vanilla essence, 3 tablespoons sugar, 1 cup flour, ½ cup chopped nuts, ½ cup chopped dates.

Method. — Cream butter and sugar, add egg (unbeaten); sift flour and baking powder together and add, then mix in nuts and fruit and essence. Take mixture in teaspoonfuls and roll in Post Toaties. Bake 10 to 15 minutes. *Mrs. G. Butterfield.*

NUTTY WONDERS

4 ozs. butter, 3 ozs. sugar, 1 teaspoon vanilla essence, 1 egg, 1 cup flour, ½ cup nuts, ½ cup sultanas, 1 teaspoon baking powder.

Method. — Cream butter and sugar, add egg then flour and baking powder, lastly fruit, nuts and essence.

Take one teaspoon of the mixture, and roll in chopped almonds or Post Toasties.

Bake for 15 to 20 minutes, until a golden brown. *Mrs. H. Mill.*

GINGER BISCUITS

4 large cups flour, 1¼ cups sugar, 6 tablespoons of butter and lard mixed, 3 tablespoons ginger, 4 teaspoons baking powder, 4 tablespoons syrup, 2 eggs and enough water to mix into a stiff paste.

Method. — Roll out and cut into shapes. Bake until browned.

Mrs. E. Pyper.

ALAND BISCUITS

Beat 6 ozs. butter to a cream with 2 ozs. icing sugar. Sift together 6 ozs. flour, 2 ozs. custard powder and a pinch of salt. Add to the butter and icing sugar, form into small balls, place on oven trays, press out with a fork and bake to a light brown colour in medium oven. Can be joined together with jam if liked. *Mrs. J. S. Moffett, Gumtree.*

TEA BISCUITS

1 lb. butter or half butter, half Holsum, ½ lb. castor sugar, 1½ lb. flour, 2 eggs, rind of lemon.

Beat butter and sugar well, add eggs, mix in flour and lemon rind until stiff dough is obtained. Roll out to $1/8$ inch thick, brush over with yolk of egg and bake in moderate oven till golden brown.

PEANUT BUTTER BISCUITS

½ cup brown sugar, ½ cup granulated sugar, ½ cup butter, 1 egg, 1 cup peanut butter, ½ teaspoon salt, ½ teaspoon soda, 1½ cups flour, ½ teaspoon vanilla.

Cream butter and sugar; beat in egg, peanut butter, salt and soda. Add flour to batter and lastly vanilla.

Roll dough into small balls, place on greased tin and flatten with a fork. Bake in moderate oven for about 15 minutes.

Makes 5 doz. biscuits.

BISCUITS AND BISCUIT PASTRY

12 ozs. (3 cups) flour, 1 cup (8 ozs) butter, 1 cup (6 ozs) sugar, ¼ tablespoon milk, ½ teaspoon bi-carbonate, pinch of salt.

Mix sugar and milk and bring to boil: add soda and allow to cool. Rub butter into flour and salt. Add cooled liquid and knead into firm dough. Roll out and cut into biscuits, or use as pastry.

THE TIRED WOMAN'S EPITAPH

Here lies a poor woman who always was tired,
She lived in a house where help was not hired,
Her last words on earth were
"Dear friends I am going
Where washing ain't done, nor sweeping, nor sewing;
But everyhing there is exact to my wishes,
For where they don't eat there's no washing of dishes,
I'll be where loud anthems will always be ringing,
But having no voice I'll be clear of the singing,
Don't mourn for me now; don't mourn for me never
I'm going to do nothing for ever and ever."

A man of words and not of deeds,
Is like a garden full of weeds.

SAVOURIES AND SNACKS

FRENCH TOAST

French toast is often used as a foundation for savouries instead of toast, biscuits or fried canapes. Cut a stale loaf of bread into fairly thick slices. Beat 1 egg with ½ cup milk, season with salt, pepper and pinch of cayenne pepper. Dip the bread into the beaten egg mixture and fry until light brown in butter or melted vegetable fat. Sprinkle with grated cheese and put into a hot oven to melt cheese. Cut into fingers and serve at once.

French toast cut into fingers may be used as a foundation for any of the following: —

(1) Sardines dipped into lemon juice and sprinkled with chopped nuts.
(2) Hard-boiled egg mashed finely and mixed with anchovy sauce, salt, pepper and a little lemon juice and forced on to the fingers of toast.
(3) Fingers of smoked salmon placed on the toast and garnished with a rose of butter creamed with lemon juice and a little chopped parsley.
(4) Chop an anchovy finely and mix with 1 tablespoon cream cheese and a little lemon juice. Moisten with mayonnaise and spread on the fingers of toast. Garnish with a dusting of paprika or chopped parsley. *"The Star".*

CHEESE ROLLS TOASTED

Cut the crust off a loaf of fresh bread, wrap in a damp cloth for a short time. Cut into slices and spread thickly with butter creamed with grated cheese, seasoned with salt and cayenne. Roll up and pack on to a baking tin, put under grill or into a hot oven and toast. Serve hot.

Salmon or sardine rolls may be made in the same way, the fish being creamed with the butter, lemon juice, salt and pepper. Anchovette too can be used.

Fish roe creamed with butter, pepper, salt and lemon juice makes another good filling for rolls. *"The Star".*

CHICKEN LIVERS IN BACON

This is a well-known snack but it is always welcomed at parties. The chicken livers should be dropped into boiling water a few minutes to firm, then cut into small pieces about 1 in. long. These are wrapped in strips of bacon, the bacon being secured with a cocktail stick. They are then placed on a shallow baking sheet and either grilled or baked in a hot oven 5 to 10 minutes, then served straight from the oven.

Prunes, cherries, or drained oysters wrapped in bacon and cooked as above are very good. A salted almond may be put into each prune before it is wrapped in the bacon. *"The Star".*

TINY FISH CAKES

Salmon, any cooked fish, or any tinned fish may be used for these. Small tin salmon or ½ lb. cooked fish, ½ lb. cooked, mashed potatoes, 1 egg, 1 oz. butter, 1 teaspoon chopped parsley; anchovy sauce to taste if cooked fish is used, salt, pepper. Mash the potatoes with the butter, mix with the flaked fish, salt, pepper, parsley and beaten egg, adding the anchovy or tomato sauce to the fish. Form into tiny round shapes about 1 inch across, dip into egg and breadcrumbs and fry either in deep, smoking hot fat or oil. Drain well, pierce with cocktail sticks and serve. These little cakes may be placed on a greased baking dish, dabbed with butter and baked for about 10 minutes, then served as above. *"The Star".*

TINY LIVER CAKES

½ lb. minced liver (chicken or calf's), or minced sheeps' kidneys, ¼ lb. mashed potatoes; ¼ lb. breakfast oats, salt, pepper, tomato sauce or Worcester sauce, 1 oz. butter, 1 egg. Pour boiling water on to the liver or kidneys, mince. The calf's liver should be minced twice if used. Mix with the breakfast oats, the hot mashed potatoes, butter, pepper, salt, sauce and beaten egg. Form into tiny cakes and either bake or dip into beaten egg and oatmeal and fry. Serve on cocktail sticks with tiny sprigs of parsley.

N.B. — The mixture may be made into tiny rolls and wrapped in rashers of bacon or pastry and baked at 450° or No 9 for 10 to 12 minutes. *"The Star".*

SARDINE OR SALMON ROLLS

Mash a tin of flaked salmon or sardines, mix with salt, pepper, a very little grated onion, and melted butter. Roll the puff pastry into a long, narrow strip, put the mixture down one side, moisten the entire length with water or beaten egg, wrap the pastry round the filling, cut into inch lengths across. Put on to a baking dish, brush over with beaten egg. Bake for 10 to 15 minutes until lightly browned. *"The Star".*

AVOCADO PEAR SAVOURY

Rounds of buttered toast. Avocado pear, sliced beetroot, ½ teaspoon grated onion, salt, pepper, lemon juice to taste.

Place a round of beetroot on each round of buttered toast, mix the avocado pear with the onion, salt, pepper and lemon juice. Pile on to the beetroot. Dust with paprika. Serve cold. This may be used as a hors d'oeuvre, or a cocktail or bridge snack. *"The Star"*.

KIPPER RAREBIT

Two boned kippers, 2 eggs, pepper, 1 tablespoon butter, hot, trimmed buttered toast.

Soak the kipper in hot water or boil a few minutes, drain and remove the flesh. Heat the butter in a saucepan, beat the eggs slightly and add pepper to taste, add to the hot butter and mix in the kipper. When it thickens put on fingers of buttered toast and serve at once. *"The Star"*.

OYSTER CANAPES

Four tinned oysters, 2 slices cooked ham or grilled bacon, salt, pepper, round of hot toast or fried bread, fried parsley.

Cut the rounds of bread a little larger than the oysters, and the ham the same size. Place a slice of ham on each round of fried bread, then put the oyster (well seasoned with salt end pepper) on top of the ham or bacon. Put a tiny dab of butter on each oyster, heat in a hot oven for 3 minutes. Remove, garnish with the fried parsley and serve at once.
"The Star".

OYSTERS SCALLOPED

Six oysters, ½ cup thick white sauce, salt and pepper, breadcrumbs, 1 hard-boiled egg.

Make a thick white sauce with 1 tablespoon butter, 1 tablespoon flour and ½ cup milk, season with salt and pepper. Have ready small individual moulds or scallop shells, well greased and thickly sprinkled with breadcrumbs. Put the oysters and chopped, hard-boiled egg equally in the small moulds. Cover with white sauce, sprinkle lightly with breadcrumbs and dabs of butter. Bake in a quick oven until nicely browned. Serve at once. *"The Star"*.

CAVIARE AND OTHER CRISPS

Cream cheese thoroughly. Add caviare and chilli sauce to desired flavour and blend well. Spread on small, crisp rounds of toast. Cherries, prunes, black olives or gherkins. Wrap in bacon, grill in oven. Spike with savoury sticks. Can be prepared previous day.
Mrs. J. Hewitson.

GREEN FILLING

Avocado pear, a little grated onion, lemon juice, pepper and salt, for sandwiches or savouries.

FILLING TO BE USED ON TOAST, BISCUITS, ETC.

(1) Shrimp, pineapple, celery, moisten with mayonnaise. (2) Hard-boiled egg, fish, pickle relish, blend with mayonnaise.

Mrs. J. Hewitson.

STEAK AND KIDNEY SNACKS

Stew 1 lb. rump steak with ½ an ox kidney. Season well and cook for 1½ hours. When ready cut up the meat into very tiny pieces and set aside in the gravy to cool.

Line some patty pans with rough puff pastry, put in a teaspoonful of the steak and kidney, cover, pierce and bake in hot oven. Serve very hot. *J. H.*

Make mutton snack in the same way, using mutton well seasoned, in place of steak and kidney.

Cut the pastry trimmings into fancy shapes and when cooked and cool, split them up and insert any savoury filling. Left over liver and bacon, seasoned with onion is particularly good. A chicken, ham and parsley mixture too is good. *J.H.*

CHEESE AIGRETTES

½ pint water, 1 oz. butter, 2 ozs. flour, 3 ozs. grated cheese, 2 eggs, cayenne and salt.

Boil water and butter, add flour and stir until mixture leaves the sides of pan. Cool and beat in cheese, seasoning and egg yolks. Lastly stiffly-beaten whites of eggs. Fry in teaspoonfuls in deep, boiling fat or oil till golden brown and crisp. *E. R.*

DEVILLED PRUNES

Take slightly tender prunes, remove the stones, then fill with finely-chopped almonds, mixed with mango chutney, salt and pepper. Wrap in thin slices of bacon, then grill. Serve on round croûtons of bread, fried a golden brown in hot butter.

A. Friend, Johannesburg.

CHEESE DROPS

4 ozs. cheese, whites of 2 eggs.

Have a dish with boiling oil. Drop portions of the mixture into oil. Let brown, then take out and drain. Serve very hot. *Mrs. W. Hamilton.*

CHEESE STRAWS

Ingredients. — 3 ozs. flour, 2 ozs. butter, 3 ozs. cheese, yolk of 1 egg, pinch salt and cayenne.

Method. — Work into thick paste. Roll thinly, cut into shapes. Brush over with little egg. Bake in very hot oven. *Mrs. V. Cullingworth.*

PUFFS FOR SAVOURIES

½ pint of water, 2 ozs. butter, 3 ozs. flour, pinch of salt, 3 eggs, cayenne and salt.

Boil water and butter, add flour and stir until mixture leaves sides of pan. Beat in seasoning and egg yolks. Lastly add stiffly-beaten whites of eggs. Drop in half teaspoons on to a greased tin and bake for about 15 minutes. When cool, split side and insert savoury filling such as prawns, minced ham or cream cheese. These fillings are nice if moistened with a little mayonnaise. *E. R.*

PETITS CHOUX SAVOURIES

To make the pastry:

Boil together 2 ozs. butter and 1 gill water.

Stir in 2½ ozs. flour, stirring well all the time, till the mixture comes from sides of pan.

Take off stove and cool slightly. Then beat in separately 2 eggs.

Roll mixture into tiny balls and bake in a moderate oven 20 to 25 minutes. Should be crisp. Cut off tops and scoop out centres if soft and fill with anchovy-flavoured, whipped cream or cream cheese. *Hazel Hawke.*

SAVOURY SNACKS

Spread brown bread and butter with anchovette paste, sandwich together and cut into fingers. Dip into milk and place on greased baking sheet, bake in quick oven for 5 to 7 minutes. Dust with curry powder and serve very hot. *Mrs. W. Hamilton.*

RELISH SNACKS

Spread wheat crispbread with butter, then cover each strip with sandwich relish and garnish with stars of beetroot.

Mrs. Hamilton.

SARDINE ROLLS

Roll out puff pastry and cut into 2-inch squares. Lay 1 or 2 sardines on each. Sprinkle a little salt and cayenne pepper over, then roll up like a sausage roll. Brush over with a little beaten egg, sprinkle some grated cheese over and bake in a hot oven.

ASPARAGUS ROLLS

Same ingredients as above, except that asparagus should be used instead of sardines. *A. Friend, Johannesburg.*

KIDNEY TOAST

Chop up 2 sheep's kidneys finely. Fry in butter 3 minutes. Then add beaten egg, mix quickly, season with salt and pepper and serve on fingers of fried bread or toast.

LIVER TOAST

Same ingredients as above, except that lambs liver should be used instead of kidneys. *A. Friend, Johannesburg.*

COCKTAIL SAVOURIES

Icecream wafers buttered.
Cover with grated cheese and chopped nuts, place in hot oven for two minutes and serve at once. *Mrs. L. Malan.*

GREEN PARSLEY BUTTER

Wash and dry parsley, mince and sieve. Mix 1 tablespoon into about 2 ozs. butter. *E. R.*

FILLINGS FOR HARD-BOILED EGGS

The eggs should be placed in cold water, brought to the boil and boiled for 10 minutes, then put into cold water and left until cold. Shell, cut in half lengthwise or rounds, remove the yolks and mash with melted butter, salt, pepper, anchovy or tomato sauce, cream cheese, grated cheese with a touch of onion, mashed sardines or salmon, minced cooked chicken, minced prawns or lobster, mayonnaise, etc., put back into the halved egg with a teaspoon or forcer. Decorate with parsley and serve on a bed of lettuce as a horse d'oeuvres or on a lettuce-lined dish for snacks. *"The Star".*

SANDWICH FILLINGS

(1) Minced stuffed olives with mayonnaise, chopped walnuts, salt and pepper, Put between bread and butter.
(2) Mix ½ cup chopped, cooked bacon with ¼ cup chopped walnuts, salt, pepper, ½ teaspoon made mustard and 2 tablespoons thick cream or softened butter. Mix well and spread.
(3) Mix 1 packet cream cheese with ¼ cup chopped nuts, ¼ cup chopped or minced gherkins and mayonnaise.

(4) Bone a small tin of sardines, then mash and mix with 2 tablespoons lemon juice, a few drops of Worcester sauce, salt and pepper, 1 teaspoon chopped parsley, 3 tablespoons softened butter. Use as required.
(5) Cream cheese with Worcester sauce and chopped nuts or olives.
(6) Cream cheese with red currant jelly.
(7) Chopped olives mixed with seedless raisins and mayonnaise.
(8) Finely minced lamb or mutton mixed with chopped mint and mayonnaise.
(9) Minced, cooked liver with chopped pickles or mixed with chutney or tomato sauce.
(10) Slices of tomato placed on bread spread with softened butter, mayonnaise and a touch of horseradish sauce.
(11) Chopped or minced ginger mixed with chopped walnuts.
(12) Chopped raisins mixed with minced or chopped celery and mayonnaise. *"The Star"*.

SAVOURY SAUSAGE AND EGG PIE

(Fish may be substituted for the sausage, if wished)

3 or 4 left-over sausages (cooked), 1 large onion, 2 hard-boiled eggs, ¾ cup grated cheese, pepper and salt to taste, 2 tablespoons flour, 1 breakfastcup of milk, or milk and water.

Butter the casserole, place the sausages (cut into rings of 1 inch) in a layer at the bottom of the dish: cover with a layer of diced hard-boiled egg, and a layer of thinly sliced onion. Repeat this until all ingredients are used and finish with a layer of onion. Cover with cheese-sauce, allowing some of the sauce to run through the mixture. Place in oven (400 degrees) until slightly browned.

CHEESE SAUCE

Place 1 large tablespoon butter in saucepan. When melted, add the flour, stirring constantly, and at the same time adding the milk a little at a time, making sure that there are no lumps. When the required thickness is reached, add salt and pepper and the grated cheese: stir well and pour over the above mixture.

*You cannot dream yourself into a character;
You must hammer and forge yourself one.*
                                            Froude.

SAVOURIES

FISH

Spread on base of savoury green butter made by mixing 2 ozs. butter, ½ tablespoon finely-chopped parsley or watercress, a squeeze of lemon juice, salt and pepper, cream well together and add a little green colouring (if any). Place ½ a sardine in centre, with spot of tomato sauce, a slice of stuffed olive or thin strips of red tomato skin placed across the sardine like ribbons.

Butter base and cover with chopped crab mixed with a little mayonnaise, pepper and salt, garnished with a little chopped cucumber, a caper and a tiny sprig of parsley.

Butter base and then spread with anchovette, and add finely chopped egg white on one half of each savoury, yellow on the other. Garnish with a little finely chopped parsley and a dash of cayenne pepper.

Prawns. — Spread with parsley butter as above. Place prawn in centre after dipping in lemon juice, garnish with 2 or 3 capers and a little chopped egg yolk or white.

Butter base and cover with chopped egg yolk, a prawn in the centre and within that a black olive with a pearl onion on top.

TOMATO

Spread with green butter, a slice of red, firm tomato, with a slice of hard-boiled egg placed on it, dusted with seasoning and a dash of cayenne.

Spread with butter and tomato sauce, sprinkle with grated cheese, put a sprig of parsley in centre and a little cayenne.

ASPARAGUS

Spread with butter and a little mayonnaise and place a tip in the centre. Garnish with a little cayenne and a little finely chopped parsley.

ASPARAGUS

Butter base and spread with tomato sauce, place an asparagus tip in the centre with pearl onions around.

BOVRIL

Butter base and spread thinly with Bovril with chopped egg white on one round, yolk on another, or mixed, chopped egg, a caper, a pearl onion or slice of stuffed olive in centre.

CHEESE

Spread with butter and cream cheese, garnish with a spot of tomato sauce in the centre and a dash of cayenne.
Mix a little grated cheese with butter and spread, dip into finely chopped egg white or yolk, garnish with thin strips of gherkin.
Spread with butter and cream cheese with a slice of tomato and a slice of stuffed olive in the centre of that.

SAUSAGE

Small Vienna sausages. Place slices of sausage in a ring with a pearl onion or small pickle in the centre. Garnish with parsley. To make a plate of mixed savouries look attractive, use a firm, red tomato, a cucumber, an egg plant, or an orange in the centre of the dish and put "warriors" in hedgehog fashion. These are made of—a slice of sausage and a cocktail onion, a black olive, a stuffed olive, a small square of cheese and a pearl onion, a cocktail sausage and a tiny pickle, etc., pierced with cocktail sticks or toothpicks.

O, Thou, in whom we live and move,
Who mad'st the sea and shore;
Thy goodness constantly we prove,
And grateful would adore.
And, if it please Thee, Power above,
Still grant us with such store
The friend we trust, the fair we love,
And we desire no more.   Burns.

O grant me then a middle state,
Neither too humble nor too great;
More than enough for nature's ends,
With something left to treat my friends.

BEVERAGES

COCKTAILS FOR YOUR WEDDING? CERTAINLY! BRIDE'S BLUSH

1 bottle K.W.V. Grapejuice, 1 soda water, 12 crystallised cherries, raspberry syrup.

Cool ingredients thoroughly in refrigerator before mixing. Pour one full-sized bottle of K.W.V. grape juice in a glass jug. Add one bottle of soda water, and one teaspoonful of raspberry syrup. Serve in cocktail glasses with a spiked cherry in each. Sufficient for 12 costs 1/6.

For toasts at a wedding of 100 guests or more, use 10 fullsized bottles of K.W.V. grape juice, 10 bottles of soda water, and 1¼ lbs. of crystallised cherries. Serve as above. Total cost 17/6.   *W.C.T.U.*

BRIDEGROOM'S JOY

2 pineapples or 2 tins shredded pineapple, 4 grenadillas, 2 lemons, sugar to taste.

Shred the pineapples with spoon and fork. Boil the hard centres and best part of rind with rather more than enough water to cover. Sweeten to taste, and add rind of two lemons. Squeeze the juice of the lemons over the shredded pineapple in a basin, add 2 piled dessertspoons of sugar. Cover basin with plate. One hour later strain the boiling syrup over the contents of the basin. When nearly cold add the grenadilla and a dozen crystallised cherries. Cool, stir well and ladle into cocktail glasses. Sufficient for 12 costs 1/6.   *W.C.T.U.*

HONEYMOON BLISS

1 cup orange juice, 4 tablespoons lemon juice, 3 tablespoons honey, few grains of salt.

Mix ingredients thoroughly. Put crushed ice into glasses, pour in mixture and serve at once, garnished with finely peeled orange rind. Sufficient for four costs 6d.   *W.C.T.U.*

BRIDESMAID'S HOPE

1 cup small strawberries, 2 oranges, 3 tablespoons lemon juice, 1 bottle soda water, 6 tablespoons powdered sugar.

Peel and remove membrane from oranges, cut segments into halves. Hull strawberries and cut into halves. Mix with orange pulp and add lemon juice and sugar. Serve very cold, one-third syrup to two-thirds soda water. Sufficient for six. *W.C.T.U.*

BESTMAN'S PUNCH

3 oranges, juice of 6 lemons, one-third grated pineapple, 1 bottle soda water, 1 cup granulated sugar.

Dissolve the sugar in 1 cup of water. Strain the juice of oranges and lemons on to the syrup and add the grated pineapple and its juice. Serve with raspberries, strawberries or crystallised cherries in cocktail glasses, using two-thirds syrup to one-third soda water. Chill and serve ice-cold. Sufficient for 12. *W.C.T.U.*

FLOWER GIRL'S FANTASY

1 cup K.W.V. Grapejuice, ¾ cup sugar, 1 cup orange juice, ½ cup lemon juice, 1 tablespoon grated lemon peel, 1 quart water, grated rind of half an orange.

Boil sugar and water for three minutes. Cool and add all the other ingredients. Blend well and chill in refrigerator before serving. Sufficient for 16 costs 8d. *W.C.T.U.*

THE PARSON'S "PEP"

This cocktail is easy to make and hard to beat.

Put the strained juice of one lemon into a large glass, add one teaspoonful of sugar syrup, then two small lumps of ice. Fill up with cold ginger ale, with a thinly cut slice of lemon on top. *W.C.T.U.*

LEMON BARLEY WATER

10 cups water, 3 cups Government sugar, 4 tablespoons Robinson's Patent Barley, rind and juice of 4 oranges and two lemons.

Boil for 15 minutes. Stir occasionally. Take from fire and cool. Add 1 packet tartaric or citric acid. Strain and bottle.

GRAPE FRUIT JUICE

3 oranges, ¼ lb. loaf sugar, 1 grapefruit, ice, 1 bottle soda water.

Rub the loaf sugar in the rind of the oranges and put into a large jug. Pour on it 1 pint of water, the strained juice of the oranges and of the grapefruit. Just before serving strain, add a lump of ice and some soda water.

MILK PUNCH

1 quart of milk, 1 lb. loaf sugar, 2 lemons, 1 wineglassful of brandy, nutmeg.

Boil together the milk and sugar. Allow to cool and stand on ice. Squeeze the juice from the lemons and add it to the brandy. Stir this into the milk and serve at once. Grate nutmeg on each glass.

MINT PUNCH

Fresh mint, 1/4 lb. castor sugar, 3 lemons, 1 orange, ice, ginger ale.

Put sugar into a large jug and pour over it the juice of the lemons. Add one lemon thinly sliced, several sprays of mint, orange peel, ice and ginger ale. *American.*

ORANGE PUNCH

1/2 pint orange juice, ice, 1 gill lemon juice, sugar to taste, 1 bottle ginger ale, 1 bottle soda water.

Put a lump of ice into a large jug. Mix orange and lemon juice, add sugar, strain and pour over the ice in the jug. Add ginger ale and soda water just before serving.

CLARET CUP

1 pint claret, 1 bottle soda water, 1 bottle lemonade, 1/2 lb. castor sugar, 1 lemon, slices of cucumber.

Put the claret into a large jug, add the cucumber and lemon sliced, stir in the sugar until it has dissolved, then stand on ice. Immediately before serving, strain and add the soda water and lemonade.

American.

LEMONADE DE LUXE

1 lemon, 1 tablespoon orange syrup, 1 wineglass sherry, chopped ice, strawberry syrup, port, soda water.

Strain the juice of a lemon into a long glass. Add the orange syrup, sherry and chopped ice. Mix in a cocktail shaker, then return it to the long glass. Add a dash of strawberry syrup and port and fill up with soda water. *American.*

GRENADILLA PUNCH

1 lemon, 1/2 pint strained grenadilla juice, loaf sugar to taste, ice, 2 bottles lemonade.

Rub the loaf sugar on the lemon rind and put it into 1/2 a pint of water with juice from lemon. Stand on ice and when ready to serve put in grenadilla juice and lemonade.

GINGER ALE PUNCH

½ pint cold tea, 4 tablespoons castor sugar, orange, lemon, 1 bottle ginger ale, 1 bottle soda water.

Mix sugar in tea and add 4 tablespoons orange juice and 2 tablespoons lemon juice. Strain and pour into a large jug, add some ice. When required add ginger ale and soda.

MIXED FRUIT CUP

Half fill a large jug with ice cubes, add the strained juice of 12 oranges, 1 or 2 grated mangoes, 2 cups grenadilla pulp, sugar to taste. Before serving, flavour with claret and fill with chilled soda water or lemonade. Mix well. *M.P.K.*

BOSTON CREAM

1 oz. tartaric acid, 1 breakfast cup sugar, 2½ cups boiling water, 2 teaspoons essence of lemon, 1 white of egg.

Pour boiling water over sugar and stir. When cold add acid and essence and well whisked white of egg, 2 fresh lemons can be substituted for essence. Bottle. Take two tablespoons to one tumbler of water, adding ¼ teaspoon carbonate of soda, if liked. *M.P.K.*

HOW TO PRESERVE LEMON JUICE

Roll lemons briskly back and forth on a table, then press the juice into a bowl and strain out the seeds. Remove the pulps from the skins and boil them in water, allowing 1 pint water to a dozen pulps. Five minutes' boiling will suffice to extract the acid. Strain the water into the juice. Allow 1 lb. of sugar to each pint of liquid. Boil for 10 minutes and bottle for use. To serve, allow 1 tablespoon of lemon syrup to each glass of water. Put melted candle fat over corks if you wish to keep bottled for a long time. *Mrs. W. Hamilton.*

GINGER BEER

1 dessertspoon ground ginger, 1 dessertspoon cream of tartar, 1 teaspoon tartaric acid, 1 lb. sugar.

Mix all ingredients in a basin and pour 1 gallon of boiling water over. Leave to cool, then add half a cake of Anchor yeast (mixed with a little of the liquid). Bottle in screwtop beer bottles and keep in refrigerator. Must be kept cold. *Mrs. R. Cruickshank, Johannesburg.*

FRUIT DRINK

Ingredients. — Juice of 4 oranges and 4 lemons, finely grated rind of 2 oranges and 2 lemons, ½ packet tartaric acid, 4 lbs. sugar, 4 pints boiling water.

Method. — Pour boiling water over rest of ingredients. Allow to cool before bottling. This drink must be stored in a refrigerator.

Mrs. Hearn.

LEMON SYRUP

Put the grated rind and juice of 6 good sized limes in a basin. Add 1½ packets citric acid and 1½ packets tartaric acid and 8 cups of water. Stir well. Then add 12 cups boiling water and stir till sugar is dissolved. This does not require to be boiled at all. Leave overnight, strain and bottle next day.

D. A. Johnson.

FRUIT SALTS

2 packets of Epsom Salts, 2 packets bicarbonate of soda, 2 packets tartaric acid, 3 tablespoons icing sugar.

Method. — Dry the salts out well in oven till a powder, then roll out all the ingredients and put in an air tight bottle, and take one teaspoon in water when needed.

Mrs. H. Mill.

ORANGE DRINK

8 oranges, 8 lemons, 5 bottles of water (quart size beer bottles), 9 lbs. sugar, 2½ packets citric acid.

Method. — Grate the rind of fruit, boil for 10 minutes with sugar and water, take off the fire, let cool for 24 hours. Then add juice of fruit and stir, but don't put back on stove. Dissolve citric acid in a cup of boiled water, which has cooled down. Mix with rest of ingredients. Stir. Then let stand for another 24 hours.
Strain through muslin cloth.
Bottled will keep for years.

Mrs. S. Watson.

ORANGE HEALTH DRINK

Ingredients. — 10 oranges, 2 lemons, 2 packets citric acid, 1 packet Epsom Salts, 5 lbs. sugar, 3 pints boiling water, rind 8 oranges.

Method. — Mix dry ingredients, orange rind, fruit juices and boiling water. Allow to stand for six hours. Strain and bottle. Dilute small quantity with cold water or soda water. This quantity makes about 5 large bottles.

Mrs. J. Knight.

ORANGE SQUASH

Juice of 8 or 10 oranges, 2 packets citric acid, 2 packets Epsom Salts, 3 pints boiling water, 5 lbs. sugar, 2 packets tartaric acid, 1 teaspoonful grated rind (heaped).

Put sugar, acids, salts, rind and juice in a bowl and stir well. Pour boiling water over and stir until dissolved. Allow to stand overnight. Next morning strain and bottle. Cork well.
Lemons may also be used.

B. C. Cleghorn.

ORANGE AND LEMON DRINK

The juice and grated rind of 3 oranges and 2 lemons. Place in a bowl with 5 cups sugar. Leave 24 hours, add 5 cups boiling water and 1 packet citric acid; bottle and use as required, diluted with water.
Mrs. Murphy.

LOGANBERRY COCKTAIL

2 cups loganberry juice (1 lb. 5 ozs. can loganberry strained — 2 cups), 1 cup orange juice, juice of 1 lemon, ¼ cup of sugar, 1 cup water.

Boil sugar and water together for 10 minutes. Mix fruit juice and syrup. Strain, cool and pour into freezing pans. Freeze to mush. Remove from tray with an ice cream scoop. Serve in sherbet glasses. Garnish with thin slices of orange and mint leaves. Set temperature selector at "1" for freezing (8 servings).
Mrs. Withiel.

TOMATO JUICE COCKTAIL

2 cups tomato, ⅛ teaspoon pepper, 2 tablespoons sugar, celery salt, 1 teaspoon salt, onion juice, ground cloves.

Strain tomatoes, add seasoning and allow to stand in refrigerator for an hour, so that flavours may mellow. Seasonings may be changed to suit individual preferences. This cocktail is improved by shaking in a beverage shaker with crushed ice.
Mrs. Withiel.

GRAPE JUICE AND RASPBERRY PUNCH

2 cups grape juice, 1 cup ginger ale, 3 cups raspberry juice or cordial, juice 6 oranges.

Mix the juices and chill. Just before serving add the ginger ale.
Mrs. Beyers (M. J. Davidtsz).

CATAWBA PUNCH

1 cup Catawba grape juice, 1 cup ginger ale, 1 cup orange juice.

Mix the fruit juices. Chill. Just before serving add the ginger ale.
Mrs. Beyers (M. J. Davidtsz).

RASPBERRY DRINK

4 lbs. sugar, 4 bottles water, 1 table jelly, ½ packet cream of tartar, ½ packet tartaric acid, 1 bottle lemon essence or any flavouring.

Bring sugar and water to boil, add table jelly before removing from fire. Then add other ingredients.
M. Grove.

CATAWBA JUICE

Crush the ripe grapes after they have been stemmed and washed. To 6 lbs. grapes add 1 lb. sugar and the juice of six lemons. Heat gradually, pressing the grapes with a wooden spoon every once in a while, to extract as much juice as possible. The heating must be a slow process. When the mixture reaches simmering point, remove from the heat. Strain out the pulp. Reheat the juice to just below boiling point. Bottle at once, and close quickly either with cork or, if fruit jars, fasten lids tightly. *Mrs. Beyers (M. J. Davidtsz).*

FRUIT PUNCH

1 cup grated pineapple, juice 4 oranges, juice 8 lemons, sugar to taste, 1½ cups ginger ale, fresh mint, 1 cup strong, freshly made tea, 1 teaspoon salt.

Combine the fruit juices, tea and salt. Pour over the mint leaves. Strain, pour over ice to chill. Just before serving add the ginger ale.

Mrs. Beyers (M. J. Davidtsz),

SPICED GRAPE FRUIT

2 cups grape juice, juice of 4 lemons, 2 cups sugar, ½ cup water, ¼ teaspoon ground cloves, ¼ teaspoon ground cinnamon, ¼ teaspoon ground ginger, ¼ teaspoon ground allspice, 1 bottle soda water.

Bring the sugar, water and spices to the boil. Cool and add the other ingredients. Leave 30 minutes to blend. Pour over ice and add the soda just before serving. *Mrs. Beyers (M. J. Davidtsz).*

CHAMPAGNE CUP

½ cup vermouth, ½ cup good rum, ½ cup maraschino, piece of cucumber rind, 2 quarts champagne, juice of 4 oranges, juice of 3 lemons, sugar to taste.

Sweeten the fruit juices slightly. Add to the other ingredients except the champagne. Leave on ice for 10 minutes to blend. Pour over ice, add the champagne just before serving. *Mrs. Beyers (M. J. Davidtsz).*

GRANNY'S FRUIT NECTAR (about 12 glasses)

1 pint weak China tea, juice of pineapple from large tin, 2 diced apples, strained juice of 3 oranges and 3 lemons, sugar to taste, about 6 ice cubes and 1 quart ginger ale.

Method. — Put strained tea into large jug with ice cubes, add the fruit juices and diced apples. Stir in the sugar to taste and add chilled ginger ale. Serve very cold. Some sprigs of mint added if liked.

Mrs. Hamilton.

LEMON SYRUP

4 large limes or lemons, ½ packet cream of tartar, ½ packet tartaric acid, ½ packet Epsom Salts, 4 large cups sugar, 4 large cups water.

Grate the rind and squeeze the juice of the lemons into a dish and add the cream of tartar, tartaric acid and Epsom Salts.

Melt the sugar in the water, boil for 2 or 3 minutes and then pour on to other ingredients. Stand overnight and in the morning strain through muslin and bottle.
Mrs. H. Mill.

WINE GUIDE

Hors d'oeuvres: Light white wine.
Oysters: Dry champagne.
Soup: Dry sherry or dry Madeira.
Fish: Champagne or dry white wine.
Entrees: Claret.
Roast Meats and Game: Burgundy.
Fowl: Dry champagne.
Sweets: Sauterne.
Cheese: Port or brown sherry.
Coffee: Liqueur or old brandy.

BY A MAN

I meant to marry a Colonial because of her meats and fruits, or
An Englishwoman because of her puddings and pies, or
A Scotswoman because of her soups and sense,
And darned if I didn't marry an Irishwoman
because I couldn't help myself.

TO A FRIEND

Thou swear's thou'll drink no more;
Kind heav'n send me
Such a cook or coachman
But no friend.
Anon.

The pattering of tiny feet,
The joy of children's laughter,
The lisping prayers, the pillowed heads,
In peaceful slumber after.
The curtained cosiness beside
The fire that brightly burns,
The joy of books and slippered ease,
When eventide returns.   *E.W.*

JAMS, JELLIES AND PRESERVES

SLICED ORANGE PRESERVE

Grate the rind off the fruit very thinly, then cut into slices, halves or quarters. Weigh the fruit and put into a large dish, allowing 1 pint of water to every pound of fruit. Leave overnight, then cook in the water for about 5 to 10 minutes, being careful not to allow them to over-cook. Lift the slices out carefully being careful not to break them. Strain the water in which they were cooked, measure it and allow 2 cups sugar to every cup of water. Bring to boil stirring until the sugar is dissolved. Boil 10 minutes, then put in the fruit a little at a time, so that it keeps on boiling. When it is boiling add the juice of 1 strained lemon to every 2 lbs. of oranges. Cook briskly until the fruit is clear and transparent and the syrup is thick. Pack into hot, dry bottles covering the fruit with the syrup. When cold cover with rounds of paper dipped in brandy or with melted paraffin wax. Seal and store in a cool, dark place.   *"The Star".*

WHOLE ORANGE PRESERVE

Grate or peel the rind off the oranges very thinly, rub the oranges with salt. Leave for half an hour, then pour boiling water over them, putting a weight to keep them under the water. Leave until the water has cooled down. Cut a cross in the top of each orange, or remove the centre with an apple corer, squeeze out the pips. Put the oranges into fresh water and leave overnight. Drop into boiling water the next day after draining well. Boil until the skin is tender and can be pierced with a straw or match. This is very important, for if the skin is not tender it will harden and will not absorb the syrup. Make a syrup, using 1 lb. of sugar to every pound of fruit and 3 cups of water to every cup of sugar. Bring to the boil, stirring until the sugar is dissolved, then strain through a sieve lined with cotton wool. Return to the preserving pan, bring to the boil, take the oranges out of the boiling water one by one and drop into the boiling syrup. When they are all in the syrup and it commences to boil again, add the strained juice of a lemon to every 2 lbs. of oranges. Boil until the fruit looks transparent and the syrup thick. Be careful to turn the fruit occasionally in the syrup so that it is covered. Put into hot, dry bottles, being careful that the fruit is covered with the syrup. When cold seal.

N.B. — All these preserves will be improved if they are sterilised at boiling point for 15 minutes after the lids have been put on and before sealing and putting away. In this case the lids should not be fixed firmly until after sterilising. *"The Star"*.

GRAPEFRUIT PRESERVE

Grate or peel the rind thinly. Allow the fruit to lie in a salt solution for 12 hours (using 1 tablespoon of salt to 6 pints water). Make a few incisions in the sides of the fruit and remove as many pips as possible, or remove the centre of the grapefruit with an apple corer and take out the pips as they make the preserves very bitter. Put into fresh water for 4 to 6 days changing the water every day. If the grapefruit are very bitter they require longer soaking than the comparatively sweet ones. Then proceed the same way as the orange preserve Grapefruit may be cooked whole, or in halves and will be done the same way as the previous recipe. *"The Star"*.

NAARTJIE PRESERVE

Grate the rind off carefully and very thinly, or peel very thinly, and make the same way as the whole orange preserve. To remove the pips from the naartjies pierce right through from side to side with a sharp-pointed knife and after boiling them until almost tender remove from the water and squeeze gently, putting the first finger on the top and the thumb at the bottom.

N.B. — All these fruits will be improved if the strained juice of lemon is added to each 2 lbs. of fruit when the fruit reaches boiling point after putting it into the syrup.

The fruit may be partly cooked in the syrup, left overnight, then next day taken out and the syrup brought to the boil. Add the fruit a little at a time and boil until clear and transparent, and proceed as in the orange preserve. This method seems to introduce more syrup into the fruit. *"The Star"*.

KUMQUAT PRESERVE

Wash the kumquats, put into boiling water mixed with bicarbonate of soda, using ½ cup of soda to 5 pints of water. Bring to boiling point. Leave in the water until it has cooled off, then drain and rinse. Wash in cold water. Make incisions right through the sides of the fruit with a sharp-pointed knife, going through to the other side. Put into sufficient boiling water to cover, and boil until tender. Drain and cool slightly, then remove the pips with a crochet hook or squeeze the fruit top and bottom. This causes the incisions to open and the pips to come out. Weigh and allow ½ lb. of sugar to every pound of fruit. Make a syrup with the sugar and allow ½ pint of water to each pound of sugar. Bring the syrup to boiling point, strain through a sieve lined with cotton wool, return to the saucepan and boil 7 minutes, then gradually add the kumquats and, when they are boiling, the strained juice of a lemon to each 2 lbs. of fruit. Boil until the kumquats are clear and transparent and the syrup is thick. This preserve is better if cooked with a lid on, as the fruit seems to swell out more. *"The Star".*

POMPELMOES PRESERVE

Peel the fruit thinly, rub with salt and leave 30 minutes. Pour boiling water over. When cooled cut a cross in the top of the fruit or make incisions in the sides and remove as many of the pips as possible. Allow to lie in fresh water for 7 to 9 days changing the water twice each day for 3 days, then once daily after that. Make the same way as orange preserve. If the fruit is very large cut into halves or quarters. *"The Star".*

TOMATO PRESERVE

Use small, firm tomatoes. Allow 1 lb. of sugar to every pound of fruit. Prick well with a darning needle. Leave in a solution of 1 tablespoon salt to 3 quarts of water for 20 minutes (if preferred, a solution of lime, using 1 tablespoon to 3 quarts of water). Rinse well. Grease the bottom of a preserving pan with oil or butter, pour in ½ cup of water and pack in alternate layers of fruit and sugar. Bring to the boil slowly, allowing the sugar to dissolve as it heats, then cook rapidy for about 2 hours or until done. Bottle into hot, dry bottles. Seal while hot. A little bruised ginger tied in butter muslin or the grated rind and juice of a lemon to each lb. of tomatoes may be added for flavouring when the sugar and fruit comes to the boil. The ginger should be removed before bottling.

N.B. — Another method is to make a syrup with 1 cup of water to each cup of sugar and after soaking the tomatoes as above for 20 minutes and rinsing them, to drop them slowly into the boiling syrup, adding the lemon juice and rind or the ginger to flavour.

"The Star".

GREEN PAWPAW PRESERVE

Peel and cut the pawpaw into pieces about 1 inch by ½ inch then steep in a lime solution, using 1 tablespoon lime to 6 pints water. Leave overnight. Next day rinse well, drop into boiling water and boil 3 to 5 minutes. Drain and put the fruit into a boiling syrup, adding a few pieces at a time and making the syrup with 1 lb. of sugar to each lb. of fruit and 1 cup of water to every cup of sugar. Flavour with bruised ginger tied in a muslin bag or with stick cinnamon, or with the grated rind and juice of 1 lemon to each 2 lbs. of fruit. Boil until the fruit is clear and the syrup thick. *"The Star"*.

HINTS ON JAM MAKING

1. — Stir with a wooden spoon.
2. — Let jam boil quickly.
3. — Remove scum — the real scum does not rise until the jam boils.
4. — To prevent jam sticking to pan or boiling over, butter the bottom of the pan freely.
5. — The better the fruit the better the jam.
6. — Under-cooked jam will neither keep nor set.
7. — Over-cooked jam will be sticky and dark in colour.
8. — To tell if jam or jelly is cooked place a little in a shallow saucer. If cooked it will jell round the edge.
9. — Too little sugar or too little cooking will cause the jam to ferment.
10. — Too much sugar or over-cooking will cause the jam to crystallise.

M.B.

QUINCE JELLY

7 lbs. quinces, sugar.

Wash and remove tops and tails. Cut up roughly, put in preserving pan and cover with water. Boil slowly 1 hour. Let it drip through a jelly bag all night (do not squeeze or your jelly will be cloudy). In the morning add 1 lb. sugar to each pint of juice. Boil until it jells.

N.B. — Apricot, plum grape and guava jelly can me made in the same way. *M.L.B.*

ORANGE AND APRICOT JAM

1 lb. dried apricots, 2 pints boiling water, 4 lbs. sugar, rind and juice of 6 sweet oranges.

Wash apricots and cut in pieces, pour over them and the grated orange rind 2 pints boiling water. Let it stand 24 hours. Add sugar and boil all together 1 hour. Orange juice should be added when sugar has dissolved. *M.L.B.*

PAWPAW AND PINEAPPLE JAM

To 6 lbs. of pawpaws (green) add 2 pineapples peeled and eyes taken out.

Cut the fruit into small pieces and add ¾ lb. sugar to every lb. of fruit. Boil until it sets. *M.L.B.*

PLUM JAM

To make red plum jam use Satsuma or Sultans.
To make light coloured jam use Kelsey or Burbanks.
To every lb. of fruit add 1 lb. of sugar.
Cut plums in half, remove stones, put into preserving pan and cover with the sugar, leave overnight. In the morning put on the stove and boil until jam sets.
N.B. — Apricot and peach can be made in the same way. *M.L.B.*

GREEN FIG KONFYT
100 figs, 7 lbs. sugar.

Peel figs thinly, cut a small cross at the end. Let them stand in cold water for 12 hours. Change the water, add a tablespoon of salt and 1 teaspoonful of alum, put on to boil. When soft take out and put into cold water for half an hour.
Prepare the syrup by allowing 2 cups of water to 1 lb. sugar, let this boil for 15 minutes, now thin the syrup a little, if necessary, add the strained fruit and boil until clear. *M.L.B.*

GUAVA JAM
1 lb. sugar to 1 lb. guava pulp.

To make the pulp, peel and slice guavas, put into pan and cover with water. Boil until fruit is tender and water thick and sticky. Rub through a sieve, add sugar and boil quickly until it jells. *M.L.B.*

ORANGE GINGER JAM

Ingredients. — 6 lbs. sweet oranges, 4½ lbs. sugar, 6 pints water, ¼ lb. lump ginger.
Method. — Wipe the oranges, peel thinly and remove all white pith from fruit, also pips. Mince peel and break fruit into sections, put into preserving pan with water. Bruise ginger, tie in muslin and add to fruit. Bring all to boil and then add sugar. Stir well, skim as required and boil until a little will jell when tested. Bottle while hot, and close bottles when jam is cold. *Mrs. J. Knight.*

ORANGE JELLY

6 lbs. oranges, 15 breakfast cups cold water. Grate rind slightly, cut up oranges roughly, and boil for 2 hours. For every cup juice allow 1 cup sugar, 1 cup rind; don't add rind until juice has boiled for some time, as it is apt to come up with the scum. Bottle while hot. *Mrs. S. Watson.*

ORANGE MARMALADE

5 large oranges, 1 lemon, 4 lbs. sugar.

Method. — Cut oranges and lemon in very thin slices. Put in saucepan with 5 breakfast cups of cold water to every 5 oranges. Leave soaking until next day, then boil 1 hour. Put away until next day, then add sugar and boil until it jellies. *Mrs. S. Watson.*

GREEN FIG PRESERVE

Scrape figs and lay in water overnight, 1 tablespoon salt to 6 pints of water. Next day place in fresh, cold water and boil until soft. Add few grape leaves; they improve the colour.
Make syrup, allowing 6 lbs. sugar and 6 pints water to 100 figs. Let syrup boil for ½ hour, then add the figs and boil quickly till the syrup is thick and fruit clear. *Mrs. S. Watson*

WATERMELON PRESERVE

Peel watermelon, take all the pink part away. Prick peel well all over with a fork, and put into lime water overnight (1 dessertspoon lime to 4 lbs. fruit and sufficient water to cover fruit). Next day wash off all the lime in fresh water and put into preserving pan. Cover with cold water and boil for 10 minutes, lift out the fruit and let it drain. Then weigh and allow 2 lbs. more sugar than fruit and 2 cups more water than sugar. Boil all together until the syrup is thick. Either of the following flavourings may be added: cinnamon or whole bruised ginger. *Mrs. S. Watson.*

RHUBARB AND FIG JAM

6 lbs. rhubarb, 8 lbs. sugar, 2 lbs. dried figs, 3 lemons, 2 teaspoonsful ground ginger.

Wipe rhubarb and cut into inch pieces. Cut up figs into small pieces. To 1 lb. of fruit use 1 lb. sugar.

Place in layers in jelly pan, and leave overnight, with the juice and rind of the lemons. Put on to boil next morning and cook until it jells. For rhubarb and ginger jam substitute preserved ginger for figs and proceed as above. *J.H.*

MARROW GINGER MARMALADE

Choose a hard-skinned marrow.

6 lbs. marrow, 6 lbs. sugar, 2 ozs. root ginger, 3 lemons.

Cut marrow into squares. Cover with sugar and leave all night. Put on to boil next morning with the ginger and lemon rind tied together loosely in a muslin bag, add lemon juice. Let it boil gently about 2 hours or until it has the appearance of preserved ginger. *M.L.B.*

MARMALADE 1

Weigh oranges first and allow to every lb., weight 3 pints water. Slice the oranges very fine and let them stand in the water for 24 hours. Boil gently 2 hours. Weigh the whole (1 pint = 1 lb.) and to every lb. weight of fruit and liquid add 1½ lbs. sugar. Boil the whole till quite transparent. To 1 dozen oranges add 3 lemons.

MARMALADE 2

16 Seville oranges cut in very thin slices, put down in 12 pints of water and let stand for 12 hours. Boil briskly 1½ hours. Add 10 lbs. sugar and boil ½ hour or until it jellies on side of pan.

MARMALADE 3

4 oranges, 2 lemons, 4 grapefruit, 11 lbs. sugar.
Cut up fruit thinly and soak in 16 cups of water for 24 hours. Boil 3 hours or until tender. Stand 24 hours. Boil again with the sugar until it jellies on the side of the pan. *M.L.B.*

MARMALADE 4

Cut up fruit. To every 5 lbs. fruit allow the juice of 1 or 2 lemons and ¼ teaspoon soda. To every basin of fruit add 2 basins of water, put into saucepan over the fire together with lemon juice and soda. Boil until tender, then measure, and add an equal amount of sugar. Boil rapidly to the jellying stage. *Mrs. Slade.*

QUINCE HONEY

5 lbs. sugar, 2 large cups water, stir together until sugar is dissolved, then boil for 10 to 15 minutes when syrup is thick and resembles honey. Add 5 large cups of minced quince. Boil fast for 25 to 35 minutes. Watch carefully. *W. E. Rowse.*

CAPE GOOSEBERRY JAM

To every pound of fruit add 1 lb. sugar. Put fruit into a preserving pan and cover with sugar. Leave overnight. In the morning put on the stove and boil until it jells. *M.L.B.*

MORE PRESERVES

Ball Brothers Coy., U.S.A.

There is, perhaps, nothing more delicious and certainly little that is more nourishing than good fruit well preserved, and this delicacy is particularly welcome during those seasons when fresh fruit is difficult to obtain. Doctors tell us that the "tired feeling" so many experience as winter draws to a close may usually be traced to an absence of fruit and vegetables in the winter diet, for these essential foods contain, probably to a greater extent than any others, the iron, phosphorus, lime, cellulose and vitamins which are so necessary to health.

In some quarters an idea is prevalent that the making of preserves is a costly and troublesome process, but we believe that, after studying the methods recommended in this article, it will be admitted that the work involved is by no means of an onerous nature nor does it involve any great expense. On the other hand, the joy of preparing bottles of luscious fruit and vegetables is great, whilst the pleasure they afford is ample reward for the effort expended.

There are certain fundamental rules for bottling which must be strictly observed if success is to be attained and these rules vary according to the method used. Two popular methodes for preserving are: (1) "Open Kettle" and (2) "The Jar Cooked". The "Open Kettle" method, as its name suggests, is that in which the food is cooked in an open container or stew pan, and it is used principally for fruits, jams, preserves and for tomatoes. It is important that each step in the process should be given careful attention and also that only firm, ripe, clean, fresh and sound products are used. The food to be bottled must be boiled for the required length of time.

While fruit is boiling, wash jars, caps and lids and completely submerge in pan of hot water. Boil jars and caps for 15 minutes. Scald rubbers and Vacu-Seal Lids. Keep in hot water until ready to use them. Place wet rubber on the hot jar. See that the rubber rests flat on the sealing surface. Fill jar to overflowing. Have shoulder of the jar and cap or lid as well as the rubber, wet when seal is made.

Fill jars to overflowing quickly with boiling product or tomatoes. Do not wipe off the top or sealing shoulder of the jars. Fully seal the jars. as son as filled. Cool as quickly as possible to room temperature. When cool, test for leaks. Do not attempt to tighten Mason caps after jars are cold — this may break the seal. Store in cool, dry place.

These are a few suggestions for "Open Kettle" preserving: —

APPLES

Wash, peel, quarter and core the apples. Drop the quarters into boiling syrup made with 1 part sugar to 1 part water and boil until tender. Add the grated yellow rind of 1 lemon for each 2 quarts of apples. Boil the apples a few minutes longer. Pack into hot Ball jars, fill to overflowing with boiling syrup and seal immediately.

FIGS (Fresh)

Use figs slightly under-ripe. Slit them on one side and soak in mild salt brine for 3 to 4 hours. Then wash thoroughly in cold water. Make a syrup of 2 cups sugar and 2 cups water to each pound (about 1 pint) of fruit. Place syrup in a kettle and when boiling, drop in figs and cook until done. Fill hot Ball jars to overflowing and seal at once.

PEACHES OR APRICOTS

Because of their rich flavour, peaches bottled by the Open Kettle method are prefered by some housewives to peaches bottled by the Jar Cooked method.

Make a syrup using 2 cups of sugar to 1 cup of water. Let the syrup come to a boil then drop in the peaches, which have been peeled and halved, cook until clear and tender. Pack carefully, cut side down, into hot Ball jars. Fill jars to overflowing with boiling syrup and seal immediately. If the peaches are weighed, a pound of sugar may be allowed for each pound of fruit. If not convenient to weigh the fruit you can start with a small amount of syrup, and if not enough, add more sugar and water in the same proportion, 2 to 1, to that already in the kettle. If this makes a heavier preserve than wanted, use a syrup of, say, 3 cups of sugar to 2 cups of water. If any syrup is left bottle the remaining peach syrup, to be used for pudding sauces, gelatine jellies, and other winter-time desserts. It also makes a delicious ice cream.

CABBAGE

Wash and boil for 10 minutes in an open kettle. Add salt to cooking water in proportion of 1 level teaspoon salt to 1 quart water. Pack hot into clean Ball jars, fill with cooking water, partly seal, and process for 40 minutes in a Steam Pressure Cooker at 10 pounds or for 1½ hours in a Hot-Water Bath. Remove from bath and seal at once.

CARROTS

Sort and grade for uniformity. Wash and scrape. Boil for 5 minutes. Slice or pack whole into hot Ball jars. Add 1 level teaspoon salt to each quart, fill with cooking water, partly seal and process for 40 minutes in a Steam Pressure Cooker at 10 pounds or for 2 hours in Hot-Water Bath. Remove from Hotwater Bath and seal immediately.

MEALIES (On Cob)

Remove husks and silk, boil for 5 minutes. Pack into hot Ball jars. Add 1 level teaspoon salt to each quart and fill with cooking water. Party seal and process for 70 minutes in a Steam Pressure Cooker at 10 lbs. or 3½ hours in a Hot-Water Bath. Remove from bath and seal immediately.

Note. — When using 2 quart jars process for 4 hours in a Hot-Water Bath, or for 2 hours in a Steam Pressure Cooker at 10 pounds. One 2-quart jar will hold 7 or 8 ears.

PEAS

Select fresh young peas. Wash pods thoroughly before shelling. Do not wash the peas. Sort, keeping those of the same size together. Cover with boiling water and boil young, tender peas for 3 minutes; more mature for 5 minutes. Pack loosely into hot Ball jars, add 1 teaspoon salt to each quart, fill with cooking water, partly seal and process for 60 minutes in a Steam Pressure Cooker at 10 pounds, or for 3 hours in a Hot-Water Bath.

Note. — Grading and sorting are necessary because the boiling period varies with the age and size of the peas. Do not attempt to bottle peas which have begun to lose their colour.

TOMATOES

Scald, peel and core, cut into pieces, add salt to taste, boil for 20 minutes, pack into clean, hot Ball jars and seal immediately.

In the Jar-Cooked method, the routine to be followed is: —

(1) Wash, then boil for 5 minutes, jars, caps and lids. Scald rubbers and vacu-seal lids. Let them stand in hot water until ready for use.
(2) Carefully examine old jars and caps and see that the sealing edges of caps or lids are not dented or chipped.
(3) Select firm, sound, fresh products. Reject any bruised and spoiled fruits or vegetables. Sort and grade for size and ripeness. Uniformity helps to secure an even distribution of heat throughout the jar and improves the appearance of the pack.
(4) Clean product thoroughly before boiling.
(5) Place new, wet rubber in position on jar or lid. See that it rests flat on the sealing shoulder.
(6) Pre-cook (boil) for necessary time. Blanch (scald), then cold dip foods such as peaches, apricots, tomatoes and beets to loosen skins.
(7) Pack product into jars loosely enough to allow for proper heat circulation; vegetables loosely enough so they will retain their shape.
(8) For fruit pack the prepared fruit into clean, hot Ball jars. Do not crush. Fill with boiling syrup to within one-half inch of top of jar to allow expansion of air and to prevent boiling over.
(9) For vegetables pre-cook (boil) for necessary time. Pack prepared vegetables into clean, hot Ball jars, add 1 level teaspoon pure salt to each quart. Fill jar with the boiling water in which the

vegetable was cooked, to within onehalf inch of top of jars. If not enough cooking water add boiling water.

Now let us give you a few recipes for "Jar-Cooked" Preserving: —

APRICOTS

Apricots may be bottled peeled or unpeeled. If bottled without peeling, remove fuzz by wiping with damp cloth. Blanch ½ minute. Halve and pip. Pack closely into Ball jars, fill with hot syrup made with 1 part sugar to 1 part water. Partly seal and process in hot-water bath for 20 minutes. Remove from bath and seal immediately.

GRAPES

Wash and stem, using only sound, firm grapes. Pack tight, without crushing, into Ball jars, fill with syrup made with 3 parts sugar to 2 parts water. Partly seal and process for 30 minutes in a hot water bath. Remove from bath and seal immediately.

PLUMS

Plums for bottling should not be too ripe. Pack tightly without crushing, and cover with boiling syrup made with 2 parts sugar to 1 part water for tart plums and a syrup made with 1 part sugar to 1 part water for sweet varieties. Partly seal and process in a hot-water bath for 20 minutes. Remove from bath and seal at once.

RHUBARB

Wash stalks and cut in pieces of uniform length. Make a syrup in the proportion of 1 cup water to 1 cup sugar. Use shallow pan with cover. Drop rhubarb into hot syrup. Cover and heat to boiling. Remove from fire and let stand 15 minutes. Pack into hot Ball Jars, cover with syrup used in precooking. Partly seal and process for 5 minutes in hot-water bath. Remove from bath and seal immediately. Rhubarb bottled by this method retains its colour and there is less shrinkage.

It is impossible in an article of this nature to deal fully with all the interesting details in regard to the bottling of fruit and vegetables, but in should be remembered that after bottling has been completed, it is essential to keep every jar or bottle absolutely airtight. Do not lift jars or bottles by the lids when removing them from the hot-water bath, as the weight of the jar is often great enough to pull the rubber ring loose, and thus allow air to enter.

Here are a few points which every woman who desires to successfully bottle foodstuffs should remember: —

The time which a product should be kept in the Hot-Water Bath or in the Pressure Cooker, varies with the elevation above sea level, and the following table should be useful in this connection: —

Above Sea Elevation Level	Extra Pound Pressure Added to Pressure Given in Pressure Cooker Time Table	Percentage To be added to Time Specified in Hot-Water Bath Time Table
2,000 feet	0 pound	20 %
3,000 "	1 "	40 %
4,000 "	1 "	60 %
5,000 "	2 "	80 %
6,000 "	2 "	100 %
7,000 "	3 "	120 %

The time for which the bottle is kept in the hot-water bath should be counted after the water is boiling, and the boiling should be kept up steadily during the entire process.

Jars or bottles should never be opened to refill with liquid; loss of liquid does not affect keeping quality provided the jar is properly sealed. If, however, the jar ring has "blown out" it must be replaced immediately with a new one and the product placed in the Hot-Water Bath again for one-third of the original time.

Satisfactory results in bottling vegetables will be assured by using fresh, sound, firm products, and bottling whilst the product is still fresh. Each jar should be placed in the Hot-Water Bath as soon as packed and kept there for the time specified, whilst the jar should be sealed immediately it is removed.

Sugarless bottling for fruit is not recommended nor is it economical. The addition of sugar during the cooking helps to develop the flavour, and the increased cost per jar is very slight.

It is unwise to subject jars to sudden temperature changes. Before use they should be first cleansed in warm water and then in boiling water. On no account place jars in a cool draught immediately after filling, nor should they be put on a cold marble or metal-top table. Several thicknesses of cloth or paper placed on the table will prevent fracture.

Ball Jars are recommended for bottling and preserving fruits, vegetables and meats. They can be obtained from all suppliers in a number of convenient sizes, and they have been used by experienced housewives for very many years.

Ball Brothers Coy., U.S.A.

DRUDGERY

I often think that drudgery is a blessing in disguise — I'm sorry for the people with no tasks in life — no ties ... The folk who plod and spend their lives in work and daily grind — they are the true philosophers — if in their work they find — the need for kindly tolerance, for patience, joy and zest — the highest qualties of man in humble things expressed ... And yet the drudge can also be an artist in his way — the worker with his muscles and the man who writes all day — the navvy and the poet and the driver in the street — can know the pride in work well done — for well-earned rest is sweet — God meant us to be drudges so that in the daily grind — we might express the finest things within the human mind ... Self-discipline and fortitude, love, humour, self-control — To lay the strong foundations in the building of the Soul.   Patience Strong.

The fate of nations depends on how they are fed.   S.A.

CHUTNEY, PICKLES AND SAUCES

PEACH PICKLE
6 lbs. yellow peaches, 6 large onions, 3 bottles vinegar, ½ breakfast cup yellow sugar, 1 tablespoon allspice, 1 tablespoon borrie, 2 tablespoons curry powder, salt to taste.

Method. — Boil all until thick but must not be too soft.

Mrs. S. Watson.

TOMATO SAUCE
8 lbs. tomatoes, ½ lb. salt, 2 large onions, 2 ozs. white pepper (whole), 1 oz. cayenne pepper, 2 lbs. brown sugar, 2 large apples (rings will do, sour), 2 bottles vinegar, 2 ozs. allspice, 1 oz. cloves.

Put all ingredients together and boil for 3 hours. Then strain by pressing through sieve and bottle.   *Mrs. E. Loveday.*

PEACH PICKLE
30 large clingstone yellow peaches, 1½ bottles of vinegar, 4 or 5 red chillies, if possible, 4 large onions, about 1 lb. sugar, a few coriander seeds, curry powder to taste.

Peel and prick peaches. Soak in very strong salt water with onions overnight. Next morning cut peaches and remove the pips, cut the onions as small as you like. Stew all ingredients for 30 minutes till syrup thickens.   *Mrs. E. Loveday.*

TOMATO CHUTNEY
3 lbs. peeled tomatoes, 2 lbs. onions, 2 lbs. sour apples (peeled), 1 lb. sugar, ½ lb. raisins, 1 bottle vinegar, 1 teaspoon cayenne, 1 tablespoon salt, 1 teaspoon ginger.

Mince all ingredients and boil until most of the liquid has boiled away (about 1¼ hours). Keep stirring towards the end or it will catch.

Mrs. Reeler.

APRICOT CHUTNEY
6 lbs. apricots, 2½ lbs. sugar, ½ tablespoon each: cayenne pepper, salt and ground ginger, 1½ lbs. onions, ½ lb. sultanas or raisins, ¾ bottle English vinegar, chillies may be added.

Cook fruit, onions, sugar together until soft, add other ingredients. Lastly before taking off the fire, add vinegar.   *Mrs. E. Loveday.*

INDIAN CHUTNEY

2 lbs apples, 2 lbs. yellow sugar, 1 lb. sultanas, 1 lb. dates, 1½ oz. garlic, 4 ozs. ginger (root), 2 ozs. salt, ¾ oz. chilli peppers, vinegar.

Have all well chopped. Pound ginger. Do not peel apples. Wash and chop them. Put all fruits except dates in enough vinegar to cover. Boil till soft then add other ingredients and boil till thick. Leave out chilli peppers and use only half quantities of the ginger if a hot chutney is not liked.
H. Michell.

CHUTNEY

4 lbs. fruit — bananas, apricots and apples. Dried apricots can be used, 4 lbs. tomatoes, 3 lbs. onions, 2 bottles vinegar, salt to taste, 2 lbs. sugar, 2 teaspoons cayenne pepper, 3 chillies cut up.

Method. — Put fruit, tomatoes and onions through mincer, add vinegar, salt, sugar, pepper, chillies. Boil 3 hours.
Mrs. S. Watson.

FRUIT CHUTNEY

4 lbs. peaches or apricots, 1¾ cups sugar, 1 dessertspoon salt, 2 teaspoons curry powder, 1½ breakfast cups vinegar, 2 large onions, 1 large apple, 4 chillies.

Method. — Grate onion and apple. Cut chillies fine; add fruit cut up in small pieces, then vinegar, salt and curry powder.
Boil 3½ hours, stirring well as it burns quickly.
Mrs. S. Watson.

TOMATO CHUTNEY

8 large tomatoes, 4 sour apples, ½ pint vinegar, 2 large onions, ¾ lb. sugar, salt, dried chillies, peppercorns, ginger, a little cayenne and any other spices.

Scald tomatoes and skin. Peel and core apples — cut up. Peel onions and cut up small. Tie spices in muslin bag. Place everything in pan except vinegar and boil for one hour, then add vinegar and boil for short time. Bottle and seal while hot.
Will keep for some time. This quantity makes five 1 lb. jars.
A. Paxton.

APRICOT CHUTNEY

1 lb. dried apricots, 1 lb. raisins, 1 lb. sugar, 2 tablespoons ground ginger, 4 bitter almonds, 2 tablespoons salt, 2 bottles vinegar, 2 small onions, a little cayenne pepper.

Method. — Stew apricots until soft and mince all the other fruit, add seasoning and vinegar. Mix well and bottle.
Mrs. W. Hamilton.

INDIAN RECIPE FOR TOMATO CHOW-CHOW

5 lbs. tomatoes (half ripe will do), 1 lb. onions.

Cut up tomatoes and onions overnight, sprinkle ¼ lb. coarse salt over them, and next morning drain off salt (put this all in an enamel basin). 1 oz. curry powder, 1 lb. golden syrup, ½ tin mustard (6 d. tins), 1½ cups vinegar.

Put these ingredients in the enamel basin, mix altogether. When boiling add tomatoes and onions and stir well and let boil for 20 minutes. Put in jars and cover when cold.

(Any fruit, such as apricots, bananas, apples can also be added).

Mrs. J. Green.

TOMATO SAUCE

1 lb. tomatoes, 1 small onion, 1 teaspoon sugar, 1 oz. butter, pinch bicarbonate soda, pepper and salt.

Slice onion and fry in butter. Add the tomatoes cut in slices, sugar, soda, salt and pepper. Cook slowly for about an hour, pass through a sieve, reheat and serve very hot. A fair quantity can be made at a time and stored in frig.

POT AND KETTLE

The books I've lent, it seems to me,
Are books I nevermore shall see;
In private thought what wrath I spill
On those who have my books — until
I find on calmer inventory
Dear me! I'm in their category.

F.P.J.

What I say about children is this.
"Have 'em. Love 'em. And then, leave 'em be."
Sidney Howard.

SWEETS

RECIPES CONTRIBUTED BY THE CHILDREN

A few sweetmaking rules.

Choose a nice wet Saturday afternoon. See that your best friend is at hand to assist. Think first of mother and see that she is carefully tucked up with a good book and the promise of a "lovely cup of tea" at 4 o'clock sharp. Close the door carefully.

Collect utensils as quietly as possible. It is never advisable to choose the best pot. Good pots have a habit of burning easily and — mothers are mothers!

Always use the longest and strongest wooden spoon for stirring, remembering that the cook has the sole right to the scrapings of the pot. It is as well to see that there is a little carron oil at hand for toffee that spurts up and a little castor oil for tastings that go down.

Remember — too many sips spoil the cook.

The droppings on the floor belong to "Spotty".

When tasting for readiness offer a small share to big brother if he promises to do the clearing up.

When sweets are quite cold, pack into tin with tight fitting lid and store in a dry place. Wash tin out next day.

It is now 4.30 p.m. Stand that pot on the sink, fill with cold water and put in a handful of soda.

Take Mummy two cups of tea and an aspirin. *Aunty Jean.*

COCOANUT ICE — PINK AND WHITE

1½ lbs. loaf sugar, ½ lb. desiccated cocoanut, ¼ pint water. Boil sugar and water together till a little sets when dropped on a saucer. Add the cocoanut and pour half into a baking tin to set. Colour the rest pink and pour it on top of other. *Blanche Roos.*

SWISS MILK TOFFEE

2 lbs. sugar, ¼ lb. butter, 2 tablespoons golden syrup, 5 tablespoons hot water.

Melt the above and bring to the boil and then add (stirring all the time), 1 tin Nestle's condensed milk. Boil for 20 minutes — no longer — stirring all the time. *Marie Roos.*

TURKISH DELIGHT

2 ozs. gelatine, 2 lbs. white sugar, juice of three lemons, 1½ cups water.

Soak gelatine in one cup of cold water for two hours. Take lemon juice, sugar and the half cup of water, bring to the boil, add gelatine and boil for six minutes, stirring all the time. Remove from heat, add flavouring (lemon essence) and colour half the mixture pale pink, adding some chopped almonds if desired. Pour into buttered dishes. When set cut into strips, roll in icing sugar, cut in squares and roll in icing sugar again. *Sheila Atherton.*

TREACLE CARAMELS

1 lb. castor sugar, 1 tablespoon treacle, 1 oz. butter, 2 tablespoons vinegar, ½ cupful water.

Put everything into a saucepan and let it boil until it cracks when tested in cold water. Pour into a buttered tin. Mark off in small squares, then wrap in greaseproof paper and eat. *Hazel Atherton.*

RUSSIAN TOFFEE

2 teacups sugar, 2 tablespoons golden syrup, 3 ozs. butter, 1 tablespoon vinegar, 1 tin sweetened condensed milk.

Method. — Melt butter in pan and add sugar, when dissolved add syrup and vinegar. Pour in milk stirring all the time. Boil till one drop will harden in water. *Nancy Harris.*

HOME-MADE TOFFEE

1½ cups sugar, 2 tablespoons syrup, ¼ cup water, 1 dessertspoon butter, 1 small teaspoon ground ginger.

Method. — Boil 15 minutes then pour into buttered dish. *Adele Harris.*

CLEAR NUT TOFFEE

2 cups sugar, ½ cup water, ½ lb. monkey nuts (peanuts), 1/8 teaspoon cream of tartar.

Method. — Dissolve the sugar in the water, add cream of tartar. Boil rapidly until a little dropped into cold water becomes brittle. Spread peanuts on greased pan, pour the boiled toffee over. Let is stand for a while, cut into 1 in. squares and leave till cool. *Louis Reinicke.*

ALMOND TABLET

1 lb. sugar, ¾ teacup milk, 3 oz. almonds (blanched and halved). Put sugar and milk into saucepan and boil for 8 minutes. Remove from fire, put the almonds into the mixture and stir for three minutes. Pour into a well buttered tin. Mark off in bars when cool.
Jennifer Travers.

HONEY CANDY

2 cups white sugar, add enough water to dissolve it then add 4 tablespoons honey. Boil till a thread will break in cold water. Add ½ teaspoon vanilla flavouring. Pour on to buttered plates and when cool enough to handle pull and cut into pieces. *Josephine Morgan.*

MELK TAMELETJIES

Melt 1 cup butter, add four cups sugar and 1 small cup water, ½ teaspoon salt and 1 tin condensed milk. Boil for ½ an hour, stirring all the time. Take off the fire and add 20 drops almond essence. Put buttered paper in roasting pan, spread toffee on paper and cut up when quite cold. *Gwynneth Morgan.*

FRUIT CANDIES

1 lb. dried apricots, 2 lbs. sugar.

Wash fruit well, cover with water and boil till tender but not broken up. Drain well in colander and press juice out gently. Return fruit to saucepan, add sugar and mix thoroughly, using a wooden spoon. Boil exactly 20 minutes, stirring all the time as it burns quickly.
Turn out on to a wet pastry board and let it stand overnight. Cut into quarter and roll in sugar. Will keep for months in tin.

Nanette Burnham.

BUTTER SCOTCH

1 lb. brown sugar, ½ lb. butter, 1 teacup water.

Boil over a slow fire until a thick syrup. Stir in the butter, boil for half an hour, stirring all the time. If it hardens in cold water it is ready. Flavour with vanilla essence. Wet a large, flat dish, pour in the mixture and cut into squares when cold. *Kathleen Baillie.*

MRS. DUNCAN'S SWISS MILK TOFFEE

Melt 2 breakfastcups of sugar with ¼ lb. butter and 1 tablespoon syrup, then pour in 1 tin condensed milk. Stir with a wooden spoon until it boils and keep stirring as the mixture burns easily. Boil for 20 minutes, take off fire and put in 1 teaspoon vanilla essence and a handful of cocoanut or chopped walnuts.

Bessie and Marion Fotheringham.

ALMOND TOFFEE

4 teacups sugar, 3 tablespoons syrup and 1¼ teacups water, 4 ozs. almonds — blanched and halved, 2 tablespoons butter.

Boil the sugar, syrup and water for twenty minutes then add the butter and boil till it hardens when dropped into cold water. Add a teaspoon lemon essence and the almonds and pour into a buttered tin.

Maureen and Margaret Blake.

MINT DELIGHT

1½ lb. castor sugar, 2 lemons, 1 dessertspoon peppermint essence, 3 ozs. fine gelatine, ½ teaspoon tartaric acid.

Put the gelatine into a saucepan with ¾ pint cold water. Dissolve over a gentle heat. Add sugar and stir until melted. Boil for 8 minutes stirring all the time. Take pan off fire, stir in the strained juice of the lemons and tartaric acid and peppermint. Turn into a wet tin and leave till next day then turn on to a board well dusted with icing sugar. Dust with sugar, cut into squares, roll again in sugar and pack in boxes. Colour with green vegetable colouring if possible. *Peggy Griffith.*

DIVINITY FUDGE

3 cups sugar, 1 cup boiling water, 1 cup syrup, salt, 3 egg whites beaten stiff, ½ teaspoon vanilla.

Mix sugar, water and syrup. Place over low heat until sugar dissolves. Boil to soft ball stage (238°). Pour slowly on egg whites, beating until thick. Flavour and pour into greased pan. Mark in squares.
If desired, add nuts, fruits or cocoanut when thick. *Yvonne Lappan.*

CHOCOLATE FUDGE

2 tablespoons butter, 2 cups sugar, 1 teaspoon vanilla, ¾ cup creamy milk, 2 squares chocolate or 4 tablespoons cocoa, ½ cup chopped walnuts.

Melt butter in pan and add sugar, milk and chocolate. Stir gently until chocolate melts. Boil without stirring at 238° or until mixture forms soft ball when tried in cold water. Remove from fire, stand until cool and add flavouring. Beat with wooden spoon or work with spatula on a marble slab. Pour ¾ inch thick in buttered pan and mark in squares.
Shirley Davel.

VANILLA CARAMELS

1 cup sugar, ⅔ cup syrup, 1½ cups cream, 1 teaspoon vanilla.

Put sugar, syrup and ½ cup cream in pan and stir until sugar dissolves. Boil, stirring gently and constantly till mixture forms soft ball when tried in cold water. Add ½ cup cream, boil as before and add remaining cream and boil until mixture forms very firm ball when tried in cold water. Pour into buttered pan. Cool, cut in squares and wrap in wax paper. If sugary, return to pan, add more cream and boil again.
Betty Hamilton.

WALNUT TOFFEE

2 ozs. butter, 1 lb. yellow sugar, 1 teacup milk, 1 tablespoon syrup, 1 teacup chopped nuts.

Put all ingredients in a pan. Stir at first, and then allow to boil. Stir again when it thickens, and boil for ¼ hour. After removing pan from stove stir till nearly cool. Pour on greased dish and when nearly cold cut into strips. *Elaine Johnson.*

MARSHMALLOWS

3 dessertspoons (¾ oz.) gelatine, ½ lb. sugar, ½ pint hot water, 1 dessertspoon lemon juice, 1 dessertspoon rose water, ½ teaspoon cream of tartar, pinch of salt.

Place sugar, water, gelatine and cream of tartar in saucepan. Simmer until the mixture forms a thread when dropped from the spoon; stir occasionally while cooking. Leave to cool. Add rosewater, lemon juice and salt. Beat thoroughly until white and thick. Cut into squares and roll in mixture of icing sugar and corn flour. (Davis' Gelatine Recipe).
Monica Johnson.

GLACES

½ lb. sugar, ½ teaspoon cream of tartar, ½ teacup water.

Boil to pale amber colour (brittle). Remove from fire. Dip cherries, nuts, raisins, dried apricots. Leave to set on waxed paper.
Helen, Jean and Allison Michell.

CANADIAN PEANUT TABLET

2 teacups brown sugar, 1 teacup milk, ¼ teaspoon salt, 2 ozs. butter, ½ teacup chopped peanuts, 1 teaspoon vanilla essence.

Boil sugar with butter and salt and keep boiling half an hour without stirring. Remove from stove, add vanilla and nuts and beat until creamy. Pour into greased tins and when cool cut into squares.
Ruth and Margaret Bennett.

PEPPERMINT CREAMS

1 lb. icing sugar, 1 large tablespoon cream or unsweetened condensed milk, white of an egg, 1 pinch cream of tartar, essence of peppermint.

Rub the icing sugar and cream of tartar through a hair sieve. Stir the cream and slightly beaten egg white into the sugar with a few drops of peppermint essence. Mix well and leave for about an hour. Knead the cream and when smooth roll out on a board sprinkled with icing sugar. Cut into rounds and leave to dry for 24 hours.
These are very nice. *Norma Retief.*

EDINBURGH ROCK

Crushed-loaf sugar, cream of tartar and water, and any of these flavourings, lemon, vanilla, raspberry, ginger or orange.

Put into a pan a pound of crushed loaf sugar and half a pint of cold water. Stir gently till sugar is dissolved. When nearly boiling add a good pinch of cream of tartar and boil without stirring until mixture forms a hard lump in cold water. Remove from fire, add colouring and flavouring and pour on to a buttered marble slab. As it begins to cool turn the ends and edges inwards with a buttered knife. When cool enough to handle, dust with powdered sugar, take it up and pull gently until it is dull. Cut in pieces with a pair of scissors. Place the rock in a warm room and let it remain there for at least 24 hours.

Lillibet Fotheringham.

MISS H. HAWKES' JUJUBES

Soak 2 ozs. leaf gelatine for 1 hour in 1 teacup of cold water.
Put into saucepan with 2 lbs. white sugar. Pour on it 1½ teacup boiling water. Boil 5 minutes stirring all the time. Take off the fire and add 2 teaspoons ground citric acid, flavour with vanilla or rose water.
Can be flavoured with 2 or 3 drops of peppermint essence and coloured green but omit acid.
Pour into shallow pans previously wet. Leave all night to set. Cut into cubes or diamonds and roll in castor sugar. To keep place in screw top jars.

Helen Hendrie.

The following recipes are contributed by Mrs. A. Marquard, Ficksburg: —

FRUIT MINCES

¼ lb. dates, ¼ lb. sultanas, ¼ lb. raisins (stoned), ¼ lb. chopped walnuts.
Mince these, mix well, roll in round or oval shapes. Place half walnut on top (or almond or cherry). Roll in desiccated cocoanut.

The following method should be applied to all the fruitsweet recipes given below after the mixtures have been boiled as directed: —
Pour into dishes, lined with grease-proof paper, to a depth of ½ in. to ¾ in. Leave till top is quite set — preferably in a draught for 6 to 10 days. Then turn out on grease-proof paper and leave till new top is quite firm. Cut into squares and roll in coarse sugar.

APRICOT SWEETS

6 lbs. ripe apricots, 2 lbs. apples, 3 lbs. sugar, 1 teaspoon salt, 1 teacup water.
Stew fruit till very soft. Rub through sieve. Return to pot and add sugar and salt. Boil 10-15 minutes.

PLUM SWEETS

5 lbs. plums, 2 lb. apples, 2½ to 3 lbs. sugar, 1 teaspoon salt.

Stew fruit till very soft; rub through sieve; return pulp to pot with sugar and salt. Boil quickly — 10-15 minutes.

PINEAPPLE SWEETS

2 lbs. pineapples, ¾ lb. apples, ½ lb. sugar, ¼ teaspoon salt, a little pineapple essence if necessary.

Boil peels, as for jelly, for a short while to extract the flavour. Strain and pour juice on minced pineapples. Add apples and boil slowly till fairly soft. Rub through sieve. Return pulp to pot adding sugar and salt. Boil quickly till thick enough.

QUINCE SWEETS

5 lbs. quinces, 1 lb. apples, 3 lbs. sugar, 1 small tea spoon salt.

Cover quinces with water and stew till very soft. Add apples and half the sugar. Stew till deep pink or red. Rub through sieve, add remainder of sugar. Boil slowly until fairly thick stirring all the time as this burns very easily.

APPLE SWEETS

2 lbs. apples, ¾ to 1 lb. sugar, ¼ teaspoon salt, cinnamon sticks to taste.

Peel and core apples, stew in water, salt and cinnamon sticks till very soft. Be careful of burning. Remove cinnamon sticks. Rub through sieve. Boil pulp and sugar quickly till mixture leaves side of pot.

RIPE FIG SWEETS

2 lbs. figs, ½ lb. apples, ¾ to 1 lb. sugar, ¼ teaspoon salt, ¾ teacup water, few sticks cinnamon.

Stew fruit till very soft. Rub through sieve. Add sugar and salt. Boil quickly 10 to 15 minutes adding cinnamon sticks for the last 5 minutes.

GOOD-NIGHT, CHILDREN!

Good-night, children! — and dream your happy dreams — forget your cares — forget your tears, and all your gallant schemes — To-morrow lies before you like an undiscovered land — with shining possibilities — the lovely things you've planned, are blurred into a

golden haze in which you play your part — in valiant adventures with a brave and fearless heart — The rabbit and the kittens and the fishes in the streams — the soldiers and the sugar mouse, go marching through your dreams — And though the darkness must descend, and toys be put away — God always sends To-morrow, when He takes away to-day.
Patience Strong.

A happy childhood is one of the best gifts that parents have in their power to bestow; second only to implanting the habit of obedience, which puts the child in training for the habit of obeying himself later on.
Children have more need of models than of critics.

There are dark shadows on the earth, but its lights are stronger in the contrast.
— *Dickens.*

WAR-TIME RECIPES
DELICIOUS WAR BREAD
The following recipe for making war bread will be welcomed by our readers and will prove that it can be so delicious that even the most critical members of the family will come a second time. 4 lbs. unsifted boermeal, 1 tablespoon salt, 2 teaspoons golden syrup, 4 ozs. butter or lard, 2 cups boiling milk, 3 cups water, 2 yeast cakes (1 oz.).

Put butter, salt and golden syrup into a basin, pour on boiling milk and stir until dissolved. Add cold water, then add yeast cakes rubbed to a paste and a little lukewarm water, stir in the meal and knead into a stiff dough. Knead thoroughly until smooth and elastic, then moisten the top with a little melted butter or warm water and put into a warm place to rise. When risen to double its bulk, knock down the dough, then form into loaves. Put into well greased pans, brush over with a little melted butter or fat and leave again in a warm place covered over. When well risen, bake in a hot oven of 450° for 50 to 60 minutes. Remove from pans, brush over with a little melted butter or use the paper in which butter was wrapped, place on a wire cake cooler, cover over with a clean cloth and leave until cold, then pack away in airtight tins.

MEALIE MEAL BROWN BREAD
2 cups mealie meal, 4 cups unsifted boermeal, ½ yeast cake (¼ oz.), 2 tablespoons butter, ¼ cup treacle or home-made caramel burnt sugar, 1 teaspoon salt, 2 cups boiling water.

Pour boiling water on to mealie meal and let it stand 10 minutes. Dissolve butter, caramel and salt over the fire until butter is melted, then stir into the mealie meal. Rub yeast cake into a paste with a little lukewarm water and add to the mealie meal mixture, which must be only lukewarm, then add unsifted meal and form into a stiff dough. Knead well until smooth and elastic, then brush over with a little melted butter and leave in a warm place, covered over until well risen. Form into loaves, put into greased pans, brush over with melted butter or fat and leave again in a warm place until double in bulk, then bake in a hot oven of 450° for 50 to 60 minutes. Turn out on to a cake cooler, brush over with a little butter or fat, cover with a clean cloth and leave until cold, then put into airtight tins.

BROWN BREAD

2 cups milk, 1 teaspoon salt, 2 tablespoons syrup or sugar, about 8 cups standard meal, ½ to 1 yeast cake soaked in ½ cup warm water, or 1 cup home-made yeast, 4 tablespoons butter or lard.

(1) Scald the milk.
(2) Add salt and sweetening and allow to cool until lukewarm.
(3) Add to yeast.
(4) Mix in well half of the meal.
(5) Stir in the melted shortening and then knead in enough meal to make a dough. (If the melted shortening is added in this way, kneading is easier. Make this bread dough fairly stiff).
(6) Knead well and allow to rise in a warm place. (If the dough cools down at any time it will rise slowly and the flavour will be affected).
(7) Knead slightly, shape loaves and let them rise, after brushing with melted butter.
(8) Bake in a hot oven for an hour. *Miss Naude.*

BROCHE: A RICH YEAST MIXTURE FOR TEA ROLLS. ROLLS, ETC.

1 cup milk, ⅔ cup butter, 1½ teaspoons salt, ½ cup sugar, 1 yeast cake soaked in ¼ cup warm water, 4 well-beaten eggs, about 4 cups standard flour.

(1) Follow the method for Brown Bread given above (Miss Naude's Brown Bread), adding the eggs to the lukewarm milk mixture.
(2) When the dough has risen once form into the desired shapes, let rise to thrice its size and bake in a hot oven. This dough can be used as follows: —

(1) *Rich Rolls:* Roll ½ in. thick, cut rounds, allow to rise and bake.
(2) *Cloverleaf Rolls:* Roll small balls of the dough between the hands and place three close together in muffin pans. Allow to rise and bake.
(3) *Pocket Book Roll:* Roll dough ½ in. thick in circles and brush with melted butter. Dent along the middle with the back of a knife, fold, allow to rise and bake.
(4) *Teawreath:* Roll the dough ⅓ in. thick, in a rectangle. Brush with melted butter and sprinkle thickly with sugar, chopped raisins and nuts, or a similar mixture. Roll from the longest side and place this roll on a greased baking dish with the ends together to form a ring. Cut with scissors from the outer edge not quite through to the inside at 1 in. intervals. Twist the pieces round to be flat, brush with melted butter and bake when it has risen. When cooled, decorate with a little water-icing poured over it. Serve with tea or coffee.

WHOLE WHEAT QUICKBREAD

3/8 cup sour or buttermilk, 1½ cups standard meal, 2 tablespoons syrup, 1 egg, ¼ teaspoon salt, ¼ teaspoon bicarbonate of soda, 2 teaspoons baking powder.

(1) Mix dry ingredients, stir in the well-beaten egg, syrup and milk.
(2) Beat well, pour into a greased pan and bake in a medium oven 30 to 40 minutes.
(3) Serve with butter.

N.B. — For variety any one of the following can be added: ½ cup **raisins**, 1/3 cup currants, ½ cup dates, ½ cup mashed banana, ½ cup stewed dried apricots or other dried fruit, as well as ¼ cup nutmeats.

"SOET-SUURDEEG" — SALT-RISING FERMENT

"Soet Suurdeeg" makes bread with a characteristic flavour which is very pleasant. It is not a method which is often used, but can be recommended as the most suitable method of making wholemeal bread.

(1) Put into a saucepan with a tight-fitting lid 1 tablespoon salt.
(2) Pour on this 2 cups boiling water and ½ cup cold water.
(3) Add 1 tablespoon sugar.
(4) Sprinkle on top 1 cup standard meal.
(5) Put on the lid, cover well with a woollen blanket and leave in a warm place overnight.
(6) Next morning, beat the mixture well with a spoon.
(7) Add 1 cup hot water, nearly boiling and enough meal to make a very thick batter.
(8) Strew a little meal over the top and set again in a warm place to rise. In one hour's time it should be ready to make into a stiff dough, as directed for salt-rising bread.

SALT-RISING BREAD

(1) Make the ferment as directed (see "Soet Suurdeeg" — Saltrising Ferment).
(2) Knead the following day, using about 5 lbs. standard meal dissolved in sufficient hot water to make a fairly firm dough.
(3) Form into loaves.
(4) Put into greased pans, and allow to rise to double its bulk, in a warm place.
(5) Bake in a hot oven about 1 hour.

BOSTON BREAD

2 cups standard meal, ½ cup sugar, 4 teaspoons baking powder, ½ teaspoon salt, 4 tablespoons butter, 2 tablespoons lard, 1 egg, 1 egg yolk, 1 cup milk less 1 tablespoon, ½ cup toasted peanuts or other nuts.

(1) Mix meal, baking powder, salt and sugar lightly. Rub in the butter and lard.
(2) Add well-beaten eggs.
(3) Add milk and nuts and beat well.
(4) Pour into greased bread tin and stand for 20 minutes.
(5) Bake for 40 minutes in a medium oven.

DATE SCONES

2 cups Pro Vita meal (or unsifted boer meal), 1 dessertspoonful of baking powder, 1 tablespoon sugar, 1 level teaspoon salt, ½ cup dates, butter and 1 egg, ½ cup milk.

Mix same as white scones.

OVEN SCONES

2 cups standard meal, ½ teaspoon salt, ¼ cup butter or lard, ⅔ cup milk, 4 teaspoons baking powder, 1 egg yolk mixed with a little milk.

(1) Rub the shortening into the dry ingredients.
(2) Make a soft dough with the milk.
(3) Roll out ½ in. thick and cut into shapes.
(4) Brush with egg mixture and bake in a hot oven for 12 to 15 minutes.

N.B. — When sour or buttermilk is used the product is finer and more tender.

WHOLEMEAL RECIPES
SHORTCRUST FOR PIES

2 level breakfast cups wholemeal, 6 ozs. butter, 1 oz. sugar ½ teaspoon baking powder, 1 egg (if desired).

Rub butter into meal, add sugar and baking powder, then mix to a paste with cold water and egg. Moderate oven.

MELDRUM BUTTER CAKE

2 cups sifted boermeal, 1 cup sugar, 1 cup butter, 1 level teaspoon baking powder, 4 eggs, ⅛ teaspoon salt, 1 teaspoon vanilla essence or grated rind of 1 orange.

(1) Cream the butter until soft, then add half of the boermeal and mix until nice and smooth.
(2) Beat the sugar and eggs for 3 minutes until light and frothy, then add half of the mixture to the creamed butter and boermeal. Mix thoroughly.

(3) Sift the rest of the boermeal with baking powder and salt, then gradually add to the creamed mixture alternately with the rest of the beaten eggs and sugar.

(4) Lastly, add the flavouring, mix well, then pour into a round cake tin lined with paper in the bottom and left ungreased. Bake 45 minutes in a moderate oven of 375° or until a nice golden brown. Turn out on to a wire cake cooler and leave to get cold.

Icing of Cake: 2 cups sifted icing sugar, 2 ozs. butter, milk or cream, 2 tablespoons plum jam, glacé cherries, cocoanut.

(1) Cream the butter until soft, add the icing sugar and, if necessary, a little hot milk or orange juice, and beat well until light and smooth. If liked, a flavouring of vanilla essence or grated rind of an orange may be added.

(2) Spread the icing smoothly over the top and sides of cake, reserving a little of the icing for decoration. Finish off the sides with the cocoanut, which may be toasted if liked, to a nice golden brown. Or instead of cocoanut, fine cake crumbs may be used.

(3) Decorate the top of cake with butter cream forced through a star tube in any simple design, using a paper bag with the point cut off and the tube inserted. Pour the jam in the centre of the cake, and finish off with glacé cherries cut in halves or quarters.

BOERMEAL RAISIN CAKE

3 cups unsifted boermeal, 6 ozs. butter, 1 cup sugar, 4 eggs, 2 teaspoons ginger, 2 teaspoons mixed spice, ½ lb. raisins, 2 level teaspoons baking powder, ¼ teaspoon salt.

Icing: 1½ cups icing sugar, 1 tablespoon caramel, 4 tablespoons butter, milk.

Collect utensils and ingredients. Line with paper the bottom of a round cake tin measuring 7½ to 8 inches in diameter, and leave ungreased. Cream sugar and butter thoroughly together until light and smooth, then break in eggs, one by one, and beat well after the addition of each. Sift together flour, baking powder and spices and stir into the creamed mixture. Mix until smooth but do not overbeat the mixture.

Lastly add the raisins which should have been thoroughly washed and dried beforehand and then cut into quarters after the seeds have been removed.

Pour into prepared tin and bake in a moderate oven of 350° Fah. for 1 hour or longer if necessary.

Icing of Cake: Cream butter until nice and soft, add caramel and mix well. Stir in the icing sugar, passed through a sieve and mixed to a nice smooth consistency, adding a little milk if necessary. Cover the top of the cake and finish off with a simple design, using a star tube and paper bag. Garnish with glacé cherries.

MRS. SLADE'S CAKE

1½ lbs. flour or boermeal, 1 lb. butter, 1 lb. Government sugar, 1 lb. raisins, 1 lb. currants, 1 lb. sultanas, ½ lb. mixed peel, 1 lb. cherries, ¼ lb. almonds, 9 eggs, 2 teaspoons nutmeg or mixed spice, 4 tablespoons caramel, juice of 1 lemon, 1 tablespoon vinegar, 1 teaspoon baking powder, 1 teaspoon bicarbonate of soda.

Cream butter and sugar, add eggs one at a time, add all liquids, then fruit and lastly the flour sieved with baking powder and soda.

Bake 3-3½ hours in medium oven.

ECONOMICAL CAKE

1 cup yellow sugar, 1 cup water, 1 cup pitted raisins, ¼ cup butter, 1 teaspoon powdered cinnamon, 1 teaspoon ground ginger, pinch of salt, 1 teaspoon bicarbonate of soda, 2 cups standard meal (sifted to remove part of the bran), 2 teaspoons baking powder.

(1) Boil together for three minutes the sugar, water, raisins, cinnamon, ginger, nutmeg, butter and salt.
(2) Allow to cool.
(3) Mix meal, baking powder and bicarbonate of soda and fold into fruit mixture.
(4) Bake in slow oven for an hour.

DUNDEE CAKE

2 cups unsifted boermeal, 1 cup brown sugar, 6 ozs. butter, 3 eggs, 1¼ teaspoons baking powder, ¼ teaspoon salt, ¼ teaspoon ground nutmeg, grated rind of 1 lemon, grated rind of 1 orange, 1 cup currants, 1 cup sultanas, 2 ozs. mixed peel, 1 tablespoon caramel, 18 almonds, milk (or orange juice).

Collect utensils and ingredients, wash currants and sultanas thoroughly in several waters, using lukewarm or hot water if on the hard side. Dry thoroughly in a clean cloth, then spread out on a baking sheet and leave in the sun or a cool oven to dry.

Cream sugar and butter thoroughly together until nice and smooth, then add eggs one by one and beat until light and spongy. Add the grated rind, caramel and fruits and mix well.

Sift together flour, baking powder, salt and nutmeg, then stir into the creamed mixture, adding enough milk or orange juice to make a fairly stiff consistency. Pour into a round cake tin lined with paper on the bottom and sides, and smooth the top of cake with the back of hand dipped in cold water. Arrange halved almonds on top then bake in a moderate oven of 350° for 2 hours.

Leave in the tin to cool before turning out.

HONEY GEMS

1½ tablespoons butter, 1 tablespoon honey, 1 egg, ½ cup milk, 1 teaspoon cream of tartar, 1 teaspoon bicarbonate of soda, 1 cup wholemeal.

Melt honey and butter, add egg and beat well together, add milk and lastly dry ingredients. Cook in muffin tins in ordinary way.

WHOLEMEAL SHORTCAKE

2 level breakfastcups wholemeal, 1 level breakfastcup flour, ¼ lb. brown sugar, 1 teaspoon baking powder, ¼ lb. melted butter, 1 egg, pinch salt, ½ teaspoon vanilla essence.

Mix dry ingredients, add beaten egg and melted butter. Mix thoroughly. Roll out on greased scone tray, bake in moderate oven about 1 hour. Cut while hot.

SPICED SHORTCAKE

1 cup wholemeal, ½ cup white flour, 6 ozs. butter, 4 ozs. brown sugar, 1 egg, 1 heaped teaspoon spice, 1 teaspoon cinnamon, 1 teaspoon baking powder.

Cream butter and sugar, add egg and then the other ingredients. Roll out and spread half with raspberry jam, cover with the other half and brush with milk. Bake slowly till nice and brown, and ice with spiced icing (1 teaspoon of spice to 4 tablespoons icing sugar), scatter with nuts.

WHOLEMEAL SPONGE

3 eggs, ¾ breakfastcup sugar, 1 level cup wholemeal, 1 teaspoon baking powder, pinch salt.

Beat sugar and eggs till light and frothy, then add wholemeal, baking powder and salt. Turn into two well-greased sandwich tins. Bake in moderate oven about 20 minutes.

DELICIOUS WHOLEMEAL BISCUITS

1 cup wholemeal, 1 teaspoon cream of tartar, ¼ lb. butter, 1 egg, ½ teaspoon bicarbonate of soda, 1 teaspoon cinnamon, ¼ lb. sugar.

Beat butter and sugar to cream, add egg yolk, mix soda, cream of tartar and cinnamon with wholemeal. Then mix with creamed butter, etc., adding a little milk if necessary. Beat white of egg lightly, roll mixture into balls and flatten. Dip in white of egg then in the sugar and place on greased, floured tray and bake in moderate oven for 20 minutes.

GOLDEN SYRUP BISCUITS

½ lb. wholemeal, 2 tablespoons golden syrup, 4 ozs. butter, ½ teaspoon baking powder, 2 ozs. sugar, pinch salt.

Cream butter, sugar and golden syrup, stir in the dry ingredients. Knead well, then roll out thinly. Bake about 15 minutes in moderate oven.

WHOLEMEAL BISCUITS

2 cups standard meal, ½ cup sugar, 3 tablespoons butter, 1 tablespoon syrup, ¼ teaspoon salt, 1 teaspoon baking powder, ½ teaspoon bicarbonate of soda, 1 tablespoon warm water.

(1) Mix dry ingredients lightly.
(2) Put in the butter.
(3) Mix soda, syrup and warm water and cut into first mixture.
(4) Knead well and leave in a cool place for a few hours or overnight.
(5) Roll out and cut into shapes.
(6) Bake in a hot oven.

Variations:

(1) Mix chopped nuts in with the dry ingredients.
(2) Place a halved nut on the top of each biscuit.
(3) Press the dough into a greased pan and spread jam thinly over it.
(4) Place the following mixture on top and bake in a medium oven. 1 cup oats, 2 tablespoons sugar, 2 tablespoons melted butter, egg to mix.

STEAMED DATE OR FIG PUDDING

1 cup boermeal, ¼ lb. stale breadcrumbs, ¼ lb. finely-chopped suet, ½ cup sugar, ½ lb. dried figs or dates, 2 eggs, 1 cup milk, 1 level teaspoon baking powder, ⅛ teaspoon salt.

Mix dry ingredients, then add well-beaten eggs and milk. The mixture should be stiff enough to just drop off the spoon. Lastly add chopped fruit, mix well, then pour into a well-greased mould. Cover with a lid or paper cap and steam 2 or 3 hours. Turn out and serve with a sweet white sauce or custard. If liked a teaspoon ground cinnamon, also a little vinegar may be added.

STEAMED WHOLEMEAL PUDDING

¼ cup butter, ½ cup syrup, ½ cup milk, 1 well-beaten egg, 1½ cups standard meal, ½ teaspoon bicarbonate of soda, ½ teaspoon salt, 1 cup raisins or dates.

(1) Melt butter, add to syrup, milk and eggs.
(2) Mix in the dry ingredients.
(3) Steam for 2¼ hours.
(4) Serve with a sauce.

NUTRITIOUS CARROT PUDDING

1½ cups wholemeal, 1 cup grated carrot, 1 cup raisins, grated rind of one orange and one lemon, 2 ozs. honey, 3 ozs. butter, 1 egg, 1 teaspoon bicarbonate of soda dissolved in ½ cup milk. Mix well and steam 2½ hours in greased and covered basin.

FRIDAY LUNCH DISH

6 cooked parsnips, 1 cup grated cheese, 1 cup breadcrumbs 1 cup milk, 1 tablespoon butter, Salt and cayenne pepper.

After slicing the parsnips thinly, place them in a buttered pie-dish in alternate layers with cheese, seasoning each layer. Place the breadcrumbs on top, add the milk slowly, and place dabs of butter on top. Bake in a quick oven until brown.

> *Were half the power that fills the world with terror,*
> *Were half the wealth bestow'd on camps and courts,*
> *Given to redeem the human mind from error,*
> *There were no need of arsenals nor forts.*
>
> — Longfellow.

A.B.C. OF HEALTH

Our health is so dependent on the food we eat, that it is only right that a little space should be accorded in a publication of this nature for reflections on health.

You should amuse your children by teaching them the A.B.C. of health. Here it is: —

"A is for Air that we breathe day and night,
 It must always be fresh to make us feel right.

B is for Bathing each day in a tub,
 Followed at once by a brisk body-rub.

C is for Cough ant its Cousin, the sneeze,
 Cover them both with your handkerchief, please.

D is for Danger, whenever you choose
 To drink from a cup that other folks use.

E is for Eyes — have good light when you read,
 And print not too fine, or glasses you'll need.

F is for Fingernails, if they were mine,
 I'd scrub them and clean them and make them look fine.

G is for Grain — Oats, Barley and Wheat,
 These are the cereals children should eat.

H is for Health, that is built day by day,
 By the Habits you form in your work and your play.

I is for Inches you'll add to your height,
 By eating and sleeping and living just right.

J is for Jaws and a good rule to follow,
 Is "Chew many times on each mouthful you swallow".

K means to Kill every fly with a swat,
 For, living, they're dangerous, dead, they are not.

L is for Loose, as your clothing should be,
 Leaving your arms and legs perfectly free.

M is for Milk, you need to drink plenty,
 But not tea or coffee before you are twenty.

N is for Neatness of dress and of hair,
 At home and at school and, in fact, everywhere.

O is for Outdoors where children should play,
 In sunshine and fresh air a part of each day.

P is for Pounds. On the scales watch your weight,
 To see if you're gaining at just the right rate.

Q is a Question you don't expect —
 Is your posture when sitting and walking, erect?

R is for Rising soon after the sun,
 Pray don't lie abed till the day's well begun.

S is for Sleep, ten hours, unbroken;
 And always, of course, with windows wide open.

T is for Teeth. Keep them shiny and white,
 By brushing them thoroughly, morning and night.
U is for Underwear, spotlessly clean;
 So change it as often as if it were seen.
V is for Vegetables — spinach and peas,
 Potatoes and carrots — eat plenty of these.
W is for Water, and Doctors all say,
 That a person should drink many glasses each day.
X is for Exercise — getting your share,
 Of playing and running out in the air.
Y is for something on which tears you shed,
 There's only one remedy: "Early to bed."
Z is the Zone wherein safety doth lie,
 Stand quietly there while the autos whiz by."

Perhaps even Mum and Dad might learn something from this little rhyme!

I wonder how some parents would answer these questions: —
(1) Does your child get proper rest? This means going to bed early every night and sleeping with the windows open, and resting during the day. (Up to ten years, he should be in bed at 7 o'clock in the winter and 8 o'clock in the summer).
(2) Does your child have his meals at regular hours?
(3) Do you plan the meals so that your child has vegetables and fruit every day?
(4) Do you see that he has a quart of milk daily either as a drink or in his food?
(5) Has your child the habit of a regular bowel movement every day?
(6) Does your child wash his hands before every meal?
(7) Does he play out of doors every day?
(8) Do you take him to the dentist twice a year to have his teeth examined and treated?
(9) Do you have him examined by a doctor at least once a year?
(10) Have you had your child immunised against diptheria, and vaccinated for smallpox?

(With acknowledgments to Metropolitan Life Insurance Co., New York).

One other point: When you read through these tasty recipes, remember — we must "eat to live and not live to eat."

H. Nelson,
Medical Officer of Health, Pretoria.

*The mind is master of the man.
And so "they can who think they can."*

HOUSEHOLD HINTS

YOUR STOVE

Prepare a dish: adjust a switch; observe the time; and you cannot fail to cook well. But there are a number of little points worth knowing, which will help you and make things easy.

A new stove should be treated in the following way: Heat up the oven by turning the switches controlling the top and bottom elements to "High" or "Full" until the temperature reaches 400°. Then turn the switches off and allow the oven to cool, with the door closed. This will remove any odours that may be in a new oven. It is a good idea to "burn out" any new cake or bread tins at the same time. Put the new tins, without greasing into the cold oven and allow them to heat up and cool again in the oven. If this is done, cakes will never stick.

In daily use, first remove the grilling pan, baking tin, and spare shelves, and see that the shelf to be used is in the proper position. Close the oven door tight and pre-heat the oven by turning the top and bottom elements on full until the required temperature is reached. In baking, the top element should be turned off as soon as the food is put into the oven; and the temperature controlled by the bottom element switch. The reason for this is easy to understand if the oven construction is examined. The top element is exposed, giving a direct, scorching heat; the bottom element is covered by a sheet of metal called baffle, which directs the heat to the sides and so distributes it evenly through the oven.

If cakes burn on top, the top element has been left on.

If cakes are browner on top than on the bottom, the shelf is too high.

If browner on bottom than top, the shelf is too low.

If cakes burn at the back the oven is too hot.

When placing food in the oven, do not leave the door open longer than necessary; this wastes heat that has to be paid for.

It is not necessary to keep watch over foods that are being cooked in the even heat of an electric oven, so avoid peeping as much as possible. A grilling pan should be used for grilling only; never use it as a baking sheet, because it fits to the sides of the oven and keeps the heat from circulating properly above it.

Once these general rules are understood using an electric stove is a simple matter. An electric stove which bakes a cake or boils a pudding at a definite temperature in a certain length of time to-day will always do so.

A dirty stove means careless use and leads to waste of heat and efficiency.
To keep your electric stove in good condition: —
Never leave switches on "High" unnecessarily.
Wipe marks off stove as soon as made.
Wipe oven while it is still warm, particularly after roasting.
Use fine steel wool — one of the aluminium cleaners — to clean off any burnt marks. *E.R.*

YOUR REFRIGERATOR

Temperature plays an important part in keeping foods fresh. For many years it was the custom to cool by evaporation and to take advantage of the cooler temperatures in cellars, etc., but rarely has it been possible to bring the cooler air below 50° F. The safety line lies between 32° F. and 50° F. Above 50° F. food begins to spoil. Cold can be controlled in an electric refrigerator, and it is therefore no longer to be considered a luxury for the home but a necessity.
Use the top shelves for butter, cheese and salad dressings; middle shelves for cooked meats, made dishes, leftovers, jellies, etc., and the lower shelves for uncooked meats, soup, stock, etc. Keep milk next to the freezing unit and fish in the defrosting tray immediately beneath the unit.
Lettuce, salad vegetables, celery and parsley taste best when crisp, and should be washed and trimmed ready for use before storing in a covered container.
Meat keeps moist if brushed over with melted fat. Keep all liquids covered.
Let foods cool before placing them in your refrigerator and allow space between articles for the circulation of the cold air. When frost becomes too thick on the freezing unit, it acts as an insulation — so defrost the unit whenever a coating ½ inch has gathered. After defrosting, wipe out the unit and empty tray into which the frost has melted.
This is also a good opportunity to clean the entire cabinet, and for this purpose warm water containing a little borax or bicarbonate of soda is best.
If your electric supply is disconnected when you are away on holiday, leave the refrigerator clean and the door open. *E.R.*

HINTS

When boiling cabbage put a small piece of butter into the water — this prevents boiling over; and a piece of bread laid on top of the cabbage prevents odour rising.
To keep your kitchen sink fresh, take 2 tablespoonfuls salt, add two pints boiling water and pour down the pipe. This removes grease. Once a week is a good plan.

A few drops of lemon juice added to the creaming of butter and sugar will make the job easier.

A thin slice of lemon cooked with cauliflower will keep it white.

A pinch of cream of tartar added to whites of eggs will make them beat up easily and quickly.

A pinch of bicarbonate of soda added to mashed potatoes makes them fluffier.

If biscuits or pastry become soft, reheat in a moderate oven for a few minutes.

Baked custards and milk puddings can be prevented from curdling by standing the piedish in a roasting pan containing ½ inch water whilst baking.

Try to avoid using bicarbonate of soda when cooking green vegetables; it kills valuable properties. Drop green vegetables slowly into fast boiling water and cook without a lid on the saucepan. Do not overcook. Peas should not be cooked in salt water, as this loosens the skins. They will keep sweet and fresh for days if shelled and kept in a covered container such as a boiling jar in your refrigerator. Wash well just before cooking.

If oranges and lemons are first warmed through by dropping them in hot water, they will yield much more juice.

To keep slices of tomato whole, dip them in seasoned flour before frying.

Prick sausages and dip them in boiling water; dry before frying. This prevents them bursting.

As a base for fruit salads, and to prevent deterioration of fruit, keep diced pawpaw, lemon juice or orange juice and sugar ready bottled in frig. Also diced or grated pineapple, pawpaw and grenadillas and lemon juice and sugar.

To soften hard butter: Cover with tepid water (not warm enough to melt) for a few minutes. Pour off water and the butter will be quite soft and will spread easily.

Buy green peas in large quantities, shell at once, place in covered glass bottle and store in refrigerator.

After roasting, make large quantities of gravy and store surplus in refrigerator.

When making sausage rolls the skins of the sausages should be removed. This is easily done by dipping them in cold water first.

A little camphorated oil smeared on globes and shades will keep flies away from them.

To air clothes in damp weather: Place the clothes on a clothes-horse with your radiator near.

A little glycerine added to jam when boiling will prevent it from getting sugary.

Spirit of camphor is good for blisters on lips and also for any hot plate marks on tables.

To clean a thermos flask and remove stuffy odour, three-quarters fill with warm water, add ½ teaspoonful of bicarbonate of soda. Shake well.
Put coffee grounds and tea leaves in pots of growing plants, or water with cold tea. Specially good for ferns.
Frost windows by brushing with a hot solution of Epsom salts and water.
Stop a leak with whitening and lemon juice.
Salt and vinegar will remove stains from discoloured teacups.
A spoonful of lemon juice put into the water in which rice is boiling will make it white and keep the grains separate.
To prevent a cake from sticking, grease the tin with suet or pastrine.
When stewing fruit, add sugar first. A little salt will reduce the quantity of sugar required.
If onions are peeled from the root end up to the stalk they will not make the eyes water. Salt rubbed on the hands before washing will remove the odour of onions, fish, etc.
See that cakes and biscuit tins are clear of crumbs before putting in a fresh stock. Line them with greaseproof paper sprinkled with a layer of white sugar at the bottom, and this will keep the cakes and biscuits fresh and crisp.
Save old powder puffs to polish silver, shoes, etc.
Rub saucepans with fat about one inch down from the top and your rice, spaghetti, etc., will not boil over.
A cube of ice in the water will keep your flowers fresh much longer. A teaspoon of salt will serve the same purpose, also a piece of camphor.
In drying curtains, leave the rods in top and bottom. It keeps edges straight.
In mending the tips of gloves drop a marble in the finger.
Wash your spinach in hot water and there will be no suspicion of grit left.
To crisp wilted lettuce lay it in hot water (not scalding) and leave it till the water is cold.
To preserve delicate colours in washing materials: Dissolve in cold water sugar of lead (1 teaspoon to 1 gallon of water). Stir with a stick until the water becomes milky white. Put the goods in dry and allow them to remain for 30 minutes, turning frequently. Lift out with a stick and rinse thoroughly in cold water. Wash with lux in lukewarm water in the usual way.
To prevent bananas from discolouring, rub in lemon juice.
When whisking whites of eggs, add a pinch of cream of tartar.
To remove motor grease stains: First scrape off as much as possible.
If material is washable, rub with lard and allow to stand before washing. Rub non-washable material with turpentine or benzine.
Internal pains can be relieved by sipping hot cinnamon or caraway seeds and water.

Scalds and Burns: Exclude air from the affected part by applying carron, olive or salad oil. Bandage lightly.

All kinds of carpets can be quickly cleaned by rubbing over with a flannel and a good lather of Sunlight soap and then rinsing with ammonia and water, the water being changed frequently.

To remove grease spots or paint stains from cotton or woollen goods sponge with turpentine. Fresh stains will disappear at once. For those of long standing, saturate the part with turpentine and leave for several hours, then rub off the paint.

FURNITURE POLISH

6 d. butter of antimony — from any chemist, ¼ pint ordinary vinegar, ¼ pint methylated spirits, ½ pint turpentine, ½ pint raw linseed oil. Mix and shake well.

Mrs. R. Steveson, 8 Brecher St., Pretoria.

ANOTHER FURNITURE POLISH

Equal quantities turpentine, vinegar, boiled linseed oil and methylated spirits.

OLD FRIENDS AND NEW FRIENDS

Make new friends, but keep the old;
Those are silver, these are gold.
New-made friendships, like new wine,
Age will mellow and refine.

Joseph Parry.

OLD FRIENDSHIP

Beautiful and rich is an old friendship,
Grateful to the touch as ancient ivory
Smooth as aged wine, or sheen of tapestry,
Where light has lingered, intimate and long.

Full of tears and warm is an old friendship,
That asks no longer deeds of gallantry,
Or any deed at all, save that the friend shall be
Alive and breathing somewhere, like a song.

Eunice Tietjins.

O woman! in our hours of ease,
Uncertain, coy, and hard to please,
And variable as the shade
By the light quivering aspen made —
When pain and anguish wring the brow,
A ministering angel thou!
Sir Walter Scott.

HOME NURSING

The bedroom should never have much in it. The bed should always be perfectly clean and no bright colours about.

Quietness, cleanliness and fresh air, without draught, are the chief factors in good nursing.

Nurses should never talk much to a patient. Talking is very exhausting. Never hesitate to wash a patient, but do not expose too much skin surface at a time. Whatever is done must be done quickly and firmly; dawdling is annoying. A patient's room should be tidied at once after washing, and the nurse herself should always be very neat and clean.

To change a bed without patient getting out: Remove all clothes except top sheet. Roll the bottom sheet in half lengthwise. If the patient can be turned over, turn patient, place roll close to back, tuck other part inside, top and bottom, turn patient, then straighten sheet and tuck in. While the patient is turned take the opportunity to well powder the back. Then place the top sheet over the top of the old one and holding on to the top one, withdraw the dirty one straight down the bed.

A thermometer should be kept in a small glass of water with a little cotton wool at the bottom to protect the end. The water should be changed every day and a handkerchief kept near on which to dry it before using. A patient must remain in bed until the temperature has been normal for 24 hours.

When a vessel is used it must be removed from the room at once. All trays should be very nicely laid — always with a cloth which must never be spotted. If a hot drink is ordered, be sure it is hot. Don't force anything. The rest and quietness in bed works wonders.

If a patient is very feverish: Ice placed in small pieces on a handkerchief tied over a basin and given with a teaspoon is very soothing. Ice to the head may be placed in a hot water bottle, but not allowed to get warm; change often.

When sponging to relieve fever, always sponge away from the head, not up and down.

To treat a patient for shock, place on a bed, raise foot of bed, apply hot water bottles, always with covers on.

Paraffin applied on a cloth stops bleeding.
Vinegar relieves a burn.
To relieve toothache, place a piece of brown paper over a saucer of water and rub ground ginger over the paper and apply to the face, tied on with a scarf. A hot water bottle applied to the seat of pain often gives relief. A small bag filled with salt and heated gives relief in a case of earache.
A. Paxton.

HINTS FOR MUMPS

As soon as mumps is detected, melt butter to lukewarm and gently rub on swollen parts every hour. It is surprising how this eases the pain and takes swelling down. *A.R.E.*

HOW TO PREPARE FOR THE DOCTOR

1. Choose suitable room for patient, notherly aspect, if possible.
2. Remove superfluous furniture — cleanse room thoroughly.
3. Prepare bed — clean linen, waterproof and draw sheet.
4. Put patient to bed comfortably.
5. Wash patient.
6. Be in readiness with history of case.
7. Have report ready for the doctor — change of temperature, bowel movements, signs and symptoms of complaint.
8. Allay anxiety of patient.
9. Have plenty of boiling water in case sterilisation of instruments is necessary.
10. Have basin, clean towel and soap ready for doctor's use.

FIRST-AID REQUIREMENTS IN THE HOME

1. Boracic lint.
2. Oiled silk.
3. Cotton wool.
4. Six triangular bandages.
5. Roller bandages: 1 in., 3 in and 4 in.
6. Packet of sterilised gauze.
7. Scissors.
8. Iodine or acriflavine.
9. Boracic powder.
10. Sal volatile.
11. Vaseline.
12. Zinc ointment.
13. Friars balsam.
14. Permanganate of potash (Condy's crystals).
15. Castor oil.
16. Tannic acid jelly (for burns).

17. Bicarbonate of soda.
18. Smelling salts.
19. Dettol or lysol.
20. Tin of mustard (for emetic).
21. Eyebath or dropper.
22. Measuring glass.
23. Enema syringe.
24. Clinical thermometer.
25. Aspirins.

(The materials to be kept in their respective packages in tin box with lid).

> *Gladness after sorrow,*
> *Sunshine after rain,*
> *Harvest after seed-time,*
> *Comfort after pain,*
> *Blossom after pruning,*
> *Victory after strife,*
> *As the way of nature,*
> *So the way of life.*
>
> — Pechy.

INVALID COOKERY

Whilst the patient has a temperature, only liquid food must be given, and that in small quantities and at frequent intervals.

All food must be nourishing and easily digested, and must be served as daintily as possible.

Never serve anything greasy, especially soup.

Albumen Water:
Beat white of an egg slightly, then add one cup cold water and shake well till thoroughly mixed.

Rice Water:
Wash 2 ozs. rice well, then sprinkle it into 4 pints boiling water, add a small piece of lemon rind and allow to cook for half an hour. Strain and sweeten to taste and leave in cool place.

Thick Barley Water:
2 ozs. Pearl barley, 1 pint water, sugar, lemon and salt.
Blanch the barley by covering with cold water in saucepan. Bring to boil, strain and rinse the barley. This prevents the drink from being dark and cloudy. Return barley to pan, cover with 1 pint water and a little thinly peeled lemon rind, and allow to cook from 1 to 2 hours. Strain, add a little lemon juice, pinch of salt and sugar to taste. Serve cold.

Mahou or Kaffir Beer:

Recommended for nursing mothers.

Make a thin porridge of 3 level tablespoons mealie meal and 1 large cup water (no salt). Boil slowly for half an hour. Add 2 tablespoons sugar and 2 pints warm water and half a cake yeast. Place in large jar or jug and stand in a warm place for two hours. Stir and strain as wanted. This is best made early in the morning and drunk during the day. *Mrs. Craddock.*

Barley Water (Clear):

2 ozs. Pearl barley, 1 pint boiling water, strip lemon rind, 3 lumps sugar.

Blanch the barley. Put barley, lemon rind and sugar into a jug and pour boiling water over. Cover and strain when cold.

Barley Water and Milk:

Mix barley water with milk — half and half. This breaks up the curd and makes milk more digestible.

Oatmeal Gruel:

Cook 1 tablespoon oatmeal in 1 pint of water or milk for half an hour. Stir frequently, then strain through piece of muslin. Add pinch of salt and sugar to taste.

Egg Flip:

1 egg, 1 dessertspoon sugar, 1 glass sherry or brandy.
Stir raw yolk of egg and sugar in a tumbler till creamy, then add the wine or brandy.
Whip white of egg stiffly and stir in lightly.
Use in cases of collapse from fatigue.

Egg Nog:

Beat egg thoroughly, then add ¾ cup milk, hot or cold, 1 tablespoon brandy or sherry, pinch of salt and sugar and nutmeg, if liked. Stir and strain before serving.

Lemon or Orangeade:

Wipe 2 oranges or lemons with a damp cloth and peel rind thinly. Put into a jug with juice and 1 pint of boiling water, add sugar to taste. Cover till cold, then strain.

Ordinary Beef Tea:

1 lb. lean beef, 1 pint cold water, salt to taste.
Remove all skin and fat. Shred meat and put into a jug or jar, cover with cold water and salt and allow to stand for an hour. Place jar in saucepan of cold water, bring water to boiling point and simmer for 3 hours. Strain through coarse strainer and remove any fat before serving.

Quickly-made Beef Tea:
½ lb. lean beef, ½ pint cold water, salt.
Put water, shredded beef and salt into an enamel saucepan. Allow to stand for 30 minutes. Stir over gentle heat and press with back of spoon to extract juice. Strain and serve.

Beef Tea and Egg:
Beat yolk of egg slightly and pour on it 1 cup of beef tea. Stir well and season. Serve with thin strips of toast.

To Thicken Beef Tea:
Use 1 teaspoon sago to 1 cup of beef tea. Soak the sago and add a quarter of an hour before beef tea is ready to serve.

Beef Tea Milk:
Add ½ cup milk to ½ cup beef tea, or according to taste.

Beef Tea Custard:
Beat 1 whole egg and 1 yolk thoroughly and add 1 cup beef tea. Pour into timbale moulds, stand them in a baking dish with a little water and bake in moderate oven till set.

Chicken Broth:
Cut a chicken into small pieces and cover well with water. Add salt and bring rapidly to the boil. Add 2 tablespoons rice and allow to simmer for 2 to 3 hours. Remove fat and strain. Add a little chopped parsley. Keep breast of chicken and stew in milk. Add beaten yolk of egg before serving.

Mutton Broth:
Made same way as chicken broth, using 1½ lbs. scrag end of mutton.

To Steam Slices or Fillets of Fish or Mutton Chop:
Place fish or meat on buttered soup-plate, sprinkle with a little salt, cover with a piece of greased paper, put another plate on top and place over a pan of fast boiling water. Cook for about 40 minutes.

Stewed Sweetbread:
1 pair calf's sweetbreads, 1 oz. flour, ½ pint milk, 1 tablespoon cream, 1 oz. butter, lemon juice, pepper and salt, toast.

Soak the sweetbreads in cold water and salt for 1 hour.

Blanch the sweetbread, then place in cold water and remove all gristle and fat.

Put into enamel pan, cover with milk and simmer gently for 1 hour. Thicken the milk with flour and add the butter, cream, seasoning and a squeeze of lemon. Pour the sauce over the sweetbread. Garnish with parsley and serve with toast.

Eggs in Ramekins:
Break an egg into a greased ramekin or Pyrex dish. Sprinkle with salt, pour in 1 tablespoon milk, put tiny piece of butter on top and set in

a tin of hot water. Cover and cook in moderate oven 10 minutes or until egg is lightly set.

Tasty steamed Fish:
Steam about 2 lbs. fish in a little water, to which is added 1 tablespoon of Dry Sherry. When tender, remove from water and flake, carefully removing all skin and bones. Use the water in which fish was steamed, adding to it sufficient milk to bring the quantity of liquid to correct amount for a white sauce — not too thick.

When the sauce is cooked, add 1 dessertspoon of butter, salt, pepper and paprika to taste, and 2—3 teaspoons of grated cheese. Mix well and pour over the fish in a pyrex dish.

Bake in a moderate oven until slightly brown on top and serve hot. Parsley may be added or extra Dry Sherry if desired.

Invalid Jelly:
½ oz. gelatine, ½ pint water, ¼ pint orange juice, 2 eggs, ½ cup sugar, lemon rind.

Place sugar, gelatine, water and rind of one small lemon in a saucepan. Stir till gelatine dissolves, then add orange juice and bring to boil. Cool the mixture and pour over beaten eggs, stirring all the time. Strain and pour into wet mould.

Arrowroot Pudding:
1 dessertspoon arrowroot, 1 dessertspoon sugar, ½ pint milk, 1 egg, pinch of salt.

Blend arrowroot with a little of the milk. Boil the rest of milk and pour over, add sugar. Cool slightly and add beaten yolk of egg. Beat white very stiffly and fold into mixture. Bake for a few minutes in a moderate oven.

Lemon Sponge:
½ pint water, ½ oz. gelatine, 1 oz. castor sugar, 1 lemon, 1 white of egg.

Heat water and add sugar and gelatine. Stir till dissolved, then add grated rind and juice of lemon. Place in refrigerator, and when on point of setting, fold in the stiffly beaten white of egg. Leave to set and serve with custard made from yolk of egg.

Junket:
Rennet for making junket can now be purchased in either liquid or tablet form, and the quantities for ½ pint milk are usually ½ teaspoon of the liquid or ½ a tablet, as the case may be. Use only fresh milk (not sterilised), sweeten to taste. Warm gently to blood heat or just lukewarm, not hotter. If tablet is used, crush and dissolve in a tablespoon of cold water. Stir rennet into the lukewarm milk. Pour into bowl or dessert cup, and allow to stand until quite cold and firm. Vanilla or other flavouring may be added. Serve with cream.

THE RIGHTS OF WOMEN

The rights of women, what are they?
The right to love and work each day,
The right to weep when others weep,
The right to wake when others sleep.
The right to dry the falling tear,
The right to stay the rising fear;
The right to smooth the brow of care,
And whisper comfort to despair.
The right to live for those we love,
The right to die that love to prove;
The right to brighten earthly homes,
With pleasant smiles and gentle tones,
Are these thy rights? Then use them well;
Thy silent influence none can tell.
If these are thine, why ask for more?
Thou hast enough to answer for. — Anon.

THE BRIDE'S CORNER

BALANCING AND PLANNING THE DIET

Two factors contribute to perfect digestion — the mental and the physical. We realise more than ever to-day the importance of the former, especially in the feeding of growing children and the sick. Cheerful surroundings and company induce good appetite, while fatigue or worry or quarrelling are known to lessen the appetite or to take it away entirely. Cleanliness and care in the preparation and service of food tend to promote good digestion. The housewife, therefore, must consider carefully these important factors that stimulate the appetite and make for good nutrition.

Good digestion depends in general upon keeping the body in good condition by plenty of fresh air, congenial work and taking suitable exercise and by cultivating cheerful mental habits.

FOOD CLASSES

Foods may be classified into the following groups, each of which plays an important part in nutrition: —

(1) Carbohydrates: These include all starches and sugars and are heat and energy yielding foods. Typical examples of starchy foods are rice, potatoes, sweet potatoes and flour. The most common of the sugars is cane sugar. It is a valuable source of energy, but must be used with discretion because taken in too large a quantity, it is irritating to the stomach. Sugar is quickly absorbed and sometimes satisfies the appetite before the need for food has been duly met. This is a common cause of malnutrition, especially among children. Sweet fruits and sweets

made from fruit are better than pure sugar as a source of energy, since they contain important mineral salts, acids and bulk as well.

(2) Proteins: These are the body-building foods, and are also necessary for the maintenance and repair of tissues, which are constantly being broken down in the wear and tear of life. They are also sources of energy, but should not be taken in too large proportion. The chief protein foods are meat, fish, eggs, milk, cheese and legumes such as dried peas and beans.

(3) Fats: The most important function of fat is to supply energy. Fat serves to protect the body and to prevent loss of heat when exposed to cold. The chief sources of fat are butter, cream, lard, monkey-nuts and cod liver oil. Certain foods not usually regarded as being fatty contain it. Examples of these are egg yolk and nearly all nuts.

(4) Mineral Salts: These are substances which are absolutely indispensable to the regulation of the body processes such as the heart beat and digestion. They are essential for the growth of bones and teeth and enter into the structure of the soft tissues and fluids of the body, largely controlling their functions. When any one of the essential mineral elements is withheld or is insufficient in quantity, growth and health are interfered with. The minerals are found chiefly in milk and its products, eggs, whole cereals, fruits and vegetables.

(5) Vitamins: These are essential for good nutrition, although they are neither building materials nor sources of energy. As a group they promote growth and make for health and vigour. Separately they provide resistance to certain infections, are responsible for normal bone and tooth development, stimulate a good appetite and protect the body from so-called deficiency diseases. Cod liver oil, fresh milk and fresh fruit and vegetables are some of the best sources of vitamins.

(6) Water: While water has no food value, it is important in the diet. It is required to dissolve the solid foods so that they can be absorbed by the tissues. A liberal supply of water is essential to good health. About six pints of liquid are considered necessary in the daily diet, part of this included in our food and the remainder in liquid form.

BALANCING THE DIET

A well-balanced diet is one consisting of foods containing all the essentials for growth, maintenance and energy. In planning the daily menus, the needs of the individual should be studied as far as possible, but the growing child should be the first consideration, as so much depends upon adequate feeding in youth. Those leading an active life will require more food than those whose life is sedentary. The following is an example of what the three daily meals should contain: —

Milk: Four cups a day for the growing child. The minimum should be two cupfuls for the adult as well. This is to ensure sufficient mineral intake for the building and preservation of bones and teeth, as well as to supply the finest protein for body building and maintenance. Milk can be given in the form of puddings, drinks, soups, etc.

Cereals: Preferably the whole ones, such as oatmeal, mealie meal, brown bread, etc. Cereals are invaluable as a source of energy and for their mineral and vitamin content.

Vegetables: Should be plentifully supplied and only one at a time of the starchy kind such as potato, rice or samp served at the same meal. Green vegetables, such as spinach, cabbage, green beans, peas and lettuce are valuable sources of iron. If possible one vegetable should be served raw in the form of a salad. In this way vitamins not contained in other foods or destroyed by cooking, are included.

Fruits are also necessary as a source of vitamins and minerals. Dried fruits are good but do not have the same high vitamin content as do the fresh.

Protein: The main dish of meat, fish, eggs, cheese or milk. It is important to remember in the feeding of children that meat is of no better value for growth than are the other protein foods, and there is danger that too much meat will make other foods seem less attractive. Meat is poor in calcium and vitamins, but it is a valuable source of iron. It is a good rule to serve meat not more than once a day and occasionally to arrange for a meatless day.

PLANNING THE MEALS

(1) Choose at least one from each of the three undermentioned groups for every meal:
(2) Use freely foods which are laxative, such as whole cereals, vegetables and fruit.
(3) Serve two or more vegetables other than potatoes or rice every day. Serve as many salads as possible.
(4) Include plenty of milk for both drinking and cooking purposes.
(5) Serve fruit at leat once a day.
(6) Plan for the day rather than for each separate meal.

REGULATING FOODS

A.— Cereals. Oatmeal, kaffir corn, mealie meal, whole meal bread.
Fruits: Any kind.
Vegetables: All but the starchy ones or those of high protein value, such as dried beans, peas, etc.
Milk: In any form.
B.— Building and Maintenance Foods: Cheese, eggs, fish, meat, milk in any form, dried beans, lentils, nuts, dried peas, monkey nuts.
C.— Energy Foods: Cereals: Whole and refined macaroni, spaghetti, sago, topioca, maizena, rice, samp. Fats.
Sugars: Dried beans, peas, lentils, potatoes, mealies, beetroot.

With a little forethought for the planning and attractive arrangement of her meals, the housewife will contribute enormously to the health and happiness of her family. *Mrs. J. van Ryneveld.*

> *Some hae meat but canna eat,*
> *And some wad eat that want it,*
> *But we hae meat and we can eat,*
> *Sae let the Lord be thankit.* *Burns.*

SOME PANTRY REQUIREMENTS

May a mouse never leave your pantry wi' a tear in its 'ee!

Tea.
Coffee.
Cocoa.
Bovril or other meat essence.
Flour.
Yeast, dried.
Boermeal.
Mabela meal or kaffir corn.
Mealie meal.
Oats.
Cereals.
Tapioca or sago, vermicelli.
Rice.
Cornflour or maizena.
Barley.
Macaroni or spaghetti.
Samp.
Dried beans.
Dried peas.
Mealie rice.
Jelly powders and assorted pudding powders.
Custard powder.
Sugar — Castor, icing and brown.
Bicarbonate of soda.
Cream of tartar.
Baking powder.
Essences — lemon, vanilla, almond, aniseed, coffee, etc.
Cochineal.
Cocoanut, almonds (ground and whole), walnuts, peanuts.
Plain cooking chocolate and chocolate grains.
Hundreds and thousands.
Currants, raisins, sultanas, prunes, assorted dried fruits
Mixed peel.
Cherries.
Mixed spice.
Ginger (whole and ground).
Cinnamon (sticks and powdered).
Cloves.
Dried herbs.
Salt and pepper — black, white and cayenne.
Mayonnaise, vinegar, salad oil, cooking oil.
Cooking fats.

Mustard and curry powder.
Browning.
Syrup and honey.
Jams and preserves.
Sauces, chutneys, pickles.
Butter, margarine.
Bacon, eggs, cheese.
Kippers or haddock.
Tinned soups, fruit, vegetables, meats and fish.
Savoury mixtures and sandwich spread.
Plain and fancy biscuits.
Paraffin.
Borax.
Household soap.
Washing soda and scouring powders.
Blue, starch, soap flakes.
Matches and candles.
Toilet paper.
Brass and silver polishes.
Floor and furniture polishes.
Ammonia.
Cooking paper.

BASIC HOUSEHOLD LINEN REQUIREMENTS

Bedroom:
1 Cotton mattress cover to each bed.
1 Thick under blanket — grey or brown, to each bed.
3 Pairs sheets to each bed.
3 Pairs pillow-cases and 2 pairs cotton covers as linings to each bed.
1 Pair blankets to each bed.
1 Rug or eiderdown to each bed.
Top cover to each bed.
2 Duchess sets.

Table:
3 Breakfast cloths.
3 Lucheon cloths.
3 Dinner cloths — all with serviettes to match, or
Breakfast cloths and two sets each luncheon and dinner mats and serviettes.
1 Large (party) table-cloth (optional).
2 Large plain table-cloths (optional).
3 Plain tea cloths
3 Fancy tea cloths
6-12 Tray cloths.

Doyleys, tea cosy covers.
Extra serviettes.

Bathroom:
2 Bath mats.
6 Bath towels.
12 Medium sized towels.
6 Hand towels (Turkish towelling)
6 Guest towels.
6 Face cloths.
6 Razor cloths.

Kitchen:
12 Dish towels.
6 Glass towels.
6 Cutlery towels.
6 Rough dish cloths.
6 Baking cloths — to cover scones, etc.
6 Oven cloths — for handling hot trays, etc.
12 Assorted dusters.
6 Fine polishing dusters.
6 Floor cloths.
Squares of old blankets for applying polish.
6 Kitchen hand towels — coarse linen — or
2 Roller towels.

SOME KITCHEN REQUIREMENTS

Electric kettle.
Electric iron.
Electric toaster.
2 Kettles — large and small.
2 Teapots — large and small.
1 Coffee pot.
1 Large soup pot — 6-8 pints.
1 Large roasting pot — oval if possible.
1 Shallow pan for stews.
Set of 6 pots for vegetables and puddings.
1 Double boiler for milk, etc.
1 Large and 1 small frying pan, 1 omelette pan.
2 Covered steaming bowls — large and small.
2 Sets oven glass baking dishes for puddings and pies.
1 Set baking bowls —6 assorted sizes.
1 Set moulds — fancy shapes.
1 Set jugs, 1 enamel jug, 1 measuring jug.
1 Measuring cup and glass, measuring spoons.
1 Doz. assorted tins or jars for cereals and dried fruits.

6 Small tins or jars for spices, etc.
Tea and coffee containers.
6 Bins (approx. 24 lbs.) for flour, sugar, meal, etc.
3 Cake tins, 2 biscuits tins, 1 scone tin.
Butter container and odd covered dishes for frig.
Roasting tins — 1 large and 1 small — for joints.
3 Shallow baking tins for cookies, scones, etc.
Set of cake tins for butter and fruit cakes (8-12 in. across and 4-5 in. in depth with loose bottoms).
2 Pairs sandwich tins for cakes, tarts, etc.
2 Flat tins with loose bottoms.
1 Round tin with funnel in centre.
3 Sets small patty pans — assorted sizes.
Wire cake trays.
Pastry and flour brushes.
3 Sifters for flour, sugar and spice.
3 Wooden baking spoons.
1 Basting spoon with long handle.
Set kitchen knives (including bread and carving knives).
Odd forks and spoons.
Scone and biscuit cutters.
Rolling pin, chopper.
Mincing machine.
Knife sharpener.
Strainers for soups, vegetables, milk, tea and coffee.
Egg beater, switch and slicer.
Scales.
Carrot and nutmeg graters, skewers.
Tin opener, kitchen scissors.
Ladles, servers, potato masher.
Bread and chopping boards, rubbing board, trays.
Pot scrapers, bottle brush.
Fly swatters.
2 Enamel basins, enamel pail and ewer.
2 Galvanised baths and buckets.
1 Rubbish container.
Long and short feather dusters.
2 Sets boot brushes.
2 Floor polishing brushes.
1 Long and 1 short scrubbing brush.
Hard and soft brooms.
Floor mop.
Coal sifter.
Enamel teapot, plates, mugs and strong pots for natives.

SUGGESTED MENUS FOR TWO

SUMMER TIME

SUNDAY:
Midday dinner (2 visitors): Chilled grapefruit. Tomato soup. Small leg of lamb (boned, stuffed and roasted), mint sauce, roast potatoes, green peas, cauliflower. Lemon snow and custard. Coffee.
Supper: Cold lamb and salads (plenty of them). Stewed fruit and cake or sponge fingers.

MONDAY:
Lunch: Cauliflower au gratin (made from cauliflower left over from Sunday). Fresh fruit.
Dinner: Remains of tomato soup. Lamb slices (see recipe for mutton slices), peas and potatoes.
Remains of stewed fruit and custard. Coffee.

TUESDAY:
Lunch: Fried fish with shredded lettuce, lemon and tomato. Fruit salad.
Dinner: Potato soup (made with milk). Mince collops (order 1 lb. steak minced, serve with croutons of bread, mashed potato and green beans. Apple sago pudding and cream. Coffee. (Apples equally good as fresh can now be bought tinned).

WEDNESDAY:
Lunch: Fish mayonnaise (made from left over fish). Grenadilla jelly and cream. Provide plenty of salad with the fish mayonnaise.
Dinner: Remains of potato soup (strained and garnished with parsley). Stuffed tomatoes (using remains mince collops). Apple sago with baked egg custard on top, flavoured with nutmeg. Fruit. Coffee.

THURSDAY:
Lunch: Maccaroni cheese or boiled mealies. Salads. Fruit.
Dinner: Vegetable soup. Crumbed fillet of steak (½ lb.), chips, fried tomatoes, spinach. Queen of puddings. Coffee.

FRIDAY:
Lunch: Savoury omelette. Remains of queen of puddings and stewed apricots.
Dinner: Vegetable soup (strained and noodles added). Baked stuffed fish, anchovy sauce, baked potatoes. Baked apples with or without cream. Coffee.

SATURDAY:
Lunch: Fish cakes, tomato sauce and green peas. Papaw and lemon.
Dinner: Cream of spinach soup. Baked ham, baked beans and potatoes (order 3-4 lbs. ham). Apricot fruit fool (made from remains of apricots stewed). Coffee.

SUNDAY:
Midday Dinner: Lentil soup. Roast chicken, stuffing, peas and potatoes. Apple tart and cream. Coffee.
Supper: Cold ham and chicken. Salad. Remains apricot fruit fool and custard. Biscuits and cheese. Tea or coffee.

MONDAY:
Lunch: Chicken patties. Lettuce and tomato salads. Fresh fruit. (Patties made from cuttings of apple tart pastry).
Dinner: Lentil soup. Chicken, ham and potato rissoles with tomato sauce and fried brinjals. Remains of apple tart. Coffee.

TUESDAY:
Lunch: Ham toast (see recipe). Fruit salad and cream.
Dinner: Giblet soup (made from chicken giblets, bones, etc.) Grilled chops (½ lb.), chips, fried tomatoes and peas. Sago custard. Fruit. Coffee.

WEDNESDAY:
Lunch: Salmon mayonnaise. Fresh fruit.
Dinner: Remains chicken soup. Hamburg steak, mashed potatoes, beans, brown sauce (order 1 lb. steak and use half). Stewed fruit and custard.

THURSDAY:
Lunch: Salmon rissoles (using left-over salmon and mashed potatoes). Remains stewed fruit.
Dinner: Clear soup. Shepherd's pie (using the ½ lb. steak minced), cabbage and pumpkin. Lemon pudding. Coffee.

FRIDAY:
Lunch: Cheese souffle and spinach, jellied fruit salad and cream.
Dinner: Clear soup with diced vegetables added. Fried fish (Kingklip), fried potatoes, lettuce and lemon. Banana whip. Coffee.

SATURDAY:
Lunch: Fish and cheese pie (see recipe). Sliced pineapple.
Dinner: Bacon and beef roll with colcannon (fried cooked cabbage and potatoes). Caramel pudding. Fruit. Coffee.

SUNDAY:
Midday Dinner: Cream of asparagus soup. Small round of beef, Yorkshire pudding, cauliflower, roast potatoes and pumpkin. Pineapple mould and cream. Coffee.
Supper: Cheese custard. Remains pineapple mould. Tea or coffee.

MONDAY:
Lunch: Cold beef and salad. Iced pawpaw.
Dinner: Cream of asparagus soup. Curry and rice. Stuffed apples (see recipe). Coffee.

TUESDAY:
Lunch: Tomato and egg. Salad. Fresh fruit.
Dinner: Chilled grapefruit. Toad-in the-hole (using ½ lb. sausages), spinach and potatoes. Semolina custard and stewed peaches. Coffee.

WEDNESDAY:
Lunch: Grilled sausage and mash.   Salad. Peaches and cream. Tea.
Dinner: Beeftea soup. Boiled salt beef and carrots, butter beans and potatoes. Junket and jelly.

THURSDAY:
Lunch: Cold salt beef. Lettuce and bean salad. Banana jelly.
Dinner: Beeftea soup with macaroni. Salt beef and potato rissoles, fresh tomato sauce and peas. Pear cream (see recipe). Coffee.

FRIDAY:
Lunch: Spinach and poached eggs. Grenadilla salad.
Dinner: Carrot soup. Fried soles and lemon, wafer chips. Remains pear cream. Fruit. Coffee.

SATURDAY:
Lunch: Mince pie (see recipe). Salad. Fruit salad or sliced melon.
Dinner: Carrot soup. Braised veal (order 2 lbs. veal), cooked with carrot, turnip, onion and celery, potatoes. Lemon meringue pie (make sufficient pastry for the two pies, but bake the mince pie in hot oven and meringue lemon pie in medium).

SUNDAY:
Midday Dinner (to serve four persons) : Giblet soup. Roast duck and green peas, roast potatoes, sage and onion stuffing. Ice cream. Coffee.
Supper: Remains mince pie and salad. Ice cream and fruit juice. Fruit. Coffee.

MONDAY:
Lunch: Cold duck and salad. Mulberries and cream.
Dinner: Giblet soup. Slices of cooked veal dipped in batter and fried lightly. Serve with gravy, fried brinjals and potatoes. Mulberry jelly and custard.

TUESDAY:
Lunch: Asparagus or egg salad or boiled mealies. Pineapple salad.
Dinner: Celery soup. Beef olives (order 1 lb. rump steak, use half), beans and potatoes. Sago custard.

WEDNESDAY:
Lunch: Cornish pasties (made from ½ lb. steak). Salad. Fruit.
Dinner: Celery soup. Roast loin or lamb (order 3 or 4 lbs., cut off 4 chops. Keep in refrigerator till needed), peas, potatoes, roasted onions, mint sauce. Remains sago custard with fruit. Coffee.

THURSDAY:
Lunch: Cold lamb and salad. Compôte of fruit.
Dinner: Leek soup. Stewed lamb with butter beans, onion, carrot and turnip. Baked custard. Coffee.

FRIDAY:
Lunch: Cheese souffle and spinach. Fruit. Coffee.
Dinner: Leek soup strained and noodles added — add plenty of parsley. Boiled fish with egg sauce and salad. Canary pudding. Coffee.

SATURDAY:
Lunch: Savoury fish omelette. Salad. Prunes and rice. Tea.
Dinner: Mixed grill, fried potatoes, tomatoes and peas. Rice custard. Coffee. Fruit.

SUNDAY:
Midday Dinner: Potato milk soup. Steak and kidney pie (order 1½ lbs. rump steak and 6 sheep's kidneys — use 2), beans, spinach and potatoes. Prune fruit fool and custard.
Supper: Remains spinach and poached eggs. Fruit fool and custard. Fruit. Coffee.

MONDAY:
Lunch: Shrimp or sardine salad. Orange and banana salad.
Dinner: Potato milk soup. Remains steak and kidney pie, macedoine carrots and peas, potatoes. Apples stuffed with dates or raisins and baked. Coffee.

TUESDAY:
Lunch: Macaroni cheese. Salad. Fresh fruit.
Dinner: Kidney soup. Sausage potatoes (using ½ lb. sausages), marrow and beans. Apple crusty pudding and cream. Coffee.

WEDNESDAY:
Lunch: Sausage rolls. Salad. Fruit.
Dinner: Kidney soup. Savoury steak and onion, potatoes and cauliflower. Vermicelli custard. Fruit. Coffee.

THURSDAY:
Lunch: Savoury pancakes (using remains savoury steak). Pineapple salad.
Dinner: Mutton broth. Boiled mutton with carrots, turnips and onions covered with white sauce and parsley, potatoes (order 2 lbs. best end neck of mutton). Add capers to sauce if liked. Stewed pineapple and vermicelli custard. Coffee.

FRIDAY:
Lunch: Cold mutton and caper sauce. Salad. Banana fritters.
Dinner: Mutton broth. Fried Cape salmon and lemon, potato balls, lettuce, parsley and tomato salad. Cape gooseberries, jelly and cream. Coffee.

SATURDAY:
Lunch: Fish custard, cream or pie. Gooseberries and cream.
Dinner: Chilled grapefruit or pawpaw. Veal cutlets with fried mushrooms and tomatoes and onion sauce, potatoes. Apricots and custard. Coffee.

WINTER MENUS
SUNDAY:
Midday Dinner: Scotch broth. Roast sirloin (3-4 lbs. take out the fillet), roast potatoes, pumpkin and sweet corn. Date pudding with custard sauce. Coffee.
Supper: Sweet corn on toast, garnished with chopped, fried bacon. Stewed fruit and sponge fingers. Tea.

MONDAY:
Lunch: Liver and bacon, tomatoes and mashed potatoes. Fresh fruit.
Dinner: Scotch broth. Rissoles (made from roast sirloin and the mashed potatoes left from lunch), gravy, mashed turnips or parsnips and spinach. Remains date pudding reheated in bowl or fried.

TUESDAY:
Lunch: Liver and bacon savoury on toast. Salad: Currant pie and coffee.
Dinner: Noodle soup. Sheep's heart stuffed, sauce, peas, potatoes. Dutch apple pudding. Coffee.

WEDNESDAY:
Lunch: Sheep's heart with salad and remains currant pie.
Dinner: Noodle soup. Savoury steak (1 lb.) and dumplings, carrots, peas, onions and tomatoes. Dutch apple pudding reheated and served with hot custard. Coffee.

THURSDAY:
Lunch: Curry remains savoury steak, rice. Fruit. Coffee.
Dinner: Leek soup. Stewed mince (1 lb.), mashed potatoes, cabbage. Pumpkin fritters. Coffee.

FRIDAY:
Lunch: Fried fish, lemon and salad. Pears and cream or custard.
Dinner: Leek soup. Savoury mince roll (made with leftover mince), beans, potatoes. Pears with chocolate sauce. Coffee.

SATURDAY:
Lunch: Tripe and onions (cooked day before). Brown Betty.
Dinner: Fish and cheese (in shells or tiny Pyrex dishes — see recipe). Pot roast chicken (very small), peas and potatoes. American raisin pie (keep left over pastry).

SUNDAY:

Midday dinner: Cream of celery soup. Roast loin of pork (3-4 lbs. and cut off 2 or 4 chops), apple sauce, roast potatoes, pumpkin and green beans. Small lemon meringue pie made with left-over pastry.
Supper: Chicken salad. American raisin pie and cream.

MONDAY:

Lunch: Cold roast pork and apple sauce, with salad. Meringue pie and coffee.
Dinner: Celery soup. Chicken and pork rissoles, apple sauce, fried tomatoes and spinach. Prune souffle.

TUESDAY:

Lunch: Savoury omelette. Salad. Fruit.
Dinner: Clear soup. Ox-tail stew (order 1 ox-tail, but stew only sufficient for two, using remainder for soup), carrots, turnips, onions, potatoes. Baked custard (made from left-over egg yolks). Coffee.

WEDNESDAY:

Lunch: Green mealies (preserved) and butter. Grenadilla fruit salad.
Dinner: Clear soup. Crumbed pork chops and apple sauce, peas and potatoes. Grenadilla fruit jelly and cream.

THURSDAY:

Lunch: Bacon and corn pancakes. Salad. Fresh fruit.
Dinner: Ox-tail soup. Rolled stuffed steak (1 lb.), onions, green beans and potatoes. Semolina custard. Coffee.

FRIDAY:

Lunch: Curried fish and rice. Orange sago.
Dinner: Ox-tail soup. Reheated stuffed steak, pumpkin and beans Remains orange sago with custard. Coffee.

SATURDAY:

Lunch: Egg and bacon pie. Honeycomb cream.
Dinner: Beef tea and noodles. Hamburg steak, fried onions and tomatoes, potato balls. Milk tart. Coffee. (Order ½ lb. steak minced for Hamburg steak).

SUNDAY:

Midday Dinner: Lentil soup. Salt beef (3-4 lbs.), dumplings, carrots in white sauce with parsley, potatoes, sweet corn. Canary pudding with syrup sauce.
Supper: Scrambled maize toast (made with sweet corn). Remains of milk tart with apricots.

MONDAY:
Lunch: Salt beef with carrot and bean salad. Hot custard and canary pudding.
Dinner: Lentil soup. Salt beef reheated in liquor in which it was boiled, carrots, onions, potatoes and dumplings. Apricots and custard. Coffee.

TUESDAY:
Lunch: Fried sweetbreads and lettuce. Fruit.
Dinner: Mulligatawny soup. Tomato bredee with boiled rice. Apple or banana fritters. Coffee.

WEDNESDAY:
Lunch: Scrambled eggs with tomatoes and fried bread. Sliced pawpaw.
Dinner: Mulligatawny soup. Steak and kidney pudding, peas and spinach. Rice custard.

THURSDAY:
Lunch: Cheese souffle and spinach. Baked apples.
Dinner: Split pea soup (made with ham shank). Remains steak and kidney pudding reheated, beans and potatoes. Gooseberries and custard.

FRIDAY:
Lunch: Finnan and cheese savoury. Salad. Fruit.
Dinner: Split pea soup. Cabbage and frikkadel with rice. Gooseberry pie. Coffee.

SATURDAY:
Lunch: Scotch eggs on lettuce (using ½ lb. sausages). Remains of gooseberry pie.
Dinner: Emergency soup. Grilled sausages, mashed potatoes and peas. Bread pudding.

SUNDAY:
Midday Dinner: Bean soup. Pork or veal and ham raised pie, apples, peas, potatoes. Lemon curd pudding. Coffee.
Supper: Cold pork pie. Apples and salad. Remains lemon curd pudding. Fruit.

MONDAY:
Lunch: Green mealie (preserved) omelette. Cheese. Fruit. Coffee.
Dinner: Bean soup. Bobotie with rice and blatjang. (Order 1 lb. mince, use $2/3$). Apple meringue.

TUESDAY:
Lunch: Remains bobotie. Salad. Fruit.
Dinner: Vegetable broth. Stuffed tomatoes (using remainder of mince), baked potatoes and spinach. Urney pudding. Coffee.

WEDNESDAY:
Lunch: Tomato and egg. Poffertjies. Fruit.
Dinner: Vegetable broth. Braised steak and onion. Green beans and potatoes. Paradise pudding and sauce.

THURSDAY:
Lunch: Savoury pancakes (using remainder braised steak, cut up). Fresh fruit.
Dinner: Carrot and potato soup. Grilled chops, green peas and potatoes. Remains paradise pudding.

FRIDAY:
Lunch: Irish stew. Apple charlotte.
Dinner: Carrot and potato soup. Fried sole and lemon. Remains apple charlotte and custard. Coffee.

SATURDAY:
Lunch: Cornish pasties. Salad. Stewed fruit and custard.
Dinner: Mixed grill with fried brinjals, tomatoes and chips. Apple pie and cream. Coffee.

SUNDAY:
Midday Dinner: Cream of spinach soup. Venison (3—4 lb. pot roast), jelly sauce, fried breadcrumbs, roasted potatoes and peas. Trifle. Coffee.
Supper: See recipe for "Tasty supper snack". Trifle. Fruit. Coffee.

MONDAY:
Lunch: Cold venison and jelly. Salad.
Dinner: Cream of spinach soup. Slices of venison dipped in batter and fried, sliced potatoes fried with a little onion, spinach. Sago custard. Coffee.

TUESDAY:
Lunch: Spinach and poached egg. Fruit.
Dinner: Cream of tomato soup. Haricot mutton with onions, carrots, turnips and haricot beans. Sago custard and stewed fruit.

WEDNESDAY:
Lunch: Salmon croquettes with lettuce and tomatoes. Stewed fruit and cream.
Dinner: Vermicelli vegetable soup. Crumbed fillet steak, fried tomatoes, peas, chips. Steamed fruit pudding. Coffee.

THURSDAY:
Lunch: Brains on toast. Salad. Fruit. Coffee.
Dinner: Vermicelli vegetable soup. Steamed liver roll, green beans, potatoes. Remains fruit pudding.

FRIDAY:
Lunch: Baked fish in tomato sauce. Apple fritters.
Dinner: Clear soup. Boiled bacon and beans, green peas and potatoes. Caramel custard. Coffee.

SATURDAY:

Lunch: Cold bacon and salad. Fruit.

Dinner: Clear soup. Savoury roly poly (made with minced bacon and onion), spinach and peas. Rhubarb and custard.

SUGGESTIONS FOR BREAKFAST

Stewed or Tinned Fruits:

A different kind every other day. Prunes, figs, dried or fresh apricots, apples, pears, peaches, grapefruit, Cape gooseberries, and pawpaws, are all good.

Cereals:

A different kind of porridge every day. Oatmeal, Tiger Oats, mealie meal, mabela meal. Post Toasties, Quaker Oats, Grape Nuts and many others.

Eggs:

Cooked in a variety of ways. Boiled, fried, scrambled, poached, baked, curried or scalloped. Bacon and egg. Scotch egg. Haddock and poached egg. Mince and poached egg. Sausage and egg. Eggs poached with tomato sauce. Eggs scrambled with chopped ham, anchovies, mushrooms, or flaked kipper.

Meat:

Mince and bacon rissole. Steak. Lamb chops. Pork fillets. Croquettes. Grilled kidneys. Ham toast. Brains on toast.

Fish:

Fried fish of all kinds. Fish cakes. Kedgeree. Kippers. Haddock. Herrings. Salmon.

Cheese:

Welsh rarebit. Tomato and cheese and egg (if liked).

Bacon:

Liver and bacon savoury. Banana and bacon.

Rissoles:

Of all kinds; prepared overnight.

Cold Meats:

Ham and tongue and cold pie and pasties.

Omelettes:

Of all kinds.

Sundries:

Savoury pancakes and fritters, toast, fried bread, scones, oatcakes, potato balls, fried bananas. Coffee, tea, milk.

MISCELLANEOUS

Remember the kettle.
Though up to the neck in hot water it continues to sing.

TO MAKE TEA
Of utmost importance, use only freshly-boiled water and a warm teapot. Rinse teapot with boiling water.
Allow one level teaspoon tea to each person and one for the pot.
Let the tea draw for two minutes. If it must stand longer, strain and pour into another warm teapot.
Use only the best tea if possible and keep it in an airtight container. Never throw away old tea; keep it for watering plants, especially ferns and use tea leaves for cleaning carpets.

TO MAKE COFFEE
Use 1 dessertspoon coffee to half a pint of water and half a pint of boiling milk. Pinch of salt.
Put coffee into warm pot with salt. Pour boiling water over and allow to stand for a few minutes, then boil for 3 minutes. Allow to settle and strain into a clean, warm jug or coffee pot. Serve with hot milk, using equal quantities.

TO MAKE COCOA
1 teaspoon cocoa, ½ teaspoon sugar, 1 cup milk or milk and water.
Mix cocoa and sugar and blend with a little milk. Stir into the hot milk and cook for 2 minutes.

PLAIN OATMEAL PORRIDGE
4 cups water, 1 cup coarse oatmeal, 1 teaspoon salt.
Boil water and salt and gradually add oatmeal. Stir constantly for 5 minutes, cover and cook slowly for 4 hours. Best made overnight. Serve with milk or cream.

Rolled Oats:
Cook in same way using same quantities but boil for 1 hour only.

MEALIE MEAL PORRIDGE
Mix 1 cup mealie meal with 1 cup cold water. Stir into 3 cups boiling water and add 1 teaspoon salt. Stir until thick and cook for 2 or 3 hours.

KAFFIR CORN PORRIDGE
Made in same way as Mealie Meal.

TO PREPARE A PUDDING CLOTH

Hold the cloth by the four corners and dip in a pan of boiling water. With the lid squeeze out the water. Spread cloth on board, rub with fat and sprinkle with flour.

BREAD CRUMBS (BROWN)

Collect all scraps of bread, crusts of toast, etc. Place on a wire tray till enough are collected — do not keep in tin. Bake in oven until golden brown. Crush with rolling pin and keep in tin till required.

BREAD CRUMBS (WHITE)

Same as brown crumbs only dry out in oven but do not allow to brown.

FRESH BREAD CRUMBS

Cut a thick slice from a loaf of bread. Remove crusts and rub the bread on a grater. Make only the amount required as these turn mouldy if kept.

FRIED BREAD CRUMBS

Melt butter in pan, stir in white breadcrumbs and fry till brown and crisp.

CROUTES OR CROUTONS

Cut slices of stale bread half an inch thick. Cut into dice. Fry in very hot fat until golden brown. Drain on kitchen paper and serve with vegetable soup.

CARAMEL (BURNT SUGAR)

Put ¼ lb. sugar in a pan, add ½ gill water and stir. Allow to boil till dark in colour and use as required.

DEVILLED ALMONDS

Blanch and dry the almonds. Fry till brown in salad oil. Toss in salt to which a little canyenne pepper has been added.

DRIPPING

To clarify:
Melt dripping and pour into large basin; add same quantity of boiling water. Stir well and leave overnight. Next morning a pure white fat will be found on top. Remove fat and throw away the water.

FAT
To render:
Any scraps of raw fat may be used. Cut the fat up in small pieces and put in a large stewpan. Cover with cold water and bring to the boil. Skim and allow to cook gently till the water has boiled away. Strain carefully.

GRAVY COLOURING
½ lb. sugar, ¼ pint cold water, ¼ pint hot water.

Put sugar into an old pan; add cold water and stir till dissolved. Stop stirring and boil fast till sugar has turned to a dark brown colour. (One stage further than caramel.) Allow to cool a little, then add boiling water, a few drops at a time. Bottle and keep for use.

GRAVY — THICKENING
Put 1 tablespoon dripping in pan: allow to become smoking hot, sprinkle in enough flour to absorb the fat and fry till flour is a golden brown, stirring all the time. Add a pint of water or stock and stir till it boils. Season, strain and serve. Over-fried flour is disagreeable and indigestible. For thin gravy add more water. Mix with sediment left in roasting or frying pan after meat has been taken out.

HINTS
Remember:
Plan your meals well ahead.
In cooking, care and variety mean everything.
Always make two days' supply of soup. To make a change the soup can be strained on the second day and a different flavouring added.
Try to buy butcher meat personally twice or three times weekly and store in frig., otherwise buy daily.
Save all cream from top of milk to serve with puddings.
Save all gravy for use in made over dishes and soups, etc.
Grate stale cheese and place in covered container in frig.
Use left-over vegetables for salads — cover liberally with mayonnaise.
In making milk puddings use very little cereal but be generous with milk (not water), eggs and butter and cook very slowly in double container or cool oven.
Keep separate tins for bread, scones, cakes and biscuits. Never keep cake and biscuits in the same tin, and do not mix sweet and plain biscuits.
Wrap fruit cake in cooking paper, keep it in an airtight tin and place half an apple in the tin. Clean all bread and cake tins once a week. Line with cooking paper and see that they are kept well supplied.

It is a good plan to set aside one morning each week for baking, preferably Friday or Saturday. Rich butter cakes, fruit cakes, gingerbread, shortbread and most biscuits keep very well indeed. Crunchies, parkins, nutty wonders and rock cakes, too, are all good "standbys". When making pastry it is better to make a fairly large quantity. That which is not required for immediate use can be wrapped in greaseproof paper and kept in frig.

Do not make a habit of cooking from tins but keep a small supply of tinned goods in case of emergency. The most useful are tins of soup, peaches, apricots, pears, Cape gooseberries, Nestle's milk and cream, salmon and sardines, green peas, beans, sweetcorn, asparagus, a good brand of tongue and ham. A very good brand of tinned apples should be kept.

When catering for two avoid buying large joints. A small amount of freshly-cooked meat is preferable to recooked meat.

Here are some of the things that can be done with small cuts of meat: —

Steak:

(1) Toad-in-the-hole, (2) beef olives, (3) rolled, stuffed steak for two days, (4) savoury steak, or will make (5) a lovely grill, if batted well and soaked in a little oil and vinegar. (If griller is not available it is possible to obtain the same result by making an electric stove plate very hot, dipping the meat into melted butter, and placing it directly on plate. Turn every 10 seconds with blade of knife and spoon. Meat will take about 8 to 10 minutes to be well cooked through. Clean stove plate at once. Serve fried onions with grilled steak and use what is left over for savoury omelettes or pancakes.

1 lb. rump steak will make a two days' stew. Add dumplings second day and cook in gravy, but only reheat the steak.

To vary, cook with different vegetables, add a dash of curry powder, add dumplings, macaroni or haricot beans or tomatoes. Can all be done in casserole and your pudding baked in oven at the same time. Even the tiniest bit of leftover steak added to a little mashed potato and chopped onion will make a delicious rissole if served with gravy (never throw away gravy) or tomato sauce. Don't forget that 2 or 3 sheep's kidneys and a little pastry added to your lb. of steak will make a grand steak and kindney pie or pudding, and writing of pastry, what about Cornish Pasties!

Mutton:

The above applies equally well to mutton, using 1 lb. of the best end of neck. Cold mutton covered with hot parsley sauce is good and curried mutton even better provided you do not re-cook but only reheat the meat. Don't forget Irish stew for cold days and when you do order a piece of loin, do not roast it all but cut off some of the chops for grilling or frying. Delicions breedes are made from mutton ribs.

Buy sufficient for a rib of mutton roast. Ribs of mutton can be boned, rolled and stuffed with curry filling. Keep the remaining mutton ribs for your bredee. When buying a leg or shoulder of lamb or mutton (the latter very good but extravagant) have them boned and rolled occasionally and make soup and mutton patties with the bones and trimmings. Cut your leg of mutton in two, pot roast the one piece and boil the other. When doing this take two fairly thick slices from the centre of the leg. Soak them in salad oil and vinegar for an hour. Drain very well, brush over with melted butter and grill for 15 minutes. Serve with tomato sauce and crisply fried potatoes and mushrooms.

Minced Steak:
What a variety of dishes can be made from a little mince. First and foremost we have our beloved South African Bobotie and cabbage Frikkadel, and then there is the Scotch Savoury Mince Pie — all three of them passports to any man's heart. Buy a lb. of steak minced and see that it is minced steak, and with the addition of a few fresh bread crumbs this will go a long way in making Hamburg Steaks, Shepherd's Pie, Stuffed Tomatoes, Stuffed Marrow, Stuffed Onions, Savoury Omelette or pancake, Patties and Rissoles, Savoury Meat Roll (made in the same way as Jam Roly Poly), and ordinary stewed mince or mince collops can be made both appetising and nourishing with the addition of a few savoury balls or dumplings. Add a little curry and a liberal helping of chutney if you want curried mince, and for supper scrambled mince or eggs poached in mince and served on hot (very hot) toast are both good. An ordinary mince rissole wrapped in bacon, secured and placed under the grill for 15 minutes, turning often, is tasty when served on hot toast. One pound of mince mixed with ½ lb. salt pork or bacon (see recipes) will make a very good meat roll.

Sausages:
From 1 lb. sausages one can have sausage and mash for lunch and Sausage Toad-in-the-Hole for supper. There are sausage rolls and Scotch eggs; a mixed grill may contain sausage, and sausage and bacon in place of liver and bacon is a change. Fry sausage cakes (skin sausages and make into cakes with egg and bread crumbs) with thick slices of tomato and apple (fry the apple) and serve with fried bread. Economical and nourishing meals can be made with brains (if we use ours and cook the sheep's), sweetbreads, heart, liver, tongue, tail, trotters, tripe, shin, marrow, kidneys.

Make good use of fish but use pork and veal sparingly and don't forget to have a meatless day occasionally. Supply plenty of well-cooked vegetables, and plenty of fresh, green salads and fruit every day. Try to avoid suet puddings and dumplings, heavy steamed puddings, rich stews, fresh and pickled pork, during hot weather, and let fruit take the place of soup.

Learn to make a good cup of tea (have the water freshly boiled and the teapot hot — I believe that is the third time I have written this) and don't spare the tea; and learn, too, to make a grill, a steak and kidney pudding, a luscious apple tart (just like Mother's, only it won't ever be quite), a Dutch milk tart, a Cornish pasty and a Scotch scone, or even shortbread (don't try haggis for a while, he would be apt to misjudge you!) and you'll have a mighty good start on the matrimonial journey — that is, of course, if you can remember to have meals varied and on time. A dainty table and a dainty person at the end of it, as dainty at 7.30 a.m. as at 7.30 p.m., the socks darned and the shirts attached to buttons regularly, a tidy house (be methodical and thorough), but leave last week's papers and books where they are and never, oh, never, give away his old trousers, coats or hats (he never has any, anyway!) without permission. Don't jump every time he drops a little ash on the carpet. Remember "a little ash on the carpet keeps the moths out and the old man in."

Be a good cook, but not just a cook, and be on your guard against slackness in any shape or form. Hang on to that sense of humour because, believe me, a juicy steak and a witty tongue can lighten the heaviest dressmaker's bill, and an apple tart on pay day is a wonderful help towards filling the tummy and emptying the pockets! During the month one's ideas are apt to soar and we forget that there are only 20 shillings in a pound. I never found more than 10 or 15 and I have also found that the Irish Sweep is not to be depended upon, so budget, and budget carefully. Extravagance can disturb the mind and wrinkle the face quicker than anything I know, and economy is the only cure.

TERMS RELATING TO COOKERY

Au Gratin: Flavoured with grated cheese, covered with crumbs and baked in oven.

Baste: To pour melted fat on meat while roasting.

Bate: To beat meat before cooking in order to soften fibre.

Bay: A hole made in flour in basin or on board, so that liquid may be poured in middle.

Bind: To moisten dry ingredients with enough liquid to hold them together.

Bisque: Soup made of shell fish.

Blanch: To bring an ingredient to the boil and then plunge in cold water.

Bobotie: A curried mince flavoured with lemon leaves.

Bouquet Garni: A bunch of sweet herbs used for flavouring.

Bredee: A stew made of thick rib of mutton, onion and a vegetable of a watery nature. Very little liquid being required.

Canapes: Bread toasted or fried in hot butter and spread with savoury fillings.

Caviare: The prepared roe of the sturgeon.

Casserole: Dish with cover, used for oven cooking.

Compôte: Stewed fruit.

Consommé: Clear soup.

Croûton: Small dice of bread toasted or fried.

Croûte: Fried bread.

Colander: A basin-shaped strainer for straining vegetables.

Cutlet: A bone of best end of neck of mutton trimmed of superfluous bone and fat.

Darriol: A small cup-shaped mould.

Devilled: Well seasoned.

Entrée: A made dish served between the fish and the joint.

Force: Forcemeat or stuffing.

Fillets: Boneless meat or fish.

Foie Gras: The prepared livers of fat geese.

Frappe: Partly frozen.

Fricasse: Meat, chicken or fish stewed in rich gravy.

Frikkadel: A rissole.

Fritter: A light batter mixture. Coat meat, fish, fruit, pumpkin, etc., and fry in deep fat.

Galantine: A cold meat dish made of boned veal or chicken. It is boiled, pressed and glazed or jellied.

Glaze: Very strong stock used for brushing over hot and cold meats.

Garnish: To decorate a savoury or meat dish.

Glace: Covered with icing.

Gruel: A thin porridge made of fine or strained oatmeal.

Hors d'Oeuvres: A small, tasty dish served before the soup.

Ingelegde: Pickled fish.

Jelly Bag: A pointed bag made of double flannel with tapes at the opening.

Julienne: Vegetables cut in fine shreds and usually added to clear soup.

Kedgeree: A rechauffe of fish, rice, butter and flavouring.

Konfyt: Fruit cooked whole or in pieces in heavy syrup.

Kromeskies: Small rissoles of meat or fish rolled in bacon dipped in batter and fried.

Larding: To pierce meat with thin strips of fat.

Legumes: Vegetables belonging to the bean family. (Beans, peas, lentils, etc.)

Macedoine: A mixture of fruit or vegetables.

Marinate: To soak meat or fish in a liquid before cooking.

Mask: To coat a substance completely with sauce.

Mosbolletjies: A light bun flavoured with aniseed and raised by "mos" or the fermented juice of the grape.

Mousse: A very light sweet or savoury mould, hot or cold.

Noodles: A kind of macaroni paste made of flour, salt, egg and water, rolled thinly, cut into fancy shapes. Used for soups, stews, etc.

Panade: A binding sauce.

Paté: A small meat pie.

Puree: Vegetables cooked, rubbed through a sieve and made into a thick soup.

Pectin: The substance in fresh fruit that causes the fruit to become jelly when cooked with sugar.

Pilau: An Indian dish of stewed fowl, garnished with rice, fried almonds and raisins.

Quennelle: A light mixture of raw fish or meat, shaped with two spoons and poached.

Ragôut: A rich stew or hash often served in a pastry case as an entrée.

Raised Pie: A pie made of hot-water crust, containing meat, game, etc. No piedish is used, the paste being moulded by hand to required shape.

Ramekin: A small china or paper case.

Rechauffé: A hot dish made of cold meat or fish.

Rissole: A mixture of minced meat or fish, bound with sauce or egg. Egged and crumbed and fried in deep fat. A Frikkadel.

Roux: A thickening for white sauces consisting of flour fried in an equal quantity of fat. To make brown roux fry the flour brown.

Salamander: A small iron plate attached to an iron rod, made red hot and used for browning scallops, etc.

Salmi: Game half roasted, cut up and cooked till tender in a rich brown sauce.

Samp: Dried whole seed of mealie.

Sosaties: Small squares of meat put on skewers, soaked in curry sauce and grilled.

Sauté: To cook a substance in fat that is not hot enough to fry it.

Savoury: A dainty dish that is not sweet, usually made of meat, cheese or fish and served after sweets and before the dessert.

Scallops: Small ramekins or shells, filled with fish, meat and sauce and browned in oven or with a salamander.

Scald: To bring milk nearly to boiling point or to pour boiling water over any substance.

Shortening: The fat used in making pastry.

Soufflé: Mixture containing fish meat or cheese as a base and made light with well-beaten eggs. A very light steamed or baked pudding.

Stock: The liquor produced by boiling down meat and bones. White: Made from chicken, veal or rabbit. Brown: Made from beef or mutton.

Stockpot: A pot used for making stock.

Truffle: An underground fungus, black, used for decorating aspics, etc. Very expensive and rarely obtainable fresh.

Zest: The fine, outer yellow rind of citrus fruit.

Beefsteak: Cut from the leg of an ox.

Fillet Steak: Cut from an undercut of the rump or from sirloin.

Rumpsteak: Cut from the rump.

Porterhouse Steak: Cut from the whole length of the sirloin.

Hamburg Steak: An artifical steak made from minced beef.

"Accurate measurements the secret of uniform results."

ALL BEHIND

"Everything's gone behind!" she said
With a sigh and a sorrowful shake of the head.
"There's not a corner that's fit to be seen;
The whole of the house wants a good spring-clean.
For nothing's been done in a skilful way,
In it's own right time, or it's own right day.
My temper is short and my forehead is lined;
No wonder! When everything's all behind!"
Just so! But think! Did you ever meet
A woman, all human and true and sweet
Who was absolutely "in front" of things?
Who never took off her eagle's wings?
A woman whose washing was always dry
Long before Monday was quite gone by;
Whose ironing was finished and put to rights,
And aired and mended on Tuesday nights?
A woman whose hall was always tidy,
Whose cupboards were always turned out on Friday,
Whose children were always asleep in bed
And dreaming, when anything private was said.
A woman who wrought with a tranquil mind
And never, no never, got all behind?
Well, I never met her! It seems to me
As long as we're this side Eternity
We are meant to strive, we are meant to grow
And we can't if life is too easy, you know.
So the only plan and the only way
Is to act as if life were but one short day,
Being gentle and nice till set of sun,
Not worrying either, o'er tasks undone.
Nor grieving over an upset plan,
Just doing as much as two hands can.
Oh, He who made us and understands
Could have given us each a hundred hands;
Have altered our houses quite unawares;
Supplied us all with hot water upstairs!
And porcelain sinks and washing-machines,
And non-staining apples, potatoes and beans,
Have kept us in garments that wax not old,
With shoes for the bairns of cast-iron mould.
He could have given us money in plenty,
With men and maid servants at least five and twenty.
In short, had He wished it, 'tis certainly true,

He could have given us — nothing to do!
But oh! God had a divine plan
For luring the better half of man.
The small cheap house and the scanty wages
Are linked up with the undying ages,
May bring forth fruit of exotic worth,
Ripened for Heaven, matured on earth.
And the poor little garden where they grew
Won't matter the tiniest bit to you.
Yes, many who here were always "last"
Will be "first" when probation time is past.
And then it will seem worth while to find
That the angels don't reckon us all behind!

Fay Inchfawn.

Go, little book, and greet my friend,
Brighten her hours and cheerful solace lend,
Then when she lays thee down at last,
And finis reads, with thanks for all the past,
Whisper to her that this is not your home,
And though your owner grants you leave to roam,
Still now the hour has struck, when, like the tide,
You make for home and there once more abide.

Name ....

INDEX

HORS D'OEUVRES

Anchovy biscuits	8	Fruit hors d'oeuvres		8
„ butter	7	Green butter		7
„ canapes	8	Parsley butter	7,	45
Canapes	8	Vegetable hors d'oeuvres		9

SOUPS

Accessories	16	Giblet	12
Bean	12	Kidney	11
Beef tea	16	Leek	13
Beetroot, iced	13	Lentil	13
Browning for soups	17	Mealie	14
Carrot and potato	11	Mulligatawny	14
Chicken broth (invalid)	16	Onion	15
Clear	13	Ox tail	13
Cock-a-leekie	11	Pea (split)	12
Cream of asparagus	14	Scotch broth	11
„ „ celery	15	Stew, left over Irish stew	15
„ „ pea	15	„ „ „ mince	15
„ „ potato	14	„ „ „ ox tail	15
„ „ rice	14	„ „ „ steak and kidney	15
„ „ spinach	15	„ „ „ vegetables	15
Custard royal	17	Tomato, Toronto	12
Emergency	12	To clarify	10
Fish	12	What to serve with soup	16
Forcemeat balls	17		

FISH

Baked in tomato sauce	18	Scalloped	19
Baked in custard	22	Sole, fried	18
Cakes	19	„ fillets in milk	18
Creamed	19	„ steamed	20
Curried	21	„ and olive sauce	20
Custard	20	Souffle	23
Finnan haddock	20	Souffle (invalid)	22
Fish and cheese	19	Stuffed, baked	19
Fish dish	22	Steamed (invalid)	21
Curried or Pickled	24	Sauce Bechamel	23
Garnishes	23	„ Hollandaise	24
Kedgeree	19, 20	„ mustard	24
Omelette	21	„ tartare	24
Pie (Cape dish)	21	„ tomato	23
Salmon mould	21	„ white	23
Sandwich	22		

MEAT AND POULTRY
Accompaniments to Meat and Poultry

Accompaniments	42	Parsey butter	7,	45
Aspic jelly	45	Stuffing, chestnut for turkey		46
Cotswold dumplings	42	„ green maize		46
Flavouring, boiled salt beef	45	„ sage and onion		46
Glaze	46	„ sausage		46
Gravy for roast meat	45	„ for chicken & turkey		46
Noodles	42	Yorkshire pudding		42
Noodle pie	42			

I

COLD MEATS

Brisket of beef	47
Brawn, pig head	47
Brawn, sheep head	48
Chaud froids	49
Galantine of fowl	48
" " turkey	48
" " veal	48
Hollandsch meat loaf	48
Jellied meat	49
Meat in aspic	49
Potted head, Scotch	47
Potted meat, or brawn, Scotch	47
Tongue, pressed, salted	49

HOT MEATS

Bacon boiled	31
Beef olives	28
Beefsteak and kidney pie	32
Beefsteak and kidney pudding	31
Beefsteak cake	37
Breakfast roll	37
Chicken, stuffed roast	41
" in casserole	42
" fried	42
" Puff	38
Chops braised	32
Corned beef ring, baked	38
Crumbed fillet or lamb chops	34
Curry	36
Cuts of meat	25, 39, 40
Cutlets baked	38
Duck roast	42
Fowl, to boil	41
Fricadelles	33
Fritters (cold meat)	36
Goose, roast	42
Grilling, suitable joints for	26
Haggis	34
Ham baked	29
" boiled	29
" croquettes	35
" in casserole	35
" toast	35
Hot-pot	28
Left overs	38
Liver and bacon	30
Liver rolled, steamed	29
Meat roll	29
" pickled dry	37
" pickled wet	37
Mixed grill	30
Mutton slices	35
Mutton ribs, salted	32
Ox heart, stuffed	31
Pickle dry	37
Pickle wet	37
Poultry and game	41
Pork and ham raised pie	31
Rissoles, carrot and liver	28
" sausage	34
" savoury rice	35
Rules for cooking	26
Salting, suitable joints for	26
Sausage potatoes	34
Scotch minced collops	33
Shepherd's pie	34
Steak and onions	28
Shoulder of mutton, rolled	29
" Porterhouse	31
" savoury	33
" stuffed	28
Stews, just	27
Stew, Irish	27
" ox tail	28
" steak and dumplings	27
Stuffed onions	33
Stuffed tomatoes	33
Sucking pig	30
Toad-in-the-hole	32
Tripe and onions	32
Turkey roast	41
Veal cutlets	31
" and ham raised pie	31
" stuffed rolled	30
Venison	36

MEAT SAUCES

Apple	44
Bread	45
Cranberry	45
Curry	45
Horseradish	44
Mint	44
Onion	44
Piquante	44
Supreme	44

VEGETABLES

Artichokes	57
Asparagus, fried (with chicken)	57
Beans, broad	53
„ haricot	54
„ French, kidney, scarlet runner	53
Beetroot	56
„ in sauce	56
„ hot	54
Brinjals, fried	56
Cabbage, tip for cooking	52
„ au gratin	53
„ another way	53
„ Illinois hot slaw	53
„ red, hot	52
„ with onions	53
Cauliflower	52
Celerie à la bourgeoisie	53
Carrots	54
Leeks	52
Marrow	54
„ stuffed	54
„ stuffed vegetable	56
„ scalloped	56
Mealies, boiled green	57
Mushrooms	55
Onions	52
Potato balls	50
„ puffs	51
Potatoes, old	50
„ new	50
„ stuffed	51
„ sweet	51
„ and cheese	51
„ eighteenth century	51
„ cold, cooked	50
Parsnips	52
Peas	52
Pumpkin	55
Pumpkin, baked	55
Rules for cooking	50
Spinach	54
Spinach souffle	57
Spuash and carrot casserole	57
Tomatoes	55
Tomato pie	55
Turnips	54
Turnips creamed	56

SALADS AND SALAD DRESSINGS

Salads

Asparagus	60
Avocado pear and banana	59
Beetroot and onion	61
Beetroot and pea	59
Cabbage	62
Cauliflower	60
Celery	62
Chicken	61
Chicken and celery	61
Corn	59
Egg	58
Eggs, stuffed	58
Eggs in aspic	58
Golden	60
Haricot bean and carrot	61
Lemon aspic	59
Macedoine	62
Macedoine in aspic	62
Orange and date	59
Pineapple	61
Pineapple, carrot and pea	61
Potato	61
Salmon mayonnaise	61
Tomato and bean	61
„ chilled	60
„ cucumber and onion	59
„ stuffed	60

Dressings

Mayonnaise	62
„ (2)	63
„ American	63
„ boiled	63
Mayonnaise quick	63
„ uncooked	63
„ without oil	64
Humorous recipe	64

BREAKFAST, LUNCH AND SUPPER DISHES

Bananas and bacon	73
Boston baked beans	73
Brains on toast	66
Cauliflower snippets	74
Cheese and fish pie	74
Cheese custards	69
„ pudding	71
„ souffle	65
„ souffle cold	74
Chicken fritters	66

III

Corn pancakes	73
Curried salmon pie	72
Egg and bacon pie	75
Finnan and cheese savoury	68
Liver and bacon savoury	69
Luncheon dish	71
Macaroni cheese	67
Macaroni with tomato	72
Mealie toast savoury	71
Mince and poached egg	68
Mushroom egg stuffed	72
Mushroom and sweetbread patties	73
Oatmeal rissoles	75
Oeufs à la Parisienne	71
Omelette delicious	69
,, green mealie	69
,, plain	70
,, puffy	70
Onion and cheese	70
Poached egg with mushroom	73
Poached egg with spinach	67
Salmon croquettes	67
,, loaf	73
,, souffle	66
,, supper dish	72
Scotch eggs	68
Scotch woodcock	73
Scrambled egg	68
Scrambled egg with tomato	68
Snack, nice supper	70
Spinach and poached egg	67
Supper dish, quick	72
Supper dish, tasty	70
Sweetbreads	66, 67
Sweetcorn supper dish	66
Tomato and cheese	68
,, ,, rissoles	75
,, ,, egg	71
Tasty Lunch Dish	75
Welsh rarebit	69

VEGETARIAN DISHES

Beans and tomatoes, curried	78
Carrots en casserole	78
Egg plant and banana savoury	78
Haricot beans	78
Leeks on toast	79
Lentil sausage	79
Nut loaf	77
Nut roast	79
Pie, onion and tomato	79
,, vegetarian	76
,, walnut	79
Potato rissoles	77

Soups

Broth	76
Clear bouillon	76
Cream of onion	76
Marrow	77
Spinach, clear	77
Spinach fritters	77

PASTRIES

Almond cut	85
Apple crusty pudding	84
,, pie deep	83
,, Pie	93
,, sauce cheese pie	91
,, tart	83, 89
,, ,, German	84
,, ,, spieced	87
Bakewell tart	85
Banana pie	91
Butterscotch pie	85
Butterscotch tart	90
Cape gooseberry flan	92
Cheese tarlets	89
Chicken patties	83
Chocolate tarts	86, 88
Cornish pasties	82
Date tart	88
Flaky Pastry	93
Fruit flans, summer	90
,, meringue tart	91
,, tart crumbly	90
German tart	86
Ginger tart	86
Lemon chiffon pie	92
,, curd tart	87
,, meringue pie	89, 92
,, pie	84
Mock mince pie	90
Mincemeat (steak) pie	82
Nougat tart	88
Pastry boiled paste for pies	81
,, Choux	82
,, Flaky	80
,, German	81
,, Plain short crust	80
,, Puff	80
,, Quickly made	81
,, Rich short	81
,, Short	81
,, Shortbread	89
,, Suet crust	81
Peach (canned) tart	93
Pineapple meringue pie	84

Pioneer tart	86
Pumpkin pie	85
Raisin pie	84
Sandringham tartlets	86
Sausage rolls	83
Savoury flan	92
Scotch mutton pie	83
Sponge tart	88
Strawberry chiffon pie	87
Swiss sacher tart	87
Swiss tart	86

PUDDINGS: HOT AND COLD
Hot Puddings

Apple and ginger	100
,, cake pudding	100
,, charlotte	102
,, dumpling	97
,, dumpling baked	97
,, fritters	103
,, poffertjies	99
,, pudding	100, 103
,, ,, Dutch	96
,, ,, Russian	101
Apples, stuffed	98
Ashfield pudding	100
Banana batter	99
,, fritters	103
,, pudding	100
Brown Betty	95
Brown pudding steamed	98
Cake and fruit pudding	99
Canary pudding	94
Cream pudding	103
Date pudding	94, 102
Date pudding, sauce for	94
Favourite	101
Fillings for pancakes	104
Foamy sauce	96
Fritter batter	103
Golden pudding	102
Last minute pudding	101
Lemon curd pudding	98
Oatmeal fritters	104
Pancakes	104
Pancakes, fillings for	104
Paradise pudding	103
Pineapple fritters	103
Plum pudding	95
Pumpkin fritters	104
Queen of puddings	102
Raisin dumplings	98
Raisin pie	95
Roly-poly	97
Roly-poly savoury	97
Sago pudding	102
Spice pudding	99
Sponge dumplings	101
Treacle pudding	95
Urney pudding	100
Velvet pudding	98
Vinegar pudding	96
Vinegar pudding, sauce for	96

Cold Puddings

Apple custard pudding	119
,, marshmallow	117
,, moulds	110
,, sago	111
Apricot delight	105
Apricot souffle	107
Banana caramel	108
,, delicous	111
,, mousse	106
,, pudding	113
,, sponge	110
,, whip	113
Charlotte russe	116
Chocolate cream	116
,, mould	113
,, mousse	109
,, pudding	111
,, special	105
Citroen cream	106
Coffee cream	117
Gold pudding	107
Cream pudding	109
Creme, brulee	122
Prepared sweet, a quickly	105
Custards:	
Apple	112
Baked cup	122
Base	115
Boiled	119
Caramel	121
Cheese, baked	119
Chocolate	121
Cocoanut pie	121
Coffee	121
Cool	122
Fruit foam	120
,, cream	116
,, jellies (basic)	114
Gold	120
Honey, baked	121

Mock butterscotch	121
Orange	107
Paw-paw	120
Quaking	120
Silver	119
Date cream	116
Date pudding	110
Fruit creams	115
Fruit fools	115
Gelatine moulds (basic)	114
Ginger cream	112
Golden cream	110
Gooseberry	119
Grenadilla mould	117
Honeycomb cream	112, 116
Jelly, egg	108
„ mottled	104
„ pudding	107
„ snow	108
„ sundaes	115
„ trifle	115
Lemon sponge	114
Lemon cream	114
Macedoine of fruit	115
Marshmallow meringue	105
Mushrooms in the field	107
Nougat cream	107
Orange sweet	106
„ pudding	108
„ cream	111
„ sponge cream	106
„ sago	112
Paw-paw mould	105
Paw-paw and passion fruit mould	108
Peach parfait	113
Peanut mould	118
Pears, chilled	114
Pear cream	109
Pineapple mould	109
Prune mould	117
Prune souffle	113
Stone cream	106
Strawberry icebox cake	118
Strawberry trifle	113
Swiss roll mould	116
Trifle	112
Vanilla cream	110, 116

Ice Creams

Caramel	123
Chocolate	123
Condensed milk	125
Custard	124
Custard foundation	123
Delicious	124
French vanilla	124
Economical	124
Marshmallow	125
Peach cream sundae	123
Uncooked	123

SWEET SAUCES

Apricot	127
Brandy	125
Caramel	127
Custard	125
Chocolate	126
Chocolate fudge	126
Foamy	126
Fruit	127
Hard	126
Lemon	126

SOUTH AFRICAN RECIPES

Biltong	130
Blatjang	135
Bobotie	134
Boerwors	133
Cabbage bredee	128
Cabbage frikkadel	129, 134
Green maize bread	130
„ „ cheese custard	132
„ „ chowder	132
„ „ cream toast	131
„ „ dishes	130
„ „ fritters	130
„ „ pudding	131
„ „ scrambled toast	131
„ „ souffle	133
Koeksisters	129
Koeksisters syrup	130
Krakelinge	133
Milk tart	135, 136
Pampoenmoes	133
Poffertjies	133
Quince mebos	136
Soetkoekies	134
Sosaties	129
String bean bredee	128
Sweet potatoes, stewed	135
Tomato bredee	128
Tomato sauce	132
Yellow rice	128

BREAD, SCONES AND BUNS

Baps	146	Buns, coffee, streusel	142
Bread, Boston	146	„ hot cross	140
„ brown	138	„ rice	146
„ directions for making	137	„ rock	146
„ fancy	140	Mosbolletjies	141
„ nut	139	Muffins	145
„ raisin	139	Rolls, breakfast	145, 146
„ white	137, 138	„ dinner	139
Biscuits, soft	146	„ frig. bread	139
Buns, butterscotch	144	Rusks	141
„ coffee	146		

Scones

Almond crescents	141	Girdle	145
Brown	143	Pancakes, Scotch	144
Butter rolls	143	Plain	142
Cheese	143	Rich	142
Cream	143	Spiced, tea	145
Date	145	Standard recipe	142
Date or raisin	143	Sweetcorn	144
Drop	144	Yeast cookies	147
Fairy	143	Quick luncheon rolls	147

CAKES

Almond cheese cakes	153	Fruit cake light	162
Apple cake	165, 168	„ „ Meg's	163
Banana bread	161	„ „ rich	163, 166
Banana loaf	161	Gingerbread	152
Bannocks, Selkirk	154	Ginger cake	152, 155
Bachelor's buttons	161	Ginger loaf	152
Black bun, Scotch	153	Hamilton's cake, Mrs. R.	163
Butter cake	159	Hazelnut cake	160
Cake making hints	149	Hilda's cake	167
Cake mixtures, standard	150	Jam cakes	155
Cheese cakes	168	Jelly cake	157
Cherry cake	163	Kisses	165
Chinese cakes	164	Lamington squares	165
Chocolate cake	153, 165, 166	Layer cake	157, 159
Chocolate fancies	171	„ „ grenadilla	159
Christmas cake	164	„ „ orange	160
Cinnamon sponge	170	„ „ pineapple	160
Coburg cakes	153	„ „ strawberry	159
Cocoanut cake	170	Lunch cake	164
„ macaroons	171	Madeline cakes	170
„ squares	168	Madeira cake	161, 168
Cream cracker cake	167	Maids of honour	169
Cumberland bun loaf	154	Orange cake	158
Date and walnut cake	153	Pound cake	162
Date and walnut loaf	161, 162	Queen cakes	153
Fairy cakes	155	Quick cake	171
French cake	171	Raspberry buns	160
Frig. cake	172	Ribbon cake	172
Fruit cake	162, 172	Rice cake	160
„ „ dark	162	Rusks, tea	170

VII

Sandwich cake	156, 158
„ „ mile-a-minute	156
„ „ mixture	156
„ „ orange	157
Shortbread	154, 155, 170
Small cakes	153
Spice cake	169
Sponge, boiling water	156
„ Queen Mary's	158
Sponge, sandwich	156
Swiss Roll	158
Temperatures, oven	150
Walnut cake	168
„ maple cake	167
„ tart	167
Weights and measures	148
Welsh cakes	171

ICINGS

Almond	176
Butter	174, 176
Caramel	176
Chocolate	175
Cocoanut	174
Coffee	176
Fondant	173
Fruit glace	175
Gelatine	175
Ginger butter	155
Jelly	173
Lemon	175
Mocha	175
Orange	175
Water	176
White mountain cream or boiled	176
Yellow	176, 177

FILLINGS

Almond	177
Butterscotch	177
Chocolate	174, 177
Cocoa almond	166
Custard	174
Fig	174
French cream	173
Fruit juice	174
Grenadilla cheese	177
Lemon curd	173, 177, 178
Mincemeat	177, 178
Mock whipped cream	174
Prune	173
Walnut	153

BISCUITS

Abernethy biscuits	181
Aland biscuits	189
Almond biscuits	181, 187
Almond rolls	187
Biscuits	186, 187
Bitter amandel koekies	188
Butterscotch biscuits	181
Cheese biscuits	182, 188
Chocolate biscuits	182
Chocolate toasties	188
Cocoanut biscuits	182
„ fingers	188
„ macaroons	180
Cornflake creams	179
Crunchies	185
Date biscuits	180
„ crackers	183
„ dainties	183
„ fingers	187
„ slices	184
„ turnovers	180
Digestive wholemeal	184
Fairy shortbread biscuits	180
Foundation recipes and variations	179
German biscuits	185
Ginger biscuits	189
„ crispies	186
„ nuts	186
„ snaps	182
Ground rice biscuits	186
Hazelnut biscuits	183
Lady fingers	184
Mabela biscuits	185
Macaroons	183
Mealiemeal biscuits	181, 186
Nut wafers	185
Nutty wonders	189
Oat squares	188
Oublietjies	179
Parkins	180
Peanut butter	190
Pastry, biscuit and biscuit	190
Sherry sticks	184
Shortbread biscuits	181, 185, 189
Tea biscuits	190
Tru-weat biscuits	188
Wine fingers	187

SAVOURIES AND SNACKS

Asparagus rolls	196
Avocado pear savouries	193
Caviare and other crisps	193
Cheese aigrettes	194
„ drops	194
„ rolls, toasted	191
„ straws	195
„ sauce	197
Chicken livers in bacon	191
Cocktail savouries	196
Eggs, hardboiled, fillings for	196
Fillings	194
Fish cakes	192
French toast	191
Green parsley butter	196
Kipper rarebit	193
Kidney toast	196
Liver cakes	192
Liver toast	196
Oyster canapes	193
Oyster scallops	193
Petit choux savouries	195
Prunes, devilled	194
Puffs for savouries	195
Relish snacks	195
Sandwich fillings	196
Sardine or salmon rolls	192
Sardine rolls	195
Savoury sausage and egg pie	197

Savouries

Asparagus	198
Bovril	199
Cheese	199
Fish	198
Sausage	199
Tomato	198
Savoury snacks	195
Steak and kidney snacks	194

BEVERAGES

Bestman's punch	201
Boston cream	203
Bride's blush	200
Bridegroom's joy	200
Bridesmaid's hope	200
Catawba juice	206
Catawba punch	205
Champagne cup	206
Claret cup	202
Flower girl's fantasy	201
Fruit drink	203
„ nectar	206
„ punch	206
„ salts	204
Ginger ale punch	203
Ginger beer	203
Grape cup, spiced	206
Grape cup and raspberry punch	205
Grapefruit juice	201
Grenadilla punch	202
Honeymoon bliss	200
Lemon barley water	201
Lemon juice, to prepare and preserve	203
Lemonade	202
Lemon syrup	204, 207
Loganberry cocktail	205
Milk punch	202
Mint punch	202
Mixed fruit cup	203
Orange and lemon drink	205
„ drink	204
„ health drink	204
„ punch	202
„ squash	204
Parson's pep	201
Raspberry drink	205
Tomato juice cocktail	205
Wine guide	207

JAMS, JELLIES AND PRESERVES

Jams

Cape gooseberry	214
Guava	212
Hints on jam making	211
Marmalade	213, 214
Marrow ginger marmalade	213
Orange and apricot	211
Orange ginger	212
Pawpaw and pineapple	211
Plum	212
Quince honey	214
Rhubarb and fig	213

Jellies

Orange	212
Quince	211

IX

Preserves

Apples	215	Naartjies	209
Apricots	216, 218	Orange	208
Cabbage	216	Pompelmoes	210
Carrots	216	Pawpaw	210
Figs	212, 213, 215	Peaches	216
Grapes	218	Peas	217
Grapefruit	209	Plums	218
Hints on preserving	214, 219	Rhubarb	218
Kumquat	209	Tomato	210, 217
Mealies	216	Watermelon	213

CHUTNEYS, PICKLES AND SAUCES

Apricot chutney	221, 222	Tomato chow-chow	223
Chutney, Indian	222	„ sauce	221, 223
Fruit chutney	222	„ chutney	221, 222
Peach pickle	221		

SWEETS

Almond tablet	225	Marshmallows	228
Almond toffee	226	Melk tammeletjies	226
Apple sweets	230	Mint delight	227
Apricot sweets	229	Nut toffee, clear	225
Butterscotch	226	Peanut tablet	228
Chocolate fudge	227	Peppermint creams	228
Cocoanut ice	224	Pineapple sweets	230
Divinity fudge	227	Plum sweets	230
Edinburgh rock	228	Quince sweets	230
Fig sweets	230	Russian toffee	225
Fruit candies	226	Swiss milk toffee	224, 226
Fruit minces	229	Treacle caramels	225
Glaces	228	Turkish delight	225
Homemade toffee	225	Vanilla caramels	227
Honey candy	226	Walnut toffee	227
Jujubes	229		

WARTIME RECIPES

Biscuits, golden syrup	239	Carrot pudding	240
Biscuits, wholemeal	238, 239	Date or fig pudding	239
Bread, Boston	234	Friday lunch dish	240
„ brown	233	Honey gems	238
„ mealiemeal, brown	232	Salt rising ferment	234
„ salt raising	234	Scones, date	235
„ war	232	Scones, oven	235
„ whole wheat	234	Shortcake, spiced	238
Broche	233	Shortcake, wholemeal	238
Cake, boermeal, raisin	236	Short crust for pies	235
„ Dundee	237	Sponge, wholemeal	238
„ economical	237	Soet suurdeeg	234
„ meldrum butter	235	Wholemeal pudding	239
Cake, Mrs. Slade's	237		

HOUSEHOLD HINTS

Furniture polish	247	Stove, the	243
Hints—Refrigerator, the	244		

HOME NURSING AND INVALID COOKING

Home Nursing

First-aid requirements 249	Mumps 249
General 248	To prepare for doctor 249

Invalid Cookery

Albumen water 250	Egg in ramekins 252
Barley water 250. 251	Fish fillets, to steam 252
Arrowroot pudding 253	Invalid jelly 253
Beef tea 251, 252	Junket 253
„ „ and egg 252	Kaffir beer 251
„ „ custard 252	Lemon or orangeade 251
„ „ milk 252	Lemon sponge 253
„ „ to thicken 252	Oatmeal gruel 251
Broth, chicken 252	Rice water 250
Broth, mutton 252	Sweetbreads stewed 252
Egg flip 251	Tasty steamed fish 253
„ nog 251	

THE BRIDE'S CORNER

Balancing and planning the diet 254, 255	Coffee, to make 271
Breadcrumbs, brown 272	Croutes or croutons 272
„ fresh 272	Devilled almonds 272
„ fried 272	Dripping 272
„ white 272	Fat 273
Breakfast, suggestions for . . . 270	Food classes 254
Caramel 272	Gravy colouring 273
Cocoa, to make 271	Gravy thickening 273

Hints

General 273, 276	Pantry requirements 258
Minced steak 275	Planning the meals 256
Mutton 274	Porridge, kaffircorn 271
Sausages 275	„ mealiemeal 271
Steak 274	„ oatmeal 271
Kitchen requirements 260	Pudding cloth. To prepare . . 272
Linen requirements 259	Regulating foods 256
Menus for two, Summer . . . 262	Tea, to make 271
Menus for two, Winter . . . 266	Terms: Cookery 277

MY HUSBAND'S CONTRIBUTION

Three prospectors were working far from the amenities of town or transport. The nearest dorp was several days trek distant, and it was only very occasionally that the trip was made.

Two of them had, however, come to the village to purchase a few of the absolute necessities of life, and, espying a cookery book in a shop, bethought themselves that their mate, who was also the cook, might, with advantage, relieve the monotony of their meals with its aid. On return to their camp they presented it to their partner with a few well chosen hints.

Alas, their expectations were not fulfilled, for after their first day at work again they found Bill in a very bad humour, and with only the usual grub prepared. On asking the reason for both these conditions, the reply was, "What was the darned good of buying a book like that? Every single recipe starts 'Take a clean dish'."

MEMO